LADY BLESSINGTON'S
Conversations of
Lord Byron

Lawrence's portrait of Lady Blessington, reproduced by permission of the Trustees of the Wallace Collection.

Lady Blessington's

CONVERSATIONS OF LORD BYRON

EDITED WITH AN
INTRODUCTION AND NOTES

by Ernest J. Lovell, Jr.

PRINCETON UNIVERSITY PRESS
PRINCETON, NEW JERSEY
1969

Publication of this book
has been aided by a grant from the
Whitney Darrow Publication Reserve Fund
of Princeton University Press

Printed in the United States of America
by Princeton University Press
Princeton, New Jersey

This book has been set in Caledonia Linotype.

148034

C O N T E N T S

PREFACE

The present volume completes a project initiated a number of years ago with the publication of *His Very Self and Voice: Collected Conversations of Lord Byron* (New York and London, 1954), which assembled for the first time all the significant accounts of Byron's conversation except the book-length reports of Thomas Medwin and of Lady Blessington, as explained in my preface. More recently, my edition of Medwin's *Conversations of Byron* has appeared (Princeton and London, 1966), as well as a biography of the author. Thus, with the publication of Lady Blessington's book on Byron, the complete conversations of the poet, as recorded by those who knew him, are now finally available in scholarly form.

The present text, collated with that of *The New Monthly Magazine and Literary Journal*, July 1832–December 1833, is based upon the London edition of 1834, published by Henry Colburn, and uses a copy annotated, underlined, and marginally marked by the Countess Teresa Guiccioli, Byron's last mistress, who was living with him when his conversations with Lady Blessington took place. When Teresa read the book, she had already met Lady Blessington and indeed had achieved a remarkable degree of insight into her mind and motives.

The "revised" edition of 1893, published by Richard Bentley, has no authority, of course, and in fact seriously disfigures the text, frequently altering paragraphing and punctuation, adding chapter divisions and headnotes, silently and sometimes doubtfully spelling out the names of persons who had originally appeared only as capital letters, and elsewhere actually "improving" the style. The introductory matter and the few notes of the 1893 edition are written in a spirit of defensive Victorian innocence, quite foreign to the essentially modern mind of Lady Blessington, and the "Contemporary Sketch of the Countess of Blessington, by her Sister" was in fact written by Lady Blessington's niece. Inasmuch as neither the relations between Byron and Lady Blessington nor the origins of her book have ever been explored in depth, the introduction to the present volume attempts to supply this deficiency. Because this edition is intended as a final companion volume to *His Very Self and Voice* and to my edition of Medwin's *Conversations of Byron*, page references in the notes are usually made to these two editions rather than to other sources.

The marginal notes of Teresa Guiccioli are normally introduced by her name, followed by a colon, and are not enclosed within quotation marks. These are of particular value, however brief, because they are usually directed not at statements of fact, which may be checked elsewhere, but at expressions of opinion and interpretations of Byron's character. Her underlinings and marginal markings, here reproduced, are quite as significant as her verbal comments, for these lines and marks, unless otherwise indicated, seem almost always to indicate her approval. (Even her marginal X's do not always mean that she disagrees or objects.) Thus they qualify greatly her generally adverse summary-judgments of the whole book and suggest clearly how seriously she took it. She was not prepared, of course, to be pleased with any biography of Byron, as she confessed to Lady Blessington on August 27, 1832, just after leaving London: "I found your remarks on my Critique [of the early installments of the *Conversations*] true and reasonable—and for some of them at least I could have scarce any other thing to reply but that you are wright [*sic*]. Yes you are wright my dear Lady Blessington when you say that on account of my sensitiveness towards Ld Byron (which has its Source not only in my devoted affection for him— but in my consciousness of all his perfections—which becomes greater the more I advance in life and experience of the world) I cannot be Satisfied of any of his biographers."[1]

It is proper here to express my grateful appreciation for the hitherto unpublished letters, journals, and marginalia incorporated in this edition: to the Curator of Special Collections in the Princeton University Library for letters of Lady Blessington to Mrs. Charles Mathews, her most intimate woman friend, for a letter from Lord Blessington to the elder Charles Mathews, and for excerpts from the diary of Charles James Mathews, who lived in the home of Lady Blessington in 1823-1824, shortly after she had known Byron; to the Curator of the Berg Collection of the New York Public Library

[1] From the autograph letter in the Miriam Lutcher Stark Library of the University of Texas at Austin.

for letters to and from Lady Blessington, most notably her correspondence with Mrs. Charles Mathews; to the Curator of the Henry E. Huntington Library for letters to and from Lady Blessington and for her "Night Thought Book," in two volumes; to Sir John Murray K.C.V.O., D.S.C., for letters of Lady Blessington, Lord Blessington, and Count D'Orsay, all addressed to Byron; to the Librarian of the University of Texas at Austin for Byron's last extant letter to Lord Blessington, for a letter from the Countess Teresa Guiccioli to Lady Blessington, and for an excerpt from the diary of Sir John F. W. Herschel the astronomer; to the Curator of Dr. Williams's Library of London for entries in the diary of Henry Crabb Robinson, referring to Byron and Lady Blessington; to the Director of the Department of Manuscripts, British Museum, for entries in the journal of Byron's friend, Henry Edward Fox, and for his letters to his mother, Lady Holland; to the Librarian of the Biblioteca Classense of Ravenna for the annotations of the Countess Teresa Guiccioli in her copy of Lady Blessington's *Conversations of Byron*; to Professor Leslie A. Marchand for photographs of selected pages from the Countess Teresa Guiccioli's manuscript "Vie de Lord Byron en Italie," here published in her original, and sometimes uncertain French; to Professor Lewis Patton for entries from the diary of William Godwin, in the Duke University microfilm of the great Lord Abinger Collection; to Lord Lytton and Mr. Malcolm Elwin for letters of Lady Blessington and Mary Millicent Montgomery, among the Lovelace Papers; and to Mrs. Joan St. George Saunders, my friend and representative in London, for favors too numerous to mention.

The University of Texas at Austin

LADY BLESSINGTON'S
Conversations of
Lord Byron

INTRODUCTION

In 1912 Miss Ethel C. Mayne, author of the then definitive biography of Lord Byron, set the twentieth century's tone of highly enthusiastic endorsement which Lady Blessington's *Conversations of Byron* has been accorded almost every since: "There is no comparison between her book, as far as it goes, and any other except [John] Galt's for the early years." She saw "deep into his true nature. . . . To quote all her admirable *aperçus* of him would be to quote nearly her whole book."[1] Ten years later, Sir John Murray, editor of *Lord Byron's Correspondence*, wrote, "Of all the ladies with whom Byron associated, Lady Blessington was perhaps the one best suited by her charm, her good sense, her intelligence, and her sympathy to be a companion of Byron if they had met in earlier days: had she been destined to be his wife his whole career would have been changed. Her *Conversations of Byron*, published in 1834 [in February, following serial publication in *The New Monthly Magazine* between July 1832 and December 1833], is one of the most interesting and illuminating accounts of him which exist."[2] Sir Harold Nicolson's *Byron: The Last Journey*, which relied heavily on her, explained in 1924: "The very real value of Lady Blessington's 'Conversations' and her 'Idler in Italy' [1839-1840] is to be looked for therefore in their reflections of the subtle reactions which the Byron of 1823 stimulated and finally allayed. She passed through those several stages of preconceived admiration, of irritated disapproval, of amused understanding, of profound and poignant sympathy, which we should traverse ourselves."[3] In 1930 André Maurois pronounced the *Conversations* to be "one of the truest and most living books ever written about Byron. . . . She has grasped him, in all his complexity, most admirably."[4] Peter Quennell in his *Byron: The Years of Fame* (1935) quoted her, without critical qualification, ten times, although Byron did not know her during the

---

[1] Ethel C. Mayne, *Byron* (New York, 1912), II, 256-57.

[2] Sir John Murray, ed., *Lord Byron's Correspondence* (London, 1922), II, 248-49.

[3] Sir Harold Nicolson, *Byron: The Last Journey* (London, 1924), p. 10.

[4] André Maurois, *Byron* (New York, 1930), p. 483.

period covered by his book; and the last ten pages of Quennell's *Byron in Italy* (1941) were drawn almost wholly from her writings: "About their association hung a pensive autumnal radiance. The tired heart . . . broke into a sedate but pleasing flutter for Marguerite Blessington. Life, long dull and automatic, became eventful and various. . . . Love might colour his emotions; it did not cloud them. . . . Two long months went by in rides, visits, dinner parties, endless conversation. . . . Behind him was a glimpse of the contentment he had always aspired to: it would pass away from him in the Blessingtons' travelling carriage on the road to Lucca. . . . On her side, Lady Blessington was both charmed and disconcerted . . . from blind admiration she had fallen back on a kind of tolerant affection. . . ."[5] In the opinion of the Marchesa Iris Origo, author of *The Last Attachment* (1949), "For all her charm, wit and beauty, he [Byron] did not fall in love with Lady Blessington. He only, for the whole ten weeks of her time in Genoa, rode with her, took tea with her, laughed and gossiped with her—and talked and talked about himself, as he had laughed and talked with no woman since Lady Melbourne. . . . She knew, unfailingly, what he was talking about; she could tell him the latest gossip about everyone he had ever met. And when—very soon—he began to talk about himself, how unfeigned was her interest, how perceptive her comments!"[6] Thus Iris Origo, who took the title of her book from Lady Blessington's account (p. 48), quoted at great length from it, even as the editors of the thirteen-volume edition of Byron's *Letters and Journals* and of his *Poetry* had done a half-century earlier. In 1952 C. L. Cline found the *Conversations* "valuable,"[7] even though his *Byron, Shelley and Their Pisan Circle* is not centrally concerned with the Byron of 1823. Samuel C. Chew, writing in 1956 in *The English Romantic Poets: A Review of Research*, described her book as one of "the two principal records of the poet's conversation," the other being Thomas Medwin's.[8] Leslie A. Marchand, author of the definitive *Byron: A Biography* (1957), agreed: Lady Blessing-

[5] Peter Quennell, *Byron in Italy* (New York, 1941), pp. 263-70.

[6] Iris Origo, *The Last Attachment* (New York, 1949), p. 341.

[7] C. L. Cline, *Byron, Shelley, and Their Pisan Circle* (Cambridge, Mass., 1952), p. 193.

[8] Samuel C. Chew, *The English Romantic Poets: A Review of Research* (New York, 1956), pp. 162-63.

ton's book, "a shrewd contemporary interpretation," is, with Medwin's account, "in many respects the most interesting of all the contemporary records."[9] Recent criticism has been influenced no less by her. To illustrate, Willis W. Pratt's *Notes on the Variorum Edition of Don Juan* (1957) quoted or referred to Lady Blessington on fourteen pages, as did Andrew Rutherford's *Byron: A Critical Study* (1961), for a total of twenty-eight separate references to her in the two books.

Similarly, the modern biographers of Lady Blessington have expressed their happy confidence in her book and their faith in the friendship of its author and her subject. J. Fitzgerald Molloy wrote in *The Most Gorgeous Lady Blessington* (c. 1897): "Byron seemed as delighted with the companionship of the Blessingtons as they were with his, and he was constantly dining or riding with them, writing to or calling on them, or sitting for his portrait to D'Orsay in their salon, and this close association enabled the countess to notice many traits in him before unsuspected. . . . Whilst at Genoa, . . . he had spoken to her unreservedly on a variety of subjects. Each time he had left her presence, it had been her habit to jot down their conversations as fully as her excellent memory would permit." It was necessary only to "transcribe and arrange" these records in order to produce the *Conversations.*[10] Michael Sadleir, author of *The Strange Life of Lady Blessington* (1933) was just as enthusiastic: ". . . she had a rare gift of understanding the complex psychology of clever men. Throughout the book one is struck by the balanced judgments which she passes on Byron's psychology, the sureness with which she distinguishes between his genuine feelings and his self-protective readiness to sneer, to wound and to shock. . . .

"And perhaps even more remarkable than the perceptiveness of Lady Blessington's reading of Byron is the fact that her judgments are for the most part very well expressed. . . . Her very use of words

[9] Leslie A. Marchand, review of Ernest J. Lovell, Jr., ed., *His Very Self and Voice: Collected Conversations of Lord Byron*, in *Keats-Shelley Journal*, IV (Winter, 1955), 97; *Byron's Poetry, A Critical Introduction* (Boston, 1965), p. 248.

[10] J. Fitzgerald Molloy, *The Most Gorgeous Lady Blessington* (London, c. 1897), pp. 85, 219. This and the other biographies of Lady Blessington are concerned only incidentally or superficially with the relations of Byron and Lady Blessington and with her book on the poet.

is different—apter and more relevant—than that displayed in her novels; the reason being, of course, that in recording conversation she was getting as near as is possible in a printed book to actual talk."[11] Willard Connely, author of *Count D'Orsay, The Dandy of Dandies* (1952), which is as much a biography of Lady Blessington as of D'Orsay, explained: "So it was that their acquaintance ripened. . . . Lady Blessington managed to ride out with Byron three or four times a week, taking down in her mind's shorthand his remarks. . . . Peter Patmore the journalist [who knew her] later observed: '. . . In Lady Blessington, Byron found a woman beautiful, not vain, intellectual enough to admire his achievement and to talk with him as an equal, and not sentimental.' . . . Byron . . . proceeded to see as much as possible of the Blessingtons. . . ."[12]

Her *Conversations* received its share of highly complimentary notices in respectable journals, although it was not reviewed as widely as Medwin's *Conversations*. In March 1833, the reviewer for *Fraser's Magazine* proclaimed: "Since the publication of Boswell's *Life of Johnson*, nothing of the kind so good as her *Conversations with Byron* has appeared. . . ." William Maginn writing in the *New Monthly Magazine* stated: ". . . by far the most solid, comprehensive, and acute estimate that has hitherto been made . . . Lady Blessington's 'Conversations of Byron' do more to explain and illustrate his mental and moral character than all the 'Lives' of him put together. . . ."[13]

But among others who knew Byron or Lady Blessington or both, opinion was somewhat more divided. Although Leigh Hunt stated that her "account of Lord Byron is by far the best and most sensible I am acquainted with,"[14] he may have been returning her compliment upon his *Lord Byron and Some of His Contemporaries*. Hobhouse, twenty years after Byron's death, and much mellowed since the days when he had nearly fought a duel with Captain Medwin, found her book "very fair and faithful." (In conversation, she

[11] Michael Sadleir, *The Strange Life of Lady Blessington* (Boston, 1933), pp. 69-70.
[12] Willard Connely, *Count D'Orsay, The Dandy of Dandies* (London, 1952), pp. 67-69, 71.
[13] *Fraser's Magazine*, VII (March 1833), 267; *New Monthly Magazine*, LVI (Second Part, 1839), 425.
[14] *The Autobiography of Leigh Hunt*, ed. J. E. Morpurgo (London, 1948), p. 436.

told him "some anecdotes, or rather sayings, of Byron, which I can easily believe to be true.")[15] Teresa Guiccioli, however, thought in a moment of irritation that Lady Blessington's book should have been called "Imaginary Conversations,"[16] and Henry Crabb Robinson, who had no reason to be partial to either side, concluded that the author by publishing did "not advance her reputation either for candour or integrity."[17] Charles C. Fulke Greville, who did not like Lady Blessington, thought that the book was "too good to be hers."[18] Contemporary rumors of the most diverse kinds circulated: that she had had assistance in writing her books and the man's name was known,[19] that she had had the manuscript of Byron's famed burned Memoirs "in her possession for weeks, and confessed to having transcribed every line of it," that "her sister, Mrs. Home Purvis, (afterwards Viscountess Canterbury,) is *known* to have sat up all one night, in which, aided by her daughters, she had a copy made."[20] The rumors associating Lady Blessington and Byron's memoirs are of particular interest because, if true, they increase the value of her book rather than diminish it. Aside from Byron himself and her good friend Thomas Moore, whom she saw in Paris in September 1822, those who had read the memoirs and who were on sufficiently good terms with her to have lent them directly to her or to Count D'Orsay include Lord Holland, Lord Kinnaird, his brother Douglas Kinnaird, Henry Luttrell, Lord John Russell, and Samuel Rogers. She might even have secured them from Moore's copyists in Paris.[21] Obviously, the glittering surface of Lady Blessington's book conceals much.

Although a comparison of the *Conversations* and the little that is known of Byron's memoirs (to which the poet referred in a letter to Lord Blessington) can prove nothing of itself, such a comparison

[15] John Cam Hobhouse, Lord Broughton, *Recollections of a Long Life*, ed. Lady Dorchester (London, 1911), VI, 104, entry for May 20, 1844.
[16] Teresa Guiccioli, "La Vie de Lord Byron en Italie," quoted by Origo, p. 341.
[17] *Henry Crabb Robinson on Books and Their Writers*, ed. Edith J. Morley (London, 1938), II, 457.
[18] *The Greville Memoirs*, ed. Lytton Strachey and Roger Fulford (London, 1938), IV, 130.
[19] *Robinson on Books and Their Writers*, I, 426.
[20] R. Shelton Mackenzie, ed., *Noctes Ambrosianæ* (New York, 1867), I, 436, note; II, 13, note.
[21] Doris L. Moore, *The Late Lord Byron* (Philadelphia, 1961), p. 46.

does demonstrate that the *Conversations* violates neither the general character of the memoirs nor the specific judgments known to have been expressed there by Byron. He stated: "The *Life* is *Memoranda*, and not *Confessions*. I have left out all my *loves* (except in a general way). . . . But you will find many opinions, and some fun, with a detailed account of my marriage and its consequences. . . ."[22] All this is essentially true of the *Conversations*, although Lady Blessington's account of Byron's marriage cannot accurately be described as "detailed." Both *Conversations* and memoirs, however, contain "reported conversation with Madame de Staël," an attack on Lady Holland, a "slighting passage" about Rogers, and a reference to Lady Jersey's ball in 1816 where Byron was cut. There are in both works only "glimpses of adventures" but a whole "gallery of sketches all personal and many satirical." Both are full of his "passions and prejudices," as he wrote of his memoirs.[23]

i

At first consideration, it would seem that the meeting of Lord Byron and the Countess of Blessington in early 1823 took place under the most auspicious conditions and promised a flowering friendship, perhaps more. Born in 1789, the year after Byron, she was now at the age of thirty-three in the full bloom of her maturity, already designated by Byron's old friend Dr. Parr as "the most gorgeous Lady Blessington." In 1822, the year before Byron met her, P. G. Patmore saw her at the Royal Academy Exhibition standing in front of her portrait by Sir Thomas Lawrence: "Unlike all other beautiful faces that I have seen, hers was, at the time of which I speak, neither a history nor a prophecy . . . but rather a star to kneel before and worship . . . an end and a consummation in itself, not a promise of anything else."[24] Clearly, the living woman outshone the famous painting. Patmore thought that she was about twenty-six at the time. The fame of her beauty as depicted by Lawrence

22 *The Works of Lord Byron. Letters and Journals,* ed. Rowland E. Prothero (London, 1898-1901), IV, 368-69; hereafter referred to as *LJ.*
23 On "The Nature of the Memoirs," see Doris L. Moore, pp. 46-53.
24 *Personal Recollections of Lamb, Hazlitt, and Others,* ed. Richard H. Stoddard (New York, 1875), p. 286.

had preceded her to Genoa, as Byron's beauty (now a little withered) had come to her attention in London, perhaps as pictured by Harlow. She had "never felt the same impatient longing to see any one known to [her] only by his works," she wrote.[25]

They had much in common, in addition to their being very nearly the same age. Both had had obscure origins, and both had been aware from early childhood of noble connections. Margaret Power's mother had claimed proud descent from the first Earl of Desmond, a name Lady Blessington gave to the model "masther" or landlord in her Irish-English novel *The Repealers*, written immediately after composition of the *Conversations*. Not unlike Byron, she had been a shy and introspective child and had early acquired a passion for reading. Richly imaginative, she had entertained not only her brothers and sisters but also her parents' friends with tales of her own composing. In 1825 she said of herself: "I have studied [poetry] since my infancy."[26]

In a family not otherwise remarkable for its literary attainments, she must have withdrawn into the world of books from the horrors of her childhood. Her drunken, brutal father, among the least of his sins, flung things at his children in his rages, once throwing a cup at Margaret's head.[27] As a child she had lived through the rebellions of 1798 and 1803, the daughter of an active English sympathizer and magistrate who vigorously and bloodily supported the establishment. "Beau" Power or "Shiver-the-Frills," as he was sometimes called because of his "full bosomed pretensious-looking shirt front, [which] flapped from side to side,"[28] had given up his Roman Catholic faith in order to become a magistrate and carry out the

[25] *His Very Self and Voice: Collected Conversations of Lord Byron* (New York, 1954), pp. 349-50; hereafter referred to as *HVSV*.

[26] R. R. Madden, *The Literary Life and Correspondence of the Countess of Blessington* (New York, 1855), I, 473, a very disorderly book which is, nevertheless, the primary published source of information about Lady Blessington and her friends. The index is unreliable, the many letters sometimes silently abridged.

[27] *The Collection of Autograph Letters and Historical Documents formed by Alfred Morrison (Second Series, 1882-1893). The Blessington Papers* (Printed for Private Circulation, 1895), p. 167, R. R. Madden's memorandum of a conversation with Lady Blessington. This collection, composed almost wholly of letters written to Lady Blessington, is now in the Carl H. Pforzheimer Library.

[28] "Lady Blessington," *The Irish Quarterly Review*, II (December 1852), 773.

law of England in Ireland with the aid of the military. He became so hated and feared that his neighbors burned his corn and killed his cattle (Lady Blessington later described the Repealers as doing this in her novel of that name). Finally Power was charged with murder, committed in the course of carrying out his duties; although he was acquitted, his name was stricken from the rolls of the magistracy. Financial ruin followed, from this and other causes. Margaret's maternal grandfather had been hanged for rebellion; his cousin, a priest convicted of murder, had been hanged, drawn, and quartered, and his head was displayed on a pike for twenty years over the porch of the jail at Clonmel,[29] where the future Lady Blessington spent a part of her childhood—and was married, at the age of fourteen.

Her intimate friend and biographer, R. R. Madden, wrote of her in 1843: "While speaking at considerable length of these lamentable events and disastrous times, . . . she was crying bitterly during the whole time that our conversation lasted." After 1818, it seems, she never agreed to return to Ireland. In the summer of 1822 she viewed a proposed return with distinct "repugnance" and persuaded Lord Blessington to go to France instead. Her sister Ellen, Madden observed, "grew up to womanhood, surrounded by the same unhappy influences and unfavorable circumstances. . . ."[30]

In 1804, when Byron was still at Harrow, Margaret was bluntly informed by her father that she was to marry a Captain Farmer, stationed nearby, a man who was known to her father, she stated later, to be subject to fits of insanity.[31] It may be that she was in effect sold into this marriage. She viewed her prospective husband with "the utmost repugnance," but even her tearful entreaties did not prevent the marriage from being solemnized on March 7, 1804, "according to the Rites and Ceremonies of the United Church of England and Ireland."[32] If no other ceremony were performed, either she had already renounced her Roman Catholic faith, or she never regarded herself as being truly married to Captain Farmer. She lived with him for about three months, she later stated, during which time he was accustomed to treat her with "personal

29 Madden, I, 13-14.
30 Madden, II, 360, note; II, 324; I, 476.
31 The Blessington Papers, p. 168.   32 Madden, I, 513.

violence; . . . lock her up whenever he went abroad, and often . . . left her without food. . . ."[33] She became convinced that he was insane.

When he received orders for a change of station, she refused to accompany him and returned to her father's house, where it seems she was received with resentment as an additional burden. However, there is evidence that she also resided at a number of other places, in none of which her father lived—Fethard, Tullow, Ringville, and Cahir, as late as 1807.[34] Her reputation may have first become seriously clouded at this time.[35] Lady Hardy informed Byron about six weeks after Lady Blessington's farewell to him: "I believe she began life as the lady fair in a most humble occasional way of the late Lord Glengall, at Cahir & supplied the absence of the lawful lady, she then succeeded in the usual routine of that life till she found the present Lord . . . ," Blessington.[36]

In 1807 or thereabouts, hearing that her husband was returning from India, she placed herself under the protection of a Captain Jenkins, a man of respectable family, generous income (between £6,000 and £8,000 a year, she said later), and some expectations. Jenkins spent so much money on her that his family feared he might be ruined. Presumably she lived with him, in Dublin and in Hampshire, until about 1816, when he, according to her own statement, accepted from Lord Blessington the sum of £10,000 "for jewels and apparel" that Jenkins had given to her during the years of his protectorate,[37] whereupon Lord Blessington set her up in a house in Manchester Square. Thus the year of Byron's downfall, 1816, was a year of great good fortune for Mrs. Farmer. When her husband conveniently killed himself by falling from the window of a London debtor's prison, Lord Blessington married her, in 1818, a change of state which she signalized by changing her name from "Margaret" to "Marguerite" and her place of residence from Manchester Square to St. James's Square. Byron's friend Joseph Jekyll, wit and ancient man about town, described the interior of the new house in a letter

[33] *The Blessington Papers*, p. 168.
[34] Madden, I, 31-32, 478.
[35] Madden, I, 32, 514.
[36] Lady Hardy to Byron, June 17, 1823, from the autograph letter in the possession of Sir John Murray.
[37] *The Blessington Papers*, p. 169.

to his sister-in-law: "Lately had a grand dinner at Lord Blessing-ton's, who has transmogrified Sir T. Heathcote's ground floor into one vast apartment, and bedizened it with black and gold like an enormous coffin,"[38] tragic foreshadowing of events to come.

It may be seen, then, that Lady Blessington, more than most women, had been dependent upon her powers of pleasing members of the opposite sex. Between 1807 and 1818 she had been a profes-sional charmer—"that despised thing, a kept mistress," as she con-fessed[39]—and she had developed to a high polish the qualities she possessed in some degree as a precocious child of fourteen: "the art of . . . entertaining as well as retaining admirers. . . . Margaret always manifested that desire to please, which gave a piquant char-acter of agreeable coquetry to her *agrèmens* [*sic*] of conversation and deportment in after-life. . . ."[40]

Meanwhile, during these earlier years, Lady Blessington had not neglected the cultivation of her mind, as her three self-revealing books published in 1822 indicate.[41] William Jerdan "advised her with her first literary production,"[42] *The Magic Lantern; or, Sketches of Scenes in the Metropolis*, one part of which appeared originally in *The Literary Gazette; and Journal of Belles Lettres, Arts, Sciences, &c.* for March 2, 1822. There it was introduced by a headnote stating that the author, still anonymous, possessed "both feminine elegance of mind and high rank in society." Two weeks earlier in the same journal, she and William Wordsworth had been juxtaposed in the column announcing books in press: his without critical comment of any kind, hers said to "give us a very favourable idea of the writer's talents. . . ."[43] It would reappear in a second edition in 1823. The scenes that she sketched are an auction of the furnishings of a great house, a Sunday stroll in the park, a visit to a life-sized model of an ancient Egyptian tomb, and an evening

[38] *Correspondence of Mr. Joseph Jekyll with his Sister-in-law, Lady Ger-trude Sloane Stanley, 1818-1838*, ed. Algernon Bourke (London, 1894), p. 123.

[39] *The Blessington Papers*, p. 169.

[40] Madden, I, 477.

[41] By February 2, 1822, she was also the author of a "lively and well written" amateur production of some kind, never published. See Madden, II, 234.

[42] *Autobiography of William Jerdan* (London, 1852-1853), III, 277.

[43] *The Literary Gazette*, March 2, 1822, p. 137; February 16, 1822, p. 108.

at the opera. For these pages, usually satiric or sarcastic, she draft-
ed the following prefatory lines, not published by her:

> If my Magic Lantern should offend,
> The fault's not mine, for scandal's not my end;
> 'Tis vice and folly that I hold in view:
> Your friends, not I, find likenesses to you.[44]

There is expressed throughout a deeply felt need (felt for many
years, presumably) to take a position of impeccable virtuousness or
moral superiority to all that is in the least degree unladylike, uncul-
tivated, unconventional, or otherwise contrary to accepted codes,
modes of behavior, or points of view. Thus her position was and
continued to be a false one, the need to assume it deeply distressing
to her. As she wrote in what "she used to speak of as her Night
Thought Book," to which she confided her secret thoughts after
retiring late from the company of her drawing room: "A false position is sustained at a price enormously expensive," exacted by society.[45] About her early life, she was, understandably, very sensitive.
Henry F. Chorley had "heard her speak of it herself once or twice,
when moved by very great emotion or injustice from without. And
what woman," he continued, "in speaking of past error, is unable to
represent herself as more sinned against than sinning."[46]

Thus, here and in her other books, she attempted to assume the
role of "a censor of society—its manners, morals, and all externals
affecting the decorum of its character," as Madden observed of her
second book.[47] In her first, interestingly, she revealed a distaste for
the "Dandy or Exquisite," an "effeminate race" which she had not
yet gotten used to, D'Orsay not yet having become a member of
her household. Assuming a tone of shocked and outraged virtue,
she condemned "this silly flirtation, commenced in folly and pursued through idleness"; she damned those ladies of easy virtue, rec-

[44] Madden, I, 215. It has not seemed necessary to footnote quotations from
any of Lady Blessington's first three books, all short.

[45] Madden, I, 244. The title of Lady Blessington's "Night Thought Book,"
the two volumes of which are now in the Henry E. Huntington Library, is
explained on an early page in an autograph note by Madden.

[46] *Personal Reminiscences by Chorley, Planché, and Young*, ed. Richard H.
Stoddard (New York, 1874), p. 17.

[47] Madden, I, 216.

ognizable by their "painted faces and scanty drapery," which "conveyed an impression not very advantageous to their purity." (Lady Blessington did not even wear perfume and seemed "to rely on the wholesomeness of soap and water. She is clean to the very essence," Haydon later recorded.)[48] Of deceiving wives and husbands, encountered in Lovers' Walk, she wrote: "I was shocked at finding the delinquents to belong to some of the most respectable families in the kingdom. . . ." Here was the bitter knowledge she lived with daily: *she* was not admitted into the company of the respectables. "Am I indeed," she continued, "in the capital of a Christian country, celebrated over all the world for its morals, its religion, and the virtues of its inhabitants, and is it thus the Sabbath is passed!"

Although she could convey the impression of being a woman of very "high church principles,"[49] Henry Edward Fox in 1827 heard her "profess without provocation, her total unbelief in Christianity,"[50] and Madden heard her say: "The doctrines of the Protestant Church never appeared to me better than those of the Catholic Church. I was educated in the doctrines of that church."[51] In 1843 her favorite niece and her sister Ellen were persuaded that she was still without religion and prayed that she might "turn to the Lord while he may be found."[52] D'Orsay thought that she had "never ceased 'in her heart' to be a Catholic,"[53] but she seldom went to any church, and he had her buried just outside the hallowed ground of an exclusively Catholic cemetery. The truth would seem to be that formal religion (or informal) played no part in her mature life, except in the most sentimental way.

One learns none of this from *The Magic Lantern*, of course, which informed her readers that she was opposed to ballet on grounds of modesty, "but if we must have a *ballet*, and nothing short of indecent exhibition can please us, let the performers, at least the female part of them, belong to any country but our own." A single

[48] *The Diary of Benjamin Robert Haydon*, ed. Willard Bissell Pope (Cambridge, Mass., 1963), IV, 263-64.
[49] Madden, I, 300.
[50] *The Journal of the Hon. Henry Edward Fox*, ed. The Earl of Ilchester (London, 1923), p. 243.
[51] Madden, I, 300-01.
[52] Madden, I, 482; see also I, 480, 483.
[53] Madden, I, 300.

stroke could thus serve for both God and country. She selected the pirouette as particularly indelicate: it "obliges all the feminine part of the audience, at least all the modest part, to withdraw their eyes, and avoid those of the gentlemen, whose libertine glances, offended modesty, at such a moment, shrinks from encountering." It is difficult, however, to imagine her withdrawing her eyes from those of Henry Edward Fox when he found her, one week before she was to meet Byron, "very vulgar and abusive," laughing at Lord Grey "for making love to her, which she says would be ridiculous to any woman but to her it would be *insolent*. She told him, 'Are you vain enough to suppose that if I was inclined to play the fool with anybody, you would be the person I should choose?' "[54] In later years she could be even more vulgar and immodest in conversation.[55]

In contrast, in her book the voice of elevated superiority is heard everywhere, even in the areas of taste and learning. "The ignorance displayed by the greater part of the visitors of the [model of the Egyptian] tomb, was truly surprising. . . . Wrapt up in their own self-satisfied ignorance, the works or monuments of antiquity hold no attention for them. . . ." Along with an uncertain sense of foreign phrase (she refers to a "cavalier servant"), she reveals a highly cultivated awareness of "the vulgar" in clothes, equipages, and riding skills. Her knowledge of the various kinds of carriages and harnesses seems quite remarkable. The "plated harness" of the horses drawing a landaulet set off the "absurd vulgarity of the carriage," and each figure in the scene is satirically sketched on the basis of his taste in transportation.

The satire is sometimes compounded with a page of sentimental benevolence or moralizing on mankind's essential goodness or badness. One example may suffice, as in "The Auction" she described the young and beautiful daughters of a financially ruined family: "Oh! bless them, bless them! well I know their goodness: they found me out when oppressed by affliction and poverty; despair had nearly overwhelmed me, and I thought Pity and Benevolence had fled the earth. They relieved my wants with a liberal hand; but, oh! what is of infinitely greater importance, they reconciled me to my fellow

[54] *Journal of Fox*, pp. 158-59.
[55] *Diary of Haydon*, IV, 180-81.

beings, and to my God. That I now live, and pursue a course of usefulness and industry, I owe entirely to their humanity: I shudder at reflecting on the fearful crisis to which poverty and despair had reduced me, when these amiable and excellent young ladies found me out." At the end of the episode the narrator learns that one lady had bought all the "furniture, books, clothes" of the needy "Misses B——" and would have them "sent to a residence which she had presented to them," while another woman was to offer her services as a domestic (presumably without pay): "My feelings glowed with delight at finding two such instances of benevolence; and I exclaimed with warmth, 'Thank heaven, all goodness has not vanished from the earth! The virtues of these two amiable women have reconciled me to my species; and I find that even the selfish vortex of an Auction cannot ingulph true virtue.'"

To Lady Blessington's credit, however, we learn from Madden, "she looked so unfavorably on 'The Magic Lantern' in her later years as seldom or never to make any reference to it."[56] And her stance of superiority had some foundation beneath it. *The Magic Lantern* also reveals a certain fashionable or dilettante knowledge of music, painting, sculpture, and rare books. The private library auctioned off contained books printed by Caxton, Wynkyn de Word [*sic*], and Elzevir. She was learning. At moments she reveals a genuine sense of the essential frivolity of much of the life around her, coupled with a lively awareness of the color and movement of a scene. But already she had suffered from "an intrepid rudeness only to be acquired by ladies of high *ton*. How often have I seen a ladylike sensitive woman, shrinking beneath the fixed gaze of some dames of fashionable notoriety. . . ." Already she had concluded that there were fewer evidences of "good breeding"—polite manners and a liberal view of a lady's past—to be found in England than in France, where she had been in 1816 and in 1821.

The preface to her second book, *Sketches and Fragments*, also published by Longmans, is dated June 12, 1822. In it, she found it necessary to "disclaim the personal satire attributed" to *The Magic Lantern*, where "general and not personal satire was the object in view." Indeed, in *Sketches and Fragments* the satiric impulse has usually been translated into didacticism or moralizing, although she

<hr />

56 Madden, I, 216.

does state that "in London . . . money is the *primum mobile*," as she had good reason to know, despite the fact that Lord Blessington's money had not propelled her into quite the sphere to which she aspired. Somewhat less revealing than her other early books, this one nevertheless suggests her familiarity, in some uncertain measure, with Locke, Robert Blair, Hume, Rousseau, Horace Walpole, Beattie, and Chateaubriand. There are pages on subjects as diverse as the choice of a proper nursemaid and the "Misrepresentation of Character," a fixed idea with her. The most revealing sketch, however, is the "Journal of a Week of a Lady of Fashion," which was reprinted in *The Literary Gazette* on June 29, 1822. It was introduced by a statement, written perhaps by William Jerdan, identifying her as the author and comparing *Sketches and Fragments* and the earlier *Magic Lantern*: "The present elegant companion to it is consequently the production of the same accomplished lady, whose taste and good feeling are perhaps still more delightfully exhibited in its pages than in those of its precursor."[57] The pages which Jerdan chose to reprint tell the story of a frivolous, flirtatious woman, grossly neglectful of husband, children, and dying mother, whose deathbed letter leads the erring daughter back to the solid virtues at the end of the sketch. The "Journal" is not a sermon, however, but another of Lady Blessington's attacks upon the frivolity or baseness of the high life in which she could not freely participate. An open assault is made upon the Lady Patronesses of Almack's, the most uncompromising of whom was Lady Jersey, who had once denied entrance to the Duke of Wellington because he was seven minutes late. On one evening the fictitious diarist found the rooms at Almack's, where Lady Blessington was not welcome, "quite filled, and narrowly escaped being locked out by the inexorable regulations of the Lady Patronesses, for it only wanted a quarter to twelve when I entered. By-the-bye, I have often wondered why people submit to the haughty sway of those ladies [and] . . . their imperious dictates. . . . There is a quackery in Fashion, as in all other things, and any one who has courage enough (I was going to write impudence,) rank enough, and wealth enough, may be a leader." The motives

---

[57] *The Literary Gazette*, June 29, 1822, p. 410. The quotation at the end of the present paragraph is from Lady Blessington's *Desultory Thoughts and Reflections* (New York, 1839), p. 72.

of the satirist may never be pure, but the truth is that English high society of the 1820's was chaotically hypocritical, and Byron and Lady Blessington could agree upon the fact. As she wrote many years later: "Modern refinement consists in a delicacy in words, and indelicacy of thoughts and actions," an expression of one form of the main theme of *Don Juan*, appearance versus reality.

To her *Journal of a Tour through the Netherlands to Paris, in 1821*, the *Literary Gazette* gave a front-page review, with copious extracts, on September 28, 1822.[58] It opened: "The pen of Lady Blesinton [*sic*] is, like herself . . . graceful and charming. . . ." The reader was assured that the *Tour* would permit him to "enjoy all the varieties of unaffected sensibility, feminine taste, and acute reflection. . . ." The reviewer thought that "Her Ladyship's taste for the Fine Arts is distinctly shown in her description of a statue recently brought to the Louvre—it is called the Venus of Milos, . . . where it was discovered but a short time ago." He then quoted her description, which distinctly shows her taste in female anatomy as much as anything else, and her outspoken frankness, when the body of a living woman was not the subject: "The neck is of exquisite beauty," she wrote; "and the chest, although it shews a little too much of the anatomy of the form, is well modelled. The bosom is small but well shaped; the right breast is compressed by the upper part of her arm, which rather impairs its beauty. . . . The waist is rather clumsy, and the stomach large. The lower part is covered with drapery, finely executed. The hips are full and gracefully turned. The face is dignified and full of calm, abstracted loveliness." The reviewer concluded: "The only effusions of Lady B.'s sentiments with which we cannot accord, are those of extreme sympathy for the late Ruler of France," a Whig affectation which Byron himself was capable of expressing at times.

The book assures the reader in its "Advertisement," signed by "The Editor," that the author has agreed to publish only at the request of friends: "The Tourist wrote for amusement, not for publication . . . [and] there has been no subsequent re-writing. . . ." Nevertheless, "the author has on former occasions been favoured with the approbation of the public, and is unwilling to lose any portion of fame which may have been acquired. . . ." It is virtually

[58] *The Literary Gazette*, September 28, 1822, pp. 607-08.

certain, from internal evidence, that the journal was either written with an eye to publication or revised for publication, perhaps both.

A new element here, not present in her earlier books, is the mention of living persons by name: Lord Hood (1753-1836); Lady Hood, whose conversation is reported; Lady Anne Hamilton, Lady-in-waiting to Queen Caroline, author of *Epics of the Ton* (1807) and, later, *Secret Memoirs of the Court* (1832), in which she published her intimacy with Byron; and Dr. and Mrs. Lushington, presumably Lady Byron's Dr. Stephen Lushington.

At this date, Lady Blessington was already an experienced picturesque tourist, a confirmed cathedral examiner, and a discriminating museum goer. She was critical of the "tawdry ornaments" in one church she visited and of statues "wretchedly and gaudily bedaubed with paint and gilding," but she wrote an informed and appreciative account of the paintings in the Musée de Lisle. Her taste for old manuscripts, rare books, and fine bindings was richly fed and flourishing. At this time, if we may believe her, she knew French well enough to enjoy (and criticize) the French theatre.

She visited Waterloo, with appropriate reflections, found reminders of Napoleon repeatedly on her tour, compared him to Croesus, and recalled Herodotus's story of Solon's somber warning to the Lydian king. Her weakness for ornate beds (so important in her life) and bathrooms was already fully developed. In the palace at Compiègne, completed by Napoleon, she found a bed "beyond every thing splendid. It is carved in fine relievo and gilt; the curtains of white satin superbly trimmed with gold fringe, held back at each side by an angel of full size, and beautifully carved and gilt." She then marveled at the magnificent circular bathroom, its walls lined with mirrors. Lord Blessington would provide her with a bed and bath quite as elaborate as these, but she later sneered in print at the gaudy bad taste of Byron's bed when Barry showed it to her in Genoa.

She was critical of women educated in France, with "shewy and superficial accomplishments, with levity and boldness of manners," unfitting them to be English wives and mothers, but their ill fortune allowed her to publish her patriotism at a time when she was

19

about to leave England to live on the Continent for eight years, from August 1822 to November 1830.

The cultivated artificiality of such sentiments as these must be balanced against the natural and attractive qualities of the woman as they were revealed to her intimates, for publication was a very special means of communication for Lady Blessington, cut off as she was from friendship with women of high social station. Her books provided her with the only way of telling them who or what she really was: a woman of education, refinement, taste, and very high moral standards. But nowhere in her early books did she reveal adequately her natural warmth, her capacity for friendship and joyous affection, her sense of humor, her talent for creating a delightful and charming life for those around her. These and related qualities emerge most clearly in the accounts of her biographer and intimate friend, Dr. Madden, who met her in 1823 in Naples, where she arrived in July; and in her letters to the actress Mrs. Charles Mathews, an old friend, and to Charles James Mathews, her son, who was a member of the Blessington party between November 1823 and November 1824.[59] Both Madden and young Mathews, then, were associated with her six months after she had known Byron, and thus their testimony is of particular value in determining the woman Byron knew. Both seem to have been infatuated by her, as were many other men who came to know her. Madden, twenty-five years old when he first met her, deserves to be heard at length, although he was never, presumably, a member of her household as Mathews was. To him Lady Blessington was "entirely free from all affectation of sentimentality," a characteristic which would recommend her most highly to Byron, of course. "There was a naturalness in her demeanor," he continued, "a grace and gentleness in her mind and manner—a certain kindliness of disposition and absence of all affection—a noble frankness about her, which left her in all circles at her ease—sure of pleasing, and easily amused by agreeable and clever people."[60] This statement appears early in his biography, before his narrative has reached that point where he describes her introduction to Byron. Thinking of her at Seamore Place, where she wrote the *Conversations*, and attempting to explain "the peculiar charm of her conversation" within her own circle, he wrote: "It was

[59] Madden, II, 409. [60] Madden, I, 61.

20

something of frankness and archness, without the least mixture of ill nature, in every thing she said, of *enjouement* in every thought she uttered, of fullness of confidence in the outspeaking of her sentiments, and the apparent absence of every *arrière pensée* in her mind, while she laughed out unpremeditated ideas, and *bon mots* spontaneously elicited, in such joyous tones, that it might be said she seldom talked without a smile at least on her lips. . . . She seldom spoke at any length, never bored her hearers with disquisitions, nor dogmatized on any subject, and very rarely played the learned lady in discourse. She conversed with all around her in 'a give and take' mode of interchange," taking care to draw out all the members of the company.[61]

At the end of his narrative of her life, Madden concluded: "Lady Blessington was naturally lively, good-humoured, mirthful, full of drollery, and easily amused. Her perception of the ridiculous was quick and keen. If there was any thing absurd in a subject or object presented to her, she was sure to seize on it, and to represent the idea to others in the most ridiculous aspect possible. This turn of mind was not exhibited in society alone; in private it was equally manifested."[62] Then Madden quoted the testimony of her personal maid of the last fifteen years of her life: "she was naturally very cheerful, droll, and particularly amusing."[63]

Most of these qualities also emerge in the correspondence of Lady Blessington and the Mathews family in 1824 and 1825. She treated Charles James Mathews, twenty years old when he was a member of her household in Naples, as if she were his loving (and intelligent) mother. She was quite sincere in her sense of loss when Charles returned to England, and she expressed it warmly to Mrs. Mathews. He wrote humorous, witty letters to her, and she replied in affectionate and motherly tone.[64] To his mother, she wrote: "pray tell him that I will yield to no other, except his mother and his wife, the place I wish to hold in his affection, as through life he may count upon me, after the two I have named, as the woman in the world the most sincerely his friend."[65] Mrs. Mathews wrote to Charles on

[61] Madden, I, 130-31.
[62] Madden, I, 198.
[63] *The Blessington Papers*, p. 173, paraphrased slightly by Madden, I, 198.
[64] Madden, II, 406-09.
[65] Madden, II, 416-17.

June 23, 1824: "While dear Lady Blesinton [*sic*] condescends to act towards you in my place . . . you *cannot err.* . . . Lady Blesinton I conceive possesses every requisite to form the mind and conduct of those about her. . . . I truly and sincerely love her as well as admire her."[66] The pleasant life she could create for those around her is suggested by Charles' diary at the time when Lady Blessington had taken the Villa Belvedere just outside Naples: "Lady B—— is more charming than ever. This is the place, with all its associations, to draw out the resources of her mind—to discover the superiority of her talents, and to be captivated by them. . . . Our evenings are charming; we have each of us a table in the same room, at which we prosecute our various studies, writing, drawing, reading, &c. All our conversations, which are frequent, are upon improving subjects: the classics, the existing antiquities around us. We write essays on various subjects proposed, which are read in the evening, opposed, and defended [a parlor game that Byron might have found somewhat formidable]. I am treated as one of the family; I make all my drawings in the same room with them, and am going to instruct Lady Blessington in architecture. It is proposed, as all of us desire to improve ourselves in Italian, that we should learn in a class, devoting an hour each day to that study. With respect to antiquarian research, we have all the ancient authors here to refer to and consult. In short, there never were any people so perfectly happy as we are. Whenever any excursion is proposed, the previous evening is employed in reading and informing ourselves thoroughly with what we are going to see."[67] This then is the lady at home in Naples, a few months after she had said farewell to Byron.

At that time and earlier she must have understood very clearly a distinction she expressed in the mid-thirties: "The desire to please half-accomplishes its object, and is in itself praiseworthy, when self-gratification is not the aim or end of it. Yet has it often been mistaken for coquetry, from which it totally differs. The first extends to our own sex as much as the other, while the second is addressed peculiarly to the male. The woman who desires to please spreads a charm over the circle in which she moves; the coquette merely

[66] *The Life of Charles James Mathews, Chiefly Autobiographical,* ed. Charles Dickens (London, 1879), I, 156.
[67] Madden, II, 443-44.

22

gratifies the vanity of men by evincing her wish to attract them."[68]

She had consciously studied her business, with great success; and between February 1818, when she married Lord Blessington, and August 1822, when she left England, soon to meet Byron, she had, within her limits, established herself as the center of a remarkable circle of men, perhaps even more substantial than that she was later to form at Seamore Place or Gore House. Of these men, more and less illustrious, Byron knew thirty-six personally, in one way or another.[69] Two dozen of them were to appear in her *Conversations*: Lord Alvanley, one of the reigning dandies of the time, friend of Brummell and the Prince Regent; Lord Blessington, remarkable in history only as the husband of Marguerite, Lady Blessington; Sir Francis Burdett, M. P. for Westminster and Byron's chosen arbitrator of the Wentworth estate; George Canning the statesman and orator, President of the Board of Control 1816-1820 and created Secretary for Foreign Affairs in 1822; George Colman the younger, the dramatist, appointed examiner of plays under George IV; John Wilson Croker, Secretary to the Admiralty since 1809, a leading contributor to the *Quarterly Review*, and one of Murray's literary advisers, about whom Byron wrote a satiric poem in 1816, which he destroyed; John Philpot Curran, the Irish orator and patriot; Edward Ellice, M. P. for Coventry and later Secretary to the Treasury and Secretary at War; Lord Erskine, orator, judge, Lord Chancellor of England, and the defender of Thomas Paine; Henry Edward Fox, son of Lord Holland and Teresa Guiccioli's lover as early as 1825; John Galt the novelist, with whom Byron had finally quarreled in 1813; William Godwin, author of *Political Justice* and father of Mary Shelley; Lord Grey, First Lord of the Admiralty and Foreign Secretary, 1806-1807, under whose ministry the Reform Bill

[68] Madden, I, 477.

[69] These mutual friends and acquaintances have been verified in Byron's letters and in sources other than Lady Blessington's *Conversations*. See Madden, I, 25, 57, 62-63, 255-56, 470; II, 511 and fol., 534; *Irish Quarterly Review*, II (December 1852), 781; P. G. Patmore, *Personal Recollections*, pp. 288-89; Thomas Moore, *Memoirs, Journals, and Correspondence*, ed. Lord John Russell (London, 1853-1856), II, 339; III, 3, 299, 343, 345. Letters or copies of letters to Lady Blessington from many of these men are preserved in the Berg Collection of the New York Public Library. Perhaps the name of Colonel Montgomery should not be in the list. He and Byron had never been introduced, but each knew who the other was, and they saw one another in Genoa, once attending the same dinner party.

of 1832 was to be passed; Lord Holland of Holland House, whose distinguished political, literary, and artistic circle Lady Blessington was attempting to rival; Joseph Jekyll, M. P., Master in Chancery, wit and elderly man about town, to whom Byron sent a copy of *Werner* in 1822; John Philip Kemble the celebrated tragedian; Douglas Kinnaird, M. P., Byron's banker, literary agent, and intimate friend; Henry Luttrell, described by Byron as "the best sayer of good things, and the most epigrammatic conversationalist I ever met," the witty author of *Advice to Julia* (1820), nicknamed by some "Letters of a Dandy to a Dolly"; Charles Mathews the comedian, father of Charles James Mathews; Colonel Hugh Montgomery, brother of Miss Mary Millicent Montgomery, friend of Lady Byron; Thomas Moore, whose *Lalla Rookh* (1817) had commanded 3,000 guineas from Longmans before it was written, witness to his immense popularity; Samuel Rogers, a founder of the *Quarterly Review*, banker and poet, whose *Jacqueline* (1814) had been published in the same volume with Byron's *Lara* and whose *Human Life* had appeared in 1819; Lord John Russell, statesman and author, who was to edit Thomas Moore's letters and journals, introduce the Reform Bill in 1831, and twice become Prime Minister; William Robert Spencer, wit and writer of *vers de société*; and John William Ward, M.P., later Earl of Dudley, a reviewer for the *Quarterly* and secretary of the Drury Lane Sub-Committee of Management when Byron was a member. Perhaps it may be assumed that Lady Blessington also had some sort of nodding acquaintance with Lady Holland and Lady Jersey, who also appear in the *Conversations*.

When Byron and Lady Blessington met, they shared at least twelve more friends and acquaintances, who do not appear in the *Conversations*: Henry Brougham, the *Edinburgh* reviewer of *Hours of Idleness* whom Byron was prepared to challenge in 1819, counsel for Queen Caroline, 1820-1821, M. P., later Lord Chancellor of England and 1st Baron Brougham; Sir George Beaumont, landscape painter, art critic, a founder of the National Gallery, and patron of Wordsworth; Castlereagh, the English statesman, whom Byron attacked repeatedly; the undistinguished 4th Earl of Darnley (1767-1831); the 5th Lord Guilford, an enthusiastic and learned philhellene; Lord Lansdowne, the liberal politician, Chancellor of the Exchequer, 1806-1807, and patron of Thomas Moore; Sir Thomas Lawrence the portrait painter, elected President of the Royal Academy in 1820; Lord Palmerston, Secretary of War, 1809-1828, and finally Victoria's Prime Minister; the learned Dr. Samuel Parr, to whom Byron once listened "with admiring ignorance and respectful silence"; James Perry, owner and editor of the *Morning Chronicle*; Dr. William Polidori, Byron's physician in 1816; and the Prince Regent.

Lady Blessington's aspirations were not merely literary and social; she also wished to influence politics. On July 12, 1819, Thomas Moore found "My lady very anxious for me to stay in town for a dinner of Opposition people, they are to have next week, is trying, with all her influence, to bring the Peer[s] over to the right side of politics, and says she is sure of succeeding."[70] Henry Fox recorded that on April 7, 1821, his father, Lord Holland, the Duke of York, "and seven Opposition peers" dined at her house.[71] In 1834 she wished "to be considered the female rallying point of the Liberals," as Benjamin Robert Haydon noted.[72] "Hardly a week passed but that the [royal] Duke of Sussex dined with her & Lord Blessington";[73] she could gather around her the masculine "*élite* of London celebrities of all kinds of distinction, the first literati, statesmen, artists, eminent men of all professions,"[74] but she was not welcome at Almack's, ruled by Lady Jersey; and when she and her lord drove Thomas Moore to Holland House at the end of an evening, they waited outside in their carriage while he went in.[75]

---

ii

And so Lady Blessington escaped, on August 25, 1822, from the closed doors of London to the less confined society of the Continent, even as Byron had done. Ladies of birth and breeding did not come to the house in St. James's Square, and Lady Blessington did not go to their houses. She lived almost entirely in a world of men. Her deep need for educated and intelligent feminine friendship, however, emerges clearly from her farewell letter to Mrs. Mathews,

[70] Moore, *Journals*, II, 339.
[71] *Journal of Fox*, p. 62.
[72] *Diary of Haydon*, IV, 197.
[73] *Diary of Haydon*, IV, 181.
[74] Madden, I, 62.
[75] Moore, *Journals*, III, 298.

written on the day of her departure for the Continent and seven months before she met Byron: "In a few days you will receive a lock of my hair, and you must consider it as a bond of amity, that I am persuaded never will be severed while we exist—I beg you will give me a similar pledge when I return. . . . I send you a little Book which is only meant to meet the eyes of my most particular friends [;] it is a crude and careless production, but you will I know attach some value to it, for sake of the Writer. . . . And now my dear Mrs. Mathews I come to the most painful word that friends can utter, or write—farewell—a word that I never yet uttered save with a faltering tongue or wrote save with an unsteady hand. May God in Heaven bless and protect you. . . ."[76]

The seven restless months between her departure and her meeting with Byron are recorded in her *Idler in Italy*, published in 1839-1840 and perhaps much revised and rewritten from her original diary. By then she had become an expert on Byron's life and words. If we may believe *The Idler*, however, her interest in Byron was already very great and the similarity of their tastes quite remarkable. Early in her first volume, recording in Paris her thirty-third birthday, she Byronically noted her passing youth and dined delightedly with Thomas Moore. "Pictures," she observed, "like music, and in truth, like all that is fine, are to be felt, and not reasoned upon. When I hear the cant of criticism, . . . I turn away in disgust, to meditate in silence on what others can talk about, but not comprehend." Of Byron she reported later in *The Idler*: "He says that he *feels* art, while others *prate* about it. . . ." He told her: "I hate cant of every kind. . . ." She waxed enthusiastic over Claude Lorraine, Titian, and Giorgione, but deplored Rubens' fleshly choice of models, even as Byron had done. On September 12, 1822, she moved on Byronically to view the Jura and the Lake of Geneva, where she awoke to think of Voltaire, Rousseau, Gibbon, Madame de Staël, Shelley,[77] and Byron, perhaps with *Childe Harold* in hand. She visited Voltaire's house at Ferney, Gibbon's house at Lausanne,

[76] From the autograph letter in the Princeton University Library.
[77] On Lady Blessington's early interest in Shelley and her extensive knowledge of him see Madden, II, 558-65. It has not seemed necessary to footnote all the many quotations from Lady Blessington's *Idler*. Volume numbers will be noted in text or notes.

Madame de Staël's estate, Coppet, and the house in Geneva in which Rousseau was born.

"The soul is lifted up from nature to nature's God," she wrote Byronically. "A deep love of nature has in it something of a religious character." Then she "made a pilgrimage to the tomb of Gessner" in Zurich, which bears an "inscription from [his] beautiful and pathetic 'Death of Abel.'" She confessed that she had read it in childhood, even as Byron had confessed of himself in his preface to *Cain*.

Back in Geneva on October 8, 1822, the party was rowed on the Lake "by Maurice, the boatman employed by Lord Byron. . . ." Maurice discussed Byron and Shelley for two pages and pointed out to her the villa Diodati and the house where Shelley had lived. At Nice, on March 15, 1823, she observed that "Byron is much in vogue in France, and a lively curiosity exists respecting him." She may well have helped to satisfy that curiosity, for it was strong in her too. About two weeks later they met.

This early interest in Byron, however much it may have been dressed up at points for publication, seems nevertheless quite genuine. The outcast Byronic hero, with his secret sin and obscure past, splendidly and scornfully defying the world, spoke very deeply and directly to her. She and Lord Blessington had discussed Byron with Galt, among others. As early as December 5, 1822, Lord Blessington knew about *The Liberal* and may have seen the first issue, published on October 15. He wrote to John Galt: "Ld. Byron seems to be a fool for working in the Liberal. It might do for Bysshe Shelley."[78] And on January 6, 1823, Galt informed her that Byron's *Heaven and Earth* was "superior in energy and passion" to Moore's *Loves of the Angels*. Then Galt reprimanded Byron because he had "'give[n] up to party,' and such a party, 'what was meant for mankind.'"[79] The reference presumably is to Hunt and *The Liberal*. Galt understood her interests, and there is no doubt of hers in Byron well before they met.

She was traveling with her younger sister Mary Ann, who would

[78] William H. Marshall, *Byron, Shelley, Hunt and The Liberal* (Philadelphia, 1960), p. 95.
[79] Madden, II, 327.

27

later make a Moll Flanders kind of marriage; the young and magnificent Count D'Orsay; and her noble lord, with whom, Byron noted, she "seemed . . . entirely bored."[80] The young Charles Mathews observed, once he joined the party in Naples, in November 1823, "Lord Blessington was not a walker, was a hater of sight-seeing and moreover a late riser, breakfasting in bed and reading his book or newspaper there till late in the day. So we saw little of him except when travelling or at mealtime."[81] This may be partially explained in terms of illness: on August 19, 1823, Mathews wrote in his diary, Lord Blessington was "laid up with gout,"[82] and the medical advice he received in Genoa, when seeing Byron, suggests the same disability, although it is impossible to estimate the extent of its seriousness. Mathews also noticed that he was, "after taking a little wine, . . . inclined to be quarrelsome."[83] Henry Fox called him a "drunkard,"[84] but this judgment seems exaggerated. Lady Blessington later wrote of her husband: "the only *téte-à-téte* we ever enjoyed during our marriage" was a fortnight on the Isle of Wight.[85] They lived surrounded, a situation of her own making presumably. She was quite aware of "the little defects" of his character, as she wrote after his death, and was "too apt to underrate" his value: she had "allowed [her] mind to be too much engrossed by [her] own selfish feelings. . . ."[86] Almost certainly she saw most of Genoa the superb without him. The death of his son, which he heard of shortly after reaching Genoa, surely did not improve relations between him and his childless wife. Moreover, it was in Genoa that he had added a codicil to his will, dated June 2, the day after his farewell to Byron.[87] The contents of it were such that he would have had to discuss them with D'Orsay and, presumably, with his wife. She could not have been pleased. The codicil provided that D'Orsay should marry one of Blessington's daughters, a mar-

[80] John Gore, " 'When We Two Parted': A Byron Mystery Re-solved," *Cornhill Magazine*, New Series, LXIV (January 1928), 51.
[81] *The Life of Charles James Mathews*, I, 78.
[82] From the autograph diary in the Princeton University Library.
[83] Madden, II, 447.
[84] *Journal of Fox*, p. 234.
[85] Madden, II, 225.
[86] Lady Blessington to Mrs. Charles Mathews, July 1829, quoted by Molloy, *The Most Gorgeous Lady Blessington*, pp. 182-83.
[87] For the codicil, see Sadleir, *The Strange Life of Lady Blessington*, pp. 75-76,

riage which Bulwer flatly stated years later, Lady Blessington was "against." "Lord Blessington enforced it. . . ."[88] This codicil, which thus put into legal form a plan formulated at least as early as March 23, 1823,[89] one week before Lady Blessington met Byron, also provided that D'Orsay should inherit Blessington's estates in the city and county of Dublin, less an annuity of £3,000 to Lady Blessington. When the will was rewritten in London three months later to incorporate the codicil, Lady Blessington's jointure was reduced to £2,000 per year—[90] this for a woman who in 1828 would live in a house on which £40,000 had been spent to decorate the walls alone! Thus was her life tied to the life of D'Orsay, her intended stepson-in-law. Dr. Madden, who considered that Blessington's unbelievably lavish expenditures were "evidence of a state of insanity . . . , partially developed," concluded: "my firm conviction, the result of my own observation, is, that at the period in question, when this will was made, Lord Blessington could not be said to be in a state of perfect sanity of mind . . ." although sane on every subject except his "family affairs."[91] It should be noted, however, that Madden was not acquainted with Lord Blessington in Genoa, could not have met him before late November 1823, when he arrived at Naples, and that the "appearance of monomania"— that is, Blessington's extravagant prodigality—which Madden described, may very well have had its source in an uxorious desire to satisfy the demands of Lady Blessington, who some years earlier had nearly bankrupted Captain Jenkins. And the will may well have been written in a mistaken effort to protect the estate against her future inroads.

The degree of Lord Blessington's sanity and prudence may be judged from a letter he wrote to the elder Charles Mathews about Mathews' son, touring in Pompeii and Paestum at the time. It was written in the year Blessington last saw Byron, and is remarkable for the sensitivity it reveals. We also learn from it that Blessington had abandoned his expensive ambition to build a castle at Mountjoy Forest, for which young Charles had drawn plans. The writer

[88] Connely, *Count D'Orsay*, p. 554.
[89] On this date Fox was told of it.
[90] For the correct text of the will, see Sadleir, pp. 323-25.
[91] Madden, I, 54, 103.

began by assuring the father of Charles' health, which "has generally speaking been extremely good." Blessington continued:

His drawing is beautiful & he is extremely accurate.

I think from his appearance & manners that he has been very happy both on the Road & since his arrival. Our Companion Sir Charles Sutton who is now at Malta has taken a strong liking to him, and Count D'Orsay says he is an amiable garcon—

There is only one thing which has occurred since his arrival which would throw a gloom over his Visions & which therefore I have not informed him of.

I discovered that Lady B[lessington] did not like our plan [for the new castle] & so without arguing the Topic I determined upon abandoning it. Knowing also how difficult if not impossible to do any thing which any body likes I determined to make a residence out of my present Cottage which every body dislikes.

Foreseeing this impediment before my departure I gave orders to build Two Rooms with three over it, on which I paid no attention to Architectural decoration—& next year I shall pull down the remaining part of the Thatch & stick up some more Rooms. Now I know this will not please either My Wife or Mr. Norman [his agent in Ireland] nor your Son, but I am encouraged to it by considering that I have laid out on the Cottage several thousand pounds. . . . I do not say any thing to Charles for sufficient to the day is the Evil thereof. . . . The balance to Charles must be that he has seen Ireland & out of Ireland saw France & Italy. Nay more, for his wishes of not returning until a later period will be realized for after leaving Rome we purpose visiting Sicily Malta the Ionian Isles Venice—the Tyrol, the Rhine Brussells & home—I really think it will be the greatest service to him for he has an inquiring mind, & after all there is nothing so useful as leaving home when the mind is imbued with virtuous Principles.

This is happily for him his case, & with virtue for the basis, and honor & gentlemanly feelings to direct and aid talent, he has also which is a blessing to you both, the most sincere love admiration & regard for his Mother & you.

When you are in low spirits think of that & it will revive you.

Think also that he is with those who cherish for you both the sincerest friendship esteem & regard. . . .

I remain your sincere friend

Blessington

C[harles] M. is making very great progress in Italian, is very tractable, attentive to good manners, obliging, good humoured, cheerful & amusing.[92]

Despite the warmth and generally evident good sense revealed here, Lady Blessington at some uncertain later date wrote a sad little poem lamenting "Unequal Marriages." In it we learn "That equal fates alone may dress/ The bowers of nuptial happiness." Love cannot exist "where ancestral pride/ Inflames, or affluence rolls its tide" over one of "humble line."[93] In her "Night Thought Book" of 1834 she wrote: "Passion! Possession! Indifference! What a history is comprised in these three words!"[94] The three reappear in her disillusioned tale of a "Honeymoon," in which the new husband, named Bellevalle, becomes bored with his wife in a fortnight: "Passion—possession—what a history is comprised in these two words! But how often might its moral be conveyed in a third— indifference!"[95] In her *Desultory Thoughts and Reflections* she concluded: "Marriage is the portal at which Love resigns his votaries to the dominion of reason," but "that union never can be happy in which the woman has more strength of mind than the man."[96] She herself regularly sat at the head of the table at this time, not Lord Blessington, who sat at her left. D'Orsay had the place of honor on her right. "The most painful and humiliating epoch in the life of a woman," she wrote in *The Repealers*, "is, when she has discovered that *he* on whom she has anchored her hopes of happiness is deficient in intellect, and yet has too much pride or too little love, to supply the deficiency by attending to her counsels."[97] In this same confessional novel, to which she supplied a key, we read the story

[92] From the autograph letter in the Princeton University Library.
[93] Madden, I, 249.
[94] Madden, I, 210.
[95] *The Works of Lady Blessington* (Philadelphia, 1838), II, 333.
[96] Quoted by Connely, p. 300.
[97] *Works*, I, 198.

of the Countess of Oriel, a woman who loses her reputation to base and baseless slander and suffers from insulting attacks in the newspapers, but whose honor, happily, is finally rehabilitated— as Lady Blessington's never was. Lady Oriel learns to evaluate the opinion of the world of fashion for what it is worth, but the Earl continues to be nervous. When she is again attacked in a newspaper, he does nothing: "His supine and reprehensible negligence, or pride, had kept him from acting as the guardian of his wife's honor. . . ."[98] Lady Blessington was not insulted in the newspapers, it appears, until after the death of her husband, but she was insulted elsewhere more than once during his lifetime, and she did not like it. There is no record that he ever did anything about it. How she felt, "whilst writhing under the insult" of a direct cut, we may also learn from *The Repealers*: "The Indian proverb says, that contempt can pierce even the shell of the tortoise. How then must it have wounded the sensitive mind of a proud woman!"[99] The woman whom Byron met was far from being happily married.

The Lord Blessington who emerges from the thirteen letters he wrote to Byron,[100] however, is a rather different man from the one seen largely through Lady Blessington's eyes. Already a pamphleteer, now writing poetry and an historical work, sensitive, affectionate, and understanding, he is seriously interested in Irish and international affairs and informed about them. Basically modest but able to address Byron the man as an equal and to meet him more than once on the equal plane of humor, he is a devoted husband and a loving father, happy to secure for his daughter, however young at the time, such a splendid catch as Alfred Count D'Orsay. In 1822, like Lady Blessington, he too had published: "Observations Addressed to the Marquess of Wellesley on the State of Ireland," "A Letter from a Representative Peer to the Marquess of Wellesley," perhaps another version of the first pamphlet, and "Observations on the Proposed North of Ireland Canal," dated January

[98] *Works*, I, 278.
[99] *Works*, I, 225.
[100] A few passages from these letters, in the possession of Sir John Murray, have been published by Doris L. Moore, *The Late Lord Byron*; they are otherwise wholly unpublished.

7, 1822.[101] In 1826 he would publish in three volumes *De Vavasour; A Tale of the Fourteenth Century.*

Lord Blessington's first letter to the poet, April 2, 1823, asked Byron to lend him copies of Galignani's English newspaper, two recent issues of which he had missed (presumably because of travel), and went on to offer Byron D'Orsay's "account of his visit to London (where his reception was equal to Grammont). . . ." Blessington thought that Byron might enjoy reading "some clever remarks on many of our friends, good descriptions of routs, Irish Ball, Court &c &c &c," and stated: "It amused me very much." Byron sent the newspapers and was delighted with the journal. Blessington wrote again on the same day to thank Byron, including in his letter remarks on Lord Liverpool and Canning, who wished to keep England out of the Franco-Spanish conflict, and on Burdett and Wilson, "Knight errants," who "wish[ed] to assume the spear & shield." Blessington "regret[ted] the line adopted by the French Cabinet," in deciding to invade Spain, but he could not "forget Wellingtons expression at the Battle of Thoulouse when in the centre a Spanish column gave way—'Did you ever see 5000 rascals run away before? Order up the 53rd.'"

Blessington's letter of April 6 announced the death of his "angelic son Mountjoy. From Letters received at Nice I had no right to hope, but yet hope lingers. Lady B[lessington] who loved him as fondly as if he had been her own first born, has suffered much and Alfred who has received his father's assent to a marriage with one of my daughters felt as if he had lost a brother." Lady Blessington hoped that Byron would "not avoid us in our misfortune." Lord Blessington then moved on to express his views on the French invasion of Spain and on reports, sent by Byron, of revolt in the French forces of the duc d'Angoulême: "With respect to the Pyrennean News I hope it is not true—strongly as I was opposed to the unjust, oppressive aggression of France, yet for Alfred's sake whom I love as if he was my own son, or Brother, I should be sorry that such Prophecies of Evil as Revolt & Insurrection should be

---

[101] The third of these pamphlets is referred to in the Blessington papers in the Berg Collection of the New York Public Library but is not listed in the catalogue of the British Museum: it may never have been published.

realised. Nor do I like the Spaniards—still if they fight for their Liberty & do not dip their hands in the blood of their King, who though a weak is I fully believe a good Man—I shall wish them success—and should feel happy to hear that the proud invader were taught a lesson of humility." With these sentiments, Byron could agree. The letter also makes clear that Byron had already revealed the rank of Teresa Guiccioli, whom Blessington referred to as "the fair Countess."

Byron sent his letter of condolence on the same day, returning a letter from his friend Dr. Parr which Blessington had allowed him to read. Indicative of the intimacy already established between the two peers, Byron observed that Dr. Parr was "a great friend of the other branch of the House of Atreus, and the Greek teacher (I believe) of my *moral* Clytemnestra. . . ." Blessington replied with several anecdotes of Parr, whom he had once heard say that Lady Byron "accented Greek better than any person he ever saw. He [Parr] then described how it came to his knowledge while at a country house." (This may have been in January 1813 at Staunton Harold, home of the Viscountess Sophia Caroline Curzon Tamworth, the niece of Lady Byron's mother.)[102] Blessington described the learned Dr. Parr as "an enthusiast—and a warm and steady friend," and continued: "When the Doctor was taken to Kensington Palace by Mr Pettigrew to see the D of Sussex Library he was astonished at his Theological Library & exclaimed 'Sir His Royal Highness rises in my estimation both in amplitude and altitude.' Now Dr Mr P added you shall taste a Bottle of his old Port. The Dr said 'Sir I never knew a Man possessed of a good Theol. Lib^y that had not also a cellar of good Port Wine.' "

Earlier in the letter Blessington had thanked Byron for his expression of sympathy upon the death of young Mountjoy and added: "it would be cruelty to ourselves to permit any selfish indulgence of sorrow to keep us from the pleasure which we feel in the society of Men of Genius; when that Genius is accompanied by kindness of heart & that we know we are sympathised with—the knowledge is sufficient—words are unnecessary." It is clear that Blessington thought he had found in Byron a true and understanding friend, and he disclosed the plan to have D'Orsay's journal privately print-

[102] See Malcolm Elwin, *Lord Byron's Wife* (New York, 1962), pp. 158-59.

ed in an edition of six copies, to be read not by "the vulgar" but by "friends read[ing] as friends." One of the six copies was to go to Byron.

On April 14, Byron was forced to decline a morning ride with the Blessington party because of applying a caustic to a wart on his lip, and Blessington replied on the same day with an expression of sympathy. Among the incidental news related was that "Lady B[lessington] went to the Theatre last night & was pleased. She says the King [of Sardinia] was dressed like a Gentleman & looked like an Englishman." Then Blessington, as "Chairman of the Acting Comm. of a Society for improving the conditions of the Irish Peasantry," asked Byron to allow his name to be used as a contributor. Byron did, and by May 24 the fund had increased from £2,200 to £4,700.

A short note on April 20, referring to a recent dinner with Byron, was followed on April 23 by another invitation: "It is not good for your Body or Mind to starve—think of Liberty & Live." Byron had already discussed his Greek plans with Blessington, who asked: "what think you of [the title] *Emperor of the Greeks?*" We learn also that Blessington had just reread with pleasure Galt's *Entail* ("too Scotch for a British audience") and purchased Byron's "works" in a number of volumes.

To this Byron replied in serious tone on the same day: "I thank you for quizzing me and my 'learned Thebans,'" the London Committee. "I assure you, my notions on that score are limited to getting away with a whole skin. . . ." The next day, April 25, Blessington explained: "I sincerely wish all to the Cause of Freedom from oppression & wish to see the Turks simple Asians or complex if you please, and if I were in London & on the Committee I would give Hon Dug [Kinnaird] & Co a Philip I beg Johnsons pardon *fillip* I should say." The man who will pun in a letter will probably pun in conversation.

On May 7, Blessington confessed that he was writing poetry as well as "Sketches of Irish History," which included "the debate on the union ending with Grattan's speech." It appears that Byron and the Blessingtons had very recently spent an "agreeable day" together. It was also on May 7 that Lady Blessington wrote to Byron about Lady Byron.

On May 22 apparently (the letter is dated "Thursday evening"), Blessington, soon to leave for England and Ireland, "determined, with Miladi's permission to comply with your wish of having [her horse] Mameluke. . . . I gave for him 2400 francs I thought that it had been 2000 but I remember, & Alfred tells me that it was Louis & not Napoleons. You may give me a Draft on Hon. Dug." These do not sound like the words of a voluntary spendthrift. Then Blessington added, a little sadly: "There are *some* that will be happy we are going & I do not know that there are many who will regret it."

Byron declined to pay more than 2,000 francs, but stated gallantly, in portions of his reply of May 23 suppressed by Lady Blessington and never before published,[103] "Who can the '*some*' be who will be 'happy that you are going'? they are not of my acquaintance. On the contrary the few people that I have seen seemed anxious that you should stay—and Mr. Barry (the banker) was going to look out a house for you.

"Do you quit your party—and return alone?

"You will let me know previously to your day of departure—that I may come and shake hands with you before you start."

This expression of friendship called forth on May 24 the longest letter Blessington wrote in Genoa to Byron: "You are very innocent about the 'Some'. Heaven preserve you so." He was uncertain of the precise date of his departure; "besides Lady B[lessington] from whom I have not been separated since our Marriage (but once & that was in leaving England she going to Calais & I by Dieppe & meeting at Rouen) feels very unwilling to let me go." Although he does not say so, her unwillingness was surely due to the fact that she knew he was going to write her out of the greater part of his will. There is nothing of this in the letter, of course, but there are references to his ill health, the advice of Dr. Alexander (no more wine, just a little weak brandy and water), the friendly habits of Mameluke ("he will follow you like a Dog when he knows you & likes Bread"), one of his pamphlets, his confidence in Byron's ability to be "of great service in Greece," his preference for

---

[103] The autograph letter is in the Miriam Lutcher Stark Library of the University of Texas at Austin. Lady Blessington, in addition to omitting portions of it, published it as two separate letters, and it so appears in *LJ*, VI, 218-19, letters numbered 1087 and 1088.

Childe Harold, recently reread, over *Don Juan* ("no favourite of mine"), his hope that Byron will have time to write in Greece: "I have thought that the career of Napoleon would make a fine Epic Poem. He certainly was a greater Man than bold Aneas, and his Ten Years Reign much more wonderful than the Siege & taking of Troy, where the Gentlemen went out to fight as one goes out for a days sport rather by shooting or hunting—some by fishing—but in my opinion it is a *private school kind* of amusement." The letter closed with remembrances from each one of the Blessington party, an offer to deliver "any message to your Corinthians" in London, and a plea to keep secret the fact that he was "trying [his] hand at verse making. I dare not call it poetry to you. . . ." It is the letter of a man who sincerely valued Byron's friendship and enjoyed his company.

Shortly before Blessington sailed on H.M.S. *Glasgow*, he decided that he wished to own Byron's *Bolivar*, with her furniture, and the books that Byron was prepared to sell. Later he tried to buy an expensive snuff box from Byron, for which he offered fifty guineas.[104] It is almost as if, at parting, Blessington was trying to tie himself to some part of Byron or Byron's life. And once at sea, he wrote a long letter to Byron on June 17, the chief purpose of which was to try to attach an Irish friend of his, Major General Sir Andrew Barnard, K.C.B., to Byron in Greece. In the course of doing so, Blessington revealed that he understood at least some of the poet's prejudices. General Barnard, he wrote, "might have several objectionable points in your consideration. Imprimis he is of the Kings Household & private friends. Second. He was one of the D of Wellingtons right hand men, & made him British Gov. of Paris. Third he is an ardent Shakespearian." Even so, Blessington recommended him as a man "generally liked," a "very good fellow," able to look at a fight "as cooly as we would at an Alderman going to cut up a Haunch of Venison." The letter closed with the information that Blessington traveled with a Galignani edition of Byron's poetical works, much "esteemed" by all those on board.

This, then, is some of the background of the conversations of Byron and Lord Blessington, almost certainly overheard by Lady

[104] From Charles F. Barry's autograph letter to Byron, January 28, 1824, in the possession of Sir John Murray.

Blessington. On Lord Blessington's side, as long as he remained in Genoa, the friendship was genuine enough. Byron's liking for Blessington during the time is witnessed by the poet's letters, including some of his best. One does not write interesting letters to a dull reader.

As for the magnificent D'Orsay, so much has been said of his supposed relations with Lady Blessington that it is difficult to think of him as not being her lover. There is, of course, no conclusive evidence. However, young Charles Mathews, after recognizing that he was "a man . . . of the finest form and most elegant manners, . . . of a noble disposition, and the bravest of the brave," observed that he was "yet quite a boy."[105] Mathews was twenty at the time, D'Orsay twenty-two. When D'Orsay was dying in Paris, he said to Madden of Lady Blessington, "with marked emphasis, *'In losing her I lost every thing in this world—she was to me a mother! a dear, dear mother! a true, loving mother to me!'* While he uttered these words, he sobbed and cried like a child. And referring to them, he again said, *'You understand me, Madden.'* " Madden believed him and concluded that he was trying to deceive neither himself nor his hearer.[106] D'Orsay's biographer, Willard Connely, concluded that "women, merely as women, were in his life a thing quite secondary." Various observers noted his effeminacy, and there was a rumor that he was impotent.[107] Byron noted ambiguously that he was "a beauty, . . . and I should suspect that the women find him more formidable than dreadful."[108] This may well mean that he was better suited to inspire awe in a woman than fear for her honor. Joseph Jekyll in 1831 described him as "an Antinous of beauty,"[109] referring to the handsome boy of whom Hadrian was so enamoured that upon his death Hadrian built and named a city for him on the Nile. Lord Blessington informed Byron on April 6, 1823, that he "love[d D'Orsay] as if he was my own son, or Brother," and that he had "a heart more valuable & *more pure* than gold. When he travelled with us first we called him Le jeune

[105] Madden, II, 443. [106] Madden, I, 299.
[107] Connely, pp. 303, 543-44.
[108] Byron to Lady Hardy, May 17, 1823, *Cornhill Magazine*, January 1928.
[109] *Correspondence of Jekyll*, p. 270.

Lion."[110] It has been suggested that Blessington's infatuation with D'Orsay was in some measure homosexual.

The young Frenchman's command of English in 1823 is suggested by the letter he wrote to Byron on April 24. The style seems to be that of neither Lord Blessington nor Lady Blessington:

My Lord

I cannot give a more convincing proof of my desire to receive a letter from your Lordship than by soliciting that honor in your language, with which I am so little acquainted, that it is not without considerable effort, and the assistance of a Dictionary, that I can write even a few lines.

The approbation you bestowed on my journal, was so flattering that it has induced me to continue my reminiscences of London, and when your Lordship has an idle hour they shall be at your disposal.

I have read with a pleasure which I can find no words to express the French Translation of your Works, which Lady B[lessington] tells me by no means renders justice to the original; I hope with her assistance in a short time to peruse them in their native language; which they will serve to immortalise.

I beg my Comp[ts] to the Cte T. G. and have the honor to subscribe myself your Lordship [sic] devoted serv[t]

Alf Cte D'Orsay[111]

Teresa stated that Byron "connut encore plus de sympathie pour lui lorsqu'il apprit qu'il venait de renoncer à sa carrière militaire pour ne pas prendre part à la guerre d'Espagne et qu'il le vit faire don de son épée et de son sabre au jeune Comte Gamba."[112] Such, then, was the second man traveling in the party of Lady Blessington when she arrived in Genoa.

Her account of her stay in Genoa and her relations with Byron, written at the time in a "MS. book" which she lent to Thomas

[110] From the autograph letter in the possession of Sir John Murray. Connely, p. 55, has suggested an attraction in some degree homosexual.

[111] From the autograph letter in the possession of Sir John Murray.

[112] From Teresa Guiccioli's autograph manuscript, "La Vie de Lord Byron en Italie," p. 1485.

Moore when he was composing his *Life* of Byron, was eventually published in her *Idler in Italy* in 1839.[113] The general authenticity of the published version is suggested by several facts, none of which, to be sure, excludes the possibility that she wrote with an eye to eventual publication or revised the original journal before publishing. She had already published her *Journal of a Tour through the Netherlands*, with actual conversation reported. However, *The Idler* could not have been written without at least lengthy notes made at the times described: there are too many details of occasion, place, and person. As for the formality or pretentiousness of the style, this is to be observed even in her letters to her most intimate correspondent, Mrs. Mathews, with whom there was no need for pretense. Further, the *Idler* account of Lady Blessington's two months in Genoa places Byron in some perspective in her life and reveals no clear evidence of padding. (There is, indeed, evidence that she deleted or shortened original entries before publishing.) She published 102 pages (about 11,220 words) describing the period, an average of 51 pages per month. The pages immediately preceding these, describing the events of September 1, 1822–March 31, 1823, average 53 per month. To describe June following her departure from Genoa, she published 57 pages and for July, the month of her arrival in Naples, 85 pages. Byron, in short, does not assume an exaggerated role in the account of her life as here recorded; and I do not find any significant falsification except for the farewell scene with Byron. He was quite capable of all the conversation attributed to him, with the exception noted. Teresa Guiccioli, that sensitive and demanding critic, thought that *"The Idler in Italy est un livre charmant—et lorsqu'elle parle de Ld Byron on y retrouve le coeur et la vérité...."*[114]

In addition, Lady Blessington's account of her sojourn in Genoa describes a great many places, persons, and activities unrelated to Byron. On March 31, the day of her arrival, she recorded her initial impressions of the city; on the next day she toured the three main streets of Genoa; on April 2 explored the flower market and jewelry shops, and on the next two days examined the Durazzo, Brignole,

[113] *The Letters of Thomas Moore*, ed. Wilfred S. Dowden (London, 1964), II, 744; *The Idler in Italy*, I, 393–II, 94.

[114] From Teresa Guiccioli's autograph manuscript, "La Vie de Lord Byron en Italie," p. 1503.

Carega, and Doria palaces and their paintings. On April 5 she enjoyed the open cook-shops on the streets and went to the Palazzo
Serra, the decorations of which, she noted, cost £44,000 exclusive
of paintings and porcelain. The next day brought the news of the
death of Lord Blessington's young son Mountjoy, and there are no
entries for the next three days. On April 11, however, she examined the Palazzo Reale, and on the day following she went with
Captain Wright, retired from the British navy and now an admiral
in the navy of Sardinia, to see the ships in the harbor. Mr. Hill,
minister to the court of Turin, called, and she watched the entry
of the King of Sardinia on his annual visit to Genoa. On April 13
and 14 she visited the cathedral of St. Laurence and the Albergo
dei Poveri, a palatial hospital. Hill dined, and the next day she
walked the streets of Genoa. On April 17, 18, and 19 she examined
the churches of St. Etienne, St. Lorenzo, and St. Ambrose, among
the thirty-eight then in Genoa, and on the day following she was
confined to her room with a headache, understandably. On April
21 Dr. Alexander, who knew Byron, called, and the next evening
Captain Wright and Mr. Barry, Byron's banker, dined with her.
There are no entries for April 24, 25, and 26: she was idle, she
noted, but on April 27 she entertained Barry again, and on the day
after Colonel Hugh Montgomery arrived. He took her to the
gardens and pavilion of M. de Negri. On May 1 and May 3 she
attended the opera, spending the next evening on the water. Hill,
Wright, and Montgomery dined on May 5, and she entertained
herself on the water and by visiting the flower and vegetable mar-
kets on May 6 and May 8. For May 2, 7, 9, 11, 12, 14, 15, 17, 18,
and 19 there are no entries, the latter three omissions "caused by
indisposition," but there are no entries and no explanations either
for May 21, 25, 26, 28, and 30. No part of her book, however, implies that she was giving her entire diary to the public. On May 22
she went to the harbor to inspect the *Glasgow* ship of war, on which
her husband would shortly sail. Its captain dined the next day
with her; she went aboard on May 24, and he dined with her
again on May 31. On June 1 she witnessed religious festivals in
Genoa and in a neighboring village. Thus did she fill up some part
of her days in Genoa, although the presence of Byron was, of course,
the greatest attraction the city offered to her.

There are some reasonable certainties concerning the relations that existed between Byron and Lady Blessington, although Byron himself was uncertain of the precise date of their first meeting: it was either on March 31 or April 1, probably the latter.[115] While she was in Genoa, he wrote fifteen surviving letters to members of her party: eight in April, six in May, and one in June; eleven were addressed to Lord Blessington, three to Lady Blessington, and one to D'Orsay. There are nineteen letters from members of the Blessington party to Byron which have been preserved: thirteen from Lord Blessington, four from Lady Blessington, and two from D'Orsay, all carefully saved by Byron and now in the possession of Sir John Murray.

By April 19, Byron had seen Lady Blessington often enough to produce in Teresa "a fit of jealousy," which had grown by May 17 —unless he was writing for dramatic effect—into "a furious fit of Italian jealousy."[116] On May 23, declining a dinner invitation, Byron excused himself on the grounds of having had "so many dinners" already with the Blessingtons: "I have already more than sufficiently abused your hospitality."[117] Teresa, who was not disposed to exaggerate the point, admitted that Byron called on the Blessingtons or dined with them "five or six" times;[118] Lady Blessington in *The Idler* claimed only seven, plus her original call upon him. Byron confessed that he had met the Blessingtons "frequently in

[115] See *LJ*, VI, 178, and *Lord Byron's Correspondence*, II, 253. The *Journal of Fox* dates the first meeting March 31; Lady Blessington, April 1.

[116] *Lord Byron's Correspondence*, II, 258-59; *Cornhill Magazine*, LXIV (January 1928), 50. Lady Hardy replied, June 7, 1823, referring to Teresa's jealousy, "Your last letter amused me very much My dear Cousin as I can imagine (& even pity) the jealousy of a Person that feels you may grow tired of the perpetual presence she has entailed on you, & seek variety in other Society. I have seen Lady Blessington in the Park & I thought her very handsome but am surprised to hear she is a Literary Lady as I believe Her first rudiments of learning were learned at Cahir in Tipperary where she was the post Masters Daughter but when Women take to write there is no saying when they will stop" (from the autograph letter in the possession of Sir John Murray; published with variants by Doris L. Moore, *The Late Lord Byron*, pp. 482-83).

[117] *LJ*, VI, 218.

[118] Madden, I, 73.

their rides about Genoa";[119] Lady Blessington in *The Idler* claimed thirteen such encounters, planned or accidental, for a total of twenty-one meetings of all kinds within the two months of her Genoa sojourn. The number does not seem excessive or exaggerated.

The degree and kind of intimacy which Byron and Lady Blessington achieved may be estimated with some exactness from his three surviving letters to her and, less certainly, from gifts and other manuscripts of his in her possession. On April 14, Byron asked Lord Blessington to "tell Lady B., with my compliments, that I am rummaging my papers for a MS. worthy of her acceptation."[120] (The choice of "acceptation" rather than the simpler and more natural "acceptance" may be significant.) One of the manuscripts given to her by Byron, she told Crabb Robinson, was a copy of Byron's letter of June 1818 to Hobhouse, written from Venice in the name and spelling of Fletcher and comically describing his own death.[121] She later showed it to Teresa. In it we read: "His nine whores are already provided for, and the other servants; but what is to become of me?"[122] There is more in a similar tone. The author of *The Magic Lantern* would not have been pleased with this gift, but Lady Blessington was hardly the same person in and out of print. If this was indeed the manuscript which he sought out for her "acceptation," it would seem to be evidence of a rather high degree of intimacy, and the gift of it clearly assumes in her a sense of humor sufficient to enjoy it. As for the poems he addressed to her, one is more gallant and one more decorous than the letter of "Fletcher." It seems that some wit in Genoa had observed, referring to the villa called "Il Paradiso," which Byron tried to persuade Lord Blessington to rent and had supposedly considered renting himself at one time: *"Il diavolo è ancora entrato in Paradiso."*[123] Byron then wrote the following impromptu lines and gave them to her:

[119] *Cornhill Magazine, loc.cit.*
[120] *LJ*, VI, 193.
[121] *Robinson on Books and Their Writers*, I, 413.
[122] *LJ*, IV, 235.
[123] Thomas Moore, *Letters and Journals of Lord Byron: With Notices of His Life* (London, 1892), p. 577, n. 1.

> Beneath Blessington's eyes
> The reclaimed Paradise
> Should be free as the former from evil;
> But if the new Eve
> For an Apple should grieve,
> What mortal would not play the Devil?

A variant of the last line appears in an anecdote reported by Madden: "Lady Blessington informed me that, on the occasion of a masked ball to be given in Genoa, Byron stated his intention of going there, and asked her ladyship to accompany him: *en badinant* about the character she was to go in, some one [Byron? Lady Blessington?] had suggested that of Eve—Byron said, 'As some one must play the devil, I will do it.' "[124] The lines he addressed "To the Countess of Blessington," at her request, are somewhat less gallant. He praised the beauty that "Lawrence has painted so well," but he described himself as one whose "feelings . . . are dry." "I am ashes where once I was fire." This is one of those poems in which the poet says he cannot write the poem that he has in fact just written, and the Byron in it, ageing before his time and emotionally drought-ridden, also appears in her *Conversations*.

Much warmer, and clearly suggestive of a genuinely romantic attraction are the lines, "But once I dared to lift my eyes—," which, in the opinion of E. H. Coleridge, editor of Byron's *Poetry*, are "probably" addressed to Lady Blessington,[125] who included them in her *Conversations* and said that Byron had given them to her. I quote them in full:

> But once I dared to lift my eyes—
>   To lift my eyes to thee;
> And since that day, beneath the skies,
>   No other sight they see.
>
> In vain sleep shuts them in the night—
>   The night grows day to me;
> Presenting idly to my sight
>   What still a dream must be.

[124] Madden, I, 73-74.
[125] *The Works of Lord Byron. Poetry*, ed. Ernest Hartley Coleridge (London, 1898-1904), IV, 564, n. 1.

A fatal dream—for many a bar
    Divides thy fate from mine;
And still my passions wake and war,
    But peace be still with thine.

Even more revealing, in estimating the nature and kind of their
relations, are his three surviving letters to her.[126] The first is dated
May 3. Behind it lies a most remarkable, an almost unbelievable
fact: her influence over him was so great that she had persuaded
him to use the services of Colonel Hugh Montgomery and his sister
Mary Millicent, whom he disliked and distrusted as friends of Lady
Byron, to secure from his wife a miniature of her "or indeed a memorial of any kind of Lady B[yron]." Further, and equally remarkable, in answer to her urgent note of May 3, stating that Montgomery would leave Genoa in two hours, that she "wish[ed] to be
accurate in conveying your wishes" and would await Byron's reply
("tell me exactly what I am to say")[127] before instructing the
Colonel, he wrote out a "message" of about 140 words specifically
designed to dispel Lady Byron's fears concerning his daughter Ada.
He was also foolish enough to give to Lady Blessington a copy of
his 1816 "Lines on Hearing That Lady Byron was Ill." She showed
the poem to Colonel Montgomery, who described it to Lady Byron
as "very severe," and Lady Blessington later published it for the
first time in her *Conversations*. But the degree of intimacy implied

[126] *LJ*, VI, 198-99, 203-05, 221-22. When Lady Blessington wrote to Colonel
Montgomery, it would seem that she paraphrased Byron's letter of May 3,
although Moore, the source of the Prothero text, may have done so himself.
However, the differences between the published text of Byron's letter and the
hitherto unpublished letter of Lady Blessington are interesting. Byron's letter
begins, "My request would be for a copy of the miniature of Lady B. . . .";
Lady Blessington wrote, "Lord Byrons anxious desire is to have a request made
to Lady Byron for a Copy of the miniature. . . ." Lady Blessington wrote also
that Byron had "heard with great regret that Lady B—— is in delicate health,"
a regret not expressed in Byron's letter. Lady Blessington concluded, "I trust
your Sister may succeed in procuring the Picture, as I believe it would be a
source of Comfort to him."
  Colonel Montgomery's malicious sister forwarded Lady Blessington's letter
with the following comments of her own: "He makes you and his unhappy fate
a frequent subject of conversation with Lord & Lady B[lessington], speaks of
you & your virtues with tears, asserts that he is to this day ignorant of the cause
of your disgust & hatred to him, and only supposes your aversion to have been
the work of ill intentioned persons who have calumniated his character & conduct &c &c &c" (from the unpublished autograph letters in the Lovelace Papers of Lord Lytton).
[127] From the autograph letter in the possession of Sir John Murray.

by this transaction and the confidence Byron reposed in her are clear.

On May 6, three days later, he sent Lady Blessington a painfully intimate letter he had written but never mailed to Lady Byron, discussing their marriage and separation. It seems to be the last letter he ever wrote to his wife. Byron explained to Lady Blessington that he had not sent it because of his "despair of its doing any good." It was accompanied by a copy of Benjamin Constant's autobiographical novel *Adolphe*, which, Byron wrote, contains "some melancholy truths" and "is too triste a work ever to have been popular." It was a most unusual gift under the circumstances, for it probes the psychology of a man tired of a long love affair but without sufficient strength of character to end it. Byron's situation was remarkably similar to that of Adolphe. Other evidence makes it clear that he had already talked to her about Teresa's jealousy.

She received his letter, along with that written to Lady Byron (now a gift from him to Lady Blessington), on May 7 and replied on the same day in a fashion that reveals much—tender interest in his marriage and separation, intimate knowledge of his daily relations and problems with Teresa—and the glance of a coquette. The postscript coyly confesses: "I dare not send you my answer to your lines on Paradise—you may guess why." This clearly implies that in her poem not sent she had expressed a willingness to play Eve to his Adam (or Satan), although to be sure she may never have written any such poem. Earlier in the letter she had asked him, referring to Teresa: "Did you get scolded yesterday? and how are you today? I have smiled more than once at the grave face of fear you put on before we parted, and I could have told you all that was at that moment passing in your mind."[128] Thus assuring him how well she understood him, she managed in one short letter to refer to his relations with both his wife and his mistress and to cast herself in the role of the naked Eve, trembling, one may say, on the verge of the Fall. It was presumably later in the same day that she replied to his five stanzas ("You have asked for a verse . . .") with five of her own—in number, form, and theme the mirror of his, beginning with the first line, "When I ask'd for a verse . . ."

[128] From the autograph letter in the possession of Sir John Murray.

In her poem she described herself as ageing, as he had described himself, and no longer able to inspire poetic fire.

> Time has press'd with rude fingers my brow,
>   And the roses have fled from my cheek
> Then it surely were folly if now
>   I the strains due to beauty should seek.
>
> But as Pilgrims who visit the Shrine
>   Of some Saint bear a relic away
> So I sought a Memorial of thine
>   As a treasure when distant I stray.[129]

Lady Blessington may well have had second thoughts about these stanzas and written a third time to Byron on the same day. In an undated note she informed him: "I find I have made a grammatical error in my lines, and tho' you may pardon bad verses, I cannot hope you will be equally lenient to bad grammar. Will you therefore return them to me that I may rectify the mistake.

> Very much yours
>
> M B[130]

On May 7 Byron wrote to Lord Blessington: "I have not returned *Miledi's* verses, because I am not aware of the error she mentions, and see no reason for the alteration; however, if she insists, I must be conformable." Evidently she did not insist, for Byron kept the poem.

All this is far removed from Lady Byron. Nevertheless, on the same day or thereabouts, Colonel Montgomery's sister forwarded Lady Blessington's letter to Lady Byron, and about a week later the Colonel, who did not like Byron, wrote himself.[131] The remarkable quality of his letter, the contents of which derived wholly from Lady Blessington, is the astonishingly sympathetic portrait that emerges, not to mention the intimate details of Byron's life with which Lady Blessington at this time was acquainted and which she supplied to the Colonel. It was she who made it possible

---

[129] From the autograph letter in the possession of Sir John Murray.
[130] From the autograph letter in the possession of Sir John Murray.
[131] Quoted by Doris L. Moore, *The Late Lord Byron*, pp. 485-86.

for Byron to represent himself to Lady Byron as emotional to the point of tears when speaking of his wife and daughter, to picture himself as the misused, calumniated husband explaining away the attacks on her in his poetry (he had been goaded into them). He is described as much thinner than he was in Venice, abstemious in private although not disagreeably so in public, studious, poetically productive, leading a regulated life, which is in some danger, for he always rides with pistols. He is, further, living virtuously, apart from Teresa, "a small, fair, delicate bashful person much more resembling a British Subject than one of any Southern nation," and he is chaperoned everywhere he goes by her brother. He wished for pictures of both wife and daughter but put first a picture of his wife, although as a father he will use as an intermediary only a man who is himself a father. He admits his faults, an "unfortunate temper which had been his ruin, & the cause of all his misfortunes," praises his wife, and protests his innocence, placing the blame not on Lady Byron but on another who had misled her. He "declar[ed] over & over again that he had no wish upon earth greater than that 'our daughter, (for she is our daughter) may resemble her mother in every thing'—Those were his exact words. . . . He added," the Colonel informed Lady Byron, "that you are the only unmarried woman he ever loved. . . ." And all of this, it may be repeated, came from Lady Blessington, who got most of these details from Byron. He could not have written a much more sympathetic letter himself, although he would not have mentioned his wearing Augusta Leigh's hair in a brooch, with a reference to which Colonel Montgomery ended his letter. Years later, Teresa was convinced that Lady Blessington was attempting to achieve a reunion between Byron and his wife and that her motive, in thus placing herself on the side of marriage and virtue, was to gain the favor of *"la société feminine aristocratique et morale de l'Angleterre qui lui tenait rigueur."*[132]

Byron's last letter to Lady Blessington was written on the day after their farewell and closed with the hope that her *"nerves are well to-day, and will continue to flourish."* She replied that they were "not better." In the account she gave to Moore, however, she

---

[132] "La Vie de Lord Byron en Italie," p. 1476. Teresa makes the same point on pp. 1470 and 1497.

stated that *he* wept.[133] As Hobhouse noted, such conduct was "very unlike him,"[134] and it seems probable that she has here reversed their roles, as she demonstrably did in terms of another detail of their parting. In the account that she gave to Moore, Byron is represented as asking her for some "memorial, some trifle which she had worn,"[135] but Byron's letter to her makes clear that it was *she* who had "wished for something *worn*. . . ." In one way or another, the scene was clearly an emotional one, and upon parting he gave her a pin, a small cameo of Napoleon, whom she greatly admired. In his letter of the next day he asked her to exchange it: "I am *superstitious*, and have recollected that memorials with a *point* are of less fortunate augury. . . ." Therefore he requested her to accept an enclosed chain, which he had "worn oftener and longer" than the pin. He explained that its only "peculiarity" was its Venetian origin: "it could only be obtained at or from Venice," the scene of his greatest sexual debaucheries, which she later deplored. But at this time she wrote to him, on June 2:

My dear Lord Byron

It is not without regret that I return you the Pin, but the chain I shall guard and I think it may form the link of a friendship that I shall sincerely prize.

My Nerves are not better today, but I shall not bore you about them. With the most unfeigned good wishes for your health and happiness, Believe me my dear Lord Byron

your obliged and sincere

M. B.

PS. I go off early tomorrow and I beg you will let me have the Book you promised, and also, that you will write your name in the one you have given me and return it before I go. If you add underneath your name that you give it to me you will oblige me. God bless you.[136]

[133] Moore, *Life*, p. 590.
[134] Hobhouse's marginalia in Moore's *Life*, published by Nicholson, *Byron: The Last Journey*.
[135] Moore, *Life*, p. 590.
[136] From the autograph letter in the possession of Sir John Murray.

She was always in need of friends; when she wrote this letter she honestly liked Byron; it is the product of a woman who was a great deal more than a mere collector of literary curiosities. One of the books that he gave her, she said, was a copy of his Armenian grammar. He had used and annotated it in 1816, the year of his debacle, when his "mind wanted something craggy to break upon."[137] By this gift he may have been subtly suggesting to her that the time had now come for her too to study Armenian. It was at Genoa that she had in effect lost her husband, who there willed the chief part of his estate not to her but to D'Orsay and whichever one of the Blessington daughters he would choose. In return for his gift, she gave Byron a ring from her finger.[138]

Teresa's version of Byron's farewell to Lady Blessington supports the emotional complexity suggested by the evidence above. She wrote, in "La Vie de Lord Byron en Italie": *Lady Bles. qui avait un réel enthousiasme pour Lord Byron se trouva si émue à l'heure des adieux qu'elle en eut une véritable attaque de nerfs; de retour à Albaro après cet adieu L. Byron se rendit chez Mme G. et lui rendit compte de ce qui venait de se passer. 'Je n'aurais pas cru mériter les regrets et la bienveillance que les Bles. m'ont témoigné. Milady a eu une attaque de nerfs. Elle a pleuré. Je ne puis voir pleurer sans souffrir. Je sentais que l'émotion allait gagner aussi mes nerfs et je me suis levé pour couper court à cette scène d'autant plus que le Comte D'Orsay ne semblait pas la regarder avec plaisir, et que Pietro l'observait avec curiosité (leurs nerfs étant probablement plus solides) et nous sommes partis.' "[139]* As early as 1829, in conversation with Lord John Russell, Lady Blessington had told the story of Byron weeping, but in the account she gave to Moore for his *Life* of Byron she stated that "all who were present in the room . . . were affected by his emotion. . . ."[140] Perhaps they both wept, although she would seem to have had the greater cause.

[137] *LJ*, IV, 10. [138] Moore, *Life*, p. 590.

[139] "La Vie de Lord Byron en Italie," pp. 1488-90.

[140] *Letters of Moore*, II, 661; Moore, *Life*, p. 590. Moore also heard another version, recorded in his "Notes for Life of Lord Byron," *Prose and Verse, Humorous, Satirical, and Sentimental*, ed. Richard Herne Shepherd (London, 1878), pp. 414-15: "B.'s scene with Lady Blessington—the B.'s near their departure—lying on the sofa while they were at dinner—burst out a-crying. Lady B., fearing that he might be ashamed of it, saying, 'One is often in that sort of mood, when one cannot help crying from nervousness.' 'Nervousness!' angry that she should think it arose from anything but feeling."

It may well be significant when one considers the evidence Byron left concerning his relations with Lady Blessington that, aside from his letters to her friends Moore and Douglas Kinnaird, written shortly after meeting her, he discussed her at length only with Lady Hardy, then in her early thirties and still the wife of Nelson's Admiral Hardy. A distant cousin, Byron had known her in 1814. She had been in Genoa in September 1822, and in the correspondence that developed they discussed, among others, James Wedderburn Webster, separated from his wife and so paying court to Lady Hardy, a situation Byron found ludicrous. He wrote to Lady Hardy that Webster, wearing a black wig that he claimed to be his own hair, had "actually (no jest I assure you) advertised [in Johnsonian terms] for an 'agreeable companion in a post chaise' in the Genoa Gazette."[141]

There must have been more than a little of the coquette in Lady Hardy, whose husband, now in his fifties, was often at sea and had not seen his wife since 1819. In addition to Webster, she had been pursued between 1814 and 1816 by Lord Buckingham, who, after being rebuffed by her, had carried on "a regular campaign of calumny against Lady Hardy in reference to her 'relations' with Lord Abercorn. . . ." In June 1816, the Admiral obtained £1,000 damages from the *Morning Herald* and then fought a duel with Buckingham.[142]

It was to her then that Byron revealed that his lines "When we two parted" actually referred to Webster's wife, with whom Byron had flirted in 1813. The point here, however, is that in his letters to Lady Hardy, Byron was also flirting or coquetting (safely, by mail). Four of his five letters to her discuss romantic love or the relations between the sexes. Typical of these passages is the following: "I have always laid it down as a maxim—and found it justified by experience—that a man and a woman can make far better friendships than can exist between two of the same sex, but *then* with this condition that they never have made or are to make love with each other. . . . Indeed I rather look on love as a sort of hostile transaction, very necessary to make or to break in order to keep the world a-going, but by no means a sinecure to the parties concerned.

[141] Byron's letters appear in the *Cornhill Magazine*, LXIV (January 1928), 39-53.

[142] John Gore, *Nelson's Hardy and His Wife* (London, 1935), pp. 49-50.

Now as *my* Love perils are I believe pretty well over and yours by all accounts are never to begin, we shall be the best friends imaginable. . . ." As for Lady Hardy, she could write to Byron, concerning the possibility of Teresa going to Greece with him, "you could not ought not to take her as a woman but you will wonder at me as a woman . . . who dont pass for a very romantic person in the eyes of the world when I say were I in her place I should try to see if I could not realise Lara's page. Would not that be heroic & troublesome to the last degree? and I should think it not unlikely such a scheme might have entered her head, as if Lady Blessington was an object of jealousy when at your elbow to counteract the spell, think what absence would create."[143]

All of this suggests something more than that Byron had merely chosen an appropriate and sympathetic correspondent with whom to discuss Lady Blessington. It was to Lady Hardy that he confessed that Lady Blessington "seemed entirely bored with her Lord, and a little sick of her Parisian Paladin also. . . ." He assured Lady Hardy, "you see there was no danger. . . ." But, one feels, he is protesting too much, for he continued: "to say truth, [I] thought that I was as well off at home." In thus comparing Teresa and Lady Blessington, then, he had assumed the possibility of replacing one with the other. He suspects that "it is only over a very young man that . . . those full blown beauties [like Lady Blessington] have the power you describe." Byron's preference for women of full figure, however, is known. Teresa was one, Lady Oxford another, and he made clear his dislike of Caroline Lamb's slight or boyish figure. "And now they are gone," he informed Lady Hardy; it is as if he had written, "And no birds sing." Teresa thought that Lady Blessington "dared not reveal all her admiration . . ." of Byron.[144]

Moore's account, based on Lady Blessington's "MS. book," states that their friendship "was a source of much pleasure" to Byron,[145] and her *Idler* account[146] is remarkable for the extent of the admiration, even affection, expressed and for the nearly complete ab-

[143] From the autograph letter, June 17, 1823, in the possession of Sir John Murray.
[144] Teresa Guiccioli, *My Recollections of Lord Byron* (New York, 1869), p. 62.
[145] *Letters of Moore*, II, 744; Moore, *Life*, p. 577.
[146] Quoted below from *HVSH*, pp. 349-51, 355-70.

sence of malice. Not that she is uncritical. She was "disappointed!" to be sure after her introduction to Byron, but chiefly or only because "the lively, brilliant conversationalist" whom she met, "witty, sarcastic, . . . lively," and flippant, with "a reckless levity of disposition," seemed "incompatible" with the "sublime passages in *Childe Harold* and *Manfred*." Even so, "his manners are very fascinating —more so, perhaps, than if they were dignified. . . ." She found his appearance "highly prepossessing" and his manner "graceful, animated, and cordial." When he looks thoughtful, "his head might serve as a model for a painter's ideal of a poet." "His voice and accent are particularly clear and harmonious. . . ." "His laugh is musical. . . ." She did not find him "ill-natured or malicious": his satiric remarks on his friends and hers proceeded from "a very uncommon degree of shrewdness and a still more rare wit. . . ."

He was without "the slightest shade of pedantry" and perfectly free "from conceit." After the death of Lord Blessington's son, she observed "a gentleness, and almost womanly softness" in Byron's manner toward her husband, "peculiarly pleasing to witness." With the "musical voice of Byron sounding in [her] ears, [her] spirits felt relieved from the gloom" of her mourning. She noticed his "passion for flowers," his charity to beggars, his manner with them "gentle and kind."

On April 30, "gay and animated," he amused them with stories of his old London life. "He tells a story remarkably well, mimics the manner of the persons he describes very successfully, and has a true comic vein when he is disposed to indulge in it." But his heart is also "capable of gentle and fond affection. . . ." He is a "gifted and remarkable man." She found that the "pertinacity with which he urged our stay [in Genoa] was very flattering . . . ,"[147] coming as it did from "his powerful mind." When he wept, as she said he did, at their parting, "he never appeared to greater advantage in

[147] In "La Vie de Lord Byron en Italie," p. 1480, Teresa explains, somewhat startlingly, Byron's reason for wishing the Blessingtons to remain in Genoa until after his own departure: *"Il lui sembla donc que la conversation si animée de cette famille Irlandaise pourrait procurer à sa jeune amie [Teresa] une distraction momentanée et ce fut dans ce but qu'il insista auprès de Milady pour qu'elle voulut changer son départ jusque après le sien."* This is the clearest evidence, of course, of the confidence that Byron placed in Lady Blessington.

our eyes than while thus resigning himself to the natural impulse of an affectionate heart; and we were all much moved."

At the very least, then, the relations between them in Genoa must be described as friendly and sympathetic, with some measure of flirtation or romantic coloring. The number and kind of letters and poems that passed between them, Teresa's jealous reaction, the number and kind of gifts exchanged, the emotional parting scene —all this and more support such an interpretation. And yet the fact is, of course, that their friendship did not outlive her departure from Genoa. After June 2, 1823, she never wrote another letter to him (who saved everything), nor, it appears, did he write to either her or her husband. One may speculate on the reasons, beginning with certain qualities of hers.

Writing to Lady Hardy a week after Lady Blessington's departure, Byron referred to her as "this new Goddess of Discord," "our Irish Aspasia."[148] Each phrase recognizes the beauty of the woman, presumably, but it was Eris's golden apple of discord, thrown significantly into the midst of a banquet to which she had not been invited and inscribed "for the fairest," which led to the judgment of Paris and the Trojan war. Here is another side of Lady Blessington, the implications of which are further clarified by the reference to Aspasia. She was, like Lady Blessington, a woman of great beauty, accomplishments, and reputation, but the comic poets regarded her as Pericles' political advisor and the cause of the Peloponnesian War. Like Lady Blessington also, she was accused of impiety and was represented as "criticizing the manners and training of the women of her time." (She was, in addition, described as a teacher of rhetoric.)[149] Associated with Eris and Aspasia, then, are the qualities of censure, strife, and discord. Byron seems clearly aware of her capacity for trouble-making. There is evidence of her taste for viciously malicious gossip in 1823, but as the evidence becomes more abundant by the mid-1830's, it will be discussed at greater length below.

It may be recalled, further, that the first three important men in the life of Margaret Power Farmer, Lady Blessington, were associated with the military—two captains and a lieutenant colonel,

[148] *Cornhill Magazine*, LXIV (January 1928), 50-51.
[149] *Encyclopædia Britannica*, 11th edn.

Lord Blessington. Indeed, the tone of her early social life, from her childhood, when the King's officers drank and dined in her father's house, had been set by the regiments stationed in Ireland. With their officers she danced at many a ball and, gossip reported, saw them under less respectable conditions as well. To them she may well have owed the "raciness" of her conversation, depending on her audience, which she did not always judge correctly. Madden, who met her in Naples in 1823, shortly after she had left Byron, noted that her "racy observations . . . never degenerate[d] into coarseness or vulgarity."[150] But the fastidious Henry Fox, heir of Holland House, on March 23, 1823, one week before she met Byron, found her "not at all pleasant, very vulgar and abusive."[151] The next day he wrote to his mother, "L^y B abuses like pickpockets all those old Lords we used to think her Lovers . . . she is not in the least pleasant & anything but clever."[152] The English in Naples christened her "the Countess of Cursington" because of her foul language.[153] In the same city in 1825, Fox observed: "The whole family bore me to extinction. My Lady has taken to be learned, and collects relics of literary value—Voltaire's pin, Ld Byron's watch-chain. . . . She writes on life and manners. I wish she would acquire some of the latter before she criticises. Her whole notion of shewing her judgment is by violent and almost *Billingsgate* censure. . . . She has a little Irish quickness and fun, and a little more brogue; but that is all. The most tiresome thing is, that she never stops on any subject when once she begins. . . ."[154]

Fox was even more severe in a letter to his mother on June 21, 1825, when he reported his delight to escape from the "persecutions of Lady Blessington. . . . I hate bad society & there is some-

---

[150] Madden, I, 236.

[151] *Journal of Fox*, p. 158.

[152] From the autograph letter, March 24, 1823, in the British Museum, Add. Mss. 51762-65.

[153] *Correspondence of Jekyll*, p. 290. Jekyll heard the story from the Misses Berry on July 18, 1831; they had recently dined with Lady Blessington's sister Ellen and her husband. Cyrus Redding, who seems not to have known Lady Blessington personally, wrote in his *Fifty Years' Recollections*: "She knew from no short practice, when it was politic to be amiable, and yet no one could be less amiable when her temper was roused; her language then being well-suited to the circumstances of the provocation, both in style and epithet" (quoted by Sadleir, *The Strange Life of Lady Blessington*, p. 331).

[154] *Journal of Fox*, p. 204.

thing so discreditable & vulgar mannered & minded in her conversation that I always feel ashamed of myself for being in the company of anything so *low* & dreadfully dull."[155] Even after she had cared for Fox for more than six weeks in her own villa, where he was laid up with a damaged ankle from October 16 to December 4, 1825, he could not like her, try as he might, and she had tried mightily, professing an "extreme partiality" for him, even though she had been "very ill." Recognizing her "beauty, talents and good qualities which far better judges than I am see and admire in her," he concluded, "she has exactly the defects that suit least with my character and that cross all my prejudices and wound all my little peculiarities of opinion and disposition." Two years later he noted again her "ribaldry."[156] Although Fox is an unfriendly witness, he was hardly a prude: he had already put Teresa Guiccioli to bed. Nor would he have invented the remarks put into his diary or mailed to his mother. Byron, who liked Fox tremendously and in general shared his background, tastes, and assumptions, may well have found the combination of Irish ribaldry and the interests of the bluestocking wildly incongruous. If she attempted to adopt the high moral tone of *The Magic Lantern* with him, it is impossible to predict the nature of his reaction. Her own "strong tendency . . . to sudden impulses of hastiness of temper"[157] would not have helped their relations either.

Their relations were probably also affected by the ostentatious vulgarity of her tastes, already suggested. It may be most clearly demonstrated by her description of her own suite in the house which Lord Blessington furnished for her in 1828, all in the most "exquisite taste." As she described the furnishings, her "silvered" bed "rests on the backs of two large silver swans, so exquisitely sculptured that every feather is in alto-relievo, and looks nearly as fleecy as those of the living bird. The recess in which it is placed is lined with white fluted silk, bordered with blue embossed lace; and from the columns that support the frieze of the recess, pale blue silk curtains, lined with white, are hung. . . ." There was a silvered sofa in the bedroom and another was in the "*salle de bain*," which had a

---

[155] From the autograph letter in the British Museum, Add. Mss. 51762-65.
[156] *Journal of Fox*, pp. 216-17, 243.
[157] Madden, I, 156.

sunken marble bath in the floor and, on the ceiling, "Flora scattering flowers with one hand, while from the other is suspended an alabaster lamp in the form of a lotus." "The effect of the whole suite," she concluded, "is chastely beautiful."[158] Less than two years before, when she had passed through Genoa again, Barry had shown her Byron's bed: it was "the most gaudily vulgar thing I ever saw," she wrote, "the curtains in the worst taste, and the cornice having his family motto of 'Crede Byron' surmounted by baronial coronets. His carriage and his liveries were in the same bad taste, having an affectation of finery, but *mesquin* in the details, and tawdry in the *ensemble*. . . ."[159] Lady Blessington's carriage has been described as "a gypsy's dream."[160] As she described it, it had "a *dormeuse à doubleressort*, with its library, soft cushions, and eiderdown pillows, its *nécessaire à déjéuner et à diner*, safely stowed in a well, and . . . innumerable other little comforts. . . ."[161] When she and her party were about to leave Paris in 1822, a French observer thought that a regiment was about to move. Her own traveling carriage was in fact basically like Byron's, which had been copied from one used by Napoleon.

The transition from Tipperary to Seamore Place, where she wrote the *Conversations*, was not accomplished in a day, but eventually Margaret Power was able to remake herself rather completely. By the time she met Byron, this process of conscious transformation had been going on for a number of years, although in 1823 the differences between her assumed and her earlier character must still have been apparent. Madden writes of her in connection with the events of July 1823: "it can not be denied that, whether discoursing in her salons, or talking with pen in hand on paper in her journals, she occasionally aimed at something like stage effects, acted in society and in her diaries, and at times assumed opinions, which she abandoned a little later, or passed off appearances for realities. This was done with the view of acquiring esteem, strengthening her position in the opinion of persons of exalted intellect or station, . . . not for any unworthy purpose, but from a desire to

158 *The Idler in France* (London, 1841), I, 119-22.
159 *Conversations of Byron*, p. 154.
160 Connely, *Count D'Orsay*, p. 56.
161 *The Idler in Italy* (London, 1839-1840), I, 43.

please, and perhaps from a feeling of uncertainty in the possession of present advantages."[162] This tendency or aim, Madden implies later in his book, "becomes in time fatal to naturalness of character, singleness, and sincerity of mind." Something of these effects must surely have been a part of her when at the age of thirty-three she met Byron. Madden concludes, without suggesting a date: "She lived, in fact, for distinction on the stage of literary society before the footlights, and always *en scene*." In order to gain such distinction, he explains, "she must become an actress there, she must adapt her manners, fashion her ideas, accomodate her conversation to the taste, tone of thought, and turn of mind of every individual around her."[163] She must possess in high degree, in other words, the power that Byron attributed to Lady Adeline Amundeville—mobility:

> Juan, when he cast a glance
> On Adeline while playing her grand role,
>   Which she went through as though it were a dance,
> (Betraying only now and then her soul
>   By a look scarce perceptibly askance
> Of weariness or scorn) began to feel
> Some doubt how much of Adeline was *real*:
>
> So well she acted, all and every part
>   By turns—with that vivacious versatility
> Which many people take for want of heart.
>   They err—'tis merely what is called mobility,
> A thing of temperament and not of art,
>   Though seeming so, from its supposed facility;
> And false—though true; for surely they're sincerest
> Who are strongly acted on by what is nearest.[164]

It is most probable that this facet of Adeline's character was indeed suggested to Byron by Lady Blessington. Teresa's note, stuck into the front of her copy of the *Conversations*, states that Byron had said to her: *"c'est un caractère que j'étudie pour* Don Juan

[162] Madden, I, 81-82.
[163] Madden, I, 205-06.
[164] *Don Juan*, XVI, xcvi-vii.

(L^y *Adeline*),"[165] and Canto XVI, in which these stanzas appear, was written between March 29 and May 6, 1823, and mailed before May 21, when Lady Blessington was still in Genoa. But that Byron had only to look within to see the quality of mobility is suggested by his obviously self-revealing note. It is perhaps significant that he used the French term: "In French, 'mobilité.' I am not sure that mobility is English, but it is expressive of a quality which rather belongs to other climates [Irish?], though it is sometimes seen to a great extent in our own. It may be defined as an excessive susceptibility of immediate impressions—at the same time without *losing* the past; and is, though sometimes apparently useful to the possessor, a most painful and unhappy attribute." Moore comments: "That he was fully aware not only of the abundance of this quality in his own nature, but of the danger in which it placed consistency and singleness of character, did not require the note

[165] From the autograph note in the Biblioteca Classense of Ravenna. Although Steffan and Pratt's variorum edition of *Don Juan* is not aware of the relation between Adeline and Lady Blessington (nor do I know that the relationship has been pointed out elsewhere), the insistence with which Teresa Guiccioli returned to the Blessingtonian debts of Adeline and the circumstantiality of Teresa's accounts strongly support the view that Byron did indeed model the Adeline of Canto XVI on the English countess. Teresa discussed the matter at least twice in her unpublished "Vie de Lord Byron en Italie," pp. 1459-61 and p. 1479: "*Il écrivait alors Don Juan—et il trouva dans ce salon des éléments de succès. Un jour entr'autres tandis que Lord Byron se trouvait chez Madame Guiccioli un courrier s'arrêta à la grille de la cour, porteur d'une invitation à dîner de la part des Blessingtons. 'Elles vous font bien la cour ces dames (lui dit la Comtesse en souriant), est-ce que vous la leur payeriez de retour?' 'Vous savez bien que non (dit-il), mais j'écris, dans ce moment pour passer des heures et m'amuser, Don Juan. Il se trouve maintenant en Angleterre au milieu de ce qu'on appelle le grand monde; j'aime assez de contrôler mes idées là-dessus avec celles des autres—et de trouver des caractères qui puissent les mettre en relief. J'ai surtout dans ce moment besoin d'une héroïne. . . .' 'Comment (reprit la Comtesse)—voudriez-vous satyriser les personnes qui vous admirent tant?' 'Oh pour cela non (dit-il). Ce que je leur emprunterais ne leur fera aucun mal et on ne connaîtra pas de quelle matière est tissée ma toile.'*"

Eighteen pages later Teresa discussed the relationship again: "*. . . pénétrer . . . dans le fond du caractère de sa charmante compatriote l'avait aidé à la création d'un type qu'il ferait vivre sous le nom d'Adeline—où toutes les circonstances de la situation réelle du type modifiées serviraient à montrer dans le poème le danger qu'il peut y avoir pour une femme charmante à se faire le mentor d'un jeune homme séduisant. Car Lady Adeline malgré sa pruderie, si le poème avait été continué—et le caractère porté à son complet dénouement devait à la fin devenir amoureuse de Don Juan et même se compromettre sans obtenir son amour puisque le coeur de Don Juan était engagé*" (from the autograph manuscript in the Biblioteca Classense of Ravenna).

on this passage to assure us. The consciousness, indeed, of his own natural tendency to yield thus to every chance impression, and change with every passing impulse, was . . . ever present in his mind. . . ."[166] He then, in danger of losing his "singleness of character," met her, who had already lost a large part of her "singleness, and sincerity of mind," and she twice accused him of "mobility," in the *Conversations* and in the *Idler*.[167] Thus, it appears, each studied the character of the other.

Other similarities between Adeline and Lady Blessington are to be found in stanzas 47, 102, and 103 of Canto XVI. She is a "Blue," who "Made epigrams occasionally too/ Upon her friends, as every body ought." She is a complete hypocrite, turning upon her guests once they are gone and leading the conversational attacks, presumably, upon "Their hideous wives, their horrid selves and dresses,/ And truculent distortion of their tresses." There is no reason to assume, however, that Lady Blessington did not also contribute to the portrait of the Duchess of Fitz-Fulke in Canto XVI, where, disguised as the ghost of the Black Friar, she becomes emblematic of the sensual draped in the robes of the spiritual. Her appearance, in stanzas 49 and 123, is more like Lady Blessington's than is Adeline's: she is "her gracious, graceful, graceless Grace,/ The full grown Hebe of Fitz-Fulke, whose mind,/ If she had any, was upon her face,/ And that was of a fascinating kind./ A little turn for mischief you might trace/ Also thereon. . . ." Her figure is of "full, voluptuous, but *not o'er*grown bulk." "But of all verse, what most insured her praise/ Were sonnets to herself. . . ."

> Her laughing blue eyes with a glance could seize
> The ridicules of people in all places—
>   That honey of your fashionable bees—
> And store it up for mischievous enjoyment;
> And this at present was her kind employment (XVI, 100).

Byron may also have been thinking of Lady Blessington when he wrote, in stanza 52, of the need to "wear the newest mantle of hypocrisy,/ On pain of much displeasing the Gynocrasy."

Controlled characters in a poem may achieve a level of illusion-

---

[166] Moore, *Life*, p. 646; see also *Don Juan*, XVII, xi.
[167] *Conversations*, p. 47; HVSV (*Idler*), p. 362.

ary reality not always possible outside the literary work. In life, when two persons of *mobilité* actually meet, as Byron and Lady Blessington met, the relations established between them must have a certain unreality, of which both actors are aware, further increasing the sense of unreality between them. Lady Blessington was aware of it and accused Byron of insincerity in her *Conversations*. Some years later, if not in 1823, she had convinced herself, as she wrote in her "Night Thought Book," kept in 1834, after the guests of her late evenings had departed: "The great majority of men are actors, who prefer an assumed part to that which Nature had assigned them. They seek to be something, or to appear something which they are not, and even stoop to the affectation of defects [as she had bitterly accused Byron of doing] rather than display real estimable qualities which belong to them."[168]

Grave irony or mystification ("humming" or "bamming") is one form which acting in society may take, and it was fashionable in certain circles in Lady Blessington's day. Byron was a master of it, but so was Lady Blessington, as well as D'Orsay.[169] Madden attributes to her as early as May 5, 1822, a "peculiar turn for grave irony, which was one of her characteristics," and quotes from the diary of Moore, who had called at St. James's Square with Washington Irving. Lady Blessington, Moore wrote, "is growing very absurd. 'I have felt very melancholy and ill all this day,' she said. 'Why is that?' I asked. 'Don't you know?' 'No.' 'It is the anniversary of my poor Napoleon's death.' "[170] Another example cited by Madden involved the simple-minded captain (Smith) of the *Bolivar*, in Naples in 1823. The captain was a captain by courtesy only and had never been promoted by the Admiralty. The countess and D'Orsay day after day enticed the poor man to explain again the reasons why he had not been posted, meanwhile suppressing their laughter as best they could. As Madden explained: "Her ladyship had a great turn and a particular talent for grave banter, for solemn irony, verging on the very borders of obvious hoaxing. . . . But it became too much of a habit, and tended, perhaps, to create a penchant for acting in society, and playing off opinions . . . for

[168] Madden, I, 242.
[169] Madden, II, 300-01.
[170] Madden, I, 61, quoting Moore, *Journals*, III, 350.

the sake of the fun of the performance."[171] Byron was capable of "bamming" such good friends as William Harness and Hobhouse, as when he told the latter: "Cain was right to kill Abel, that he might not have the bore of passing 200 years with him."[172] According to the *Conversations*, the playful poet conversed in this mode with Lady Blessington. It is clear that she did not like it. For only one can play this game of grave irony; the other must be the victim.

Aside from such matters, Byron had within himself at the time a sufficiency of reasons for withholding some part of himself from Lady Blessington—for Teresa, for Greece, for the sake of his reputation, which he thought, rightly enough, was about to rise from the ashes on military wings. Greece was uppermost in his mind almost from the first day of the Blessingtons' stay in Genoa. On April 5 he had talked with Blaquiere, and on April 7 he had first offered his services, in person, to both Hobhouse and Kinnaird. As Teresa observed: "every person who was near him at the time can bear witness to the struggle which his mind underwent," as the time of his departure for Greece neared. Under these conditions, the Blessington party, frivolous or worse, may well have seemed a little too much even for Byron. Lord Blessington had now for the second time courted another man's wife and then married her (he had two illegitimate children by the woman who became his first wife); Byron knew that Lady Blessington had been a kept mistress before her marriage to Blessington and knew also of the plan for D'Orsay to marry one of Blessington's daughters,[173] regarded by Henry Fox as "only a blind" for the two suspected lovers, Lady Blessing-

[171] Madden, I, 89-90; see also I, 159-64, 215-17, 310.
[172] *HVSV*, p. 316.
[173] Byron to Lady Hardy, June 10, 1823, *Cornhill Magazine*, LXIV, 51; Lord Blessington had informed Byron of D'Orsay's marriage plans. Lady Hardy wrote to Byron on June 17, 1823, of Lady Blessington: "I believe she began life as the lady fair in a most humble occasional way of the late Lord Glengall, at Cahir & supplied the absence of the lawful lady, she then succeeded in the usual routine of that life till she found the present lord in deep despair at his first wife's death who though what is called in England a *Naughty* Woman, was I believe as near an Angel as possible. I knew a person that knew her well & from his Account she was an example to other women of every high & noble feeling though she had lived as Lord Mountjoys Mistress for two years before he married her. I hope I dont shock you by being *too liberal* to others" (from the autograph letter in the possession of Sir John Murray).

ton and D'Orsay.[174] All this, then, may have been in some degree repugnant to Byron's moral sense or sense of seriousness at the time.

The failure of any lasting friendship to develop is also witnessed by the fact, noticed earlier, that there is no surviving letter from Byron to any member of the Blessington party after its departure on June 3, although Lord Blessington wrote to him once on June 17. Byron received the letter, quoted from above, but either he did not reply to it, or his reply was suppressed or destroyed by one of the Blessington party. On November 19, 1823, Barry informed Byron that Lord Blessington's draft for 400 guineas, the price of the *Bolivar*, had been dishonored by his bank, and on January 14, 1824, Barry wrote again to Byron: "I am sorry to say that my Lord Blessington's acceptance continues in the Hands of our Bankers in London unpaid. I don't like the look of it at all—it is clear you knew him better than I did. He has ordered me to sell the Bolivar even at half what he *agreed* to give you—but this is not a *Market* for pleasure boats. . . ."[175] On April 9, 1824, Byron instructed Barry to inform Lord Blessington that unless the bill was paid speedily, the affair would be made public and "other steps [taken] which will be agreeable to neither" party.[176] So ended, on this unpleasant note, the friendship of Lords Blessington and Byron, with its inevitable effect on Lady Blessington, to whom money and reputation were very important. Her early dislike of the *Bolivar*, recorded by young Charles Mathews, is probably a reflection of this financial episode, although the bitterness and other peculiar qualities of the *Conversations* are to be explained only on the basis of her life after its connections with that of Byron.

---

iv

The years between Lady Blessington's last meeting with Byron and the writing of the *Conversations* are quite as important as any others in her life; for in part they throw light on the woman Byron knew, and in other part they made the woman who wrote the book, who was by no means the same woman Byron knew.

[174] *Journal of Fox*, p. 158.
[175] From the autograph letter in the possession of Sir John Murray.
[176] *LJ*, VI, 374-75.

As she moved toward Naples, where she would live for nearly three years, the thought of Byron came back to her frequently, according to the second volume of *The Idler in Italy*. By the time she had completed the diary from which it and *The Idler in France* derive, she was as well prepared, by her travels and by her friends and Byron's, to write a book about him as any person who had ever known him. In Florence, the sight of a portrait of the banished Dante recalled to her the banished Byron, both victims of "the baleful passion of envy," which she understood, having suffered from it herself. In Florence, she saw the old Countess of Albany, who reminded her of Alfieri, who reminded her of Byron, because of the "great similarity between the[ir] characters," which Medwin had noticed several years earlier. Both poets, she wrote, were "haughty, even to insolence," lacked prudence, and suffered from "an undue and overweening self-esteem. . . ." However, at Rome she quoted *Childe Harold*, IV, 78, and observed: "These beautiful lines embody the sentiment, with which every feeling mind must contemplate Rome. I experienced their truth today. . . ." She viewed the Coliseum by moonlight and in the light of *Childe Harold*, IV, 143-144, which she quoted: "Byron has afforded a better notion of the Coliseum . . . than all who have written on it, before or since." There "the few words spoken were uttered in whispers; as if we feared to disturb the holy calm of the place, or to awaken a profane echo in such a spot." Her mood and conduct were very different, but no less genuine, presumably, when she was back in Rome in 1828 and Henry Fox observed her and her party one evening in the Coliseum: "The hallos and clapping of hands and shouts of vulgar laughter that they made rendered this enchanting spot detestable. I remained, however, till the . . . rioters were gone, and enjoyed a full hour amidst these grand ruins while the moon was casting long shadows and bright light upon its overgrown masonry."[177] All things considered, Byron might well have preferred Lady Blessington's "shouts of vulgar laughter" to Fox's picturesque meditations.

The Idler for 1823, after quoting *Childe Harold*, IV, 146-147, continues: "Byron has left nothing to be said of the Pantheon except by matter-of-fact travellers. . . . I never visit any of the places on

177 *Journal of Fox*, pp. 294-95.

which Byron has written, without involuntarily repeating to my self the lines: . . . his name and his verses will be associated with the Eternal City and its treasures as long as our language shall last." True to her principles, she wrote: "Never will English eyes at least dwell on the Gladiator without Byron's description recurring to memory. Glorious privilege of genius! thus to identify itself with the beautiful and sublime."

She arrived in Naples in July 1823, and in November dined with her "old friend, good, kind Lord Guildford," [sic] whom Byron at one time described as "the most illustrious humbug of his age and country." She rightly associated the two men, both dedicated to Greece: "Byron has been mocked for going to fight for the Greeks; Lord Guildford is derided for educating them!" In May 1824, Guilford would become the first Archon of the Ionian University in Corfu, which he had founded and endowed. In April 1824, among her other "old friends" who had come to Naples to escape the winter in Rome, was Byron's friend Ward, whom she found "as clever, amusing, and eccentric as ever," and presumably as rich, with an annual income reported to be £40,000, larger than Lord Blessington's.

In May, eleven months after she had parted from Byron, she heard of his death and remembered him tenderly. "This sad news has thrown a gloom over us all. We have been recalling to memory every word, every look of his during our last interview," which she described again. His "looks, his voice," returned to her, as she read "over the notes of his conversations . . . and could almost fancy, in those well-remembered accents of his, I heard his lips utter the words noted down." She then composed twenty-four "Lines of the Death of Byron," in closed couplets. The theme is the loss of "Britain's noblest Poet," not necessarily her noblest man. Even so, "At thirty-seven, Byron had acquired a self-control, and a distaste for the luxurious indulgences to which so many of even a more advanced age give way . . . ; his mind [had been] released from the thraldom of the senses. . . ." She then discussed him with Sir William Gell, "who was well acquainted with Byron some years ago," and they agreed, presumably, that Byron had been "most scurvily treated by the greater part of his contemporaries. . . ." In June Byron was still "continually recurring to [her] memory," although "while he lived [she] thought of him but rarely," and at "a gay musical party" she composed five stanzas on him: "I think upon that scornful mouth/ That rarely smiled, yet smiled with me." In June she dined aboard the *Bolivar*, which may have been paid for at this time but had not been at the time of Byron's death. She thought "Byron wrote much of his *Don Juan*" while aboard. "It brought Byron back to my recollection most vividly. He was very partial to this vessel. . . ." Perhaps so, before Shelley's death, but she was not, in fact. Charles James Mathews, traveling with her, reported: "Lord Blessington was an enthusiastic sailor of the *Bolivar*, his lady bored with it."[178] Presumably by this date she knew that Byron had threatened to make public Lord Blessington's unpaid bill. In November 1824, Henry Fox, Byron's "halting angel, who has tripped against a star," dined with her. She found him, whom she courted as the son of Lord Holland, "lively, intelligent, and *très-spirituel*; [he] seizes the points of ridicule in all whom he encounters, at a glance; and draws them out with a tact that is very amusing to the lookers-on." For his part, it was at this time that he found her lacking in good manners, full of "Billingsgate censure," and tiresomely repetitious.[179] Perhaps they discussed Byron. A son of Lord Carlisle, Byron's guardian, dined with them on the same day.

The Idler does not reveal that she thought of Byron again until May 1825, when she gave the subject of the poet's death to an *improvisatore*, who "instantly" produced a sonnet. Between October 16 and December 4, however, Fox was her invalid house guest, while he recovered from an injured ankle. Her *Idler* account is of curiously mixed tone and is misdated August. She attributed to Fox the quality which the French call *malice* and explained that the French term "must not be taken in the sense of the broader and stronger one of the word malice, in our language. The French phrase means simply a roguishness or slyness, that induces a person to play tricks, and draw out, and exhibit the follies of his acquaintances, for the sake of exciting a laugh, without being impelled by any desire of injuring them. Henry Fox gives such admirable imitations of the peculiarities of his absent acquaintances,

---

[178] *Life of Mathews*, I, 108.
[179] *Journal of Fox*, p. 204.

that those present are infinitely amused; forgetting that they in turn will furnish subjects for the talent they are now admiring." She and Fox seem to have been evenly matched in their capacity for malice, in the English sense of the word. His journal entry states his feelings toward her directly: ". . . she has exactly the defects that suit least with my character. . . ."[180] He then referred to the "ridicules" of her character which he had observed earlier.

The woman Byron knew is further revealed by the friendships she formed in Naples, where she rented the villa of his friend Ward. Here she sought out and achieved intimacy with three men of very learned or antiquarian tastes—Sir William Drummond, Sir William Gell, and Keppel Craven. Each was significantly older than she: Craven by ten years, Gell by twelve, and Drummond by twenty-nine. She described Craven as "a person of the greatest versatility of knowledge," a "scholar";[181] Drummond she thought "one of the most intellectual men of his day,"[182] and Gell wrote learned, witty, and lengthy letters to her from 1823 until 1835, the year of his death. Her talent for the outrageous compliment is to be seen in a letter she wrote to Drummond on April 24, 1825. She had just read his unfinished *Odin*. After comparing it to the work of Michelangelo, Shakespeare, and Milton, being "persuaded that we have no living poet who could write a sequel" to it, she concluded: "Hitherto, my dear Sir William Drummond, I have looked on you as one of the first scholars and most elegant prose writers of the present day; permit me to say, that I regard you as *the first poet*."[183] Henry Fox said of Drummond at this time: "He hates the Bible, but has more spite against the Old than the New Testament." Gell diverted Fox "with his sarcasm and philosophic determination to take the whole world as a lively comedy. He cares very little for anybody, and is never unhappy but from his . . . gouty pains."[184]

She left Naples in February 1826, recalling Childe Harold "dragging at each remove a lengthening chain," for a brief stay in Florence, where she met Lamartine, whom she greatly liked: "He is very good-looking and distinguished in his appearance, and dresses so perfectly like a gentleman, that one never would suspect him to

[180] *Journal of Fox*, p. 217.
[182] Madden, I, 386.
[184] *Journal of Fox*, pp. 205, 211.

[181] Madden, I, 416.
[183] Madden, I, 473.

67

be a poet." In every way that she observed, he was quite unlike Byron, about whom he asked her "many questions." In December she returned briefly to Genoa, where "every object around recalls poor Byron so vividly" that she could hardly believe he was dead. She called on Barry, who read her "several letters and MSS. of Byron's," some of which, "for the sake of the living and the dead," she hoped would never be published. One of these was "a lampoon on a brother poet—a poet, too, for whom Byron once professed no common esteem. I remember well his repeating these identical verses to me, and offering me a copy, which I declined to accept, . . . because I was on habits of intimacy with the person attacked: a scrupulousness which excited the raillery of Byron." Yet she owned a copy of Byron's attack on Rogers, "Question and Answer," first published in January 1833 in *Fraser's Magazine*, then edited by D'Orsay's friend (and hers too, presumably) William Maginn. Crabb Robinson reported in 1836: "She says that Lockhart [who in the *Quarterly Review* for September 1835 had attacked her friend Nathaniel P. Willis] gave the infamous verses against Rogers to [Hugh] Fraser, who insinuates they came from Lady Blessington."[185] There is no clear reason why Lockhart, editor of the *Quarterly*, should publish an attack on Rogers, one of its founders, or should make a gift of this kind to the founder of *Fraser's Magazine*; but on April 1, 1834, Crabb Robinson wrote in his diary: ". . . of Rogers she said that his malignity in speech at least was such as to justify Lord Byron's satire—he spared nobody."[186] On the same day that she saw Barry in Genoa, to return to the sometimes unreal world of *The Idler*, she also talked with Byron's friend Lord John Russell, a man of "good sense, a considerable power of discrimination, a highly cultivated mind, and great equality of temper. . . ."

In Pisa in December 1826, where she remained until June of the next year, "the delicately formed hands and feet" of the Duchesse de Guiche reminded her of "Byron's favorite hypothesis," that there are "infallible indications of noble birth." Here she saw Lamartine again, "as amiable as he is clever," unlike Byron; "with great sensibility, . . . he possesses sufficient tact to conceal, in general society,

[185] *Robinson on Books and Their Writers*, II, 506.
[186] *Robinson on Books and Their Writers*, I, 440.

every attribute peculiar to the poetical temperament, and to appear only as a well-informed, well-bred, sensible man of the world." She also noted that he was a devoted husband. In April 1827, she paid a call upon Prince Carragia and his Turkish wife, who lived in the Palazzo Lanfranchi, Byron's former residence. "I was glad of an opportunity of seeing the rooms he inhabited; and the scene I beheld in them reminded me of him: *he* would have been struck with it," for the Prince and his Princess were dressed in Turkish costume, and the room was decorated in "barbaric" Turkish splendor.

In the summer of 1827 she returned to Florence, where she soon formed a friendship with Landor. It illustrates her ability to maintain over many years the devotion of a literary man of some genius. She declared him to be "one of the most remarkable writers of his day, as well as one of the most remarkable and original of men."[187] In 1836, however, talking with Henry Crabb Robinson, "she quoted absurd judgments given by Landor, whose critical decisions are ludicrously bad, as she herself and Chorley affirmed. She quoted him as affirming that [George Payne Rainsford] James is the greatest writer of the age. . . . Yet Landor is her dear friend—I believe she really admires him . . . ," wrote the puzzled Robinson.[188] She had now long practiced the art of flattery, and Landor visited her in Florence every evening from eight until eleven, while he talked fearlessly on every subject and she listened to the outpourings of "a mind that has never submitted to the ignoble fetters that a corrupt and artificial society would impose," as she wrote to him years later when encouraging him to give to the world his autobiography. It would, she told him, teach "the timid and . . . the weak . . . to rely on their intellectual resources instead of leaning on that feeble reed, the world, which can wound but not support those who rely on it."[189] He was over fifty years of age when she met him, and she did not care that he neglected his clothes, for his manner toward her, unlike that of Byron, exhibited a "manly tenderness," "a more than ordinary politeness,"

[187] Madden, I, 101.
[188] *Robinson on Books and Their Writers*, II, 506.
[189] Molloy, *The Most Gorgeous Lady Blessington*, p. 145.

which was "grave and respectful" and which arose from his own "natural dignity," a quality she did not find in Byron.

In October 1827, *The Idler* states, she spent an evening with the scholarly Henry Hallam, author of *Europe in the Middle Ages*, a book which her *Conversations* indicates she had discussed with Byron. She was delighted and impressed by Hallam's "acute mind" and "the manner in which he unconsciously sifted circumstances detailed in the conversations to which he listened. His appears to be a mind that never trifles, but sets seriously to work on whatever subject engages his attention." In the same month, on October 23, Henry Fox described a very different kind of evening with the Blessingtons: "L^d. B. got quite drunk, and said rude things to me about H[ollan]d H[ou]se, which I did not answer, because the correction of a drunkard in his own house seems to me impossible for one of his guests to undertake; and when not drunk he is below contempt." This did not deter Fox from dining with the Blessingtons two days later: present was Lamartine, "a poet, a dandy and a diplomat, in about the 3^d or 4th classes of each department. . . . The dinner was dull. The hostess, d'Orsay, and even that besotted idiot Ld B., recounted as usual the universal flattery and admiration with which they are hourly dosed, and scrupled not to assure us how well they deserved what they did receive and more to boot."[190]

In early November, 1827, the Blessingtons moved on to Rome, "very proud," Fox recorded, "of having taken two floors in the Palazzo Negroni, which act of magnificence they think likely to strike the hearers dumb with awe." Later in the same month Fox dined with them and heard Lady Blessington "profess without provocation, her total unbelief in Christianity. . . . I am sorry to see that they have made poor Lady Harriet (who was before well educated) listen with childish pleasure to the heartless doctrines and selfish ribaldry of her worthless mother-in-law." On December 9, Fox was told of the marriage of Lady Harriet Gardiner, Lord Blessington's daughter by his first wife, to D'Orsay. The bride was fifteen years old. Fox wrote: "They are just returned from Naples, where they have triumphantly effected the nefarious marriage of poor Lady H. Gardiner. They are proud of what they have done

[190] *Journal of Fox*, pp. 234, 235-36.

and expect me to congratulate and approve. I behaved as civilly as I could, feeling as I do the strongest detestation and contempt for Lady B., and great sorrow at d'Orsay's weakness and folly in being humbugged and blinded by the machinations of that b[itch]."[191]

The marriage had not been an easy one to arrange: Lady Blessington had had to travel for it and suffer for it. The original plan had been to have it performed in Florence before she left in November. Yet when she called at the English legation there to make arrangements for the two ceremonies, Anglican and Roman Catholic, she was reminded that English doors could slam in her face even in Italy. The English minister, Lord Burghersh, the brother of Lady Jersey and the stepson of Lady Westmorland, chose rudely to disapprove of the marriage and insulted Lady Blessington to her face. One of the difficulties imposed by Lord Burghersh took the form of an order that the Anglican ceremony must precede the Roman Catholic, and he was able to impose his will in Rome also. Thus, twice defeated, Lady Blessington traveled to Naples again, where the British minister was Byron's friend Hill, whom she had met in Genoa; the marriage was performed, and she took her revenge by attacking Lord Burghersh's sister, Lady Jersey, in her *Conversations*. D'Orsay took his by writing an insulting letter to Burghersh. Early in 1828, his stepmother, Lady Westmorland, the former Jane Saunders, of dubious past, became incensed because the Duc de Laval had received Lady Blessington socially and tried to persuade "the English ladies [in Rome] to refuse going to his house in a body," as Fox noted. Thus it was, when D'Orsay's wife left her husband and Lady Blessington's house in London, in August 1831, Lady Jersey was delighted to tell Lady Holland, who wrote to her son Henry Fox, that Harriet "had quitted her worthless companion & joined her aunt. . . . L[y] J[ersey] says L[d] Burghersh refused to allow the marriage they celebrated [in Naples] in his house in Florence, in consequence of a private message from Lady Harriet declaring her reluctance to the union."[192] None of this appears, of course, in *The Idler*, which describes a very different kind of world.

[191] *Journal of Fox*, 238, 243, 250.
[192] The difficulties associated with Harriet's marriage are summarized from Connely, *Count D'Orsay*, pp. 106-14, 179.

71

There, in early 1828, Lady Blessington was very happy, it appears from her account, as she moved among nobility and ex-royalty, including the Duc de Laval, the French Ambassador; Hortense, the former Napoleonic queen of Holland; and Jerome Bonaparte, the former king of Westphalia. She even met Napoleon's mother. Henry Fox saw them at a costume ball given by the Duc de Laval on January 29: "The Blessingtons there gorgeously dressed as Turks; L^y B., however, looked like one of her profession." On February 7, he found the conversation at her house "frivolous and vulgar. L^y B. had the good taste to tell with indignation the story of a Mrs Fletcher at Florence forcing her way into society, in the same manner she is doing here—quite a counterpart to her own adventures. The politeness of her guests could hardly prevent them from laughter." On February 16, seeing her at a masked ball given by Queen Hortense, he described her simple and direct methods: "L^y Blessington uninvited, though Hortense had foolishly granted permission for two unknown masks to come, had the effrontery to force herself upon the society." Such conduct, he indicated, was normally only a "venial misdemeanour," but not for one of her "trade, who, having persuaded a drivelling drunkard to marry her, dishonours him and makes the future misery of his young daughter by sacrificing her at 15 years old to a worthless adventurer, whom, as the husband of this poor child, she may contrive to keep in the house on the score of the relationship. It is one of the basest and most barbarous transactions I ever knew." Meanwhile, "Lord Blessington describes to [Lady Elinor Butler, who repeated to Fox on March 23] the extreme chastity of each member of his family. L^y B. has a spine complaint, which prevents him from exercising his matrimonial duties. D'Orsay has not and will not consummate his marriage, and he himself does not think le jeu vaut la chandelle to make any search among dirty Italian women."[193] Thus chaste, D'Orsay was able to sublimate his energies, presumably, and between February and April sketched Gell, Hallam, Luttrell, and Lord Blessington,[194] all of whom appear in Lady Blessington's *Conversations,* as do most of those mentioned in this essay.

[193] *Journal of Fox,* pp. 265, 267, 268, 281.
[194] Connely, *Count D'Orsay,* pp. 565ff., lists the chronology of D'Orsay's drawings.

The night before she left Rome in May 1828, she talked for the first time, it seems, with Teresa Guiccioli. The place was Queen Hortense's house. Lady Blessington found Teresa's "manners remarkably distinguished, and her conversation *spirituelle* [like that of Fox] and interesting," she wrote in her *Idler*. She did not leave any record of what she said to Teresa, for it would not have been seemly of the Idler to have done so: but Henry Fox did. After the queenly party, he wrote in his journal, May 9: "I went to T. G. She gave me a fresh proof of Lady Blessington's malice. In order to distress her, and also perhaps in hopes of making us quarrel, she told T. G. of Ld Byron, in 1823, having said to me at Genoa that one of his reasons for going to Greece was to get rid of her and her family—which he meant, I conclude, by saying he wished to cut cables in Italy and go either to Greece or England in order to regain his liberty." Later, using a different pen and a lighter ink, he wrote above the last line: "of course I denied it tho' it is true."[195]

It is clear that Byron's "new Goddess of Discord" still lived and reigned in 1828, although the reasons why Henry Fox so persistently sought out her company are far from clear. Strangely, if we may believe the *Idlers*, from this time on the image of Byron was increasingly in her mind. Perhaps the stimulus was her meeting with Teresa. Perhaps she traveled with the complete works of Byron in her library, as she made her leisurely journey in the direction of Paris,[196] going over much of the ground of Childe Harold and his author. On her way out of Rome she visited the grave of Sir William Drummond and there in the Protestant cemetery saw that of Shelley too. She "thought of Byron" as she gazed at the cataract of Terni—"painted . . . in never fading colours" by the poet—and then quoted four stanzas from *Childe Harold*, IV, 69-72. At Ravenna she stayed at the very inn used by Byron when he first arrived, in pursuit of Teresa, quite ill. "How well I remember," she wrote, "his declaration to me of the fervor and devotion of his attachment, at that period. 'I do assure you,' would he say, 'that I thought of nothing but her; and had she ceased to exist, I believe that I should not have survived.'" Perhaps so, but she may

[195] From the autograph journal in the British Museum, Add. Mss. 52080-52102.
[196] The third volume of *The Idler in Italy* begins at this point.

have been remembering Moore's *Life* rather than Byron. She questioned her hosts at the inn about Byron; she visited the Palazzo Guiccioli, pausing in the very rooms occupied by Byron when he wrote Canto V of *Don Juan*, "which he told me he discontinued at the request of the Countess Guiccioli." She was "enabled, by a perfect recollection, to bring back to the mind's eye, the exact image of the man. . . ." "The tones of his voice come back to me as fresh as if heard yesterday." Then she compared the lives of Byron and Dante, discussed his interest in the Carbonari movement and his *mobilité*, and listened to the custodian praise his acts of charity, as she questioned the man about Byron's habits. In the room in which Byron slept and wrote, "it was with a sentiment approaching reverence that we paused before the spot where the table once stood, on which he wrote poems that have found their way all over Europe. . . ." Altogether, she composed a passage of ten printed pages on Byron and Teresa at Ravenna, one of the most sympathetic accounts of him she ever wrote. If one cannot believe every word of them, the mere fact that she visited so many places with which he was associated is clear evidence of her lively interest in the details of his life and her knowledge of them.

In Ferrara, "with melancholy interest," she saw the name of "our own Byron" on the wall of Tasso's prison and, perhaps inspired by Byron's *Lament of Tasso*, she wrote a "Soliloquy of Tasso," four pages of rhymed couplets. She also saw in Ferrara "the court-yard where Parisina and Ugo . . . were executed," remembering Byron's source (Gibbon) more accurately than the poem, in which the nature of Parisina's end is left uncertain. In Venice the ducal palace reminded her of Byron's *Marino Faliero*. Byron had "thrown a halo" over the title character. " 'I stood at Venice on the Bridge of Sighs' today," she continued, "and involuntarily repeated Byron's fine lines on the subject," four stanzas of which she then quoted, comparing their author to Shakespeare. After visiting the Palazzo Mocenigo, then a tourist attraction, she deplored the character of Byron's life there: recollections of it "haunted" her while she was in the palace. As bad as Byron's Venetian life was, however, his "fearless delineation" of it was worse, for it corrupted others: a policy of "careful concealment, though it may be termed hypocritical," is much to be preferred. "I could not divest myself of the recollection of the orgies, more than hinted at by our *cicerone*, which had polluted the palace of Byron, and never felt so little interest about him, as while in it. He, too, never recurred to Venice without expressing a sort of horror of it. . . ." One recalls the chain of Venetian manufacture which he gave to her upon parting, obtainable nowhere except "at or from Venice," the Armenian grammar annotated at Venice, and the letter of "Fletcher" written in Venice. She remembered, at length, Byron's account of Moore's visit to Venice, which "had an intoxicating effect on him," allowing him to escape into the memories of his carefree London years and allowing her to dispose of the distressing subject of Byron's dissipations. She moved on to describe an expensive antique shop.

Her life next touched Byron's when she made a trip to the island of St. Lazzaro to see the Armenian convent, where she "enquired for, and conversed some time with, Father Pasquali [Father Pasquale *or* Paschal Aucher], from whom poor Byron took lessons [in Armenian] when at Venice." The monk "spoke in terms of warm regard" for Byron; she observed again the poet's effortless power to charm those around him and recalled the grammar which he had given her in Genoa. Returned to Venice, she "went over" the Manfrini Palace and there saw the painting by Giorgione which Byron had admired in *Beppo*, stanza xii, a line from which she quoted: "But such a woman! love in life." This time she approved his taste in pictures. A visit to the Foscari palace in Venice produced a long and appreciative discussion of Byron's play and the historical Foscari.

Leaving Venice with regret, which was greatly and Byronically "increased . . . by the knowledge [that the city was] fast decaying," she visited the tomb of Petrach at Arqua, noted the name of "our own Byron" in the album, with Teresa's, and recalled that he had told her of his visit, with dialogue which she reproduced. In Milan, at the Ambrosian library, she saw a lock of the golden hair of Lucretia Borgia, which reminded her of the medallion which she said Byron always wore, containing about "twenty fair hairs" from the head of this Pope's daughter, whose court, despite the heinous crimes attributed to her, became a center for artists, poets, and scholars. Teresa firmly denied that Byron wore the hair of Lucretia

Borgia (one of "une foule d'impossibilités")[197] and referred to his letter of November 6, 1816, to Moore: "I took one single hair of it as a relic." Lady Blessington, who also collected artists, poets, and scholars, defended Lucretia Borgia; what she did not confess was that she herself owned "a small tress of this golden hair of the too celebrated Lucretia," as Madden wrote, given to her at the time she toured the Ambrosian library. It came into the hands of Madden along with her papers.[198] Here, then, is another curious example of the transfer of roles with Byron that Lady Blessington arranged more than once. Before she left Milan she also saw Guarino's [i.e., Guercino's] painting of Hagar and made the curious observation that she was "a woman who has 'loved, not wisely, but too well,' and like all who have so done, been punished by him who caused the sin." This reminded her that Byron had told her that he too "had been greatly struck with this picture," as he had also revealed to Stendhal and to Moore and to Murray, the first of these accounts to be published being Stendhal's, in 1824.[199]

At Bologna she met the famous linguist Mezzophanti, said to be a master of forty languages. "Byron might well say of Mezzofanti," she wrote, "that he would have been a most useful person at the building of the Tower of Babel, to serve as interpretor." Although this is a paraphrase from Byron's "Detached Thoughts," No. 53, not published presumably until 1830, in Moore's *Life*, perhaps she was not trying to mislead the reader into thinking that Byron had spoken in conversation with her of the linguist. It does demonstrate, however, that the *Idler* at this point was revised for publication.

The third and last volume closes, appropriately, with her return to Genoa. "How many recollections come crowding on memory at the sight of this place, and the well known objects that every where meet my view! In each, and all, Byron bears a prominent part, and . . . I feel my regret for his loss renewed afresh." She seemed to hear again "the sound of that clear, low, and musical voice. . . ." It was early summer again, the time of year when she had parted from Byron, but now five years later, 1828. The sight of Lady

[197] "La Vie de Lord Byron en Italie," p. 1500.
[198] Madden, I, 113.
[199] See *HVSV*, pp. 198-99.

Byron and Ada on the street "affected [her] strangely," as indeed it might. She dined with Barry "and felt a mournful interest in inspecting the apartments occupied by Lord Byron," where Barry now lived, with some of the poet's furniture, books, and manuscripts. She listened to Barry's account of Byron's return on July 14, 1823, when the *Hercules* was becalmed in the Gulf of Genoa; considered Sardanapalus, in love with both wife and mistress; and concluded, "by dying only could he [Byron] be faithful to both." The sight of Lady Byron must have been a little too much for her. "Such is one of the bitter consequences resulting from the violation of ties, never severed without retribution," she observed, from her own experience. Protesting "the kind and gentle feelings still entertained" toward the memory of Byron, she confessed that he had been "sceptical of their friendship," the only such admission in *The Idler in Italy* and the last time the poet's name appears in her book. The evidence of 1823, while she was in Genoa, suggests nothing of such scepticism, and the possible cause of her change in attitude toward him which developed years later will be considered shortly. Meanwhile, before she left in 1828, "the kind-hearted and excellent Lord Burghersh" and his lady arrived in Genoa, and by the purest chance Lord Blessington presented to Lady Blessington a very curious gift, but one bestowed in "a princely way." It was a *calèche* newly arrived from England, copied from one driven in Florence by Lady Burghersh, which Lady Blessington had admired. At their departure, Mr. and Mrs. Barry saw them off.

In June 1828, the Blessingtons were in Paris, where she lived until November 1830, a period described in *The Idler in France*, the two volumes of which were published in 1841. Although Byron was never in France, the references to him continue to be abundant, as time moved on to the point when she would write her *Conversations*. It was here in Paris that Lord Blessington rented for her the magnificent Hôtel Ney, "the decorations of its walls alone cost[ing] a million of francs." Here too her "most gallant of all gallant husbands" decorated her "chastely beautiful" bedroom and bath, with its silvered swan bed and Flora scattering flowers from the ceiling. Although Byron was far distant, a remarkable number of his friends and acquaintances were in Paris. "Our old friend, Mr. Douglas Kinnaird—'the honourable Dug,' as poor Lord Byron used to call him—paid . . . a visit," but he was not looking very well and induced in her the reflection that Londoners seem to have eaten of the lotus and forgotten the past, "so wholly are they engrossed by the present, and by the vortex in which they find themselves plunged." In his state of ill health, Kinnaird, who had spent the intervening years as a sober man of business and who would die in 1830, may not have wished to discuss Byron. Sir Francis Burdett, also to appear in the *Conversations*, called with Colonel Leicester Stanhope, who gave Lady Blessington "some interesting details of poor Byron's last days in Greece, and seems to have duly appreciated his many fine qualities, in spite of the errors that shrouded but could not eclipse them." One of those "errors" may have been some hint from Stanhope that Byron had disclaimed his friendship with Lady Blessington, a possibility which will be considered below.

Lord Darnley, an acquaintance of Byron, dined, and Lord Charlemont, father of the beautiful Lady Anne admired by Byron, both men looking much older than Lady Blessington had remembered them. Lord Lansdowne, who called with Count Flahault, very probably appears anonymously in the *Conversations*, his name left a blank, although the coloring of the sketches in the two books is quite different. Byron's unnamed lord owed his political success to a "fortune [that] puts him out of the possibility of being suspected of mercenary motives" and to his "high rank." His supposed "high character" consists merely in his "having an even temper, thanks to a cool head and a colder heart!—and a mediocrity of talents that insures his being 'content to live in decencies for ever'. . . ."[200] Lady Blessington's Lansdowne is described in *The Idler in France* as follows: "With a fortune that exempts him from incurring even the suspicion of mercenary motives for holding office, and a rank which precludes that of entertaining the ambition of seeking a higher, he is free from . . . angry passions. . . . The sole thing wanting is . . . warmth and cordiality of manner. . . ."[201] Somehow this patron of Thomas Moore had displeased Lady Blessington.

At a large dinner party the witty Mr. ——, who had acquired a certain reputation for his *bon mots* and "caustic wit," agreed with the opinion she had "often heard Lord Byron give, that the

[200] *Conversations of Byron*, pp. 135-36.
[201] *The Idler in France*, I, 146-47.

78

society in English country-houses [to which she was not invited] is any thing but agreeable. . . . Byron, had he not been a poet, would have become a wit in society; and, instead of delighting his readers, would have wounded his associates."

William Spencer dined;[202] she received news of "an admirable speech" on the Catholic question made by Lord Grey, "one of the friends in England whom I most esteem"; she read the "exquisite" poems of Mrs. Hemans, which affected her "like sacred music." All three persons would appear in the *Converstions*.

In October 1829, Rogers and Luttrell called, reminding her of her "many pleasant days in St. James's Square," now to be no more, for Lord Blessington had died suddenly on May 25, changing her life completely. "Mr. Rogers talked of Byron, and evinced a deep feeling of regard for his memory. He little knows the manner in which he is treated in a certain poem. . . . I hope that it may never be published, and I think no one who had delicacy or feeling would bring it to light.

"Byron read this lampoon to us one day at Genoa. . . . He offered us a copy, but we declined to accept it. . . . Byron, however, found others less scrupulous, and three or four copies of it have been given away."

"Brief as was the period Byron had lived in what is termed fashionable society in London, it was long enough to have engendered in him a habit of *persiflage*, and a love of uttering sarcasms, (more from a desire of displaying wit than malice,) peculiar to that circle in which, if every man's hand is not against his associates, every man's tongue is." Here once more is the curious reversal of roles. The Byron of the *Conversations*, discoursing on the evils resulting from an unmerited loss of reputation (which indeed he understood) is made to say, ". . . malevolence and injustice having set the condemned seal on the reputation of him who has been judged without a trial, he is driven without the pale of society, a sense of injustice rankling in his heart; and if his hand be not against each man, the hand, or at least the tongue, of each man is against him."[203] Thus again, they saw eye to eye. Society had unjustly condemned them both; the tongue of every man was against them.

[202] The second volume of *The Idler in France* begins at this point.
[203] *Conversations*, p. 216.

79

Through his voice she could attack the malicious gossip which she feared and hated, and in her own person she could condemn him for engaging in it, at the very time that she was blackening his reputation for "putting on paper [his] epigrammatic malice." By contrast, she knew "no more agreeable member of society than Mr. Luttrell. His conversation, like a limpid stream, flows smoothly and brightly along." The Byron of the *Conversations* also thought that Luttrell was "a most agreeable member of society. . . ." The last of Byron's friends to appear both in Paris and in the *Conversations* was Lord John Russell; she took him, with Luttrell and Rogers, to the Louvre, on a day when the general public was not admitted, for a tour guided personally by the Baron Cailleux, the head of the museum.

v

She was putting up a courageous front, for already she had been deeply hurt by the most scurrilous attacks against herself and her relations with D'Orsay. These had appeared in August, September, and October 1829, in the *Age*, edited by Charles M. Westmacott, and another would appear in March 1830.[204] By October 7, 1829, her sister Ellen, respectably married for about nine months to the Speaker of the House, Manners Sutton, had already fallen away from her, leaving a terrible hurt that grew into a general disillusionment. Of her sister, also of dubious past, she wrote to Mrs. Mathews: "I have no longer any illusion as to the real feelings of one whom for so many years I considered as my second self. . . . She can not dislike my going to England as much as I do. . . . I wish that she could be persuaded that *business* alone could take me, and that I never can accept [her] civilities or hospitality. . . . Her convictions are to us all, a subject of as much indifference as are those of her husband. I however heartily agree with her on one point, which is, that I think it would be desirable that Lady H[arriet] should have a family, and nothing would be more gratifying to me, because it might produce a stronger degree of interest and affection between the husband and wife, than has hitherto ex-

[204] See Connely, *Count D'Orsay*, pp. 142-44, 150.

isted; but should Providence deny her this boon, I see no reason why Mrs. M[anners] Sutton should put any evil construction on it. I have been twice married and never was in the family way. Lady H[arriet]'s mother never was in the family way by her first husband, but it is too absurd to reply to, or reflect on such folly; and Mrs. Sutton may be certain that her opinion is counted for less by us all than that of any other individual of our acquaintance, and that not one single step shall we ever take to change it."[205] Mrs. Mathews was in fact acting as a courier between the two sisters, and it is clear that Mrs. Manners Sutton had subscribed to the gossip linking Lady Blessington with D'Orsay and the childless state of his wife. Two days later, on October 9, she again confessed her anguish to Mrs. Mathews: ". . . it is dreadful to be deceived by those whom we loved and trusted, more especially friends we never can totally efface from our hearts; an affection that has grown with our growth, and strengthened with our strength, it is so natural to love a Sister, as I did love her, so truly, and endeavoured to prove it all my life, that not all the feelings of wounded pride and affection can heal the wounds her conduct has, and will continue, to inflict on my Peace."[206] The pain here is genuine. On November 30, 1829, she wrote just as revealingly: "I have experienced such ingratitude and unkindness, that . . . I really dread becoming a misanthrope, and that my heart will shut itself up against all the world. If you knew the bitter feelings the treatment I have met with has excited in my breast, you would not wonder that it has frozen the genial current of life. . . . Had God spared me my ever-dear and lamented husband, I could have borne up against the unkindness and ingratitude of friends estranged. . . ."[207] She had written to Lord Blessington's solicitor and on December 14 informed Mrs. Mathews: "I heard from Mr. Powell yesterday, and find he has as yet done nothing either in discovering the author of the scandalous attacks against me, or in preventing a renewal of them."[208] Her bitter tears continued to fall into 1830. On January

[205] From the autograph letter in the Berg Collection of the New York Public Library.
[206] From the autograph letter in the Berg Collection of the New York Public Library.
[207] Madden, II, 428.
[208] Madden, II, 419.

18 she described herself to Mrs. Mathews as a woman "alone, with estranged and ungrateful friends."[209]

In the spring of the year, however, her false sister tempted her to return to England. On March 26 she wrote: "I can no more understand why my Sister now writes me such frequent and affectionate letters, than I could penetrate the mystery of her former dereliction. Do you fathom this secret? I hope this warmth on her part may last, for I have suffered too much, not to be most vulnerable to unkindness."[210] By May 7, 1830, she was seriously considering the move and on that day wrote again to Mrs. Mathews: "My Sister advises my coming to fix in England, and so my Medical people advise also, as my health is so indifferent. She has grown more kind, and invites me to Mistly, pray write and tell me if this seeming affection *be real*, or to what you attribute the change. You may write *Soeur ouvert*, as no eyes but mine shall see your letter . . . , but I really wish to know *on what I may* count, as I have been so often deceived that I am become doubtful."[211] Her sister would deceive her again.

Before she left Paris she poured forth, in three volumes, her sense of grief, deception, and isolation in her first novel, *Ella Stratford; or, The Orphan Child.* It is a tired work of a woman at bay, hounded and harassed beyond endurance, with no succor in sight. The main character is not only an orphan but also the only child of parents who were themselves orphaned only children. Left alone and unprotected in a world in which the titled or privileged persons, with rare exception, are heartless or worse, she is pursued by unfeeling roués through a dreary succession of jobs as governess or *femme de chambre*, resigning repeatedly in order to protect her honor. In the end, still virtuous, she is left hopefully anticipating marriage with a young curate of a neighboring parish. Up until the last few pages, Ella Stratford is a woman alone, beset by the unhallowed desires of most of society. The subtitle asserts that the novel was "Founded on Facts."

Foolishly, Lady Blessington returned to London in November

[209] Madden, II, 420.
[210] From the autograph letter in the Berg Collection of the New York Public Library.
[211] From the autograph letter in the Huntington Library.

1830, moved into Seamore Place, and attempted to establish a continental salon which would rival the splendors of Holland House. But 1831 was to become her year of greatest sorrows. By July it became known that her sister Ellen and her husband Manners Sutton had "thrown my Blessington overboard,"[212] presumably because of the gossip concerning her relations with D'Orsay. In the same month she had been publicly vilified in the *Satirist* by the second Lord Glengall, who moved in or on the edge of Lady Jersey's circle. This was the son of the Lord Glengall who, Lady Hardy informed Byron in 1823, had made Margaret his mistress while she was postmistress of Cahir, a position he may have secured for her. Thus, if true, were the sins of the father avenged by the son.[213] In August, Harriet D'Orsay left her husband, taking with her her income, upon which Lady Blessington and D'Orsay depended, and the small degree of respectability which her presence had thrown over the presence of D'Orsay in the house. He was forced to move. On August 14, Lady Blessington wrote to Mrs. Mathews: ". . . your letter found me suffering under all the nervous excitation natural for a sensitive person to feel, under such painful and embarrassing circumstances as I find myself placed in by the separation of Comte, and Lady H—— d'Orsay. . . ." Lady Blessington explained that Harriet's behaviour had been such that D'Orsay told her she must either change "her modes and conduct" or "go and reside with her Aunt. This latter alternative she has adopted, and in a manner no less offensive, than heartless, and the result is, as you may well imagine, most painful to my feelings. . . ." Also involved were "the machinations of [her] relations,"[214] the Blessingtons. But as the legal adviser of Lady Harriet wrote many years later, when declining to assist Madden with his biography, "She has suffered much from the late Countess. . . ."[215] In the autumn Lord Blessington's illegitimate son Charles Gardiner, acting for all the family, brought suit to break his father's

[212] *Correspondence of Jekyll*, p. 290. Jekyll heard the story from the Misses Berry, who had dined with Ellen and her husband.
[213] Connely, *Count D'Orsay*, pp. 173-74, mistakenly assumes that the verses in the *Satirist* were written by the 1st Earl of Glengall, but he had died in 1819; the 2nd Earl, born in 1794, lived until 1858.
[214] From the autograph letter in the Berg Collection of the New York Public Library.
[215] *The Blessington Papers*, p. 172.

will. The gossip was mounting, along with D'Orsay's debts. On November 15, she described herself to Mrs. Mathews as one who had "drunk the cup of bitterness to the very dregs. . . . Alas I have too *keenly, deeply,* felt the want of *friends* to consider the rank or position of any one. . . ."[216] On December 7, 1831, she wrote despairingly and misanthropically again to Mrs. Mathews: "when I have felt myself the dupe of those for whom I sacrificed so much, and in return asked only for affection, it has soured me against a world where I feel alone. . . ."[217] She had been *"deceived,"* she wrote two weeks later,[218] underlining the word for emphasis, and by the time the second installment of her *Conversations* had appeared in *The New Monthly,* her "heart [had been] only preserved from corroding, by knowing that such hearts as yours exist, though like Angel visits they are few and far between—Rochefoucault says that there is always something consoling in the misfortunes of our friends, I used to deny this assertion, but I find that on reflecting on the treatment you have experienced from your Sisters, I cease to be so much surprised or wounded at the conduct of mine, as I am conscious I never hurt your sweetness of temper, or forbearance, consequently there is some consolation in the misfortunes of friends—"[219] By 1834, the year when the *Conversations* appeared in book form, "London fashionable society [had become] that Dead Sea which destroys the energies of all who float over it," she wrote to Bulwer.[220] Her heart had become "like a frozen fountain," she confided to her "Night Thought Book," and then she referred to her "knowledge of the nothingness of life."[221]

This manuscript notebook, kept in 1834, with its epigrammatic expressions of bitterness, fear, cynicism, and misanthropy, is so revealing of the woman who wrote the *Conversations of Byron* that her narrative must be interrupted at this point for a selection from

216 From the autograph letter in the Berg Collection of the New York Public Library.
217 Madden, II, 422.
218 From the autograph letter in the Princeton University Library, to Mrs. Mathews, December 22, 1831.
219 From the autograph letter in the Princeton University Library, to Mrs. Mathews, August 15, 1832.
220 Quoted by Connely, *Count D'Orsay,* p. 224.
221 Madden, I, 250.

its unpublished passages.[222] These were the secret thoughts of the still beautiful Lady Blessington, still able to draw to her some of the most distinguished men of England.

They only can compassionate with misfortune who have drunk of its bitter Cup, for unmixed prosperity by keeping us ignorant of it, prevents our Sympathy.

We seldom attain virtue until we have been tried and purified in the school of affliction, as only Martyrs become Saints.

Une des choses les plus marquantes de nos jours est le grand mépris des principes joints au grand respect pour les convenances.

So inherent is ingratitude in Man, that it is only in affliction that he lifts his Soul to his Creator, in joy and prosperity he forgets Him.

We never address our Souls with such true fervour to Heaven, as when all hope on Earth has failed us.

Calumny is the offspring of Envy.

Anger banishes reflection though its consequences give rise to it.

The most certain mode of making people content with us, is to make them content with themselves.

A knowledge of life is the least enviable of all species of knowledge, because it can only be acquired by painful experience.

The young turn their thoughts often to Heaven, unknowing the Sins and Crimes of Earth, and the old fix theirs on it, because they know them too well.

The prayers of the young spring from innocence, and those of the old from Experience.

The Genius and talents of a man, may be judged of by the quantity of his Enemies, and his mediocrity, by the number of his friends.

[222] The two volumes of the "Night Thought Book," now in the Huntington Library, contain a total of 316 pages, each page approximately 4 by 6½ inches. A small selection of these, perhaps one-third, appeared in the very rare *Desultory Thoughts and Reflections* (1839), a little sextodecimo of 97 pages. The published versions of Lady Blessington's night thoughts are almost always revised for the worse, diluted for her public.

Mountains appear more lofty, the nearer they are approached, but great Men resemble them not in this particular.

Vice is often more courageous than Virtue, because it has less to lose, and that modesty, the constant attendant of the latter, is often mistaken for shame, which follows the former.

Memory retains but the voice which makes us weep.

Genius—a barrier of polished steel, that rises up between its possessor, and society, gaining for him first, fame—and then—Hatred.

Those who make their happiness depend on the futile pleasures of society, instead of on the resources of their own mind, resemble the insects who feed on the dust, and whom the feet of the passengers crush, and destroy.

The passions which urge us to sin, for their indulgence, die, and leave us sensible of our transgressions, without the motive that led to them, As fevers in the physical frame, subside and leave only the weakness and langour that follow them, a prostration of force, more sensibly felt from the undue vigour that preceded it.

Like a Bird, with wearied pinions, flying over the Sea, and feeling the languor of exhaustion stealing on him while yet nought but the interminable ocean meets his eye, is he who yet ere half lifes course is passed, is forsaken by hope, and with a bruised heart, and languid mind trembles on beholding the dreary waste of existence over which he has yet to wander.

As honey is found in the most bitter flowers, such as Aloes, Colocynthis, and others, so is some redeeming trait of goodness to be found even in what are considered to be the worst natures.

Horne Took said of intellectual philosophy that he had become better acquainted with the Country through having had the good luck, sometimes, to lose his way. May not the same be said of Virtue? Which is never so truly known, or appreciated as by those who having strayed from its path, have at length regained it.

One passion neutralises twenty virtues.

The misfortunes and trials that seem so insupportable while we are enduring them, are often reflected upon in after times, with much the same feeling with which we peruse a fictitious Tale of Sorrow, and the French Actress's exclamation, while recurring to the desertion of a faithless Lover in her youth, "Ah! c'etait le bon tem[p]s! j'etois bien malheureuse," was not unnatural.

When one sees at every side the respect paid to riches, a respect that even precludes any reference as to how they have been acquired, can we wonder that the obtaining them, should induce Men to commit actions which no sophistry can disguise or extenuate. Such Men probably reason as did Odant, a Piedmontese conspirator for Catharine, when he said, "I see there is no regard for any thing but money, and money I will have, and when I have got enough I will return to my own Country, and there live like an honest Man."

If Age deprives us of our pleasures, it also deadens our sense of misfortunes, by subduing the acuteness of our Sensibility.

People are often ridiculous, who were only meant to be commonplace, but who sighing for notoriety, have sought it by the affectation of eccentricity.

Middle age is the bridge of Life, whence we see the shadow of our youth, and the approach of age with all its unloveliness. We look with trembling at the future, where nought is distinct, save gloom and lassitude and we begin to search for some anchor to arrest the progress of our bark, into the dreary gulph to which it is hurrying.

The Aristocracy are apt to ridicule the elevation of Men of the middling classes to high official situations, not reflecting, that if Gentlemen cannot be formed into Ministers, Ministers must be formed into Gentlemen.

Destiny is a phantom of our own creation, like the Monsters children imagine, and tremble at. Our Conduct forms our Destiny, and that conduct is much more frequently guided by our weaknesses, than by our Vices.

Society like Wine, should be used in moderation, too much of either, impairs the mind, but taken moderately exhilirates [sic].

To find some kindred mind some refuge—some sure stay. . . .

Reason destroys the illusions of life, but gives us little consolation for their loss.

Those who cannot exalt themselves, are prone to pull down others, hence the world will always be filled with Levellers.

Do we not betray a knowledge of the world, by the established usage, which all follow of withdrawing from it, the moment that misfortune or affliction overtakes us.

All that we give in Pity, to the unfortunate, we decrease in respect. Hence he who would be respected, must conceal his cares, for once known, they become pitied, and he no longer respected, or else they are ridiculed, and he is despised.

There are two trials, to which all are subject, but which the World have agreed to consider the greatest crimes—Poverty, and affliction. To be esteemed in the world, both must be carefully concealed, for if once discovered the next step will be to endeavour to discover some vice or crime that led to them, and which of course precludes necessity of Pity—or assistance.

Be prosperous, and gay, require our services—never, and we will be your friends. This is not what Society says, but it is the principle on which it acts.

We never more fully display our own characters than when we assail those of others.

So little formed are we for happiness, that if the present offers nothing to torment us, we look back to the past, and forward to the future, for some cause of chagrin.

—— respects truth so much that she seldom even approaches it. Nay you are wrong, for she is said to take great liberties with it.

We ourselves make the path of life weary, plant all the thorns that intersect its course and continually pierce us, while the few flowers that cheer us, come from others.

Flattery is always acceptable, however we may despise the flatterer, because it implies an acknowledgment of our superiority. A flatterer whatever may be his station always places himself in an inferior position to those he condescends to flatter.

Husbands to strictly fulfill their duties, should be Janus like, blessed with two heads, one to guard over the happiness of a Wife in Society, and the other to watch it in its secret recesses of the mind.

Women with their bright imaginations, tender hearts, and unsullied minds, make unto themselves Idols, on whom they lavish their worship, making their hearts temples in which the false God is adored. But alas! the Idol is proved to be of base clay, instead of pure gold, and though pity would still conceal its defects, and cherish it even with them, Virtue, reason, and justice destroy the false Idol, but in doing so, injure for ever the temple where it was enshrined.

How often do we let the sacred fire of love expire in our hearts, because purity, the vestal that ought to have guarded it, has left her charge.

How many are there, capable of committing all the faults that passion leads to, without the capability of redressing them, by one grand, or generous action.

How difficult is it to enjoy repose, when the heart retains all the freshness of youth, and the mind has arrived at the wisdom of age. Vain wisdom, which only shows us our weakness without teaching us how to subdue it—Will all its whispers still the throbbings of despair, or give force to resist the sorrows that lacerate the heart?

The Past, the only good of which false friends cannot deprive us. They may imprison the present, and cloud over the future, but to the past we can still turn for consolation, and call back its enjoyment to enable us to bear the cheerless present and to meet the gloomy future.

The sacrifices we make for others, are cheerfully borne, as long as those for whom they are made appreciate them, but when we discover that they are not valued, our generosity receives a check that often influences the character through after life.

Reputation has often survived virtue, but virtue more rarely out-lives reputation, except in superior minds who know it for itself, and not for its name.

En France, l'amour propre mène à la passion, et en Angleterre la passion mène à l'amour propre.

We suffer more from imaginary, than real wants, never reflecting that it is easier to moderate our desires, than to attain their ful-fillment.

More than half our lives are passed with persons who have neither the power to make us think or feel, nay who often impair our capabilities of doing either.

There is no knowledge for which so great a price is paid as knowl-edge of the world and no one ever became an adept in it, except at the expense of a hardened or a wounded heart.

Hell must be the place where one is sure to meet the pleasantest company, if, as is believed, the clever people, Wits, Men of Pleasure, and lively Roués, are condemned to abide there.

There is one thing which we all desire to receive, and yet which no one will directly ask for—Praise.

A man of ordinary capacity best conceals his stupidity by silence, as too short a robe is best concealed by its wearer remaining seated.

Misery lengthens our nights, but shortens our days.

The noblest characters only shew themselves in their real light; all others act comedy with their fellow men, even unto the grave.

Most people escape the weight of obligations by Ingratitude.

Dr. Madden summed up: ". . . I renewed my acquaintance with Lady Blessington in Seamore Place [into which she moved in early 1831 and where she wrote the *Conversations* in 1832]. It was evi-dent that another great 'change had come over the spirit of her dream' of life since I had last seen her. [The quotation is from Byron's "The Dream."] Cares, and troubles, and trials of various kinds had befallen her, and left, if not visible external traces, at least perceptible internal evidences of their effects."[223] She was a bitter and defeated woman, but few were allowed to know this, for she was also a proud and courageous woman, of many faces. To intimates like Madden, Mrs. Mathews, and Landor, she could reveal herself, writing to the latter in the summer of 1832: "I live in a world where friendship is little known, and were it not for one or two individuals like yourself, I might be tempted to exclaim with Socrates, 'My friends, there are no friends.'" Then she referred to "the modern Babylon" in which she lived, "where thinking and feeling are almost unknown."[224] As for Socrates, she attributed the same quotation to the Byron of the *Conversations*. Closing this letter to the celebrated author of *Imaginary Conversations*, she wrote, almost inevitably: "I shall be glad to hear what you think of the 'Conversations.' I could have made them better, but they would no longer have been what they now are, genuine." He replied: "Thanks upon thanks for making me think Byron a better and wiser man than I had thought him."[225] Her first installment had appeared in July 1832.

In the spring of the year, driven by necessity, she had offered her services to *The New Monthly Magazine*, founded by Colburn, who in 1824 had published Medwin's *Conversations of Byron*. Her friend Bulwer had recently succeeded Campbell as editor, and Samuel Carter Hall, an assistant editor, was sent to call upon her. She received him with "kindness and courtesy" and talked to him about the books of his wife, with which she was "well acquainted," he was pleased to observe. Hall's account continues: "But the subjects she suggested for the magazine were not promising. Some objects in her charmingly furnished drawing-room led to remarks concerning Byron, of whom she related to me some striking anecdotes. It was natural to say, as I did say, 'If you desire to write for the *New Monthly*, why not put on paper the stories you are telling me about the great poet?' Out of that simple incident arose the 'Conversations with Lord Byron.'"[226] Perhaps it had all been cleverly

[223] Madden, I, 157.
[224] Quoted by Molloy, *The Most Gorgeous Lady Blessington*, p. 227.
[225] *The Blessington Papers*, p. 113.
[226] Samuel C. Hall, *Retrospect of a Long Life* (New York, 1883), p. 367, where the date is given as 1831. In Hall's *Book of Memories of Great Men and Women of the Age, from Personal Acquaintance* (London, 1871), p. 401, the date is given as 1832.

planned by her, and he never knew it. By June 24, 1832, she could inform Mrs. Mathews that she had "disposed of my journal of Conversations with Lord Byron, very advantageously. . . ."[227] On July 16 she wrote again: "I have been so constantly and fatiguingly occupied in Copying and correcting since I last saw you that I have not had a moment to myself. . . ."[228] This timing was fortunate but not accidental. In 1831 her sister Mary Ann, now past thirty, had married the Count Saint Marsault, twice her age. Like Moll Flanders and her husband, each discovered too late that the other was without fortune, and they separated after a few months. Another "one of the causes of [her] low spirits," she explained on March 30, 1832, was that her brother Robert, who had formerly supported her father, had lost his job as agent of the Blessington estates in Dublin, "which threw him and his large family, out of comfort and competence, to struggle with all the miseries of an income much too small for their wants."[229] It was necessary for her to send money to Ireland. D'Orsay's extravagances had already become a matter of concern to her. The *Conversations of Lord Byron* was written because she needed money, and it could have been written in a single month, for it is shorter by one-third than *The Two Friends* (1835), the composition of which had cost her only six weeks.[230] She wrote the last 600 of the 980 pages of *The Repealers* between March 4 and March 31, 1833.[231]

The change in her feelings toward Byron, as one moves away from the evidence dating from the period of their friendship, is clearly marked in the *Conversations* and calls for explanation. The closing pages are especially hostile, as she discusses the effect of Byron on "those around him," one of these being Lady Blessington. "Sensitive, jealous, and exigent himself, he had no sympathy or forbearance for those weaknesses in others." His "natural flippancy" or "incontinence of speech" made his "display of reserve on other

[227] Madden, II, 423.
[228] Madden, II, 427; the date is supplied from the autograph letter in the Berg Collection of the New York Public Library.
[229] From the autograph letter in the Princeton University Library, to Mrs. Mathews.
[230] N. Parker Willis, *Pencillings by the Way* (New York, 1852), p. 516.
[231] Madden, II, 258.

points still more offensive." "It was as though he said, I think aloud, and you hear my thoughts; but I have no feeling of friendship towards you, though you might imagine I have from the confidence I repose. . . ." She found in him no "reciprocity of feelings," and it was this "that deprived him of the affection that would otherwise have been unreservedly accorded to him. . . ."[232] The episode involving payment for the *Bolivar*, which had occurred nine years, presumably, before she wrote the *Conversations*, does not seem enough to account for this severe tone. A much more likely and probable explanation is that she had heard of some uncomplimentary remark supposedly or actually made by Byron about her. It seems significant that in four places in the *Conversations* she decried Byron's habit of disclaiming friendships, three of the four within ten pages very near the end of her book.[233] The most revealing of these passages points with some clarity to the possibility that she had indeed heard that Byron had disclaimed his friendship with her, as he had done in effect in letters to Hobhouse and Lady Hardy. She wrote in the *Conversations*: "This habit of disclaiming friendships was very injudicious in Byron, as it must have wounded the *amour propre* of those who liked him, and humiliated the pride and delicacy of all whom he had ever laid under obligations, as well as freed from a sense of what was due to friendship, those who, restrained by the acknowledgment of that tie, might have proved themselves his zealous defenders and advocates." As she did not prove herself in her book to be one of his "zealous defenders and advocates," so the word "delicacy" is one more frequently used in reference to women than to men, and Teresa stated that Lady Blessington's "*amour propre*" had indeed been wounded by Byron.[234] Teresa, in her copy of the *Conversations*, also underlined the phrase "humiliated the pride" in the sentence quoted above. It seems virtually certain that this is in fact what happened and that it happened long after Byron and Lady Blessington were together in Genoa. It is also quite significant that she, fearfully anticipating an announced "dissection" of her book and attempting

[232] *Conversations*, pp. 227-28.
[233] *Conversations*, pp. 100, 222, 223, 228.
[234] Teresa Guiccioli, *My Recollections*, p. 62.

to ward it off, wrote to P. G. Patmore in late 1832: "It was one of the worst traits in Byron, to receive persons in private, and then deny the acquaintance to those whom he considered might disapprove of it."[235] In conversation with Haydon and in a letter to Joseph Jekyll, she brought the same charge against Byron.[236]

The knowledge that Byron had disclaimed his friendship with Lady Blessington might have reached her from any of a number of sources, but several likely ones emerge rather clearly. In December 1832, Lady Hardy was back in London and was seeing Lord Melbourne,[237] who had no reason to love Byron, even though Lady Caroline Lamb, his wife, had been dead for four years. And he had even less reason to care for Lady Blessington, who gossiped viciously about him and Mrs. Caroline Norton.[238] As for Lady Hardy, she had only to repeat what Byron had written to her about Lady Blessington. Another very likely source is Colonel Leicester Stanhope or his wife. He did not wholly admire Byron and quarreled with him in Greece. Stanhope knew Lord Blessington at some time before February 1, 1825,[239] and Lady Blessington's *Idler in France* records that Stanhope called on her in Paris in 1828 and that they discussed Byron.[240] Mrs. Stanhope, another gossip, told Haydon in 1835 that "she had seen a letter from Byron saying, 'Can any one relieve me of Lady Blessington or rather Count D'Orsay?' "[241] The highminded Stanhope, a Benthamite reformer, frequented Mrs. Norton's circle, where it was customary to disapprove of Lady Blessington; and it is certainly possible that Byron minimized the intimacy of his relations with Lady Blessington or even denied the acquaintance to Stanhope. However all this may be, the least possibility of any such gossip would drive Lady Blessington to protect herself by taking the position that Byron had the "habit of disclaiming friendships" and that she had only a highly qualified admiration of him.

[235] P. G. Patmore, *Personal Recollections*, pp. 303-04
[236] *Diary of Haydon*, IV, 264; *Correspondence of Jekyll*, p. 306.
[237] *Diary of Haydon*, IV, 23.
[238] *Diary of Haydon*, IV, 239-40, 254-55, 271.
[239] Madden, II, 483.
[240] *Idler in France*, I, 142-43.
[241] *Diary of Haydon*, IV, 264.

The woman who appears in the *Conversations* is not the same woman whom Henry Crabb Robinson met in 1832 and whom Benjamin Robert Haydon met in 1833. To one she turned her literary side and showed her malice; with the other she flirted and showed her malice, more coarsely, although no less dangerously. With both she discussed Byron. As P. G. Patmore expressed it: "Lady Blessington's intercourse with Byron, so pleasantly and characteristically described . . . in her conversations at Seamore Place and Gore House, formed an era in her life, and probably contributed not a little to the unique position which she afterwards held in London society. . . ."[242] In short, she was trading on the name of Byron; and with Robinson, a friend of Coleridge, Wordsworth, and Southey, she seems to have said what she thought he would like to hear. Thus in conversation with him on September 28, 1832, she attacked Byron, an enemy of Southey, at length.[243] Moore, far removed from the so-called Lake School, of course, and at this date neither highly regarded by Robinson as a poet nor on friendly terms with him,[244] she attacked by having Byron attack him. She used the same technique on Rogers, whose conversational powers and breakfast parties rivaled those of Robinson. Rogers and Robinson saw each other frequently in company, but Robinson did not fully trust the sincerity of the other's professions of friendship.[245] No one present knew Claire Clairmont or Medwin, who had returned to England in early 1831; thus she felt free to attack them too. She made a tactical error in attacking the vulgarity of Mary Shelley, which Robinson denied but Landor, also present, asserted. Thus she could entertain her guests, she thought, and give vent to her own spleen or malice at the same time, for she had her own reasons for attacking those whose names she introduced into the conversation.

[242] P. G. Patmore, *Personal Recollections*, p. 290.
[243] This, Robinson's first meeting with Lady Blessington, is described in *Robinson on Books and Their Writers*, I, 411-13.
[244] *Robinson on Books and Their Writers*, I, 292; II, 550.
[245] *Robinson on Books and Their Writers*, II, 728.

It is very important to remember, however, that in 1832 (and presumably in earlier and later years), "Lady Blessington could not bear any one to speak disparagingly of Byron in any respect but herself. . . ."[246] It was on this rock that Thomas Campbell foundered; in talking with her, he "could see nothing to admire, to pity, or to spare in Byron." The result was that "the acquaintance [was] dropped," and it seems clear that she owed nothing to Campbell for assistance in getting her *Conversations* published in the *New Monthly*, which he had ceased to edit in 1830. Campbell, we are told by Madden, "had a sort of instinctive apprehension of any person who was supposed to be an admirer of Byron."[247] This, it may be noted, was very shortly before the publication of the first installment of her *Conversations*.

But on September 28, 1832, Robinson, finding her to be "a great talker," observed: "Nearly the whole conversation was about Lord Byron. . . . She is, however, by no means an extravagant admirer of Lord Byron, at least not of his character, and makes such admissions concerning him as will satisfy the enemies of Lord Byron." Landor, D'Orsay, and Lady Blessington's sister Mary Ann, who had also known Byron, were the only other persons present. "She went so far as to say that she thinks Leigh Hunt [author of *Lord Byron and Some of his Contemporaries*, 1828] gave in the main a fair account of Lord Byron—not that she knows Leigh Hunt: she keeps aloof from all the literary connections of Lord Byron. . . ." This was an excellent defensive measure, whether she knew it or not.

Then she "spoke with great bitterness of Moore, against whom she is incensed. She mentioned among the causes of offense a note in the tenth volume to a poem copied from Lady Blessington's *Conversations* implying that it was not intended for the public— Moore having himself printed so many much worse of which the same may be said." She may not have liked the implications of Moore's note to Byron's "Lines on hearing that Lady Byron was Ill," suggesting the impropriety of Lady Blessington in publishing it. And she could hardly have been pleased with Moore's comments in his *Life* of Byron on two poems which Byron had addressed to her.

[246] Madden, II, 274.
[247] *Loc.cit.*

One, "Beneath Blessington's eyes," Moore described as "hardly worth transcribing," and the other, "You have asked for a verse," he thought "might well [have been] warmer."[248] But she had other reasons for attacking Moore. In late 1829, when he was collecting materials for his *Life* of Byron, he wrote to her that Lord John Russell had told him that she had seen "a good deal of Lord Byron during his last days in Italy," had anecdotes and "some verses addressed to yourself by Lord Byron, which were very pretty and graceful—in short, in every way worthy of the subject.

"Now, my dear Lady Blessington, . . . sit down instantly and record for me, as only a woman *can* record, every particular of your acquaintance with Byron, from first to last. You may depend upon what you write never meeting any eye but my own. . . .

"Above all, too, do not forget the verses. . . ."[249] Lord Blessington had been dead nearly six months by then, and Moore did not know it, but surely Lady Blessington knew that whatever she chose to give him would certainly meet other eyes than his own. She complied with his request, however, sending him letters and a manuscript book. He failed to present her with a copy of his *Life* of Byron, forgot to return her letters and manuscript book (for which she had to write), thought that he had torn up Lord Blessington's letters, and displeased her by publishing what he called "the very harmless allusions in Byron's letter to the very harmless pursuits of Lord Blessington's youth." The tone of her letter to Moore, written in April 1832, had "surprised and pained" him.[250] None of this implies, to be sure, that she was prepared to end her long friendship with Moore; when he could be useful she would call upon him. As editor of *The Book of Beauty* she asked him, in February and in June 1834, to contribute verses to her annual, inviting him to dinner in the latter month.[251]

[248] Moore, *Life*, p. 577.
[249] *Letters of Moore*, II, 661-62.
[250] *Letters of Moore*, II, 744.
[251] Madden, I, 254; *Letters of Moore*, II, 785. N. P. Willis, *Pencillings by the Way*, pp. 511-13, describes a conversation of 1834 or 1835 in which Lady Blessington defended Moore at length in the face of charges of "worldliness and passion for rank." She did not deny these weaknesses but talked of his honorable behavior in connection with his deficit in Jamaica and upon the occasion of his being offered a seat in Parliament, with an annual salary of £1,200 attached.

Meanwhile, on September 28, 1832, Robinson heard her threaten "to expose" Moore, "which she could do [and was doing] by repeating Lord Byron's contemptuous words and epigrams against him. One she mentioned. Lord Byron used to say: 'Tommy makes pretty *sweet* verses—sweet indeed, no wonder—he was fed on plums and sugar-candy by his father, the Dublin grocer.' It seems, according to Lady Blessington, that Lord Byron was incapable of loving any one with constancy." Lady Blessington had known Moore since 1809, and N. P. Willis thought that Moore had been her "lover when she was sixteen," writing "some of the sweetest of his songs" to her.[252] It is pertinent to observe here, however, that Byron had ridiculed Moore behind his back in conversations with Hobhouse, Medwin, and Leigh Hunt.[253]

Next, to return to Henry Crabb Robinson and Lady Blessington, she "repeated a most ferocious and scornful epigram against Rogers by Lord Byron. . . ." This must have been Byron's "Question and Answer," for the publication of which she was presumably responsible. On December 28, 1832, she described this poem to Robinson and quoted from it.[254] Then on March 26, 1833, she and Robinson again "talked on the old topics, Landor and Lord Byron. . . . Lady Blessington spoke with bitterness of Rogers; she says he is most malignant. . . ." It was not until April 1, 1834, that she told Robinson that Rogers' "malignity in speech at least was such as to justify Lord Byron's satire—he spared nobody," like Byron, as she had reported him.[255]

[252] Madden, I, 254; N. P. Willis, *Pencillings by the Way*, p. 518.

[253] *HVSV*, pp. 77-78, 214-15, 314, 548, 619, n. 74; Ernest J. Lovell, Jr., *Captain Medwin, Friend of Byron and Shelley* (Austin, 1962), *passim; Leigh Hunt's Literary Criticism*, ed. Lawrence H. and Carolyn W. Houtchens (New York, 1956), pp. 335-43.

[254] *Robinson on Books and Their Writers*, I, 420-21 and n. 1. Lady Blessington gave Robinson a copy of "Question and Answer" which differs from the accepted version.

[255] *Robinson on Books and Their Writers*, I, 423, 440. Joseph Jekyll reported on August 1, 1832, and January 9, 1833 (*Correspondence*, pp. 298, 309): "She [Lady Blessington] recited to me most dreadful verses by Byron against his friend Rogers, but will not publish them, or the poet must inevitably plunge into the Serpentine. . . . I was alarmed enough to ask if I was safe. She said, to my comfort, that she [*sic*] spoke of me as a favourite."
"Rogers has lost a favourite brother, and in the midst of his sorrows was assailed by the dreadful verses of Byron against him, a copy of which has appeared in *Fraser's Magazine*, and of which I always heard only three were known to exist. . . . Rogers . . . will feel this deeply."

Concerning the reasons why, on September 28, 1832, Lady Blessington should attack Mary Shelley and Claire Clairmont, one can only speculate. She most certainly knew that Mary had been acquainted with Byron longer and more intimately than she. Mary was also an authoress, more successful than she until the publication of the *Conversations*. And Mary, now completely respectable, had made the mistake of requesting Lady Blessington to treat her with "forbearance" in the *Conversations*. She had, with the result that it is impossible to recognize the two descriptions, the written and the conversational,[256] as being those of the same person. Lady Blessington knew, almost certainly, that Mary had been Shelley's mistress before becoming his wife[257] and so, the Countess must have reasoned, was no better than herself. Teresa Guiccioli had come to London in the spring of 1832; she and Lady Blessington were eventually to become friends of a sort and Teresa would visit in her home. But Mary Shelley wrote of the danger of Teresa's visiting her: "I have such a dread of her coming to see me here— imagine the talk,"[258] and the two women never developed very satisfactory relations in England. It was from Teresa, presumably, that Lady Blessington heard the story she told Robinson: "Mrs. Shelley is said to be a great liar. This was Lord Byron's opinion of her, and she is accused of treachery in having opened a packet of letters from Lord Byron to Countess Guiccioli entrusted to her by Count Gamba, from which she supplied extracts to Moore. With difficulty the Guiccioli has got back the letters and means now, at some future time, to publish them and take her revenge on Mrs. Shelley." After this, it must have seemed relatively harmless to hear Lady Blessington "speak of the habitual insincerity of Lord Byron and the immorality of his habits. . . . She says Lord Byron was aware that Medwin meant to print what he said and purposely

---

[256] *Robinson on Books and Their Writers*, I, 412-13; *Conversations*, p. 53. Edward L. Bulwer wrote to Mary Shelley on July 23, 1832: "I beg to thank you for your kind letter. I fear that in the present sheet of Lady Blessington's journal, there are a few words about you, and it was printed off before I received your letter. But there is not a syllable the most fastidious could object to. . . . You may rely on nothing more about you appearing in the *New Monthly* without at least your seeing it" (*Shelley and Mary* [For Private Circulation Only, 1882], III, 1164).
[257] See Madden, II, 558.
[258] Quoted by Origo, *The Last Attachment*, p. 409, n.

hummed him." Then she "praised excessively" Thomas Hope's *Anastasius*, which the Byron of the *Conversations* also praises. In Robinson's diary entry for September 28, 1832, this is the only unqualified praise of anyone which is attributed to her. Robinson remembered the book as "odious," which it is. He "doubt[ed] the propriety of keeping up my acquaintance with her, so very bad are the stories told of her"; but eventually they achieved terms of such intimacy that "she told me tales," he wrote, "of the Honourable Mrs. Norton, whom she declared to be the mistress of Lord Melbourne," already prime minister.[259] On December 28, 1832, "Lady B spoke of the late King. . . . He asked the most disgusting and filthy questions concerning Lady Conyngham of an old lover of hers—she spoke with great indignation of the treatment of the late Queen. The Duchess of Devonshire prevented the Pope's allowing her a Guard of Honour. She was forced home."[260] And by January 26, 1835, Robinson and Lady Blessington were on such terms that she "related a mot of her own. The Queen is said to be enceinte but her children are weak and never live—she said when she heard of it, 'The Queen is as ladies wish to be who love their Lords Chamberlain.' "[261]

Her letter to the young Charles Mathews written in the summer of 1833, after she had become editor of *The Book of Beauty*, states her position clearly. He had submitted to her a love poem, the publication of which she had to decline. She wrote to him, who had traveled with her in 1823 and 1824 and with whom there was no need of pretense, for they honestly liked each other: "A thousand thanks, my dear Charles, for the verses, which are beautiful, but, alas! a *leetle* too warm for the false prudery of the public taste, though not for mine. Were I to insert them, I should have a host of hypercritical hypocrites attacking the warmth of the sentiments of the lines, and the lady editor, and therefore I must ask you to give me a tale, or verses more prudish. . . . I have been so long a mark for the arrows of slander and attack, that I must be more particular than any one else. . . . What a misery it is, my dear Charles, to live in any age when one must make such sacrifices

[259] *Robinson on Books and Their Writers*, I, 420; II, 458.
[260] From the autograph diary in the Dr. Williams's Library.
[261] From the autograph diary in the Dr. Williams's Library.

to cant and false delicacy, and against one's own judgment and taste."[262] Thus it was that the Byron of the *Conversations* attacks repeatedly the cant and false prudery of the day, which she hated, and just as repeatedly is reprimanded for it by the fair author. Elsewhere, and privately, she damned "the ridiculous prudery of a pack of fools."[263] She saw herself as one whose "contempt for the world has induced me to set its laws at defiance whenever I found them based on hypocrisy. . . . I dare to be honest in avowing opinions that few of my sex have the moral courage to acknowledge."[264] But her defiance of the world, like Byron's, had been nurtured in large part by necessity. She saw more of herself in him than she could admit, and she did not always like what she saw.

The suffering Lady Oriel of Lady Blessington's novel *The Repealers* "had yet to learn [what the author, somewhat ungrammatically, had long ago persuaded herself of], that severity towards the errors, real, or supposed, of others, rarely proceeds from a love of virtue or detestation of vice, but are the modes in which jealousy and envy delight to avenge themselves. . . . An error in conduct may be overlooked, provided the sinner is neither young, beautiful, nor clever. . . ."[265] Repeatedly she placed Byron in the same position and explained him in the same terms. In the *Idler*, discussing his separation and the enemies who then revealed themselves to him, she wrote of "those who, envious of his literary fame, and jealous of the homage it received, armed themselves with an affected zeal in her [Lady Byron's] cause, and a hypocritical pretense of morality, to decry and insult him." Byron, she said, "dwelt with bitter scorn on the desertion of many summer friends. . . . He still writhes beneath the recollection. . . ."[266]

The basic similarity of their situation, as she understood it at the time of her *Conversations*, is startlingly suggested by two of her letters, one written shortly before she started her book, the other

---

[262] Madden, II, 413-14.
[263] Lady Blessington to Captain Marryat, quoted by Sadleir, *The Strange Life of Lady Blessington*, p. 209.
[264] Lady Blessington to Edward L. Bulwer, quoted by Sadleir, p. 215.
[265] *Works*, I, 254.
[266] *HVSV*, p. 362; see also pp. 367-68.

shortly after its publication.[267] To Mrs. Mathews she wrote on December 7, 1831: "if, in my near relations, I had met with only kind usage or delicacy, I should now not only be happier, but a better woman, for happiness and goodness are more frequently allied than we think." On March 16, 1835, she wrote of Byron to Landor, who had belatedly received her *Conversations*: "Had ten years been added to his existence, he would have been a *better* and *happier* man. Are not goodness and happiness the nearest approach to synonymous terms?" To Mrs. Mathews she continued: "But I confess to you, my beloved friend, a great part of the milk and honey of nature with which my heart originally overflowed is turned into gall. . . ." Of Byron, she wrote in her *Conversations*: "The milk and honey that flowed in his breast has been turned to gall by the bitterness with which his errors have been assailed. . . ."[268] Of her own "bitterness," she wrote to Mrs. Mathews that she had "not power to prevent its corroding my own heart, and rusting many of the qualities with which Nature had blessed me." Correspondingly, in the *Conversations*: "let us remember what must have been the heart-aches and corroding thoughts of a mind so sensitive as Byron's. . . ."[269] To Landor she explained: "[Byron] was one of the many proofs of a superior nature spoiled by civilization. . . . But then there were outbreakings of the original goodness. . . ." She herself had "enough goodness left to prevent its [her heart's] bitterness from falling even on those who have caused it . . . ," she informed Mrs. Mathews. Byron, of course, did not. In the *Conversations*, however, after he had been greatly moved by the sound of English sailors singing "God save the King," she wrote of him, sympathetically: "And this is the man that I have heard considered unfeeling! How often are our best qualities turned against us. . . ."[270] As for herself, she wrote to Mrs. Mathews, she felt "alone—misunderstood—with my very best qualities turned against me." Both Byron and Lady Blessington, then, had begun

[267] Madden, II, 106, 422.

[268] *Conversations*, p. 217.

[269] *Conversations*, p. 217. Similarly, she wrote to Mrs. Mathews on August 15, 1832, that her "heart . . . is only preserved from corroding, by knowing that such hearts as yours exist . . ." (from the autograph letter in the Princeton University Library).

[270] *Conversations*, p. 47.

life in simplicity and goodness of heart, had become the victims of envy and jealousy in a hypocritical society, ever ready to attack persons of superior talent, had suffered bitterly from this, and had become bitterly disillusioned upon the loss of supposed friends. Under other conditions, it followed, both would have been happier and better persons, for happiness and goodness are closely allied, if not synonymous.

That Byron would have agreed to the main line of this argument seems highly probable, and that there were such significant affinities between Lady Blessington and the poet places her among his most acute and understanding commentators, provided her book is read with some understanding of its obvious biases. A better and a happier man, milk and honey turned to gall, character corroded, natural goodness spoiled by civilization, our best qualities turned against us—the very fact that she used such clichés suggests the depth of her identification with Byron. Although she knew, as she wrote of such persons as Lady Holland and Lady Jersey, that he was really of their party, not hers, the violence of some of her conversational attacks on him suggests that they proceeded from her deep awareness of their similarities of position, her own bitterness expressing itself in terms of her psychological and social double, as it were. The coarseness of some of the stories attributed by her to Byron (but never in print, to be sure), may be explained in terms of her rebellion against the prevailing prudery of the day and her efforts to escape from it.

Light of a different kind is also thrown on the author of the *Conversations* by Benjamin Robert Haydon, who met her a year after Robinson had and found her on October 7, 1833, "sweet & refined & unaffected." Later in the month, he sketched her as she sat, and she "amused [him] excessively. She has a fine head, full of feeling. She spoke of Lawrence [who had painted her most famous portrait] with contempt & said she was certain no woman ever loved him. She told me Byron was hideously affected."[271] Haydon saw her chiefly in 1834 and 1835. His diary entries are particularly interesting because they describe the strange combination in her of sweetness and bitterness, refinement and coarseness, amiability and malice, nature and artifice. Here the difficulty of distinguishing the

[271] *Diary of Haydon*, IV, 131, 137.

natural from the affected in her is compounded by the suspicion that love and spite lie partly in the eye of the beholder, Haydon, who on March 10, 1834, for example, had had an unpleasant time with Lord Grey as he sat for his portrait. At that time, Haydon had recalled "Lawrence's advice, 'Never have any mercy on your sitters.'" Lord Grey had been self-conscious about his legs. Four days later Haydon "sketched Lady Blessington. She was delightfully amiable, and we had a regular & delicious 'chat amiable.'

"She amused me excessively about Lord Grey. She said his vanity was excessive, that there was no bodily perfection he did not believe he possessed, that you could never make his hands small enough or his feet small enough, that he was flattered morning, noon, and night by his family, who believed him the ne plus ultra of perfection. She said he used constantly to be about her, and that she called him 'petit garcon,' that once she praised Lord Angelsey & his daughters, whom she met in the park, & that Lord Grey, quite spitish, said, 'Do you mean to say they are a finer family than my own?'—and staid away for two days!

"She said, 'I wonder he had not fallen in love with Mrs. Norton.'" Later Lady Blessington told Haydon that Grey "was so much touched that if she quizzed & scolded him, he would pout like a boy & stay away."[272]

The tone of this is very different from that of Lady Blessington's easily unlocked novel *The Repealers* (1833), where Lord Grey the prime minister appears as Lord Rey the premier, first encountered when he is talking with Lady Guernsey (Lady Jersey): "What a dignified air and distinguished bearing he has! He seems the very personification of aristocracy, from his intellectual looking head to his finely formed legs and feet. . . . Lady Rey was always cited as an example for mothers and wives; and her daughters emulated her virtues. Married in early youth to a nobleman no less distinguished for his high character than for his brilliant and solid talents as a statesman, and who sought for happiness and repose from his political duties, where only it can be truly found, in the bosom of his family—the domestic circle of Lord Rey had become proverbial for the exhilarating example it furnished of harmony and rational enjoyment. Even he, the supposed misanthropic poet

[272] *Diary of Haydon*, IV, 178, 180, 328.

[Byron] . . . never recurred to the family of the Premier without commendations whose warmth proved their sincerity. . . ."[273] This is in fact a cross-reference to the *Conversations*, page 40, where Byron says that in the opinion of Madame de Staël, "Lord Grey and his family were the personification of her *beau idéal* of perfection, as I must say they are of mine. . . ." After a reference to his "dignity," Byron referred to Lady Grey's "mild and matron graces, her whole life offering a model to wives and mothers. . . ." In spite of the fact that Grey had been infatuated with Lady Blessington at one time (Mrs. Cowper told Haydon he "was so much in love with Lady Blessington he offered to go to America with her"),[274] he appears, as paterfamilias, with his wife and fifteen children, to be a particularly pleasant person and seems to have drawn his strength from them.[275] Lady Blessington may have been provoked with Lord Grey for political reasons, but simple envy and resentment seem more probable reasons for her conversational attacks. He had flirted with her; now he was only one of the "occasional guests" at Seamore Place;[276] his devoted wife moved freely in a world of respectability, surrounded by all her children.

On the same day that she attacked Lord Grey in conversation with Haydon, March 14, 1834, she also attacked the beautiful Mrs. Caroline Norton, granddaughter of Sheridan, eighteen years younger than she, a bluestocking and published author, separated from her husband, and like all the Sheridans devoted to Harriet D'Orsay. In 1836 Mrs. Norton's husband would sue Lord Melbourne for seduction of his wife. Haydon's diary is of interest at this point for the shockingly coarse stories Lady Blessington could tell. Haydon recorded: "She then told me of Mrs. Norton's being at [the 9th] Lord Kinnaird's, & that she behaved so coarsely, the Ladies determined never again to meet her, that she talked in the grossest manner of the infidelity of husbands, and made a very pretty little Woman cry, who believed in the fidelity of hers.

"She said she [Mrs. Norton] used to go up with the Ladies as far as the Landing place, & then come down & sit with her husband

[273] *Works*, I, 250-51.
[274] *Diary of Haydon*, IV, 328.
[275] See Lloyd Sanders, *The Holland House Circle* (London, 1908), pp. 138-39.
[276] Madden, II, 511.

105

and the men, that Lord ——, being exceedingly provoked at her gross remarks on his person, told her if she made another, he would attack her, that she did, & then he said, 'Now Norton, excuse me, but I will dissect your wife.'

"That he said, 'You have the damdest skin Woman was ever cursed with. Your upper lip is that of a negress, your under an animal. Your hands are those of a Porter and your feet like a dray Horse, and as to your talent, it is damned humbug.' She then burst into tears!" Haydon commented: "This was told me with a sort of gusto—I do not like to hear these things."[277] But this did not deter Lady Blessington from telling similarly coarse stories to him later, similarly blind to the very coarseness in herself that she condemned in others. Mrs. Norton appears in her *Repealers* as Mrs. Grantley, a name chosen presumably because Mrs. Norton had married the brother of Lord Grantley. There we read of "the celebrated Mrs. Grantley, no less remarkable for her beauty, than for her genius and talents. Does she not look the very personification of a muse?"[278] There is more.

Later in March Lady Blessington sat again for her portrait and again "amused [Haydon] excessively. She seemed to complain of the Whigs bitterly. She told me many things—how she used to receive notes from Lord Grey begging her to get Lord Blessington to vote or give him his proxy. She said there was hardly a week passed but that the Duke of Sussex dined with her & Lord Blessington, that the Duke used to complain of his poverty & that he could not afford to buy [a] star in diamonds, & that Lord Blessington bought him a star in diamonds, & gave it to him—that then they enjoyed 41,000 a year, but that she had only 2000 now, & once a year the Duke of Sussex left his card. She abused him & seemed very much mortified." The sense of ingratitude was strong in her, and she bitterly resented the loss of friends. Haydon concluded that she was "clever, spirituelle, & totally unaffected—perhaps the most unaffected, except Lady Seymour [the sister of Mrs. Norton], in High Life." When she left she told him she had been married at fourteen and would be forty on her

[277] *Diary of Haydon*, IV, 180.
[278] *Works*, I, 249.

next birthday, an understatement of five years. In June he found her "just as unaffected & sweet as ever."[279]

She was still, in 1835, a woman to give a man pause. On February 16, Haydon wrote, after returning from Seamore Place: "I was with her an hour before any one came in. She looked superb. She had on a gray satin with large black flowers, her beautiful arms and hands encircled with jewels, while a superb jewel divided her hair. She was lounging in a soft chair, her beautiful complexion engoldened by the luxurious light of an amorous sleepy lamp, her whole air melting, voluptuous, intellectual, and overwhelming! . . . It is a devil of a business—to be alone with a beautiful Woman of Fashion. What is a man to do with a Woman alone? I always feel inclined immediately to kiss—the horror of infidelity always checks me. I make up my mind to a certain kind of conduct. I am married; I love; I will not swerve from my duty. . . ." Before he left, she had told him that "Byron was not sincere; that when she asked him about the Hunts, he always affected never to have seen them above once or twice a week. . . . She said his nose was not handsome, one eye decidedly larger than the other, but his mouth exquisite."

When he introduced into the conversation the subject of suicide and the Miltonic concept of freedom of the will, she found it "a puzzler. 'Good heavens,' said Lady Blessington, 'such subjects in modern Society would create a dead stare.' "[280] Four years later Fulke Greville wrote of an evening spent at her house: "There is a vast deal of coming and going, and eating and drinking, and a corresponding amount of noise, but little or no conversation, discussion, easy quiet interchange of ideas and opinions. . . . The reason for this is that the woman herself, who must give the tone to her own society, and influence its character, is ignorant, vulgar, and commonplace. Nothing can be more uninteresting than her conversation, which is never enriched by a particle of knowledge, or enlivened by a ray of genius or imagination."[281] Yet in 1834 Benjamin Disraeli wrote to her for advice on the modern French novelists: ". . . is it worth my while to read them, and if

[279] Diary of Haydon, IV, 181, 197.   [280] Diary of Haydon, IV, 263-66.
[281] The Great World: Portraits and Scenes from Greville's Memoirs (1814-1860), ed. Louis Kronenberger (New York, 1964), p. 153.

so, what do you recommend me? . . . I ask these questions because you will give me short answers, like all people who are masters of their subject."[282] He remained her friend for life. Haydon
wrote of her in 1835: "She is the center of more talent & gaiety
than any other Woman of Fashion in London, Fashion of the highest kind."[283] But to her it seemed "a cold and artificial atmosphere"
in which she lived,[284] although she herself helped to make it so
and in fact deliberately chose it as a way of life.

On May 11, 1835, Haydon recorded: "Lady Blessington told us
yesterday that the Guiccioli used to watch Byron with a Telescope
when he went out.

"She (Lady B.) asked Lord Byron why he did not take her out,
& he drawled out in his usual way, 'Consider what a fright she
would be in a habit.'

"She asked him if he thought her handsome. He replied, 'She is
a horror—she has *red* hair'—which is not true. She said, 'Why do
you not walk with her?' He replied, 'She shuffles like a Duck & I
am lame—a pretty couple!' She said, 'Do you ever tell her
this?' 'Yes.' 'What does she say?' 'She scra-a-a-tches me,' replied
Byron."[285]

At the time of this conversation, Teresa was in England. Later in
the summer, she, Lady Blessington, and D'Orsay vacationed together at Anglesey. Afterwards, she wrote to Teresa: "We often
think and talk of the pleasant hours passed in your society at Anglesey, when your charming voice and agreeable conversation gave
wings to them."[286] This was Teresa's third trip to England; she
and Lady Blessington were already friends of a sort, and would become closer. But Lady Blessington could not easily admit to herself the full implications of Teresa's liaison with Byron. As Madden,
who knew both women, delicately put it: "Lady Blessington appeared to remember that the Guiccioli claimed a property in the
memory of Lord Byron which was not altogether compatible with
the feelings of the author of 'Conversations with Lord Byron.'

[282] William F. Monypenny, *The Life of Benjamin Disraeli* (New York,
1916), I, 257.
[283] *Diary of Haydon*, IV, 271.
[284] To Sir Thomas N. Talfourd, from the autograph letter in the Huntington
Library.
[285] *Diary of Haydon*, IV, 284-85. Cf. Willis, *Pencillings by the Way*, p. 473.
[286] Madden, II, 21.

Lady Blessington courted the society of Madame Guiccioli, it is true, . . . but any little peculiarities of the Italian lady were seized hold of eagerly, and made the most of in society, and laughed at in it."[287]

Madden and Lady Blessington thought that Teresa had no understanding of anything like irony or a joke, but when in 1832 Lady Blessington rather cruelly showed her Byron's humorous letter to Hobhouse, written in the name and spelling of Fletcher, Teresa found it to be "a very curious thing, and it amused me a great deal."[288] She understood much more about Lady Blessington and her book than the English countess realized. Her reconstruction, years later, of the relations between Byron and Lady Blessington is consistent with much of what can be learned of them elsewhere, although her remarks must be read with some caution, of course. She wrote: ". . . il jugea cette charmante dame à la première séance; il la trouva belle et spirituelle, mais peu naturelle. Il se méfia donc de sa sincérité . . . et lorsque la conversation ayant roulé sur les connaissances communes, il trouva dans l'esprit de la dame une tendance à le relever par des observations fines et caustiques."[289] Here, clearly, at their very first meeting, is Byron's "new Goddess of Discord." Teresa also explained that in Byron's opinion D'Orsay was too young to have been the author of the famous journal: it had probably been written by Lady Blessington. Byron thought the journal was "un travail assez spirituel —mais d'un bout à l'autre satyrique et portant l'empreinte d'un fond d'esprit caustique—moqueur, et même aigri par quelqu'hostilité sociale."[290] This is Lady Blessington's recognizable style, of course. According to Teresa, Byron said to her: " 'Evidemment il est un oeuvre dicté—écrit en français mais pensé en anglais—il doit être une traduction des idées de Milady.' Il y trouvait même les tendances de l'esprit de la dame, 'et cela est heureux pour le jeune Français (dit-il) car une telle précoce perte des illusions serait un grand mal pour un homme si jeune.' "[291] The precise nature of Lady Blessington's relation to the journal is perhaps not important;

[287] Madden, II, 10.   [288] Madden, II, 27.
[289] From the autograph manuscript of "La Vie de Lord Byron en Italie," p. 1452.
[290] "La Vie," p. 1456.   [291] "La Vie," p. 1457.

it is clear, however, that a number of its characteristics, as analyzed by Teresa, were those of Lady Blessington.

In "La Vie de Lord Byron en Italie" Teresa restated her conviction that Byron found the English countess *"un peu artificielle—et par conséquence il soupçonnait sa sincérité. . . . Le défaut de naturel que Lord Byron trouvait chez Lady Blessington ne pouvait cependant pas lui venir de sa nature, car elle n'etait pas seulement charmante, elle était vraiment sensible, généreuse, douée de sentiments élevés; il ne pouvait qu'être la conséquence de la fausse position que des circonstances—et une jeunesse tourmentée et malheureuse lui avaient fait subir; et que pesaient sur sa couronne de Comtesse—et la lui faisait (laissait) ternir par les regards de l'envie et de la médisance."* Few sentences have expressed more insight into Lady Blessington than this one. Then Teresa explained that Byron studied her character in order to draw that of Adeline. On two later pages, however, she stated, more generously, *"Son enthousiasme pour lui* [him] *était donc aussi sincère que naturel . . . ,"* and confessed that Byron was by no means bored or always on guard in the company of the Blessington party: *"tout en leur sâchant gré de leur hospitalité trouvant les dames charmantes, les messieurs aimables, leur conversation agréable, car il pouvait s'amuser à leur entendre passer en revue les individus de la société qu'il avait lui même si bien connue."*[292]

Teresa concluded of the *Conversations:* *"Mais ce qui est blâmable est d'avoir mis dans la bouche de Lord Byron (quand il ne pouvait plus s'en défendre) ce qu'elle pensait d'une foule de choses et de personnes pour sa satisfaction personnelle—et pour se soustraire ainsi à la responsabilité de leur rancunes."* Among such subjects, Teresa observed, are Lady Holland, Holland House, and Lady Jersey. It is important, therefore, to consider her qualification of this judgment: *"mais néanmoins il est juste d'ajouter que dans ce livre il y a aussi la partie vraie et qu'il est ingénieux, car elle a réussi à peindre souvent Lord Byron avec des traits réels de son caractère et à former des Conversations qui peuvent être crues."*[293] This is rather high praise, from Teresa.

[292] "La Vie," pp. 1459, 1461-63, 1480-82.
[293] "La Vie," pp. 1498-1500.

In her copy of the *Conversations*, Teresa wrote a note upon the last sentence that applies to many another passage as well: "*Heureusement ses flatteries à l'hypocrisie et au cant n'ont pas profité à l'auteur; n'ont pas produit les consequences qu'elle esperer* [sic] *de ces insinuations et exaggerations.*" On a slip of paper placed into the front of the book, Teresa wrote, perhaps later: "*Evidemment Lady Blessington a écrit ce livre pour faire servir L. B*[yron] *à ses vues personelles. Elle a mis dans la bouche de L. B. une foule de choses* mauvaises *qu'elle pensait de l'Angleterre, attirant sur lui le blâme, et ensuite elle s'est posée en apologiste de l'Angleterre pour gagner* les bonnes graces de la haute société, choses où elle a du échouer. *Elle a voulu aussi laisser entrevoir que L. B. avait conçu pour elle une grande sympathie—rien de plus faux! Elle a fait tout ce qu'elle a pu pour séduire son esprit (au moins) mais L. B. a compris l'artifice et il me a dit, en ajoutant, c'est un caractère que j'étudie pour Don Juan (L^y Adeline).*"[294]

If this is the worst that may be said of Lady Blessington's *Conversations* by a contemporary of Byron, what final judgment of the book can be reached in the twentieth century? Written because the author needed money, the book is sometimes diffuse, padded to swell her purse. It sometimes expresses her own bitter feelings toward London society and some of its prominent members, notably Lady Jersey, Lady Holland, and her son Henry Fox. These women had received Byron but had refused her, and one of them, the divorced Lady Holland, she probably felt was no better than herself. Madden saw clearly, along with the virtues of the book, the "secret feeling of pique and annoyance" expressed in it. As Gell, who had known Byron in London, wrote to her: "in the 'Conversations,' I reverence you infinitely more than the poet . . . as I have more respect for Homer than for Agamemnon. . . ." (The compliment, to be sure, was somewhat ambiguous: was Byron the poet, or was he Agamemnon, commanding general of all the Greeks?) This Homeric art, as Madden analyzed it, depended on there being "no commendation . . . without a concomitant effort at depreciation."[295] His opinion is supported by that of the anonymous writer

[294] From Teresa's autograph note in her copy of the *Conversations*, in the Biblioteca Classense of Ravenna.
[295] Madden, II, 106; I, 218, 370-71, 71.

in *The Monthly Review* for January 1834: ". . . nothing in the way of praise by Lady Blessington is ever uttered without its accompanying antidote. . . ."[296] Thus Lady Blessington's sentences show a high degree of antithesis, as at her worst she writes condescendingly of Byron. And occasionally she places in Byron's mouth expressions of admiration for those she wishes to praise, like Lord Blessington or Mrs. Hemans.[297]

At best, however, her insights into Byron's character are often impressive and convincing, and the conversational attacks attributed to him are, by no means, always to be understood as her fabrications. Her own sarcasm in Genoa may well have betrayed him into some kind of similar response, his *mobilité* responding to her malice, reenforced by that of the D'Orsay of the satiric journal so much admired by Byron, and strengthened even by Lord Blessington, who did not hesitate at his own table to insult Holland House before its very heir, Henry Fox. And as she wrote, her identification with her subject became quite remarkable, although this does not always result in a flattering portrait. By and large, however, as the many scholarly compliments to her book quoted at the opening of this essay indicate, her portait is drawn with a substantial degree of sympathy, creating the illusion, at least, of objectivity or balanced judgment. Long before William J. Calvert's *Byron: Romantic Paradox* (1935), she recognized Byron as the complete man of paradoxes—the poet-soldier, attempting to live in two worlds at once; selfish in trifles, giving his life and fortune for Greece; the sentimentalist fearful of sentiment, in whom reason and sensibility were ever at war; the aristocratic democrat, proclaiming universal freedom out of his pride of rank; the satirist of appearances who delighted in "mystification"; the Romantic poet who

---

[296] *The Monthly Review*, CXXXIII (January 1834), 103.

[297] As for the French phrases placed in the mouth of Byron, he employed twenty-eight French words scattered throughout the twenty-six letters written while the Blessingtons were in Genoa and printed in *LJ*. See, however, W. M. Rossetti, "Talks with Trelawny," *The Athenaeum*, July 15, 1882, p. 79, where Trelawny is reported as saying: "When they (Byron and Shelley) spoke English, they heedfully avoided interlarding it with foreign words or phrases, and Lady Blessington's book about Byron is unfaithful in giving the contrary idea." But this proves nothing, of course, about Byron's conversational style with Lady Blessington: he may well have tailored it to fit her.

worshipped Pope; in short, a thorough chameleon. Calvert concluded that Lady Blessington had discovered "the surest guide to his [Byron's] character."[298]

The value of the *Conversations* lies also in its uniqueness. No other woman described Byron's conversation at book length. Teresa's *Recollections* as well as her unpublished "Vie" report very little of it at first hand. The few other women of Byron's acquaintance who described his conversation did so sketchily or fragmentarily, in letters or diaries. Lady Byron was obsessed and wrote with her lawyers (and her own self-justification) in view. And only with Lady Blessington did he talk at such length about literary matters, a fact supported by Byron's letters: to Moore he wrote, "Miladi seems highly literary . . .," and to Lady Hardy he stated, self-defensively, that his association had been "literally literary."[299] In short, she drew from him a response quite different from any other. Nor did any other reporter of his conversation at book length come so completely, however illegitimately, out of his old London background. One result is that the book gains substantial, additional value from its many vignettes of persons more and less prominent at the time.

Although she was often unable to write convincing dialogue and the long speeches of Byron are to be understood in no sense as accurate transcriptions of his words, her book is an important record of her impressions, distilled over a decade, cast into dramatic form, and greatly enriched by her association over the years with many of Byron's friends, acquaintances, and enemies. The book provides major evidence, in short, of the way in which Byron dealt with and affected a very beautiful, very complex woman with a literary bent and clouded past. The notes to this edition are witness to the usual accuracy of her account.

After she fled Gore House in 1849 and left its furnishings to her creditors, her intimate friend Edward Bulwer bid £7 at the auction for her set of Byron's works, "with her arms on the binding, and with the landscapes painted on the edges of the leaves."[300] Then

[298] Calvert, p. 54.
[299] *LJ*, VI, 180; *Cornhill Magazine*, LXIV (January 1928), 50.
[300] Connely, *Count D'Orsay*, p. 506.

he sent the volumes to her in Paris. Bulwer knew her true feelings as well as anyone during these last years of her life. His gift is witness to the genuine if strange attraction she still felt toward the long dead poet, whom she had met and flirted with at the height of her beauty and whom she had written a book about in her time of need, with middle age, however resplendent, upon her.

LADY BLESSINGTON'S
Conversations of
Lord Byron

PREFACE

THE deep and general interest with which every detail connected with Lord Byron has been received by the public, induced the writer to publish her Conversations with him. She was for a long time undecided as to adopting this measure, fearful that, by the invidious, it might be considered as a breach of confidence; but as Boswell's and Mrs. Piozzi's disclosures, relative to Dr. Johnson, were never viewed in this light, and as Lord Byron never gave, or implied, the slightest injunction to secrecy,[1] she hopes that she may equally escape such an imputation.

The many pages suppressed, filled with poems, epigrams, and sallies of Lord Byron, in which piquancy and wit are more evident than good-nature, bear testimony, that a wish to avoid wounding the feelings of the *living*, or to cast a darker shade over the reputation of the *dead*, has influenced the writer much more than the desire to make an amusing book; and she trusts, that in portraying Lord Byron, if she has proved herself an unskilful, she incurs not the censure of being considered an unfaithful, limner.

[1] Cf. *Medwin's Conversations of Lord Byron . . . Annotated by Lady Byron . . . and Others Who Knew the Poet Personally*, ed. Ernest J. Lovell, Jr. (Princeton, 1966), p. xvi: "They were communicated . . . without any injunctions to secrecy. . . ." All future references to Medwin's *Conversations* are to this edition.

JOURNAL

OF THE

CONVERSATIONS OF LORD BYRON

WITH THE

COUNTESS OF BLESSINGTON.

Wo du das Genie erbilickst
Erbilickst du auch zugleich die Marterkrone.

GOETHE.

Genoa, April 1st, 1823.

SAW Lord Byron for the first time. The impression of the first few minutes disappointed me, as I had, both from the portraits and descriptions given, conceived a different idea of him. I had fancied him taller, with a more dignified and commanding air; and I looked in vain for the hero-looking sort of person with whom I had so long identified him in imagination. His appearance is, however, highly prepossessing; his head is finely shaped, and the forehead open, high, and noble; his eyes are grey and full of expression, but one is visibly larger than the other;[1] the nose is large and well shaped, but from being a little *too thick*, it looks better in profile than in front-face: his mouth is the most remarkable feature in his face, the

---

[1] The fact that one of Byron's eyes was smaller than the other is confirmed by Medwin, *Conversations,* p. 8, and by Augusta Leigh. See Malcolm Elwin, *Lord Byron's Wife* (New York, 1962), p. 356. The entire account of Lady Blessington's first meeting with Byron should be compared with that in her *Idler in Italy* (London, 1839-1840), reprinted in *His Very Self and Voice: Collected Conversations of Lord Byron,* ed. Ernest J. Lovell, Jr. (New York, 1954), pp. 349-51, hereafter referred to as *HVSV;* cf. also the accounts of Henry Edward Fox and Teresa Guiccioli, *HVSV,* pp. 351-55.

5

upper lip of Grecian shortness, and the corners descending; the lips full, and finely cut. In speaking, he shows his teeth very much, and they are white and even; but I observed that even in his smile—and he smiles frequently—there is something of a scornful expression in his mouth that is evidently natural, and not, as many suppose, affected. This particularly struck me. His chin is large and well shaped, and finishes well the oval of his face. He is extremely thin,[2] indeed so much so that his figure has almost a boyish air; his face is peculiarly pale, but not the paleness of ill-health, as its character is that of fairness, the fairness of a dark-haired person—and his hair (which is getting rapidly grey) is of a very dark brown, and curls naturally: he uses a good deal of oil in it, which makes it look still darker.[3] His countenance is full of expression, and changes with the subject of conversation; it gains on the beholder the more it is seen, and leaves an agreeable impression. I should say that melancholy was its prevailing character, as I observed that when any observation elicited a smile—and they were many, as the conversation was gay and playful—it appeared to linger but for a moment on his lip, which instantly resumed its former expression of seriousness. His whole appearance is remarkably gentlemanlike, and he owes nothing of this to his toilet, as his coat appears to have been many years made, is much too large—and all his garments convey the idea of having been purchased ready-made, so ill do they fit him. There is a *gaucherie* in his movements, which evidently proceeds from the perpetual consciousness of his lameness, that appears to haunt him; for he tries to conceal his foot when seated, and when walking, has a nervous rapidity in his manner. He is very slightly lame, and the deformity of his foot is so little remarkable that I am not now aware which foot it is.[4] His voice and accent

[2] Cf. Byron to Thomas Moore, April 2, 1823: "I am thin,—perhaps thinner than you saw me, when I was nearly transparent, in 1812 . . ." (*The Works of Lord Byron. Letters and Journals*, ed. Rowland E. Prothero [London, 1898-1901], VI, 181, hereafter referred to as *LJ*).

[3] For accounts of Byron's physical appearance, including his pale face and the use of Macassar oil on his hair, see my "Byron and the Byronic Hero in the Novels of Mary Shelley," the University of Texas *Studies in English*, XXX (1951), 165-66 and n. 1, and Medwin's *Conversations*, p. 8.

[4] When writing his *Life* of Byron, Thomas Moore also discovered that he did not know whether Byron's right or left foot was lame and appealed to Mary Shelley. See *The Letters of Thomas Moore*, ed. Wilfred S. Dowden (London, 1964), II, 627. Byron was born with a deformed right foot.

are peculiarly agreeable,[5] but effeminate—clear, harmonious, and so distinct, that though his general tone in speaking is rather low than high, not a word is lost. His manners are as unlike my preconceived notions of them as is his appearance. I had expected to find him a dignified, cold, reserved, and haughty person, resembling those mysterious personages he so loves to paint in his works, and with whom he has been so often identified by the good-natured world: but nothing can be more different; for were I to point out the prominent defect of Lord Byron, I should say it was flippancy, and a total want of that natural self-possession and dignity which ought to characterise a man of birth and education.

Albaro, the village in which the Casa Saluzzo, where he lives, is situated, is about a mile and a half distant from Genoa; it is a fine old palazzo, commanding an extensive view, and with spacious apartments,[6] the front looking into a court-yard and the back into the garden. The room in which Lord Byron received us was large, and plainly furnished. A small portrait of his daughter Ada, with an engraved portrait of himself, taken from one of his works, struck my eye. Observing that I remarked that of his daughter, he took it down, and seemed much gratified when I discovered the strong resemblance it bore to him.[7] Whilst holding it in his hand, he said, "I am told she is clever—I hope not; and, above all, I hope she is not poetical:[8] the price paid for such advantages, if advantages they be, is such as to make me pray that my child may escape them."

The conversation during our first interview was chiefly about our mutual English friends, some of whom he spoke of with kind interest. T. Moore, D. Kinnaird, and Mr. E. Ellice[9] were among those

[5] Cf. Henry Edward Fox in his diary, April 1, 1823 (reprinted in *HVSV*, p. 353): "The tones of his voice are as beautiful as ever. . . ." See also Medwin's *Conversations*, pp. 132, 133n., 263n., and his *Angler in Wales* (London, 1834), II, 212.

[6] Spacious enough to allow the Gambas a private apartment.

[7] When Lady Blessington returned to Genoa in 1828, she said that she recognized Ada on the street with her mother from the resemblance the child bore to her father. See also Medwin, *Conversations*, p. 101.

[8] Cf. Byron to Augusta Leigh, October 12, 1823: "I hope that the Gods have made her [Ada] anything save *poetical*—it is enough to have one such fool in the family" (*LJ*, VI, 264).

[9] Moore and Douglas Kinnaird were old friends not only of Lord Byron but also of Lady Blessington, who made "a grand eulogium" of Kinnaird and his "*beauty* (a sign that you wear well)" on the first day she met Byron. He wrote to both men the day afterwards, describing the Blessington party (*Lord*

7

whom he most distinguished. He expressed himself greatly annoyed by the number of travelling English who pestered him with visits, the greater part of whom he had never known, or was but slightly acquainted with, which obliged him to refuse receiving any but those he particularly wished to see:[10] "But," added he, smiling, "they avenge themselves by attacking me in every sort of way, and there is no story too improbable for the craving appetites of our slander-loving countrymen."

Before taking leave, he proposed paying us a visit next day;[11] and he handed me into the carriage with many flattering expressions of the pleasure our visit had procured him.[12]

April 2nd.—We had scarcely finished our *déjeuné à la four-chette* this day when Lord Byron was announced: he sent up

Byron's Correspondence, ed. John Murray [London, 1922], II, 252-53; *LJ*, VI, 178-83). In a letter to Lady Blessington, Moore implied that their friendship had begun in 1809 (Madden, I, 254). Edward Ellice appears in her novel *The Repealers*, written immediately after the *Conversations*, as Errice, the "brother-in-law of Lord Rey [Lord Grey]" (*The Works of Lady Blessington* [Philadelphia, 1838], I, 255).

[10] Cf. Medwin, *Conversations*, p. 2, who refers to Byron's "known refusal at that time [late 1821, in Pisa] to receive the visits of strangers, even of some who brought him letters of introduction. . . ."

[11] Verified by Byron's letter to Thomas Moore, April 2, 1823 (*LJ*, VI, 178).

[12] The diary of Henry Edward Fox (*HVSV*, pp. 351-52) describes a very different situation. He wrote: "To my great dismay the family of Blessington were forcing their way, and his Lordship had already gained admittance. I found Lord Byron very much annoyed at their impertinence and rather nervous. . . . While the B's staid, the conversation rather flagged. As soon as they were gone he talked most agreeably and most openly on every subject." Cf. Byron on Fox and Lord and Lady Holland as reported by Blessington, pp. 10-13. Although Lady Holland, the divorced wife of Sir Godfrey Webster, and Lady Blessington were social rivals and the latter obviously enjoyed writing her pages on Lady Holland, it is also true that Byron had mentioned Lady Holland's name "in an unfair manner" in his destroyed Memoirs (Thomas Moore, *Memoirs, Journal, and Correspondence*, ed. Lord John Russell, London, 1853-1856, III, 251).

Writing to Moore, a friend of the Blessingtons, Byron said of this first meeting with them that he found them "very agreeable personages. . . . Miladi seems highly literary. . . . She is also very pretty even in a morning . . . (*LJ*, VI, 179-80). However, Teresa Guiccioli, who never consented to be introduced to Lady Blessington in Genoa and who was indeed "seized with a furious fit of Italian jealousy," Byron wrote, commented that Byron even at this first meeting "distrusted her sincerity, and he was even more on his guard against her when he found out that she had made her entrance into literature with a novel. . . ." See Teresa's full account, *HVSV*, pp. 353-55.

two printed cards, in an envelope addressed to us, and soon followed them. He appeared still more gay and cheerful than the day before—made various inquiries about all our mutual friends in England[13]—spoke of them with affectionate interest, mixed with a badinage in which none of their little defects were spared;[14] indeed candour obliges me to own that their defects seemed to have made a deeper impression on his mind than their good qualities (though he allowed all the latter), by the *gusto* with which he entered into them.

He talked of our mutual friend Moore, and of his "Lalla Rookh," which he said, though very beautiful, had disappointed him,[15] adding, that Moore would go down to posterity by his Melodies, which were all perfect. He said that he had never been so much *affected* as on hearing Moore sing some of them, particularly "When first I met Thee," which he said, made him shed tears:[16] "But," added he, with a look full of archness, "it was after I had drunk a certain portion of very potent white brandy." As he laid a peculiar stress on the word *affected*, I smiled, and the sequel of the white brandy made me smile again: he asked me the cause, and I answered that

[13] See my introduction, pp. 23-25. These mutual friends and acquaintances numbered at least thirty-six persons.

[14] Crabb Robinson reported in 1832, "Lady Blessington says Lord Byron spared no one, mother, wife, or friend; it was enough to raise his bile to praise any one in his presence; he would instantly fall abusing the friend that left him" (*HVSV*, p. 372). It is possible that in later years someone may have reported to Lady Blessington Byron's remarks upon her (see my introduction, pp. 92-94.

[15] Byron's many references to *Lalla Rookh* appear in letters to Moore or in his semi-public letters to Murray. With one qualified exception, these references are complimentary, but it was immediately after reading the poem that Byron wrote: "With regard to poetry in general, I am convinced, the more I think of it, that he [Moore] and *all* of us—Scott, Southey, Wordsworth, Moore, Campbell, I,—are all in the wrong, one as much as another; that we are upon a wrong revolutionary poetical system, or systems, not worth a damn in itself . . ." (*LJ*, IV, 169). Byron goes on to say that he had examined Moore's poems, side by side with Pope's, and found Pope's to be immeasurably superior. See also Hobhouse's diary for December 13, 1817 (*HVSV*, pp. 214-15), and Robinson's diary (*HVSV*, p. 371).

[16] N. P. Willis, *Pencillings by the Way* (New York, 1852), p. 525, has described Moore's style and its effect upon his audience: "He makes no attempt at music. It is a kind of admirable recitative, in which every shade of thought is syllabled and dwelt upon, and the sentiment of the very song goes through your blood, warming you to the very eyelids, and starting your tears, if you have soul or sense in you. I have heard of women's fainting at a song of Moore's. . . ."

his observation reminded me of the story of a lady offering her condolence to a poor Irishwoman on the death of her child, who stated that she had never been more affected than on the event: the poor woman, knowing the hollowness of the compliment, answered, with all the quickness of her country, "Sure, then, ma'am, that is saying a great deal, for you were always affected." Lord Byron laughed, and said my apropos was very wicked; but I maintained it was very just. He spoke much more warmly of Moore's social attractions as a companion, which he said were unrivalled, than of his merits as a poet.

He offered to be our cicerone in pointing out all the pretty drives and rides about Genoa; recommended riding as the only means of seeing the country, many of the fine points of view being inaccessible, except on horseback; and he praised Genoa on account of the rare advantage it possessed of having so few English, either as inhabitants or birds of passage.

I was this day again struck by the flippancy of his manner of talking of persons for whom I know he expresses, nay, for whom I believe he feels a regard. Something of this must have shown itself in my manner, for he laughingly observed that he was afraid he should lose my good opinion by his frankness; but that when the fit was on him he could not help saying what he thought, though he often repented it when too late.

He talked of Mr. [Fox], from whom he had received a visit the day before, praised his looks, and the insinuating gentleness of his manners, which, he observed, lent a peculiar charm to the little tales he repeated: he said that he had given him more London scandal than he had heard since he left England; observed that he had quite talent enough to render his malice very *piquant* and amusing, and that his imitations were admirable. "How can his mother do without him?" said Byron; "with his *espièglerie* and malice, he must be an invaluable coadjutor; and Venus without Cupid could not be more *délaissée* than *Milady* [Holland] without this her legitimate son."

He said that he had formerly felt very partial to Mr. [Fox]; his face was so handsome, and his countenance so ingenuous, that it was impossible not to be prepossessed in his favour; added to

10

which, one hoped that the son of such a father could never entirely degenerate: "he has, however, degenerated sadly," said Byron, "but as he is yet young he may improve; though, to see a person of his age and *sex* so devoted to gossip and scandal, is rather discouraging to those who are interested in his welfare."[17]

He talked of Lord [Holland]; praised his urbanity, his talents, and acquirements; but, above all, his sweetness of temper and good-nature.[18] "Indeed I do love Lord [Holland]," said Byron, "though the pity I feel for his domestic thraldom has something in it akin to contempt. Poor dear man! he is sadly bullied by *Milady*;[19] and,

[17] Byron's two letters of April 2, 1823, one to Moore and one to Douglas Kinnaird, express nothing but unqualified approval of Henry Edward Fox and delight in his visit: "If to those [personal or social accomplishments] he can add hereditary talents, he will keep the name of Fox in all its freshness for half a century more, I hope" (*LJ*, VI, 178). See also *Lord Byron's Correspondence*, II, 253: "On Monday I saw Henry Fox (Lord Holland's son) and was delighted in him; he seems to me, on so slight a glimpse, the *ne plus ultra* of the amiable; even to the very features of his face." It is true, however, that Fox delighted in scandal (his diary is full of it) and that his parents had an illegitimate son before his birth. But it is also true that D'Orsay, on his first trip to London, had insulted Lady Holland in her own house (Connely, p. 26), and by the time the *Conversations* came to be written the author had suffered much at the hands of her rival, Lady Holland (see my introduction). D'Orsay and Fox had also quarreled.

Fox, born in 1802, is described by the Earl of Ilchester, the editor of his *Journal* (London, 1923), as a man of strongly marked likes and dislikes, inclined to jump to conclusions about people. His "critical perception of the faults of his intimates tended to limit him in his choice" of friends. Fox's "studied dislike of anything savouring of dishonesty or sordidness caused him to discard those who proved themselves inferior to his self-accepted standard. . . . Yet at times a querulous spark in his character would shine out . . ." (pp. 13-16). There were attractive compensating qualities, however, in the man.

[18] Lord Holland was proverbial for these qualities. See *LJ*, I, 184, n. 1, for the many tributes paid him; also D'Orsay's tribute (Madden, I, 138), and Lloyd Sanders, *The Holland House Circle* (London, 1908), especially Chapter V. Byron dedicated *The Bride of Abydos* to him. Lord Holland dined at the home of Lord and Lady Blessington, but as far as I know Lady Holland was never a guest there (Fox, *Journal*, p. 62).

[19] A Mrs. Trench thus describes Lady Holland's dictatorial treatment of her husband: "She lies in easy posture on a sofa. . . . Her husband has the honour of being fag-in-chief. . . . 'Now shut two windows and open one door. No, open two doors and shut one window. Lord Holland, seal my letters. Settle those newspapers according to their dates—tell me which of them I have read. Now, do bring me my gloves—not those. . . . Lord Holland, I believe you are deaf—did you not hear me call?'" (Willard Connely, *Count D'Orsay: The Dandy of Dandies* [London, 1952], p. 25; see also p. 582; Sanders, *The Holland House Circle*, Chapter V; and R. R. Madden, *The Literary Life and Correspondence of the Countess of Blessington* [New York, 1855], I, 139-40.)

11

what is worst of all, half her tyranny is used on the plea of kindness and taking care of his health. Hang such kindness! say I. She is certainly the most imperious, dictatorial person I know—is always *en reine*; which, by the by, in her peculiar position, shows tact, for she suspects that were she to quit the throne she might be driven to the antichamber; however, with all her faults, she is not vindictive— as a proof, she never extended her favour to me until after the little episode respecting her in 'English Bards;' nay more, I suspect I owe her friendship to it. Rogers persuaded me to suppress the passage in the other editions.[20] After all, Lady [Holland] has one merit, and a great one in my eyes, which is, that in this age of cant[21] and humbug, and in a country—I mean our own dear England—where the cant of Virtue is the order of the day, she has contrived, without any great resemblance of it, merely by force of—shall I call it impudence or courage?—not only to get herself into society, but absolutely to give the law to her own circle.[22] She passes, also, for being clever; this, perhaps owing to my dulness, I never discovered, except that she has a way, *en reine*, of asking questions that show some reading. The first dispute I ever had with Lady Byron was caused by my urging her to visit Lady [Holland]; and, what is odd enough," laughing with bitterness, "our first and last difference was caused by two very worthless women."[23]

[20] *English Bards*, 11, 552-59, to which Byron attached a note: ". . . we know from good authority that the manuscripts [sent to the *Edinburgh Review*] are submitted to her perusal—no doubt for correction" (*The Works of Lord Byron. Poetry*, ed. E. H. Coleridge [London, 1898-1904], I, 341; hereafter referred to as *Poetry*).

[21] Lady Blessington has a great deal to say about Byron's hatred of cant, a word which appears repeatedly in his writings. Cf. Byron in his "Letter . . . on . . . Bowles's Strictures" (*LJ*, V, 542): "The truth is, that in these days the grand *'primum mobile'* of England is *cant*; cant political, cant poetical, cant religious, cant moral; but always *cant*, multiplied through all the varieties of life." See also *LJ*, V, 557, n., and *HVSV*, p. 357, on "the cant of the love of nature." She also suffered from the social or moral hypocrisy of the time and so hated and feared it.

[22] The Earl of Ilchester explains, in *Elizabeth, Lady Holland to Her Son, 1821-1845* (London, 1946), p. vii: "As a divorcee [with an illegitimate son by Lord Holland], she was only received in a limited number of the great houses, comprising those of her husband's relatives and of the great Whig magnates. Consequently, the masculine sex predominated at the gatherings over which she presided." Lady Blessington suffered from a similar limitation and was not received at Holland House.

[23] The other was probably Mrs. Clermont. Lady Byron declined to call on Lady Holland because she was a divorcee, presumably.

12

Observing that we appeared surprised at the extraordinary frank-ness,[24] to call it by no harsher name, with which he talked of his *ci-devant* friends, he added:—"Don't think the worse of me for what I have said: the truth is, I have witnessed such gross selfish-ness and want of feeling in Lady [Holland], that I cannot resist speaking my sentiments of her."—I observed: "But are you not afraid she will hear what you say of her?"—He answered:—"Were she to hear it, she would act the *aimable*, as she always does to those who attack her; while to those who are attentive and court her, she is insolent beyond bearing."[25]

Having sat with us above two hours, and expressed his wishes that we might prolong our stay at Genoa, he promised to dine with us the following Thursday,[26] and took his leave, laughingly apolo-gizing for the length of his visit, adding, that he was such a recluse, and had lived so long out of the world, that he had quite for-gotten the usages of it.

He on all occasions professes a detestation of what he calls *cant*; says it will banish from England all that is pure and good; and that while people are looking after the shadow, they lose the substance of goodness; he says, that the best mode left for conquering it, is to expose it to *ridicule*, the only *weapon*, added he, that the English climate cannot rust. He appears to know every thing that is going on in England; takes a great interest in the London gossip; and while professing to read no new publications, betrays, in various ways, a perfect knowledge of every new work.

[24] For Byron's imprudence in conversation, see Moore, *Life*, p. 574, and *The Idler in Italy*, I, 295.

[25] When Moore gave Byron's Memoirs to Lady Holland to read, on July 6, 1821, telling her that Byron "had mentioned her name in an unfair manner somewhere, she said, 'Such things give me no uneasiness; I know perfectly well my station in the world: and I know all that can be said of me. As long as the few friends that I *really* am sure of speak kindly of me (and I would not believe the contrary if I saw it in black and white), all that the rest of the world can say is a matter of complete indifference to me'" (Moore, *Journal*, III, 251). Lady Blessington is the only one of Byron's conversationalists to whom he revealed any dislike of Lady Holland. The only evidence in his letters is a single reference to her ill-nature (*Correspondence*, I, 171, August 18, 1813, to Lady Melbourne).

[26] Unless Byron saw the Blessingtons three days in a row, this is April 10. Cf. the *Idler* account, *HVSV*, 356, there dated April 4.

"MY DEAR LORD,

"I send you to-day's (the latest) Galignani. My banker tells me, however, that his letters from Spain state, that two regiments have revolted, which is a great vex, as they say in Ireland. I shall be very glad to see your friend's journal. He seems to have all the qualities requisite to have figured in his brother-in-law's ancestor's Memoirs. I did *not* think him old enough to have served in Spain, and must have expressed myself badly. On the contrary, he has all the air of a *Cupidon déchaîné*, and promises to have it for some time to come. I beg to present my respects to Lady B—, and ever am your obliged and faithful servant,

"NOEL BYRON."

When Lord Byron came to dine with us on Thursday, he arrived an hour before the usual time, and appeared in good spirits. He said that he found the passages and stairs filled with people, who stared at him very much; but he did not seem vexed at this homage, for so it certainly was meant, as the Albergo della Villa, where we resided, being filled with English, all were curious to see their distinguished countryman. He was very gay at dinner, ate of most of the dishes, expressed pleasure at partaking of a plum pudding, *à l'Anglaise*, made by one of our English servants; was helped twice, and observed, that he hoped he should not shock us by eating so much: "But," added he, "the truth is, that for several months I have been following a most abstemious *régime*, living almost entirely on vegetables; and now that I see a good dinner, I cannot resist temptation, though to-morrow I shall suffer for my gourmandise, as I always do when I indulge in luxuries." He drank a few glasses of champagne, saying, that as he considered it a *jour de fête*, he would eat, drink, and be merry.

He talked of Mr. [Hill], who was then our Minister at Genoa.[27]

[27] William Noel-Hill, later 3rd Lord Berwick, English minister to the Kingdom af Sardinia, had followed the king and his court on their annual visit to Genoa, from Turin. Hill thought that Byron was "most delightful . . . but most vindictive when he takes dislikes" (quoted in *LJ*, VI, 158). Hill was later minister in Naples, where D'Orsay and Lord Blessington's daughter were finally married, after being disappointed in Florence and Rome, as a result of the influence of Lord Burghersh, the minister at Florence (see my introduction).

"H[ill]," said he, "is a thorough good-natured and hospitable man, keeps an excellent table, and is as fond of good things as I am, but has not my forbearance. I received, some time ago, a *pâté de Perigord*, and finding it excellent, I determined on sharing it with H[ill]; but here my natural selfishness suggested that it would be wiser for me, who had so few dainties, to keep this for myself, than to give it to H[ill], who had so many. After half an hour's debate between selfishness and generosity, which do you think" (turning to me) "carried the point?"—I answered, "Generosity, of course."—"No, by Jove!" said he, "no such thing; selfishness in this case, as in most others, triumphed: I sent the *pâté* to my friend H[ill], because I felt another dinner off it would play the deuce with me; and so you see, after all, he owed the *pâté* more to selfishness than generosity." Seeing us smile at this, he said:—"When you know me better, you will find that I am the most selfish person in the world; I have, however, the merit, if it be one, of not only being perfectly conscious of my faults, but of never denying them; and this surely is something, in this age of cant and hypocrisy."

The journal to which Lord Byron refers was written by one of our party, and Lord Byron, having discovered its existence, and expressed a desire to peruse it, the writer confided it to him.

"MY DEAR LORD,   "April 14th, 1823.

"I was not in the way when your note came. I have only time to thank you, and to send the Galignani's. My face is better in fact, but worse in appearance, with a very *scurvy* aspect; but I expect it to be well in a day or two. I will subscribe to the Improving Society.

                              "Yours in haste, but ever,
                                        "NOEL BYRON."

"MILOR,   "April 22nd, 1823.

"I received your billet at dinner, which was a good one—with a sprinkling of female foreigners, who, I dare say, were very agreeable. As I have formed a sullen resolution about presentations, which I never break (above once a month), I begged —— to

15

dispense me from being introduced, and intrigued for myself a place as far remote as possible from his fair guests, and very near a bottle of the best wine to confirm my misogyny. After coffee, I had accomplished my retreat as far as the hall, on full tilt towards your *thé*, which I was very eager to partake of, when I was arrested by ——— requesting that I would make my bow to the French Ambassadress, who it seems is a Dillon, Irish, but born or bred in America; has been pretty, and is a *blue*, and of course entitled to the homage of all persons who have been printed. I returned, and it was then too late to detain Miss P—— over the tea-urn. I beg you to accept my regrets, and present my regards to Milady, and Miss P——, and Comte Alfred, and believe me ever yours,

"Noel Byron."

"April 23rd, 1823.

"my dear lord,

"I thank you for quizzing me and my 'learned Thebans.' I assure you, my notions on that score are limited to getting away with a whole skin, or sleeping quietly with a broken one, in some of my old Glens where I used to dream in my former excursions. I should prefer a grey Greek stone over me to Westminster Abbey; but I doubt if I shall have the luck to die so happily. A lease of my 'body's length' is all the land which I should covet in that quarter.

"What the Honourable Dug* and his Committee may decide, I do not know, and still less what I may decide (for I am not famous for decision) for myself; but if I could do any good in any way, I should be happy to contribute thereto, and without *éclat*. I have seen enough of that in my time, to rate it at its value. I wish *you* were upon that Committee, for I think you would set them going one way or the other; at present they seem a little dormant. I dare not venture to *dine* with you to-morrow, nor indeed any day this week; for *three* days of dinners during the last seven days, have made me so head-achy and sulky, that it will take me a whole Lent to subside again into anything like independence of sensation

* His abridgment for Douglas Kinnaird.

16

from the pressure of materialism.   *   *   *   *   But I shall take my chance of finding you the first fair morning for a visit. Ever yours,

"NOEL BYRON."

"May 7th, 1823.

"MY DEAR LORD,

"I return the poesy, which will form a new light to lighten the Irish, and will, I hope, be duly appreciated by the public. I have not returned *Miledi's* verses, because I am not aware of the error she mentions, and see no reason for the alteration; however, if she insists, I must be conformable. I write in haste, having a visitor.

"Ever yours, very truly,

"NOEL BYRON."

"May 14th, 1823.

"MY DEAR LORD,

"I avize you that the Reading Association have received numbers of English publications, which you may like to see, and as you are a Member should avail yourself of early. I have just returned my share before its time, having kept the books *one* day instead of *five*, which latter is the utmost allowance. The rules obliged me to forward it to a Monsieur G——, as next in rotation. If you have anything for England, a gentleman with some law papers of mine returns there to-morrow (Thursday), and would be happy to convey anything for you. Ever yours, and truly,

"NOEL BYRON.

"P.S. I request you to present my compliments to Lady Blessington, Miss Power and Comte D'Orsay."

"May 23rd, 1823.

"MY DEAR LORD,

"I thought that I *had* answered your note. I ought, and beg you to excuse the omission. I should have called, but I thought my chance of finding you at *home* in the environs, greater than at the hotel.   *   *   *   *   I hope you will not take my *not* dining

17

with you again after so many dinners, ill; but the truth is, that your banquets are too luxurious for my habits, and I feel the effect of them in this warm weather for some time after. I am sure you will not be angry, since I have already more than sufficiently abused your hospitality. ＊ ＊ ＊ ＊ I fear that I can hardly afford more than two thousand francs for the steed in question, as I have to undergo considerable expenses at this present time, and I suppose that will not suit you. I must not forget to pay my Irish Subscription. My remembrances to *Miledi*, and to Alfred, and to Miss P——. Ever yours,

"NOEL BYRON."

"May 24th, 1823.
"MY DEAR LORD,

"I find that I was elected a Member of the Greek Committee in March, but did not receive the Chairman's notice till yesterday, and this by mere chance, and through a private hand. I am doing all I can to get away, and the Committee and my friends in England seem both to approve of my going up into Greece; but I meet here with obstacles, which have hampered and put me out of spirits, and still keep me in a vexatious state of uncertainty. I began bathing the other day, but the water was still chilly, and in diving for a Genoese *lira* in clear but deep water, I imbibed so much water through my ears, as gave me a *megrim* in my head, which you will probably think a superfluous malady.

"Ever yours, obliged and truly,
"NOEL BYRON."

In all his conversations relative to Lady Byron, and they are frequent, he declares that he is totally unconscious of the cause of her leaving him,[28] but suspects that the ill-natured interposition of Mrs.

---

[28] This was Byron's usual pose of ignorance. He said to Henry Edward Fox on April 1, 1823, concerning the separation, that "he had no conception what it was for . . ." (*HVSV*, p. 352). Cf. Lady Blessington as summarized or quoted by Thomas Moore, *Letters and Journals of Lord Byron: with Notices of His Life* (London, 1892), pp. 580-81: "This negotiation [involving Colonel Montgomery] . . . led naturally and frequently to conversations on the subject of his marriage . . . —and the account which he then gave, as well of the circumstances of the separation, as of his own entire unconsciousness of the immediate causes that provoked it, was [like his other accounts]."

Charlemont[29] led to it. It is a strange business! He declares that he left no means untried to effect a reconciliation, and always adds with bitterness, "A day will arrive when I shall be avenged. I feel that I shall not live long, and when the grave has closed over me, what must she feel!" All who wish well to Lady Byron must desire that she should not survive her husband, for the all-atoning grave, that gives oblivion to the errors of the dead, clothes those of the living in such sombre colours to their own too-late awakened feelings, as to render them wretched for life, and more than avenges the real or imagined wrongs of those we have lost for ever.

When Lord Byron was praising the mental and personal qualifications of Lady Byron, I asked him how all that he now said agreed with certain sarcasms supposed to bear a reference to her, in his works.[30] He smiled, shook his head, and said they were meant to spite and vex her, when he was wounded and irritated at her refusing to receive or answer his letters;[31] that he was not sincere in his implied censures, and that he was sorry he had written them; but notwithstanding this regret, and all his good resolutions to avoid similar sins, he might on renewed provocation recur to the same vengeance, though he allowed it was petty and unworthy of him. Lord Byron speaks of his sister, Mrs. Leigh, constantly, and always with strong expressions of affection; he says she is the most faultless person he ever knew, and that she was his only source of consolation in his troubles on the separation.

Byron is a great talker; his flippancy ceases in a *tête-à-tête*, and he becomes sententious, abandoning himself to the subject, and seeming to think aloud, though his language has the appearance of stiffness, and is quite opposed to the trifling chit-chat that he enters into when in general society. I attribute this to his having lived so much alone, as also to the desire he now professes of applying

[29] Medwin, *Conversations*, pp. 41 and 43n., confused Mrs. Clermont with "Mrs. Charlment."

[30] Cf. Colonel Montgomery, who secured his information from Lady Blessington, in his letter to Lady Byron, May 1823 (Mrs. Doris L. Moore, *The Late Lord Byron* [Philadelphia, 1961], p. 485): "He has been told that you are ever abusing him and vilifying his character & to the reports of your calumnies are to be attributed the Various attacks upon you that have appeared in his Works."

[31] Cf. Byron as reported by Lady Blessington in Moore's *Life*, p. 581: "Lady Byron . . . has refused to answer my letters."

19

himself to prose writing. He affects a sort of Johnsonian tone,[32] likes very much to be listened to, and seems to observe the effect he produces on his hearer. In mixed society his ambition is to appear the man of fashion; he adopts a light tone of badinage and persiflage that does not sit gracefully on him, but is always anxious to turn the subject to his own personal affairs, or feelings, which are either lamented with an air of melancholy, or dwelt on with playful ridicule, according to the humour he happens to be in.

A friend of ours, Colonel M[ontgomery], having arrived at Genoa, spent much of his time with us. Lord Byron soon discovered this, and became shy, embarrassed in his manner, and out of humour. The first time I had an opportunity of speaking to him without witnesses was on the road to Nervi, on horseback, when he asked me if I had not observed a great change in him. I allowed that I had, and asked him the cause; and he told me, that knowing Colonel M[ontgomery] to be a friend of Lady Byron's, and believing him to be an enemy of his, he expected that he would endeavour to influence us against him, and finally succeed in depriving him of our friendship; and that this was the cause of his altered manner.[33]

---

[32] This tone was by no means usual or typical with Byron, although Leigh Hunt records: "He liked to imitate Johnson, and say, 'Why, Sir,' in a high mouthing way, rising, and looking around him" (*HVSV*, p. 328). James Kennedy reminds us that "his conversation and manners varied according to his company" (*HVSV*, p. 480).

[33] Byron had the most excellent reasons to dislike and distrust Colonel Hugh Montgomery and his unmarried sister Mary Millicent. She was a childhood friend of Lady Byron, an orphaned invalid, and in 1814, in a letter to Byron, Annabella had cast him in the fictitious role of her suitor. Byron, recorded Annabella in 1812, "seemed to have received an unpleasant impression from MM's countenance though he spoke of the cleverness it indicated." Both brother and sister had been confidants of Annabella and her mother for many years, and following the separation they became most spiteful and trouble-making partisans (see Malcolm Elwin, *Lord Byron's Wife* [New York, 1962], pp. 85, 117, 214, 215).

At Venice, at Contessa Benzoni's, when Byron tried to speak to Mary Millicent, she "cut him dead," and Mengaldo spread the story "all over Venice." It reached Stendhal, who thought that Colonel Montgomery had challenged Byron (Iris Origo, *The Last Attachment* [New York, 1949], p. 34). At that time, the Colonel informed Annabella that Byron was "extremely fat . . . bloated and heavy" (Ethel Colburn Mayne, *The Life and Letters of Anne Isabella, Lady Noel Byron*, p. 277). Mary Millicent thought that he was "a very bad man" (Doris L. Moore, *The Late Lord Byron*, p. 485).

In Genoa, Byron saw the Colonel, to whom he had never been introduced, at a dinner given by Mr. Hill, where they "sat at the opposite side[s] of a wide table. . . ." Of this encounter Montgomery wrote: "I thought at first he

I endeavoured, and at length succeeded, to convince him that Colonel M[ontgomery] was too good and honourable a man to do anything spiteful or ill-natured, and that he never spoke ill of him; which seemed to gratify him. He told me that Colonel M[ontgomery]'s sister was the intimate and confidential friend of Lady Byron, and that through this channel I might be of great use to him, if I would use my influence with Colonel M[ontgomery], to make his sister write to Lady Byron for a copy of her portrait, which he had long been most anxious to possess.[34] Colonel M[ontgomery], after much

did not know me, but afterwards I found that he spoke about me to Lord Blessington, saying that I was a great friend of his Wife, & that he would have procured an introduction, but did not know whether it would be agreeable. In this he conjectured right, & I took very good care to avoid anything of the kind afterwards" (Doris L. Moore, *The Late Lord Byron*, p. 473). This dinner may have been that of March 15 (*Correspondence*, II, 251), although Lady Blessington in *The Idler* states that Byron dined with Hill on April 21 (*HVSV*, p. 360). It does not necessarily follow, as Mrs. Moore argues (p. 473), that Lady Blessington "surprised him [Byron] on the 29th with the news of the Colonel's arrival." Byron may well have reacted in surprised embarrassment merely because she mentioned his name as that of a friend, in a city where there were so few English that Montgomery saw Byron "frequently."

Byron, then, was quite correct in believing Montgomery to be an enemy of his. Montgomery's letter to Lady Byron following that of his sister's by about a week, informed her not only that Byron wanted her picture but also that he wore a strand of Augusta Leigh's "hair in a large brooch" (Mrs. Moore, pp. 485-86). For her part, Lady Blessington showed Montgomery a copy of Byron's "Lines on Hearing that Lady Byron was Ill," which he described in his letter as "very severe."

[34] This passage provides some opportunity to study the relation between Lady Blessington's original diary, *The Idler*, and the *Conversations*. On April 15, 1832, the Blessington "letters and MS. book," which she had lent to Thomas Moore for his *Life* of Byron, were still in his possession. She had asked for their return and presumably received them at once (*The Letters of Thomas Moore*, II, 744). The first installment of her *Conversations* appeared in the July 1832 issue of *The New Monthly*. I do not think there is any reason to assume that Moore rewrote Lady Blessington in any significant way, except to recast her account in the third person. We read, then, in Moore, *Letters and Journals of Lord Byron: with Notices of his Life* (London, 1892), p. 580: "A gentleman, whose sister was known to be the confidential friend of Lady Byron, happening at this time to be at Genoa, and in the habit of visiting at the house of the poet's new intimates, Lord Byron took one day an opportunity, in conversing with Lady Blessington, to say that she would render him an essential kindness if, through the mediation of this gentleman and his sister, she could procure for him from Lady Byron what he had long been most anxious to possess, a copy of her picture." In *The Idler* (*HVSV*, p. 363, italics mine), this appears as "Byron has asked me to use my influence with Colonel M. to induce him, *through the* medium *of his sister*, who is *the* intimate *friend of Lady Byron*, to *procure a copy of* Lady B's portrait, which her Lord has *long* wished to *possess*." The sense of the two sentences is the same; the

21

entreaty, consented to write to his sister on the subject, but on the express condition that Lord Byron should specify on paper his exact wishes; and I wrote to Lord Byron to this effect, to which letter I received the following answer. I ought to add, that in conversation I told Lord Byron that it was reported that Lady Byron was in delicate health, and also that it was said she was apprehensive that he intended to claim his daughter, or to interfere in her education:[35] he refers to this in the letter which I copy.*

Talking of literary women, Lord Byron said that Madame de Staël was certainly the cleverest, though not the most agreeable woman he had ever known. "She declaimed to you instead of conversing with you," said he, "never pausing except to take breath; and if during that interval a rejoinder was put in, it was evident that she did not attend to it, as she resumed the thread of her discourse as though it had not been interrupted."[36] This observation

---

* Here follow the letters in Moore's Journal, p. 644-46 [*LJ*, VI, 198-99].

italicized words in the second sentence are common to both. This becomes in the *Conversations*: "He told me that Colonel Montgomery's sister was *the intimate* and confidential *friend of Lady Byron*, and that *through* this channel I might be of great use to him, if I would *use my influence with Colonel* Montgomery, to make *his sister* write to Lady Byron for *a copy of* her *portrait, which* he had *long* been most anxious *to possess*." The italicized words are those which also appear in *The Idler*.

[35] Moore: "It having been represented to him, in the course of the same, or a similar conversation, that Lady Byron was said by her friends to be in a state of constant alarm lest he should come to England to claim his daughter, or, in some other way, interfere with her, he professed his readiness to give every assurance that might have the effect of calming such apprehensions . . ."

The Idler, with words common to both sentences italicized: "This request has given me an opportunity of telling Byron, that *Lady Byron was* apprehensive that he might *claim* their *daughter, or interfere in some way with her*. Byron was greatly moved, and after a few minutes' silence, caused evidently by deep emotion, he declared that he never intended to take any step that could be painful to the feelings of Lady Byron."

Conversations, with words common to *Idler* passage italicized: "I ought to add, that in conversation I told Lord Byron that it was reported that Lady Byron was in delicate health, and also that it was said she *was apprehensive that he* intended to *claim* his *daughter, or to interfere in* her education. . . ."

[36] Madame de Staël was famous for the kind of conversation here described, and there are numerous references to it in Byron's letters and journals. He wrote of her to Lady Byron in 1813 (*LJ*, III, 408): "Do you know her? I don't ask if you have heard her?—her tongue is the perpetual motion." Byron lent Lady Blessington a copy of Benjamin Constant's *Adolphe* and informed her that many supposed de Staël to be the heroine (*LJ*, VI, 204; see below, p. 27).

from Byron was amusing enough, as we had all made nearly the same observation on him, with the exception that he listened to, and noticed, any answer made to his reflections. "Madame de Staël," continued Byron, "was very eloquent when her imagination warmed, (and a very little excited it;) her powers of imagination were much stronger than her reasoning ones, perhaps owing to their being much more frequently exercised; her language was recondite, but redundant; and though always flowery, and often brilliant, there was an obscurity that left the impression that she did not perfectly understand what she endeavoured to render intelligible to others.[37] She was always losing herself in philosophical disquisition, and once she got entangled in the mazes of the labyrinth of metaphysics; she had no clue by which she could guide her path—the imagination that led her into her difficulties could not get her out of them; the want of a mathematical education, which might have served as a ballast to steady and help her into the port of reason, was always visible, and though she had great tact in concealing her defeat, and covering a retreat, a tolerable logician must have always discovered the scrapes she got into. Poor dear Madame de Staël! I shall never forget seeing her one day, at table with a large party, when the busk (I believe you ladies call it) of her corset forced its way through the top of the corset, and would not descend though pushed by all the force of both hands of the wearer, who became crimson from the operation. After fruitless efforts, she turned in despair to the valet de chambre behind her chair, and requested him to draw it out, which could only be done by his passing his hand from behind over her shoulder, and across her chest, when, with a desperate effort, he unsheathed the busk. Had you seen the faces of some of the English ladies of the party, you would have been like me, almost convulsed; while Madame remained perfectly unconscious that she had committed any solecism on *la décence Anglaise*. Poor Madame de Staël verified the truth of the lines—

> Qui de son sexe n'a pas l'esprit,
> De son sexe a tout le malheur.

[37] Cf. Medwin's *Conversations*, p. 184: "She was very indefinite and vague in her manner of expression. In endeavouring to be new she became often obscure, and sometimes unintelligible."

She *thought* like a man, but, alas! she *felt* like a woman; as witness the episode in her life with Monsieur Rocca, which she dared not avow, (I mean her marriage with him,) because she was more jealous of her reputation as a writer than a woman, and the faiblesse de cœur, this alliance proved she had not courage to *affiche*.[38] A friend of hers, and a compatriot into the bargain, whom she believed to be one of the most adoring of her worshippers, gave me the following epigrams:—

Sur la Grossesse de Madame de Stael.

Quel esprit! quel talent! quel sublime génie!
En elle tout aspire à l'immortalité;
Et jusqu'à son hydropisie,
Rien n'est perdu pour la postérité.

Portrait de Madame de Stael.

Armande a pour esprit des momens de délire,
Armande a pour vertu le mépris des appas:
Elle craint la railleur que sans cesse elle inspire,
Elle évite l'amant que ne la cherche pas:
Puisqu'elle n'a point l'art de cacher son visage,
Et qu'elle a la fureur de montrer son esprit,
Il faut la défier de cesser d'être sage
Et d'entendre ce que'lle dit.

"The giving the epigrams to me, a brother of the craft of authors,[39] was worthy of a friend, and was another proof, if proof were wanting, of the advantages of friends:

No epigram such pointed satire lends
As does the memory of our faithful friends.

I have an exalted opinion of friendship, as you see. You look incredulous, but you will not only give me credit for being sincere in

---

[38] Compare Medwin's *Conversations*, p. 185: "She was vain; but who had an excuse for vanity if she had not? I can easily conceive her not wishing to change her name, or acknowledge that of Rocca."

[39] Writing may have been regarded as a craft by Lady Blessington, but probably not by Byron (*LJ*, IV, 238): "Did you read his [Leigh Hunt's] skimble-skamble about Wordsworth being at the head of his own *profession*, in the *eyes* of *those* who followed it? I thought that poetry was an *art*, or an *attribute*, and not a profession. . . ." See also below, pp. 186, 191, and elsewhere.

24

this opinion, but one day arrive at the same conclusion yourself. 'Shake not thy *jetty* locks at me:' ten years hence, if we both live so long, you will allow that I am right, though you now think me a cynic for saying all this. Madame de Staël," continued Byron, "had peculiar satisfaction in impressing on her auditors the severity of the persecution she underwent from Napoleon: a certain mode of enraging her, was to appear to doubt the extent to which she wished it to be believed this had been pushed, as she looked on the persecution as a triumphant proof of her literary and political importance, which she more than insinuated Napoleon feared might subvert his government.[40] This was a weakness, but a common one. One half of the clever people of the world believe they are hated and persecuted, and the other half imagine they are admired and beloved. Both are wrong, and both false conclusions are produced by vanity, though that vanity is the strongest which believes in the hatred and persecution, as it implies a belief of extraordinary superiority to account for it."

I could not suppress the smile that Byron's reflections excited, and, with his usual quickness, he instantly felt the application I had made of them to himself, for he blushed, and half angry, and half laughing, said:—"Oh! I see what you are smiling at; you think that I have described my own case, and proved myself guilty of vanity." I allowed that I thought so, as he had a thousand times[41] repeated to me, that he was feared and detested in England, which I never would admit. He tried various arguments to prove to me that it was not vanity, but a knowledge of the fact, that made him believe himself detested: but I, continuing to smile, and look incredulous, he got really displeased, and said:— "You have such a provoking memory, that you compare notes of all one's different opinions, so that one is sure to get into a scrape." Byron observed, that he once told Madame de Staël that he considered her "Delphine" and "Corinne" as very dangerous productions to be put into the hands of young women. I asked him how she received this piece of candour, and he answered:—"Oh! just as all such candid avowals

---

[40] Cf. Medwin's *Conversations*, p. 184: "I cannot believe that Napoleon was acquainted with all the petty persecutions that she used to be so garrulous about, or that he deemed her of sufficient importance to be dangerous. . . ."

[41] Teresa Guiccioli: *en combien de jours?*

25

are received—she never forgave me for it. She endeavoured to prove to me, that, *au contraire,* the tendencies of both her novels were supereminently moral. I begged that we might not enter on 'Delphine,' as that was *hors de question,* (she was furious at this,) but that all the moral world thought, that her representing all the virtuous characters in 'Corinne' as being dull, common-place, and tedious, was a most insidious blow aimed at virtue, and calculated to throw it into the shade. She was so excited and impatient to attempt a refutation, that it was only by my volubility I could keep her silent. She interrupted me every moment by gesticulating, exclaiming—'*Quel idée!*' '*Mon Dieu!*' '*Ecoutez donc!*' '*Vous m'impatientez!*'—but I continued saying, how dangerous it was to inculcate the belief that genius, talent, acquirements, and accomplishments, such as Corinne was represented to possess, could not preserve a woman from becoming a victim to an unrequited passion, and that reason, absence, and female pride were unavailing.

"I told her that 'Corinne' would be considered, if not cited, as an excuse for violent *passions*, by all young ladies with imaginations *exalté*, and that she had much to answer for. Had you seen her! I now wonder how I had courage to go on; but I was in one of my humours, and had heard of her commenting on me one day, so I determined to pay her off. She told me that I, above *all people*, was the last person that ought to talk of morals, as nobody had done more to deteriorate them.[42] I looked innocent, and added, I was willing to plead guilty of having sometimes represented vice under alluring forms, but so it was generally in the world, therefore it was necessary to paint it so; but that I never represented virtue under the sombre and disgusting shapes of dulness, severity, and *ennui*, and that I always took care to represent the votaries of vice as unhappy themselves, and entailing unhappiness on those that loved them; so that *my moral* was unexceptionable.[43] She was perfectly outrageous, and the more so, as I appeared calm and in earnest, though I as-

[42] Cf. Medwin's *Conversations*, p. 12: "Somebody possessed Madame de Staël with an opinion of my immorality. . . . Madame de Staël took the liberty to read me a lecture before this crowd; to which I only made her a low bow." Lady Blessington uses the word *lecture* later in this paragraph.
[43] Cf. Byron to Murray, December 25, 1822 (*LJ*, VI, 155): "*Don Juan* will be known by and bye, for what it is intended,—a *Satire* on *abuses* of the present states of Society, and not an eulogy of vice. . . ."

sure you it required an effort, as I was ready to laugh outright at the idea that *I*, who was at that period considered the most *mauvais sujet* of the day, should give Madame de Staël a lecture on morals; and I knew that this added to her rage. I also knew she never dared avow that *I* had taken such a liberty. She was, notwithstanding her little defects, a fine creature, with great talents, and many noble qualities, and had a simplicity quite extraordinary, which led her to believe every thing people told her, and consequently to be continually hoaxed, of which I saw such proofs in London.[44] Madame de Staël it was who first lent me 'Adolphe,' which you like so much: it is very clever, and very affecting. A friend of hers told me, that she was supposed to be the heroine, and I, with my *aimable franchise*, insinuated as much to her, which rendered her furious.[45] She proved to me how impossible it was that it could be so, which I already knew, and complained of the malice of the world for supposing it possible."

Byron has remarkable penetration in discovering the characters of those around him, and he piques himself extremely on it: he also thinks he has fathomed the recesses of his own mind; but he is mistaken: with much that is *little* (which he suspects) in his character, there is much that is *great*, that he does not give himself credit for: his first impulses are always good, but his temper, which is impatient, prevents his acting on the cool dictates of reason; and it appears to me, that in judging himself, Byron mistakes temper for character, and takes the ebullitions of the first for the indications of the nature of the second. He declares that, in addition to his other failings, avarice is now established.[46]

This new vice, like all the others he attributes to himself, he talks of as one would name those of an acquaintance, in a sort of deprecating, yet half-mocking tone; as much as to say, you see I know all my faults better than you do, though I don't choose to correct

[44] Cf. Byron in his "Detached Thoughts" of 1821 (*LJ*, VI, 423): "I liked the Dandies; they were always very civil to *me*, though in general they disliked literary people, and persecuted and mystified Mᵉ. de Staël . . . damnably."

[45] Cf. Byron to Lady Blessington, May 6, 1823 (*LJ*, VI, 204): "The first time I ever read it [*Adolphe*] . . . was at the desire of Madame de Staël, who was supposed by the good-natured world to be the heroine;—which she was not, however, and was furious at the supposition."

[46] Cf. Byron as reported by Henry Edward Fox (*HVSV*, p. 352): "He says he now is taking to be fond of money, and he has saved £3,000."

them: indeed, it has often occurred to me, that he brings forward his defects, as if in anticipation of some one else exposing them, which he would not like; as, though he affects the contrary, he is jealous of being found fault with, and shows it in a thousand ways.

He affects to dislike hearing his works praised or referred to; I say affects, because I am sure the dislike is not real or natural;[47] as he who loves praise, as Byron evidently does, in other things, cannot dislike it for that in which he must be conscious it is deserved. He refers to his feats in horsemanship, shooting at a mark, and swimming, in a way that proves he likes to be complimented on them; and nothing appears to give him more satisfaction than being considered a man of fashion, who had great success in fashionable society in London, when he resided there.[48] He is peculiarly compassionate to the poor, I remarked that he rarely, in our rides, passed a mendicant without giving him charity, which was invariably bestowed with gentleness and kindness; this was still more observable if the person was deformed, as if he sympathised with the object.[49]

Byron is very fond of gossiping, and of hearing what is going on in the London fashionable world: his friends keep him *au courant,* and any little scandal amuses him very much. I observed this to him one day, and added, that I thought his mind had been too great to descend to such trifles! he laughed, and said with mock gravity, "Don't you know that the trunk of an elephant, which can lift the most ponderous weights, disdains not to take up the most minute? This is the case with my *great* mind, (laughing anew,) and you must allow the simile is worthy the subject. Jesting apart, I do like a little scandal—I believe all English people do. An Italian lady, Madame Benzoni, talking to me on the prevalence of this taste among my compatriots, observed, that when she first knew the English, she thought them the most spiteful and ill-natured people in the world, from hearing them constantly repeating evil of each

[47] Contrast Byron in his 1813 journal: "She [de Staël] always talks of *myself* or *herself,* and I am not (except in soliloquy, as now,) much enamoured of either subject—especially one's works" (*LJ,* II, 363-364). Teresa Guiccioli rejected Lady Blessington's assertion with a single word: "No!"

[48] Cf. Medwin, *Conversations,* pp. 265-66: "He never shews the author, prides himself most on being a man of the world and of fashion, and his anecdotes of life and living characters are inexhaustible."

[49] On Byron's generosity, see Moore, *Life,* pp. 45, 418.

other; but having seen various amiable traits in their characters, she had arrived at the conclusion, that they were not naturally *méchant*; but that living in a country like England, where severity of morals punishes so heavily any dereliction from propriety, each individual, to prove personal correctness, was compelled to attack the *sins* of his or her acquaintance, as it furnished an opportunity of expressing their abhorrence by words, instead of proving it by actions, which might cause some self-denial to themselves.[50] This," said Byron, "was an ingenious, as well as charitable supposition; and we must all allow that it is infinitely more easy to decry and expose the sins of others than to correct our own; and many find the first so agreeable an occupation, that it precludes the second—this, at least, is my case.

"The Italians do not understand the English," said Byron; " indeed, how can they? for they (the Italians) are frank, simple, and open in their natures, following the bent of their inclinations, which they do not believe to be wicked; while the English, to conceal the indulgence of theirs, daily practise hypocrisy, falsehood, and uncharitableness; so that to *one* error is added many crimes." Byron had now got on a favourite subject, and went on decrying hypocrisy and cant,[51] mingling sarcasms and bitter observations on the false delicacy of the English. It is strange, but true as strange, that he could not, or at least did not, distinguish the distinction between cause and effect, in this case. The respect for virtue will always cause spurious imitations of it to be given; and what he calls hypocrisy is but the respect to public opinion that induces people, who have not courage to correct their errors, at least to endeavour to conceal them; and Cant is the homage that Vice pays to Virtue.* We do not value the diamond less because there are so many worthless imitations of it, and Goodness loses nothing of her intrinsic value because so many wish to be thought to possess it. That nation may be considered to possess the most virtue where it is the

* Rochefoucault [misquoted].
[50] On the "gaiety, vitality, and ardour" of the aging Contessa Benzoni, who had had a cavalier servente for the greater part of her life, see Moore, *Life*, p. 415, and Origo, *The Last Attachment*, p. 38. She disapproved not of Byron's affair with Teresa Guiccioli but of the way he conducted it.
[51] It was also a favorite subject of Lady Blessington.

most highly appreciated; and that the least, where it is so little understood, that the semblance is not even assumed.

About this period the Duke of Leeds and family arrived at Genoa, and passed a day or two there, at the same hotel where we were residing. Shortly after their departure, Byron came to dine with us, and expressed his mortification at the Duke's not having called on him, were it only out of respect to Mrs. Leigh, who was the half-sister of both. This seemed to annoy him so much, that I endeavoured to point out the inutility of ceremony between people who could have no two ideas in common; and observed, that the *gêne* of finding oneself with people of totally different habits and feelings, was ill repaid by the respect their civility indicated.[52] Byron is a person to be excessively bored by the constraint that any change of system would occasion, even for a day; but yet his *amour propre* is wounded by any marks of incivility or want of respect he meets with. Poor Byron! he is still far from arriving at the philosophy that he aims at and thinks he has acquired, when the absence or presence of a person who is indifferent to him, whatever his station in life may be, can occupy his thoughts for a moment.

I have observed in Byron a habit of attaching importance to trifles, and, *vice versâ*, turning serious events into ridicule; he is extremely superstitious, and seems offended with those who cannot, or will not, partake this weakness. He has frequently touched on this subject, and tauntingly observed to me, that I must believe myself wiser than him, because I was not superstitious. I answered, that the vividness of his imagination, which was proved by his works, furnished a sufficient excuse for his superstition, which was caused

[52] Sidney Godolphin Osborne, son of the 5th Duke, Secretary of the Seven Islands, based in Corfu, was the stepson of Augusta Leigh's mother. In January 1821, he wrote to Byron from Ancona to invite him to Corfu and did in fact come to Cephalonia at the end of 1823 to visit Byron, of whom he seems to have been very fond, as Byron was of him. It does not appear likely that he would have passed through Genoa without looking Byron up, nor indeed that he was even in Genoa, for on April 5 Byron gave to Edward Blaquiere, on his way to Greece, a letter of introduction to him. It would appear, further, that Byron and Osborne were not "people of totally different habits and feelings," with "no two ideas in common," as Lady Blessington asserts. Byron said to Kennedy: "He is a merry fellow, and has some fine qualities," and later, "I really wish you could convert this wild fellow of a lord, he has as much need of it as I have" (*HVSV*, pp. 453, 456; see also *LJ*, V, 186; VI, 322 and n.; *Correspondence*, II, 255).

by an over-excitement of that faculty; but that *I*, not being blessed by the *camera lucida* of imagination, could have no excuse for the *camera oscura*, which I looked on superstition to be. This did not, however, content him, and I am sure he left me with a lower opinion of my faculties than before. To deprecate his anger, I observed that Nature was so wise and good that she gave compensations to all her offspring: that as to him she had given the brightest gift, genius; so to those whom she had not so distinguished, she gave the less brilliant, but pershaps as useful, gift of plain and unsophisticated reason. This did not satisfy his *amour propre*, and he left me, evidently displeased at my want of superstition. Byron is, I believe, sincere in his belief in supernatural appearances;[53] he assumes a grave and mysterious air when he talks on the subject, which he is fond of doing, and has told me some extraordinary stories relative to Mr. Shelley, who, he assures me, had an implicit belief in ghosts. He also told me that Mr. Shelley's spectre had appeared to a lady, walking in a garden, and he seemed to lay great stress on this.[54] Though some of the wisest of mankind, as witness Johnson, shared this weakness in common with Byron, still there is something so unusual in our matter-of-fact days in giving way to it, that I was at first doubtful that Byron was serious in his belief. He is also superstitious about days, and other trifling things,—believes in lucky and unlucky days,—dislikes undertaking any thing on a Friday, helping or being helped to salt at table, spilling salt or oil, letting bread fall, and breaking mirrors;[55] in short, he gives way to a thousand fantastical notions, that prove that even *l'esprit le plus fort* has its weak side. Having declined riding with Byron one day, on the plea of going to visit some of the Genoese palaces and pictures, it furnished him with a subject of attack at our next interview; he declared that he never believed people serious in their admiration of

[53] For Byron's belief in spectral appearances, see his letter to Murray, November 9, 1820 (*LJ*, V, 118), although when Shelley argued in favor of their existence in 1816, Byron was capable of taking the other side (*HVSV*, p. 191).

[54] Byron told one such story to John Cowell in October, 1822 (*HVSV*, p. 325); he told him that he had seen Shelley ten days before his death when Shelley was elsewhere.

[55] On Byron's various superstitions, see Medwin, *Conversations*, pp. 103-04, 107; also Byron to Lady Blessington (*LJ*, VI, 221): "I am *superstitious* . . . ," and Arthur Palmer Hudson, "The 'Superstitious' Lord Byron," *Studies in Philology*, LXIII (October 1966), 708-21.

pictures, statues, &c., and that those who expressed the most admiration were "Amatori senza Amore, and Conoscitori senza Cognizione." I replied, that as I had never talked to him of pictures, I hoped he would give me credit for being sincere in my admiration of them: but he was in no humour to give one credit for anything on this occasion, as he felt that our giving a preference to seeing sights, when we might have passed the hours with him, was not flattering to his vanity. I should say that Byron was not either skilled in, or an admirer of, works of art; he confessed to me that very few had excited his attention, and that to admire these he had been forced to draw on his imagination. Of objects of taste or virtù he was equally regardless, and antiquities had no interest for him; nay, he carried this so far, that he disbelieved the possibility of their exciting interest in any one, and said that they merely served as excuses for indulging the vanity and ostentation of those who had no other means of exciting attention.[56] Music he liked, though he was no judge of it:[57] he often dwelt on the power of association it possessed, and declared that the notes of a well-known air could transport him to distant scenes and events, presenting objects before him with a vividness that quite banished the present. Perfumes, he said, produced the same effect, though less forcibly, and, added he, with his mocking smile, often make me quite sentimental.

Byron is of a very suspicious nature; he dreads imposition on all points, declares that he foregoes many things, from the fear of being cheated in the purchase, and is afraid to give way to the natural impulses of his character, lest he should be duped or mocked. This does not interfere with his charities, which are frequent and liberal; but he has got into a habit of calculating even his most trifling personal expenses,[58] that is often ludicrous, and would in England expose him to ridicule. He indulges in a self-complacency when talking of his own defects, that is amusing; and he is rather fond than reluctant of bringing them into observation. He says that money is wisdom, knowledge, and power,[59] all combined, and that this con-

[56] See *English Bards*, ll. 1027-34, and *Childe Harold*, IV, liii.
[57] See *The Idler*, under date of April 16, 1823 (*HVSV*, p. 359), and Byron's diary, February 2, 1821 (Moore, *Life*, p. 486).
[58] Cf. Medwin, *Conversations*, p. 266: "Miserly in trifles . . ."
[59] Byron in *Don Juan* frequently sings a song of money: see XII, xiv, and XIII, c.

viction is the only one he has in common with all his countrymen. He dwells with great asperity on an acquaintance to whom he lent some money, and who has not repaid him.

Byron seems to take a peculiar pleasure in ridiculing sentiment and romantic feelings;[60] and yet the day after will betray both, to an extent that appears impossible to be sincere, to those who had heard his previous sarcasms: that he is sincere, is evident, as his eyes fill with tears, his voice becomes tremulous, and his whole manner evinces that he feels what he says. All this appears so inconsistent, that it destroys sympathy, or if it does not quite do that, it makes one angry with oneself for giving way to it for one who is never two days of the same way of thinking, or at least expressing himself. He talks for effect,[61] likes to excite astonishment, and certainly destroys in the minds of his auditors all confidence in his stability of character. This must, I am certain, be felt by all who have lived much in his society; and the impression is not satisfactory.

Talking one day of his domestic misfortunes, as he always called his separation from Lady Byron, he dwelt in a sort of unmanly strain of lamentation on it, that all present felt to be unworthy of him;[62] and, as the evening before, I had heard this habitude of his commented on by persons indifferent about his feelings, who even ridiculed his making it a topic of conversation with mere acquaintances, I wrote a few lines in verse, expressive of my sentiments,[63] and handed it across the table round which we were

[60] This characteristic of Byron was frequently noted, by Medwin, Trelawny, Moore, Teresa Guiccioli, and Galt, among others. See my *Byron: The Record of a Quest* (Hamden, Conn., 1966), "Byron's Laughter," especially pp. 63-66.
[61] Cf. James Kennedy: "He often spoke for effect" (*HVSV*, p. 481).
[62] Cf. Colonel Hugh Montgomery to Lady Byron, May, 1823, reporting Lady Blessington: "He was always talking about you and Ada, with tears *running down* his cheeks—"(Mrs. Moore, *The Late Lord Byron*, p. 485).
[63] Mrs. Moore, p. 475, clearly implies, without explanation or evidence, however, that Lady Blessington did not give Byron the verses below but five complimentary quatrains, which she quotes, "immensely different from those scornful ones she published." However, the five quatrains were clearly written in reply to Byron's five quatrains "To the Countess of Blessington," which also rhyme alternately. Byron's poem begins, "You have asked for a verse . . ."; Lady Blessington begins, "When I ask'd for a verse . . . ," in a poem that very nearly parodies Byron's own. Mrs. Moore, in a footnote on the next page, finally seems to have realized that the Blessington poem she quotes is a reply to Byron's, although her argument is not always clear. Even so, one may doubt that Lady Blessington presented to Byron the three stanzas below.

33

seated, as he was sitting for his portrait.[64] He read them, became red and pale by turns, with anger, and threw them down on the table, with an expression of countenance that is not to be forgotten. The following are the lines, which had nothing to offend; but they did offend him deeply, and he did not recover his temper during the rest of his stay.

> And canst thou bare thy breast to vulgar eyes?
>> And canst thou show the wounds that rankle there?
> Methought in noble hearts that sorrow lies
>> Too deep to suffer coarser minds to share.
>
> The wounds inflicted by the hand we love,
>> (The hand that should have warded off each blow,)
> Are never heal'd, as aching hearts can prove,
>> But *sacred* should the stream of sorrow flow.
>
> If *friendship's* pity quells not real grief,
>> Can *public* pity soothe thy woes to sleep?—
> No! Byron, spurn such vain, such weak relief,
>> And if thy tears must fall—in secret weep.

He never appeared to so little advantage as when he talked sentiment:[65] this did not at all strike me at first; on the contrary, it excited a powerful interest for him; but when he had vented his spleen, in sarcasms, and pointed ridicule on sentiment, reducing all that is noblest in our natures to the level of common every-day life, the charm was broken, and it was impossible to sympathise with him again. He observed something of this, and seemed dissatisfied

[64] D'Orsay made at least three sketches of Byron and one portrait. See Connely, *Count D'Orsay*, pp. 565, 575. A full-length sketch is reproduced as the frontispiece to *LJ*, V; a half-length sketch is reproduced in Marchand's *Byron*, facing p. 1214. Teresa (*HVSV*, p. 354) states that Byron first agreed to sit for his sketch when he called to introduce Pietro, April 12; one or more of these were finished by May 6 (*LJ*, VI, 204). Teresa, in her judgment of D'Orsay's talent ("La Vie," pp. 1485f.), may refer to the sketch used as the frontispiece to Lady Blessington's *Conversations*: "*Ce jeune français avait naturellement l'Amour et l'intelligence des arts, mais quant à l'exécution, on peu dire qu'elle était encore chez lui à l'état latent. On comprend donc facilement que avec ces premiers essais, qu'un talent d'amateur, talent méchanique, ne venant ni de l'âme ni du coeur, ce portrait n'offre pas la moindre idée de Lord Byron.*"

[65] Contrast Lady Blessington's account of Byron's sentimental parting with her, *HVSV*, p. 369: "He never appeared to greater advantage. . . ."

and restless when he perceived that he could no longer excite either strong sympathy or astonishment. Notwithstanding all these contradictions in this wayward, spoiled child of genius, the impression left on my mind was, that he had both sentiment and romance in his nature; but that, from the love of displaying his wit and astonishing his hearers, he affected to despise and ridicule them.[66]

From this period we saw Lord Byron frequently; he met us in our rides nearly every day, and the road to Nervi became our favourite promenade.[67] While riding by the sea-shore, he often recurred to the events of his life, mingling sarcasms on himself with bitter pleasantries against others. He dined often with us, and sometimes came after dinner, as he complained that he suffered from indulging at our repasts,[68] as animal food disagreed with him. He added, that

[66] James Kennedy made this point (*HVSV*, pp. 481-82).

[67] If we may accept Lady Blessington's dates, she first met Byron on April 1, 1823; he returned the call at her hotel the next day and dined with the Blessingtons on April 3. On April 10 and 12, they rode together, and the next day Byron introduced Pietro. They rode on the 16th, 17th, and 22nd, on the latter day to the Lomelini gardens, when Byron introduced Mr. Barry his banker. They may have ridden on April 28, a date under which Lady Blessington discusses Byron in *The Idler*. On April 29 they talked about Colonel Montgomery, and on the evening of April 30 Byron drank tea with the Blessingtons. On May 1 she rode with Byron and Pietro, who promised to lend her a copy of *The Age of Bronze*. On May 3, she writes, Byron asked her to use her influence with Colonel Montgomery. On May 4 Byron dined with them and on the next day took them to see Il Paradiso. On May 10 she met Byron riding; he talked of going to Greece. On May 13 he dined with them. They rode on May 16 and May 20, the latter an accidental meeting, when Byron talked about Trelawny. They may have seen each other on May 22, under which date in *The Idler* she discusses the purchase of the *Bolivar* and the sale of Mameluke. He dined with them on May 29 and paid his farewell visit on June 1. According to Lady Blessington, then, she talked with Byron on at least twenty or twenty-one separate occasions within two months, an average of one meeting every third day. Byron's own statements on the number of times that he saw Lady Blessington are contradictory, at least on the surface. On May 17, 1823, Byron wrote to Lady Hardy of the Blessingtons: "I met them frequently in my rides about Genoa." After their departure he wrote to Lady Hardy, who had warned him against falling in love with a "post Master's Daughter" from "Cahir in Tipperary": "I saw very little of them especially latterly." If Byron's "especially" is a protective screen, his two statements are quite consistent, for between May 17 and June 1 he did indeed see the Blessingtons only three times or perhaps four. Although he surely did not trust her at all times and knew something of her past, before her marriage to Lord Blessington, he was clearly conscious of the charm and beauty of "our Irish Aspasia," as he called her (see my introduction).

[68] Lady Blessington's *Idler* claims four dinners and one evening after dinner to drink tea. Teresa admits "four or five formal dinners" (*HVSV*, p. xxxii). Byron wrote to Lord Blessington, May 23 (*LJ*, VI, 218): "I hope you will not

even the excitement of society, though agreeable and exhilarating at the time, left a nervous irritation, that prevented sleep or occupation for many hours afterwards.[69]

I once spoke to him, by the desire of his medical adviser,[70] on the necessity of his accustoming himself to a more nutritious regimen; but he declared, that if he did, he should get fat and stupid, and that it was only by abstinence that he felt he had the power of exercising his mind. He complained of being spoiled for society, by having so long lived out of it; and said, that though naturally of a quick apprehension, he latterly felt himself dull and stupid. The impression left on my mind is, that Byron never could have been a brilliant person in society, and that he was not formed for what generally is understood by that term: he has none of the "small change" that passes current in the mart of society; his gold is in ingots, and cannot be brought into use for trifling expenditures; he, however, talks a good deal, and likes to *raconter*.

Talking of people who were great talkers, he observed that almost all clever people were such, and gave several examples: amongst others, he cited Voltaire, Horace Walpole, Johnson, Napoleon Bonaparte, and Madame de Staël. "But," said he, "my friend, Lady [Jersey],[71] would have talked them all out of the field. She, I sup-

---

take my *not* dining with you again after so many dinners, ill; but the truth is, that your banquets are too luxurious for my habits. . . ."

[69] Cf. Byron to Lady Blessington, May 6 (*LJ*, VI, 205): "One of the reasons why I wish to avoid society is, that I can never sleep after it, and the pleasanter it has been the less I rest."

[70] Dr. James Alexander, to whom Byron had been introduced by Mr. Hill at Genoa (see Marchand, *Byron*, n. to p. 1052, l. 30, and Mrs. Moore, p. 486).

[71] Lady Jersey, described by George Ticknor as a "beautiful creature, with a great deal of talent, taste, and elegant knowledge," was indeed "independent in her principles," as Lady Blessington reports—so independent and so influential in society that she denied the Duke of Wellington admission to Almack's in 1819 because he came seven minutes late, and she stared down the Prince Regent when he tried to cut her at another party. Byron paid tribute to her beauty in his "Condolatory Address to Sarah Countess of Jersey, on the Prince Regent's Returning her Picture to Mrs. Mee," where he sang "The glossy darkness" of her hair; and in the same year, 1814, in his "Fragment of an Epistle to Thomas Moore," he observed that she was as "lovely as ever," as she danced with the Czar, to the Prince Regent's displeasure. On these matters, as well as her conversational powers, see *LJ*, II, 112-14, n. 1. Lady Jersey was Byron's (and Augusta's) champion to the extent of inviting him to a large party on April 8, 1816 (where he and Augusta were cut by a

pose, has heard that all clever people are great talkers, and so has determined on displaying, at least, *one* attribute of that genus; but her ladyship would do well to recollect that *all* great talkers are not clever people—a truism that no one can doubt who has been often in her society."

"Lady [Jersey]," continued Byron, "with *beaucoup de ridicule,* has many essentially fine qualities; she is independent in her principles—though, by-the-bye, like all Independents, she allows that privilege to few others, being the veriest tyrant that ever governed Fashion's fools, who are compelled to shake their caps and bells as she wills it. Of all that coterie," said Byron, "Madame de [Flahault],[72] after Lady [Jersey], was the best; at least I thought so, for these two ladies were the only ones who ventured to protect me when all London was crying out against me on the separation, and *they* behaved courageously and kindly; indeed Madame de [Flahault] defended me when few dared to do so, and I have always remembered it. Poor dear Lady [Jersey]! does she still retain her beautiful cream-coloured complexion and raven hair? I used to long

---

number of people), and serving as a sponsor at the baptism of Augusta's fifth child on June 3, 1816 (Marchand, p. 598; Elwin, p. 438, n. 1).

Although Byron had every reason to be grateful to Lady Jersey, Lady Blessington had none, and it may be assumed that the attack placed in the mouth of Byron is fiction. According to Lady Holland, writing to her son Henry Fox in August 1831: "Lady Jersey had heard that Ly Harriet D'Orsay had quitted her worthless companion [her husband] & joined her aunt, the wife of an Irish bishop. I wish she (Harriet) may be able to annul her imperfect marriage & recover the enjoyment of her property. Ly J[ersey] says Ld Burgersh [Lady Jersey's brother] refused to allow the marriage they celebrated (in Naples) in his house in Florence, in consequence of a private message from Lady Harriet declaring her reluctance to the union" (quoted by Connely, *Count D'Orsay,* p. 179, from the Earl of Ilchester, ed., *Lady Holland to her Son,* p. 112).

Lady Jersey appears in *The Repealers* as Lady Guernsey, where she also has a "cream coloured skin" and "dark" hair (*The Works of Lady Blessington,* I, 250). In a letter to Murray, November 25, 1816, Byron referred to her "dark glossy hair" (Moore, *Life,* p. 333). See also the *Gentleman's Magazine,* CLV (April 1834), 352; Medwin, *Conversations,* pp. 48, 50; and E. B. Chancellor, *Memorials of St. James's Street* (London, 1922), pp. 211-12, 217-19, 224-27.

[72] On the support and regard of Madame de Flahault, the former Margaret Mercer Elphinstone, for Byron, see Marchand, pp. 598-99; *LJ,* III, 253, n. 1; V, 212 (one of "about a dozen others of that sex . . . who stuck by me in the grand conflict of 1815 [*sic*]"). See also Moore, *Life,* p. 303.

to tell her that she spoiled her looks by her excessive animation; for eyes, tongue, head, and arms were all in movement at once, and were only relieved from their active service by want of respiration. I shall never forget when she once complained to me of the fatigue of literary occupations; and I, in terror, expected her ladyship to propose reading to me an epic poem, tragedy, or at least a novel of her composition, when, lo! she displayed to me a very richly-bound album, half filled with printed extracts cut out of newspapers and magazines, which she had selected and pasted in the book; and I (happy at being let off so easily) sincerely agreed with her that literature was very tiresome. I understand that she has now advanced with the 'march of intellect,'[73] and got an album filled with MS. poetry, to which all of us, of the *craft*,[74] have contributed. I was the first; Moore wrote something, which was, like all that he writes, very sparkling and terse; but he got dissatisfied with the faint praise it met with from the husband before Miladi saw the verses, and destroyed the effusion: I know not if he ever has supplied their place. Can you fancy Moore paying attention to the opinion of Milor on poesy? Had it been on racing or horse-flesh he might have been right; but Pegasus is, perhaps, the only horse of whose paces Lord [Jersey] could not be a judge."[75]

Talking of fashionable life in London, Lord Byron said that there was nothing so vapid and *ennuyeux*. "The English," said he, "were intended by nature to be good, sober-minded people, and those who live in the country are really admirable. I saw a good deal of English country life, and it is the only favourable impression that remains of our mode of living; but of London, and *exclusive* society, I retain a fearful recollection.[76] Dissipation has need of wit, talent,

[73] Thomas Moore wrote ironically of "the march of intellect" to Lady Blessington in his letter of November 18, 1829, requesting materials for his life of Byron (*The Letters of Thomas Moore*, II, 661 and n. 1). The *Oxford Dictionary* observes that the phrase was common between 1827 and 1850. However, Keats used it in his Mansion of Life letter, May 3, 1818: "there is really a grand march of intellect." Lady Blessington uses the phrase three times in one paragraph in *The Repealers* (*Works*, I, 307-08), and again in a letter to Mrs. Mathews, August 9, 1830 (Madden, II, 421).

[74] See above, p. 24, n. 39.

[75] The Earl of Jersey was twice appointed Master of the Horse to Queen Victoria.

[76] For Byron on town life versus country life, see his letter to Lord Blessington, April 5, 1823 (*LJ*, VI, 187), where the boredom of country life is

and gaiety to prevent reflection, and make the eternal round of frivolous amusements pass; and of these," continued Byron, "there was a terrible lack in the society in which I mixed. The minds of the English are formed of sterner stuff. You may make an English woman (indeed Nature does this) the best daughter, wife, and mother in the world; nay, you may make her a heroine; but nothing can make her a genuine *woman of fashion!*[77] And yet this latter *rôle* is the one which, *par preference*, she always wishes to act. Thorough-bred English gentlewomen," said Byron, "are the most distinguished and lady-like creatures imaginable. Natural, mild, and dignified, they are formed to be placed at the heads of our patrician establishments;[78] but when they quit their congenial spheres to en- act the leaders of fashion, *les dames à la mode*, they bungle sadly; their gaiety degenerates into levity—their hauteur into incivility— their fashionable ease and nonchalance into *brusquerie*—and their attempts at assuming *les usages du monde* into a positive outrage on all the *bienséances*. In short, they offer a coarse caricature of the airy flightiness and capricious, but amusing, *légèreté* of the French, without any of their redeeming *espièglerie* and *politesse*. And all this because they will perform parts in the comedy of life for which nature has not formed them, neglecting their own digni- fied characters.[79]

"Madame de Staël," continued Lord Byron, "was forcibly struck by the factitious tone of the best society in London, and wished very much to have an opportunity of judging of that of the second class. She, however, had not this opportunity, which I regret, as I

---

described. See also my *Byron: The Record of a Quest*, especially Chapter III, "Town versus Country." Byron's letters contain numerous references to the dissipation of London life.

[77] This discussion of women of fashion seems more Blessingtonian than Byronic. It should be recalled that by the time Lady Blessington wrote the *Conversations*, "*les dames à la mode*" would not accept invitations to her house. Note the profusion of French phrases in the paragraph.

[78] Cf. Byron in his diary, January 15, 1821 (Moore, *Life*, p. 479), on one of Lord Grey's daughters, who had "much of the *patrician, thorough-bred look* of her father, which I dote on. . . ."

[79] There are a number of bitter attacks in *The Repealers* on the exclusive and heartless high society of London. See her *Works*, I, 202-04, 229-31, 247-49. The novel is concerned in part with the sufferings of Lady Oriel, whose repu- tation is ruined by false gossip. Her husband is too weak, sensitive, and proud to protect her honor properly.

think it would have justified her expectations. In England, the raw material is generally good; it is the over-dressing that injures it; and as the class she wished to study are well educated, and have all the refinement of civilization without its corruption, she would have carried away a favourable impression. Lord Grey and his family were the personification of her *beau idéal* of perfection, as I must say they are of mine," continued Byron, "and might serve as the finest specimens of the pure English patrician breed, of which so few remain.[80] *His* uncompromising and uncompromised dignity, founded on self-respect, and accompanied by that certain proof of superiority—simplicity of manner and freedom from affectation, with *her* mild and matron graces, her whole life offering a model to wives and mothers—really they are people to be proud of, and a few such would reconcile one to one's species."

One of our first rides with Lord Byron was to Nervi, a village on the sea-coast, most romantically situated, and each turn of the road presenting various and beautiful prospects. They were all familiar to him, and he failed not to point them out, but in very sober terms, never allowing any thing like enthusiasm in his expressions, though many of the views might have excited it.[81]

His appearance on horseback was not advantageous, and he seemed aware of it, for he made many excuses for his dress and equestrian appointments. His horse was literally covered with various trappings, in the way of cavesons, martingales, and Heaven knows how many other (to me) unknown inventions. The saddle was *à la hussarde* with holsters, in which he always carried pistols.[82] His dress consisted of a nankeen jacket and trousers, which

[80] The second Earl Grey was a friend of both Lady Blessington and Byron, who called him "the *Capo Politico* of the remaining Whigs" (*LJ*, V, 174-75). Grey used his influence with the Lord Chancellor in 1821 to secure an injunction prohibiting the performance of *Marino Faliero*, and in 1822, following the death of Lady Noel, Byron directed Hanson to appoint Grey his referee if Burdett declined to serve. He appears in *The Repealers* as Lord Rey, the premier, "the very personification of aristocracy" (*Works*, I, 250). His family is also commended in the novel (*Works*, I, 251).

[81] *The Idler* describes this episode, with Byron's remarks on "the cant of the love of nature" (*HVSV*, pp. 356-57). Teresa Guiccioli approved in the margin: "*Vrai.*"

[82] So Lady Blessington also told Colonel Montgomery: "rides (always with pistols) till 6," setting out on a typical day, it seems, at two (Mrs. Moore, p. 486, Montgomery's letter to Lady Byron).

40

appeared to have shrunk from washing; the jacket embroidered in the same colour, and with three rows of buttons; the waist very short, the back very narrow, and the sleeves set in as they used to be ten or fifteen years before; a black stock, very narrow; a dark-blue velvet cap with a shade, and a very rich gold band and large gold tassel at the crown; nankeen gaiters, and a pair of blue spectacles, completed his costume, which was any thing but becoming.[83] This was his general dress of a morning for riding, but I have seen it changed for a green tartan plaid jacket. He did not ride well,[84] which surprised us, as, from the frequent allusions to horsemanship in his works, we expected to find him almost a Nimrod. It was evident that he had *pretensions* on this point, though he certainly was what I should call a timid rider. When his horse made a false step, which was not unfrequent, he seemed discomposed; and when we came to any bad part of the road, he immediately checked his course and walked his horse very slowly, though there really was nothing to make even a lady nervous. Finding that I could perfectly manage (or what he called *bully*) a very highly-dressed horse that I daily rode, he became extremely anxious to buy it; asked me a thousand questions as to how I had acquired such a perfect command of it, &c. &c. and entreated, as the greatest favour, that I would resign it to him as a charger to take to Greece, declaring he never would part with it, &c. As I was by no means a bold rider, we were rather amused at observing Lord Byron's opinion of my courage; and as he seemed so anxious for the horse, I agreed to let him have it when he was to embark. From this time he paid particular attention to the movements of poor Mameluke (the name of the horse), and said he should now feel confidence in action with so steady a charger.[85]

During our ride the conversation turned on our mutual friends and acquaintances in England. Talking of two of them, for one of whom he professed a great regard, he declared laughingly that they

[83] Lady Blessington had expressed very firm notions on proper and improper or vulgar riding habits and harnesses in *The Magic Lantern* (1822), the sketch of "The Park."

[84] Cf. *The Idler*, May 22 (*HVSV*, p. 368): ". . . he is *not* . . . a good horseman." See Medwin, *Conversations*, pp. 14 and 15, n. 32.

[85] Cf. the briefer account in *The Idler* (*HVSV*, p. 368), under date of May 22.

41

had saved him from suicide.[86] Seeing me look grave, he added, "It is a fact, I assure you: I should positively have destroyed myself, but I guessed that ——— or ——— would write my life, and with this fear before my eyes, I have lived on. I know so well the sort of things they would write of me—the excuses, lame as myself, that they would offer for my delinquencies, while they were unnecessarily exposing them, and all this done with the avowed intention of justifying, what, God help me! cannot be justified, my *unpoetical* reputation, with which the world can have nothing to do! One of my friends would dip his pen in clarified honey, and the other in vinegar, to describe my manifold transgressions,[87] and as I do not wish my poor fame to be either *preserved* or *pickled*, I have lived on and written my Memoirs, where facts will speak for themselves, without the editorial candor of excuses, such as 'we cannot excuse *this* unhappy error, or defend *that* impropriety!'—the mode," continued Byron, "in which friends exalt their own prudence and virtue, by exhibiting the want of those qualities in the dear departed, and by marking their disapproval of his errors. I have written my Memoirs," said Byron, "to save the necessity of their being written by a friend or friends, and have only to hope they will not add notes."[88]

[86] On suicide, see Byron to Murray, April 9, 1817 (Moore, *Life*, p. 350).
[87] Perhaps Moore and Hobhouse. Lady Blessington told Henry Crabb Robinson in 1832 that Byron said: "Tommy makes pretty sweet verses—sweet indeed, no wonder—he was fed on plums and sugar-candy by his father, the Dublin grocer" (*HVSV*, p. 371). As early as February 1814, Byron had in fact appointed Moore his "Editor and Historiographer (in case any enraged husband should be the death of you)," as Moore put it in a letter (*Letters of Moore*, I, 306). Hobhouse's qualifications as the other candidate are impressive. As he told Moore on April 29, 1822: "I know more of Byron than anybody else, and much more than I should wish anybody else to know." Lady Byron requested him to write a memoir of Byron, following the poet's death, in conjunction with her and other members of the family. Hobhouse, a kind of embodiment of the British conscience, as Marchand describes him, repeatedly told Byron of his faults and transgressions and was the best friend Byron ever had. Byron suggested Hobhouse as his biographer when talking with Stanhope in Greece (Iris Origo, *The Last Attachment*, p. 521, n. 112).
[88] Cf. Byron to Annabella, December 31, 1819: "You will perhaps say *why* write my life?—Alas! I say so too—but they who have traduced it—& blasted it—and branded me—should know that it is they—and not I—are the cause—It is no great pleasure to have lived—and less to live over again the details of existence—but the last becomes sometimes a necessity and even a duty—" (quoted by Mrs. Moore, p. 47, from *Astarte*).

42

I remarked, with a smile, that at all events he anticipated his friends by *saying* beforehand as many ill-natured things of *them* as they could possibly *write* of *him*. He laughed, and said, "Depend on it we are equal. Poets (and I may, I suppose, without presumption, count myself among that favoured race, as it has pleased the Fates to make me one,) have no friends. On the old principle, that 'union gives force,' we sometimes agree to have a violent friendship for each other. We dedicate, we bepraise, we write pretty letters, but we do not deceive *each other*. In short, we resemble you fair ladies, when some half dozen of the fairest of you profess to love each other mightily, correspond so sweetly, call each other by such pretty epithets, and laugh in your hearts at those who are taken in by such appearances."

I endeavoured to defend my sex, but he adhered to his opinion. I ought to add that during this conversation he was very gay, and that though his words may appear severe, there was no severity in his manner. The natural flippancy of Lord Byron[89] took off all appearance of premeditation or bitterness from his remarks, even when they were acrimonious, and the impression conveyed to, and left on my mind was, that for the most part they were uttered more in jest than in earnest. They were however sufficiently severe to make me feel that there was no safety with him, and that in five minutes after one's quitting him on terms of friendship, he could not resist the temptation of showing one up, either in conversation or by letter, though in half an hour after he would put himself to personal inconvenience to render a kindness to the person so shown up.

I remarked, that in talking of literary productions, he seemed much more susceptible to their defects, than alive to their beauties. As a proof, he never failed to remember some quotation that told against the unhappy author, which he recited with an emphasis, or a mock-heroic air, that made it very ludicrous. The pathetic he always burlesqued[90] in reciting; but this I am sure proceeded from an affectation of not sympathizing with the general taste.

[89] Noted in *The Idler* under date of April 1, 1823 (*HVSV*, p. 350).
[90] Both E. E. Williams and Medwin observed this trait in Byron (see *HVSV*, pp. 283, 311; see also Moore, *Life*, p. 181, and Medwin, *Conversations*, p. 238).

43

April —. Lord Byron dined with us to-day. During dinner he was as usual gay, spoke in terms of the warmest commendation of Sir Walter Scott, not only as an author, but as a man, and dwelt with apparent delight on his novels, declaring that he had read and re-read them over and over again, and always with increased pleasure.[91] He said that he quite equalled, nay, in his opinion surpassed, Cervantes.[92] In talking of Sir Walter's private character, goodness of heart, &c., Lord Byron became more animated than I had ever seen him; his colour changed from its general pallid tint to a more lively hue, and his eyes became humid; never had he appeared to such advantage, and it might easily be seen that every expression he uttered proceeded from his heart. Poor Byron!—for poor he is even with all his genius, rank, and wealth—had he lived more with men like Scott, whose openness of character and steady principle had convinced him that they were in earnest in *their goodness*, and not *making believe*, (as he always suspects good people to be,) his life might be different and happier.

Byron is so acute an observer that nothing escapes him; all the shades of selfishness and vanity are exposed to his searching glance, and the misfortune is, (and a serious one it is to him,) that when he finds these, and alas! they are to be found on every side, they disgust and prevent his giving credit to the many good qualities that often accompany them. He declares he can sooner pardon crimes, because they proceed from the passions, than these minor vices, that spring from selfishness and self-conceit. We had a long argument this evening on the subject, which ended, like most arguments, by leaving both of the same opinion as when it commenced. I endeavoured to prove that crimes were not only injurious to the perpetrators, but often ruinous to the innocent, and productive of misery to friends and relations, whereas selfishness and vanity carried with them their own punishment, the first depriving the person of all sympathy, and the second exposing him to ridicule, which to the vain is a heavy punishment, but that their effects were not destructive to society as are crimes.

He laughed when I told him that having heard him so often de-

[91] Byron's admiration for Scott is well known; it does not appear that Lady Blessington was personally acquainted with him.
[92] On Cervantes, see *Don Juan*, XIII, viii-xii.

claim against vanity, and detect it so often in his friends, I began to suspect he knew the malady by having had it himself, and that I had observed through life, that those persons who had the most vanity were the most severe against that failing in their friends. He wished to impress upon me that he was not vain, and gave various proofs to establish this; but I produced against him his <u>boasts of swimming</u>, his evident desire of being considered more *un homme de société* than a poet, and other little examples, when he laughingly pleaded guilty, and promised to be more merciful towards his friends.

We sat on the balcony after tea: it commands a fine view, and we had one of those moonlight nights that are seen only in this country. Every object was tinged with its silvery lustre. In front were crowded an uncountable number of ships from every country, with their various flags waving in the breeze, which bore to us the sounds of the as various languages of the crews. In the distance we enjoyed a more expanded view of the sea, which reminded Byron of his friend Moore's description, which he quoted:

The sea is like a silv'ry lake.

The fanal casting its golden blaze into this silvery lake, and throwing a red lurid reflection on the sails of the vessels that passed near it; the fishermen, with their small boats, each having a fire held in a sort of grate fastened at the end of the boat, which burns brilliantly, and by which they not only see the fish that approach, but attract them; their scarlet caps, which all the Genoese sailors and fishermen wear, adding much to their picturesque appearance, all formed a picture that description falls far short of; and when to this are joined the bland odours of the richest and rarest flowers, with which the balconies are filled, one feels that such nights are never to be forgotten, and while the senses dwell on each, and all, a delicious melancholy steals over the mind, as it reflects that, the destinies of each conducting to far distant regions, a time will arrive when all now before the eye will appear but as a dream.

This was felt by all the party; and after a silence of many minutes, it was broken by Byron, who remarked, "What an evening, and what a view! Should we ever meet in the dense atmosphere of London, shall we not recall this evening, and the scenery now be-

45

fore us? but, no! most probably *there* we should not feel as we do here; we should fall into the same heartless, loveless apathy that distinguish one half of our dear compatriots, or the bustling, impertinent importance to be considered *supreme bon ton*[93] that marks the other."

Byron spoke with bitterness,[94] but it was the bitterness of a fine nature soured by having been touched too closely by those who had lost their better feelings through a contact with the world. After a few minutes' silence, he said, "Look at that forest of masts now before us! from what remote parts of the world do they come! o'er how many waves have they not passed, and how many tempests have they not been, and may again be exposed to! how many hearts and tender thoughts follow them! mothers, wives, sisters, and sweethearts, who perhaps at this hour are offering up prayers for their safety."

While he was yet speaking, sounds of vocal music arose; national hymns and barcaroles were sung in turns by the different crews, and when they had ceased, "God save the King" was sung by the crews of some English merchantmen lying close to the pier. This was a surprise to us all, and its effect on our feelings was magnetic. Byron was no less touched than the rest; each felt at the moment that tie of country which unites all when they meet on a far distant shore. When the song ceased, Byron, with a melancholy smile, observed, "Why, positively, we are all quite sentimental this evening, and *I—I* who have sworn against sentimentality, find the old leaven still in my nature, and quite ready to make a fool of me. 'Tell it not in Gath,'[95] that is to say, breathe it not in London, or to English ears polite, or never again shall I be able to *enact* the stoic philosopher. Come, come, this will never do, we must forswear moonlight, fine views, and above all, hearing a national air sung. Little does his gracious Majesty Big Ben, as Moore calls him,[96] imagine what

[93] We read in *The Magic Lantern*, p. 101, of "an intrepid rudeness only to be acquired by ladies of high *ton*."

[94] Much of the bitterness must be Lady Blessington's.

[95] From 2 Samuel, I:20. Cf. Byron's "Letter . . . on . . . Bowles" (*LJ*, V, 541): ". . . don't say this in Gath. . . ."

[96] A reference to Moore's "Epistle from Tom Crib to Big Ben," the Prince Regent, which Byron also mentioned to Medwin (*Conversations*, p. 240).

loyal subjects he has at Genoa, and least of all that I am among their number."

Byron attempted to be gay, but the effort was not successful, and he wished us good night with a trepidation of manner that marked his feelings. And this is the man that I have heard considered unfeeling! How often are our best qualities turned against us, and made the instruments for wounding us in the most vulnerable part, until, ashamed of betraying our susceptibility, we affect an insensibility we are far from possessing, and, while we deceive others, nourish in secret the feelings that prey *only* on our own hearts!

It is difficult to judge when Lord Byron is serious or not. He has a habit of mystifying, that might impose upon many; but that can be detected by examining his physiognomy; for a sort of mock gravity, now and then broken by a malicious smile, betrays when he is speaking for effect, and not giving utterance to his real sentiments.[97] If he sees that he is detected, he appears angry for a moment, and then laughingly admits that it amuses him to *hoax* people, as he calls it, and that when each person, at some future day, will give their different statements of him, they will be so contradictory, that *all* will be doubted,—an idea that gratifies him exceedingly! The mobility of his nature is extraordinary,[98] and makes him inconsistent in his actions as well as in his conversation. He introduced the subject of La Contessa Guiccioli and her family, which we, of course, would not have touched on. He stated that they lived beneath his roof because his rank as a British peer afforded her father and brother protection, they having been banished from Ravenna, their native place, on account of their politics. He spoke in high terms of the Counts Gamba, father and son; he said that he had given the family a wing of his house, but that their establishments were totally separate, their repasts never taken together, and that such was their scrupulous delicacy, that they never would accept a pecuniary obligation from him in all the difficulties entailed on them by their exile.[99] He represented La Contessa

[97] See my *Captain Medwin, Friend of Byron and Shelley* (Austin, 1962), pp. 100-03. For Lady Blessington's own habit of mystifying, see the introduction to this volume.

[98] Cf. *Don Juan*, XVI, xcvii, and Byron's note, on Lady Adeline's mobility; also, on Lady Blessington's mobility, the introduction to this volume.

[99] Teresa declined to be mentioned in Byron's will.

47

Guiccioli as a most amiable and lady-like person,[100] perfectly disinterested and noble-minded, devotedly attached to him, and possessing so many high and estimable qualities, as to offer an excuse for any man's attachment to her. He said that he had been passionately in love with her, and that she had sacrificed everything for him; that the whole of her conduct towards him had been admirable, and that not only did he feel the strongest personal attachment to her, but the highest sentiments of esteem. He dwelt with evident complacency on her noble birth and distinguished connexions,—advantages to which he attaches great importance. I never met anyone with so decided a taste for aristocracy as Lord Byron,[101] and this is shown in a thousand different ways.

He says the Contessa is well educated, remarkably fond of, and well read in, the poetry of her own country, and a tolerable proficient in that of France and England.[102] In his praises of Madame Guiccioli, it is quite evident that he is sincere, and I am persuaded this is his last attachment. He told me that she had used every effort to get him to discontinue "Don Juan,"[103] or at least to preserve the future cantos from all impure passages. In short, he has said all that was possible to impress me with a favourable opinion of this lady, and has convinced me that he entertains a very high one of her himself.

[100] This is a favored term of approbation in Lady Blessington's vocabulary: "a lady-like sensitive woman, shrinking beneath the fixed gaze of some dames of fashionable notoriety," appears in *The Magic Lantern*, p. 69.

[101] In the 1820's Lady Blessington made every effort, in England and in Europe, to cultivate the aristocracy.

[102] That Teresa at this date could read English poetry with any ease seems doubtful. Byron's first note to her in English was dated July 22, 1823; his last letter to her, March 17, 1824, states: "I write to you in English without apologies—as you say you have become a proficient in that language of birds" (Marchand, pp. 1092, 1199). In the summer of 1822 Byron translated for her parts of *Don Juan*, VI (Marchand, p. 1014). She had read the first two cantos in French translation (*LJ*, V, 321).

[103] Byron announced to Murray on July 6, 1821, that Teresa had persuaded him *"not* to continue *Don Juan"* (*LJ*, V, 320). However, "Sir H[umphrey Davy] mentioned that Lord Byron had told him at Venice that he did not mean to publish any more of Don Juan that its intention had been mistaken by the public, he having meant it as a moral tale!" (From the autograph diary of Sir John F. W. Herschel the astronomer, December 9, 1820, in the Academic Center Library of the University of Texas at Austin.) This statement must refer to cantos I-II, published July 15, 1819; cantos III, IV, and V were not published until 1821. Byron saw Sir Humphrey in Ravenna in April 1820 (*LJ*, V, 11), not, it seems, in Venice. See also Moore's diary for May 19, 1820 (*Memoirs*, III, 118).

Byron is a strange *mélange* of good and evil,[104] the predominancy of either depending wholly on the humour he may happen to be in. His is a character that Nature totally unfitted for domestic habits, or for rendering a woman of refinement or susceptibility happy. He confesses to me that he is not happy, but admits that it is his own fault, as the Contessa Guiccioli, the only object of his love, has all the qualities to render a reasonable being happy. I observed, *apropos* to some observation he had made, that I feared La Contessa Guiccioli had little reason to be satisfied with her lot. He answered, "Perhaps you are right; yet she must know that I am sincerely attached to her; but the truth is, my habits are not those requisite to form the happiness of any woman: I am worn out in feelings; for, though only thirty-six, I feel sixty in mind,[105] and am less capable than ever of those nameless attentions that all women, but, above all, Italian women, require. I like solitude, which has become absolutely necessary to me; am fond of shutting myself up for hours, and, when with the person I like, am often *distrait* and gloomy. There is something I am convinced (continued Byron) in the poetical temperament that precludes happiness, not only to the person who has it, but to those connected with him. Do not accuse me of vanity because I say this, as my belief is, that the worst poet may share this misfortune in common with the best. The way in which I account for it is, that our *imaginations* being warmer than our *hearts*, and much more given to wander, the latter have not the power to control the former; hence, soon after our passions are gratified, imagination again takes wing, and, finding the insufficiency of actual indulgence beyond the moment, abandons itself to all its wayward fancies, and during this abandonment becomes cold and insensible to the demands of affection. This is our misfortune, but not our fault, and dearly do we expiate it; by it we are rendered incapable of sympathy, and cannot lighten, by sharing, the pain we inflict. Thus we witness, without the power of alleviating, the anxiety and dissatisfaction our conduct occasions. We are not so totally unfeeling as not to be grieved at the unhappiness we cause;

[104] A quality shared by many of the Byronic heroes: see *Lara*, ll. 289-90.
[105] Cf. *The Idler* (*HVSV*, p. 357): "Though now but in his thirty-sixth year, Byron talks of himself as if he were at least fifty." See also Byron's lines "To the Countess of Blessington."

but this same power of imagination transports our thoughts to other scenes, and we are always so much more occupied by the ideal than the present, that we forget all that is actual. It is as though the creatures of another sphere, not subject to the lot of mortality, formed a factitious alliance (as all alliances must be that are not in all respects equal) with the creatures of this earth, and, being exempt from its sufferings, turned their thoughts to brighter regions, leaving the partners of their earthly existence to suffer alone. But, let the object of affection be snatched away by death, and how is all the pain ever inflicted on them avenged! The same imagination that led us to slight, or overlook their sufferings, now that they are for ever lost to us, magnifies their estimable qualities, and increases tenfold the affection we ever felt for them—

> Oh! what are thousand living loves,
> To that which cannot quit the dead?

How did I feel this when Allegra, my daughter, died! While she lived, her existence never seemed necessary to my happiness; but no sooner did I lose her, than it appeared to me as if I could not live without her.[106] Even now the recollection is most bitter; but how much more severely would the death of Teresa afflict me with the dreadful consciousness that while I had been soaring into the fields of romance and fancy, I had left her to weep over my coldness or infidelities of imagination. It is a dreadful proof of the weakness of our natures, that we cannot control ourselves sufficiently to form the happiness of those we love, or to bear their loss without agony."

The whole of this conversation made a deep impression on my mind, and the countenance of the speaker, full of earnestness and feeling, impressed it still more strongly on my memory. Byron is right; a brilliant imagination is rarely, if ever, accompanied by a warm heart; but on this latter depends the happiness of life; the other renders us dissatisfied with its ordinary enjoyments.

[106] According to Teresa, as reported by Hubert E. H. Jerningham, Byron had a positive dislike for Allegra: "Each time she came into her father's presence, he used to turn away in disgust and exclaim, 'Enlevez la: elle ressemble trop à sa mère'" (HVSV, p. 252). But Teresa also recorded Byron's grief at the time of her death (see HVSV, pp. 288-89, 635, n. 34, and Moore, Life, p. 422).

He is an extraordinary person, *indiscreet* to a degree that is surprising, exposing his own feelings, and entering into details of those of others, that ought to be sacred, with a degree of frankness as unnecessary as it is rare. Incontinence of speech is his besetting sin. He is, I am persuaded, incapable of keeping any secret, however it may concern his own honour or that of another; and the first person with whom he found himself *tête-à-tête* would be made the confidant without any reference to his worthiness of the confidence or not. This indiscretion proceeds not from malice, but I should say, from want of delicacy of mind. To this was owing the publication of his "Farewell," addressed to Lady Byron,—[107] a farewell that must have lost all effect as an appeal to her feelings the moment it was exposed to the public—nay, must have offended her delicacy.

Byron spoke to-day in terms of high commendation of Hope's "Anastasius;"[108] said that he wept bitterly over many pages of it, and for two reasons,—first that *he* had not written it, and secondly, that *Hope* had; for that it was necessary to like a man excessively to pardon his writing such a book—a book, as he said, excelling all recent productions, as much in wit and talent, as in true pathos. He added, that he would have given his two most approved poems to have been the author of "Anastasius."

From "Anastasius" he wandered to the works of Mr. Galt, praised the "Annals of the Parish" very highly, as also "The Entail," which we had lent him, and some scenes of which he said had affected him very much.[109] "The characters in Mr. Galt's novels have an identity," added Byron, "that reminds me of Wilkie's pictures."[110]

[107] On "The publication of the 'Separation Poems,' " see Mrs. Moore, pp. 162-66.

[108] For Byron's admiration of Thomas Hope's *Anastasius* (1819), see *LJ*, V, 58, 81. Published anonymously, the book was reviewed as Byron's in *Blackwood's*, September 1821. Lady Blessington also liked it (*Henry Crabb Robinson on Books and Their Writers*, ed. Edith J. Morley [London, 1938], I, 413).

[109] On Byron and Galt, see *HVSV*, pp. xii-iv. The indexes to *LJ, Poetry, Correspondence*, and *HVSV* list no reference to any one of the novels of Galt, with whom Byron quarreled in 1813 but with whom Lady Blessington had been on friendly terms since 1822. Lord Blessington, however, reported to Galt that Byron had said he had read *The Entail* three times (*The Life of Lord Byron* [London, 1830], p. 268).

Lady Blessington in 1834 thought that Byron had treated Galt "shockingly" (N. P. Willis, *Pencillings by the Way* [New York, 1852], p. 471).

[110] The indexes to *LJ, Poetry, Correspondence*, and *HVSV* list no reference by Byron to Sir David Wilkie, the painter, but Lady Blessington had long been on friendly terms with him.

As a woman, I felt proud of the homage he paid to the genius of Mrs. Hemans,[111] and as a passionate admirer of her poetry, I felt flattered, at finding that Lord Byron fully sympathized with my admiration. He has, or at least expresses, a strong dislike to the Lake school of poets, never mentions them except in ridicule, and he and I nearly quarrelled to-day because I defended poor Keats.[112]

On looking out from the balcony this morning with Byron,[113] I observed his countenance change, and an expression of deep sadness steal over it. After a few minutes' silence he pointed out to me a boat anchored to the right, as the one in which his friend Shelley went down,[114] and he said the sight of it made him ill.—"You should have known Shelley," said Byron, "to feel how much I must regret him. He was the most gentle, most amiable, and *least* worldly-minded person I ever met; full of delicacy, disinterested beyond all other men, and possessing a degree of genius, joined to a simplicity, as rare as it is admirable. He had formed to himself a *beau idéal* of all that is fine, high-minded, and noble, and he acted up to this ideal even to the very letter. He had a most brilliant imag-

[111] Was Byron "mystifying" Lady Blessington? Although in 1816 he admired Mrs. Hemans' *Restoration of the Works of Art to Italy* (*LJ*, III, 368), as the years passed he held her poetry increasingly in contempt. Her *Modern Greece* he thought "good for nothing" (*LJ*, IV, 164); in 1820 he decided that her poetry was "too stiltified and apostrophic" (*LJ*, V, 38) and directed Murray, her publisher, to send him no more of it (*LJ*, V, 64). Hers was a "false stilted trashy style, which is a mixture of all the styles of the day, which are *all bombastic* . . . neither English or poetry" (*LJ*, V, 82). For Lady Blessington's admiration of Mrs. Hemans' poetry, see R. R. Madden, *The Literary Life and Correspondence of the Countess of Blessington*, II, 82. In May 1835, she wrote to Talfourd: "I am very sad today, for I have heard of the death of Mrs. Hemans, whose works have taught me to love her" (from the autograph letter in the Huntington Library).

[112] See my *Byron: The Record of a Quest*, Chapter II, "Byron's Laughter." Byron, who clearly distinguished, of course, between the Lake poets and the "Cockney school," paid impressive tribute to Keats in *Don Juan*, XI, lx, written in Genoa in October 1822. Lady Blessington had read Byron's attack on Keats in Moore, *Life*, p. 464.

[113] It seems doubtful that Byron would call on Lady Blessington in the morning. Colonel Montgomery, whose information came from Byron's physician, through Lady Blessington, described the poet's daily routine at this time as follows: "he rises at 9, reads writes &c till 2 . . ." (Mrs. Moore, p. 486). If Lady Blessington had called on him in the morning, presumably he would not have liked it. The first call made by the Blessingtons took place about two o'clock (*HVSV*, p. 351).

[114] The *Don Juan* was owned at one time by its builder, Captain Daniel Roberts (Mrs. Moore, p. 216).

ination, but a total want of worldly-wisdom.[115] I have seen nothing like him, and never shall again, I am certain. I never can forget the night that his poor wife rushed into my room at Pisa, with a face pale as marble, and terror impressed on her brow, demanding, with all the tragic impetuosity of grief and alarm, where was her husband! Vain were all our efforts to calm her; a desperate sort of courage seemed to give her energy to confront the horrible truth that awaited her; it was the courage of despair. I have seen nothing in tragedy on the stage so powerful, or so affecting, as her appearance, and it often presents itself to my memory. I knew nothing then of the catastrophe, but the vividness of her terror communicated itself to me, and I feared the worst, which fears were, alas! too soon fearfully realized.[116]

"Mrs. Shelley is very clever, indeed it would be difficult for her not to be so; the daughter of Mary Wollstonecraft and Godwin, and the wife of Shelley, could be no common person."[117]

Byron talked to-day of Leigh Hunt, regretted his ever having embarked in the "Liberal," and said that it had drawn a nest of hornets on him; but expressed a very good opinion of the talents and principle of Mr. Hunt, though, as he said, "our tastes are so opposite, that we are totally unsuited to each other. He admires the Lakers, I abhor them; in short, we are more formed to be friends at a distance, than near." I can perceive that he wishes Mr. Hunt and his family away. It appears to me that Byron is a person who, without reflection, would form engagements which, when condemned by his friends or advisers, he would gladly get out of without considering the means, or, at least, without reflecting on the humiliation such a desertion must inflict on the persons he had associated with him. He gives me the idea of a man, who, feeling him-

[115] Cf. Byron to Moore, March 4, 1822 (*LJ*, VI, 32): "As to poor Shelley . . . he is, to my knowledge, the *least* selfish and the mildest of men—a man who has made more sacrifices of his fortune and feelings for others than any I ever heard of."

[116] Mary Shelley's account, in a letter to Maria Gisborne, is in essential agreement (*HVSV*, pp. 304-05).

[117] Lady Blessington told Crabb Robinson that Byron had described Mary as "vulgar," "a great liar," of "artificial character and worthlessness." "She was hated intensely by Lord Byron . . ." (*HVSV*, pp. 371-72). Mary had requested in writing that she not be mentioned in the *Conversations* (see my "Byron and Mary Shelley," *Keats-Shelley Journal*, II [January 1953], 35-49, and the introduction to the present volume).

self in such a dilemma, would become cold and ungracious to the parties with whom he so stood, before he had mental courage sufficient to abandon them. I may be wrong, but the whole of his manner of talking of Mr. Hunt gives me this impression, though he has not said what might be called an unkind word of him.[118]

Much as Byron has braved public opinion, it is evident he has a great deference for those who stand high in it, and that he is shy in attaching himself publicly to persons who have even, however undeservedly, fallen under its censure.[119] His expressed contempt and defiance of the world reminds me of the bravadoes of children, who, afraid of darkness, make a noise to give themselves courage to support what they dread. It is very evident that he is partial to aristocratic friends; he dwells with complacency on the advantages of rank and station, and has more than once boasted that people of family are always to be recognised by a *certain air*, and the smallness and delicacy of their hands.[120]

He talked in terms of high commendation of the talents and acquirements of Mr. Hobhouse; but a latent sentiment of pique was visible in his manner, from the idea he appeared to entertain that Mr. Hobhouse had undervalued him. Byron evidently likes praise: this is a weakness, if weakness it be, that he partakes in common with mankind in general; but he does not seem aware that a great compliment is implied in the very act of telling a man his faults— for the friend who undertakes this disagreeable office must give him whom he censures credit for many good qualities, as well as no ordinary portion of candour and temper, to suppose him capable of hearing their recapitulation of his failings.[121] Byron is, after all, a spoiled child, and, the severe lessons he has met with being disproportioned to the errors that called them forth, has made him

[118] Crabb Robinson reported in 1832: "She went so far as to say that she thinks Leigh Hunt gave in the main a fair account of Lord Byron" (*HVSV*, p. 371). William H. Marshall's *Byron, Shelley, Hunt and The Liberal* (Philadelphia, 1960) provides the most detailed account of the relations of Byron and Hunt.

[119] Lady Blessington had also "braved public opinion"; she had deferred for years to those who stood high in the world; and she knew painfully the position of one who had "fallen under its censure."

[120] Byron wrote to his mother in 1809 (*LJ*, I, 251), of Ali Pasha: "He said he was certain I was a man of birth, because I had . . . little white hands. . . ."

[121] See Hobhouse's account of his last visit with Byron, September 15-20, 1822 (*HVSV*, pp. 313-16).

54

view the faults of the civilized world through a false medium; a sort of discoloured magnifying-glass, while his own are gazed at through a concave lens.[122] All that Byron has told me of the frankness and unbending honesty of Mr. Hobhouse's character has given me a most favourable impression of that gentleman.

Byron gave me to-day a MS. copy of verses, addressed to Lady Byron, on reading in a newspaper that she had been ill. How different is the feeling that pervades them from that of the letter addressed to her which he had given me! a lurking tenderness, suppressed by a pride that was doubtful of the reception it might meet, is evident in one, while bitterness, uncompromising bitterness, marks the other. Neither were written but with deep feelings of pain, and should be judged as the outpourings of a wounded spirit, demanding pity more than anger. I subjoin the verses, though not without some reluctance. But while to the public they are of that value that any reasons for their suppression ought to be extremely strong, so, on the other hand, I trust, they cannot hurt either her feelings to whom they are addressed, or his memory by whom they are written:—to her, because the very bitterness of reproach proves that unconquerable affection which cannot but heal the wound it causes: to him, because who, in the shattered feelings they betray, will not acknowledge the grief that hurries into error, and (may we add in charity!)—atones for it.

TO * * * * *

And thou wert sad—yet I was not with thee;
And thou wert sick, and yet I was not near;
Methought that joy and health alone could be
Where I was not—and pain and sorrow here!
And is it thus?—it is as I foretold,
And shall be more so; for the mind recoils
Upon itself, and the wreck'd heart lies cold,
While heaviness collects the shatter'd spoils.

[122] Contrast Lady Blessington in her "Night Thought Book" (Madden, I, 209-10): "England is the only country in Europe where the loss of one's virtue superinduces the loss of all. I refer to chastity. A woman known to have violated this virtue, though she possess all the other virtues, is driven with ignominy from society into a solitude rendered insupportable by a sense of the injustice by which she is made a victim to solitude, which often becomes the grave of the virtues she brought to it."

It is not in the storm nor in the strife
We feel benumb'd, and wish to be no more,
But in the after-silence on the shore,
When all is lost, except a little life.

I am too well avenged!—but 'twas my right;
Whate'er my sins might be, *thou* wert not sent
To be the Nemesis who should requite—
Nor did Heaven choose so near an instrument.

Mercy is for the merciful!—if thou
Hast been of such, 'twill be accorded now.
Thy nights are banish'd from the realms of sleep!—
Yes! they may flatter thee, but thou shalt feel
A hollow agony which will not heal,
For thou art pillow'd on a curse too deep;
Thou hast sown in my sorrow, and must reap
The bitter harvest in a woe as real!
I have had many foes, but none like thee;
For 'gainst the rest myself I could defend,
And be avenged, or turn them into friend;
But thou in safe implacability
Hadst nought to dread—in thy own weakness shielded,
And in my love, which hath but too much yielded,
And spared, for thy sake, some I should not spare—
And thus upon the world—trust in thy truth—
And the wild fame of my ungovern'd youth—
On things that were not, and on things that are—
Even upon such a basis hast thou built
A monument, whose cement hath been guilt!
The moral Clytemnestra of thy lord,
And hew'd down, with an unsuspected sword,
Fame, peace, and hope—and all the better life
Which, but for this cold treason of thy heart,
Might still have risen from out the grave of strife,
And found a nobler duty than to part.

But of thy virtues didst thou make a vice,
Trafficking with them in a purpose cold,
For present anger, and for future gold—
And buying other's grief at any price.
And thus once enter'd into crooked ways,
The early Truth, which was thy proper praise,
Did not still walk beside thee—but at times,
And with a breast unknowing its own crimes,
Deceit, averments incompatible,
Equivocations, and the thoughts which dwell
In Janus-spirits—the significant eye
Which learns to lie with silence—the pretext
Of Prudence, with advantages annex'd—
The acquiescence in all things which tend,
No matter how, to the desired end—
All found a place in thy philosophy.
The means were worthy, and the end is won—
I would not do by thee as thou hast done!

It is evident that Lady Byron occupies his attention continually; he introduces her name frequently; is fond of recurring to the brief period of their living together; dwells with complacency on her personal attractions, saying, that though not regularly handsome, he liked her looks. He is very inquisitive about her; was much disappointed that I had never seen her, nor could give any account of her appearance at present. In short, a thousand indescribable circumstances have left the impression on my mind that she occupies much of his thoughts, and that they appear to revert continually to her and his child. He owned to me, that when he reflected on the whole tenour of her conduct—the refusing any explanation—never answering his letters, or holding out even a hope that in future years their child might form a bond of union between them, he felt exasperated against her, and vented this feeling in his writings; nay more, he blushed for his own weakness in thinking so often and so kindly of one who certainly showed no symptom of ever bestowing a thought on him. The mystery attached to Lady Byron's silence has piqued him, and kept alive an interest that, even now, appears as lively as if their separation was recent. There is something so humiliating in the consciousness that some dear object, to whom we thought ourselves necessary, and who occupies much of our thoughts, can forget that we exist, or at least act as if she did so, that I can well excuse the bitterness of poor Byron's feelings on this point, though not the published sarcasms caused by this bitterness; and whatever may be the sufferings of Lady Byron, they are more than avenged by what her husband feels.

It appears to me extraordinary, that a person who has given such interesting sketches of the female character, as Byron has in his works, should be so little *au fait* of judging feminine feeling under certain circumstances. He is surprised that Lady Byron has never relented since his absence from England; but he forgets how that absence has been filled up on his part. I ventured to suggest this, and hinted that, perhaps, had his conduct been irreproachable during the first years of their separation, and unstained by any attachment that could have widened the breach between them, it is possible[123] that Lady Byron might have become reconciled to him; but that no woman of delicacy could receive or answer letters written beneath the same roof[124] that sheltered some female favourite, whose presence alone proved that the husband could not have those feelings of propriety[125] or affection towards his absent wife, the want of which constitutes a crime that all *women*, at least, can understand to be one of those least pardonable. How few men understand the feelings of women! Sensitive, and easily wounded as we are, obliged to call up pride to support us in trials that always leave fearful marks behind, how often are we compelled to assume the semblance of coldness and indifference when the heart inly bleeds; and the decent composure, put on with our visiting garments to appear in public, and, like them, worn for a few hours, are with them laid aside; and all the dreariness, the heart-consuming cares, that woman alone can know, return to make us feel, that though we may disguise our sufferings from others, and deck our countenance with smiles, we cannot deceive ourselves, and are but the more miserable from the constraint we submit to! A woman only can understand a woman's heart—we cannot, dare not, com-

123 Teresa Guiccioli: No!   124 Teresa Guiccioli: *et où?*
125 Teresa Guiccioli: *ce la à-t'il eu lieu?*

58

plain—sympathy is denied us, because we must not lay open the wounds that excite it; and even the most legitimate feelings are too sacred in female estimation to be exposed—thus while we nurse the grief "that lies too deep for tears," and consumes alike health and peace, a man may with impunity express all, nay, more than he feels—court and meet sympathy, while his leisure hours are cheered by occupations and pleasures, the latter too often such as ought to prove how little he stood in need of compassion, except for his vices.

I stated something of this to Lord Byron today, *apropos* to the difference between his position and that of his wife. He tried to prove to me how much more painful was his situation than hers; but I effected some alteration in his opinion when I had fairly placed their relative positions before him—at least such as they appeared to me. I represented Lady Byron to him separating in early youth, whether from just or mistaken motives for such a step, from the husband of her choice, after little more than a brief year's union, and immediately after that union had been cemented by the endearing, strengthening tie of a new-born infant! carrying with her into solitude this fond and powerful remembrancer of its father, how much must it have cost her to resist the appeals of such a pleader!—wearing away her youth in almost monastic seclusion, her motives questioned by some, and appreciated by few—seeking consolation alone in the discharge of her duties, and avoiding all external demonstrations of a grief that her pale cheek and solitary existence are such powerful vouchers for! Such is the portrait I gave him of Lady Byron—his own I ventured to sketch as follows.

I did not enter into the causes, or motives, of the separation, because I know them not, but I dwelt on his subsequent conduct:— the appealing on the separation to public sympathy, by the publication of verses which ought only to have met the eye of her to whom they were addressed, was in itself an outrage to that delicacy, that shrinks from, and shuns publicity, so inherent in the female heart.[126] He leaves England,—the climate, modes, and customs

[126] It is perhaps enough to recall that immediately after finishing the *Conversations*, Lady Blessington wrote *The Repealers*, supplied the publisher with a key to thirty-three characters (most of them outrageously complimented, others outrageously attacked), and assigned the names of living persons to

of which had never been congenial to his taste,—to seek beneath the sunny skies of Italy, and all the soul-exciting objects that classic land can offer, a consolation for domestic disappointment. How soon were the broken ties of conjugal affection replaced by less holy ones! I refer not to his attachment to La Contessa Guiccioli, because at least it is of a different and a more pure nature, but to those degrading *liaisons* which marked the first year or two of his residence in Italy, and must ever from their revolting coarseness remain a stain on his fame.[127] It may be urged that disappointment and sorrow drove him into such excesses; but admitting this, surely we must respect the grief that is borne in solitude, and with the most irreproachable delicacy of conduct, more than that which flies to gross sensualities for relief.

Such was the substance, and I believe nearly the words I repeated to him to-day; and it is but justice to him to say that they seemed to make a deep impression. He said that if my portrait of Lady Byron's position was indeed a faithful one, she was much more to be pitied than he; that he felt deeply for her, but that he had never viewed their relative situations in the same light before; he had always considered her as governed wholly by pride.

I urged that my statement was drawn from facts; that, of the extreme privacy and seclusion of her life, ever since the separation, there could be no doubt, and this alone vouched for the feelings that led to it.

He seemed pleased and gratified by the reflections I had made, insensibly fell into a tone of tenderness in speaking of Lady Byron, and pressed my hand with more than usual cordiality. On bidding me good bye, his parting words were, "You probe old and half-healed wounds, but though you give pain, you excite a more healthy action, and do good."

His heart yearns to see his child; all children of the same age remind him of her, and he loves to recur to the subject.

Poor Byron has hitherto been so continually occupied with dwelling on, and analyzing his own feelings, that he has not reflected on those of his wife. He cannot understand her observing such a total

others: Lord and Lady Lansdowne, Mrs. Samuel C. Hall, Moore, Luttrell, and the Lord-Lieutenant of Ireland.

[127] Teresa Guiccioli: liaisons Poh!! *not at all!*

60

silence on their position, because he could not, and cannot, resist making it the topic of conversation with even chance associates: this, which an impartial observer[128] of her conduct would attribute to deep feelings, and a sense of delicacy, he concludes to be caused by pride[129] and want of feeling. We are always prone to judge of others by ourselves, which is one of the reasons why our judgments are in general so erroneous. Man may be judged of by his species *en masse*, but he who would judge of mankind in the aggregate, from one specimen of the genus, must be often in error, and this is Byron's case.[130]

Lord Byron told me to-day, that he had been occupied in the morning making his will; that he had left the bulk of his fortune to his sister, as, his daughter having, in right of her mother, a large fortune, he thought it unnecessary to increase it; he added, that he had left La Contessa Guiccioli £10,000, and had intended to have left her £25,000, but that she had suspected his intentions, and urged him so strongly not to do so, or indeed to leave her anything, that he had changed the sum to £10,000. He said that this was one, of innumerable instances, of her delicacy and disinterestedness, of which he had repeated proofs; that she was so fearful of the possibility of having interested motives attributed to her, that he was certain she would prefer the most extreme poverty to incurring such a suspicion.[131] I observed, that were I he, I would have left her the sum I had originally intended, as, in case of his death, it would be a flattering proof of his esteem for her, and she had always the power of refusing the whole, or any part of the bequest she thought proper. It appeared to me, that the more delicacy and disinterestedness she displayed, the more decided ought he to be, in marking his appreciation of her conduct. He appeared to agree with me, and passed many encomiums on La Contessa.

He talked to-day of Sir Francis Burdett, of whose public and private character he entertains the most exalted opinion. He said that it was gratifying to behold in him the rare union of a heart and

---

[128] Teresa Guiccioli: Bah!   [129] Teresa Guiccioli: *nonsense.*
[130] Teresa Guiccioli: No!
[131] This will was never written (see *Correspondence*, II, 284); Lady Blessington may have learned her details from Moore's *Life* (see p. xix, a letter from Barry to Moore, which, however, states that Byron had discussed with Lord Blessington a bequest of £10,000 to Teresa, who had declined it).

head that left nothing to be desired, and dwelt with evident pride and pleasure on the mental courage displayed by Sir Francis in befriending and supporting him, when so many of his professed friends stood aloof, on his separation from Lady Byron.[132] The defalcation of his friends, at the moment he most required them, has made an indelible impression on his mind, and has given him a very bad opinion of his countrymen.[133] I endeavoured to reason him out of this, by urging the principle that mankind, *en masse*, are everywhere the same, but he denied this, on the plea that, as civilization had arrived at a greater degree of perfection in England than elsewhere, selfishness, its concomitant, there flourished so luxuriantly,[134] as to overgrow all generous and kind feelings. He quoted various examples of friends, and even the nearest relations, deserting each other in the hour of need, fearful that any part of the censure heaped on some less fortunate connexion might fall on them. I am unwilling to believe that his pictures are not overdrawn, and hope I shall always think so—

Where ignorance is bliss, 'tis folly to be wise.

"Talking of friends," said Byron, "Mr. Hobhouse has been the most impartial, or perhaps (added he) *unpartial* of all my friends; he always told me my faults, but I must do him the justice to add, that he told them to *me*, and not to others." I observed that the epithet impartial was the applicable one; but he denied it, saying that Mr. Hobhouse must have been *unpartial*, to have discerned all the errors he had pointed out; "but," he added, laughing, "I could have told him of some more which he had not discovered, for even, then, *avarice* had made itself strongly felt in my nature."[135]

Byron came to see us to-day, and appeared extremely discomposed; after half-an-hour's conversation on indifferent subjects, he at

[132] See Burdett's letter to Douglas Kinnaird (*LJ*, VI, 19, n.), written in early 1816, praising Byron and criticizing Lady Byron ("strangely perverted in intellect"). Byron chose Burdett as one of the two arbitrators of the Wentworth estate. Lady Blessington knew Burdett before she met Byron, was still on intimate terms with him in 1832, when she was writing the *Conversations* (Madden, I, 62; II, 253).

[133] Cf. *The Idler* (*HVSV*, p. 362). Teresa Guiccioli asks in the margin: "Was he wrong?"

[134] Teresa Guiccioli: Most true!   [135] Teresa Guiccioli: but laughing!

length broke forth with, "Only fancy my receiving to-day a tragedy dedicated as follows—'From George —— to George Byron!'[136] This is being cool with a vengeance. I never was more provoked. How stupid, how ignorant, to pass over my rank! I am determined not to read the tragedy; for a man capable of committing such a solecism in good breeding and common decency, can write nothing worthy of being read." We were astonished[137] at witnessing the annoyance this circumstance gave him, and more than ever convinced, that the pride of aristocracy is one of the peculiar features of his character. If he sometimes forgets his rank, he never can forgive any one else's doing so; and as he is not naturally dignified, and his propensity to flippancy renders him still less so, he often finds himself in a false position, by endeavouring to recover lost ground. We endeavoured to console him by telling him that we knew Mr. George —— a little, and that he was clever and agreeable, as also that his passing over the title of Byron was meant as a compliment—it was a delicate preference shown to the renown accorded to George Byron the poet, over the rank and title, which were adventitious advantages ennobled by the possessor, but that could add nothing to his fame. All our arguments were vain; he said, "this could not be the man's feelings, as he reduced him (Lord Byron) to the same level as himself." It is strange to see a person of such brilliant and powerful genius sullied[138] by such incongruities. Were he but sensible how much the *Lord* is overlooked in the *Poet* he would be less vain of his rank: but as it is, this vanity is very prominent, and resembles more the pride of a *parvenu* than the calm dignity of an ancient aristocrat. It is also evident that he attaches importance to the appendages of rank and station.[139] The trappings of luxury, to which a short use accustoms every one, seem to please him; he observes, nay, comments upon them, and oh! mortifying conclusion, appears, at least for the moment, to think more highly of their possessors. As his own mode of life is so extremely simple, this seems the more extraordinary; but everything in him is contradictory and extraordinary. Of his friends he remarks, "this or that person is a man of family, or he is a *parvenu*, the marks of which char-

[136] A somewhat similar reaction, involving verses by W. S. Rose, is recorded in Moore, *Life*, p. 378, n. 2.
[137] Teresa Guiccioli: Pah!   [138] Teresa Guiccioli: Pah!
[139] Teresa Guiccioli: Nonsense.

acter, in spite of all his affected gentility, break out in a thousand ways." We were not prepared for this; we expected to meet a man more disposed to respect the nobility of genius than that of rank; but we have found the reverse. In talking of Ravenna, the natal residence of La Contessa Guiccioli, he dwells with peculiar complacency on the equipage of her husband; talks of the six black carriage-horses, without which the old Conte seldom moved, and their spacious palazzo; also the wealth of the Conte, and the distinguished connexions of the lady. He describes La Contessa as being of the middle stature, finely formed, exquisitely fair, her features perfectly regular, and the expression of her countenance remarkable for its animation and sweetness, her hair auburn, and of great beauty. No wonder, then, that such rare charms have had power to fix his truant heart; and, as he says that to these she unites accomplishments and amiability, it may be concluded, as indeed he declares, that this is his last attachment. He frequently talks of Alfieri, and always with enthusiastic admiration. He remarks on the similarity of their tastes and pursuits, their domesticating themselves with women of rank, their fondness for animals, and, above all, for horses; their liking to be surrounded by birds and pets of various descriptions, their passionate love of liberty, habitual gloom, &c. &c. In short, he produces so many points of resemblance, that it leads one to suspect that he is a copy of an original he has long studied.[140]

This, again, proceeds from a want of self-respect; but we may well pardon it, when we reflect on the abuse, calumny, envy, hatred, and malice, that, in spite of all his genius, have pursued him from the country that genius must adorn.

Talking of Alfieri, he told me to-day, that when that poet was travelling in Italy, a very romantic, and, as he called her, *tête montée* Italian Principessa, or Duchessa, who had long been an enthusiastic admirer of his works, having heard that he was to pass within fifty miles of her residence, set off to encounter him; and having arrived at the inn where he sojourned, was shown into a room where she was told Alfieri was writing. She enters, agitated and fatigued,— sees a very good-looking man seated at a table, whom she con-

[140] Medwin had made this comparison (*Conversations*, p. 268, n.); Moore (*Life*, p. 644) developed it.

64

cludes must be Alfieri,—throws herself into his arms,—and, in broken words, declares her admiration, and the distance she has come to declare it. In the midst of the lady's impassioned speeches, Alfieri enters the room, casts a glance of surprise and *hauteur* at the pair, and lets fall some expression that discloses to the humbled Principessa the shocking mistake she has made.

The poor Secretary (for such he was) is blamed by the lady, while he declares his innocence, finding himself, as he says, in the embraces of a lady who never allowed him even a moment to interrupt her, by the simple question of what she meant! Alfieri retired in offended dignity, shocked that any one could be mistaken for him, while the Principessa had to retrace her steps, her enthusiasm somewhat cooled by the mistake and its consequences.

Byron says that the number of anonymous amatory letters and portraits he has received, and all from English ladies, would fill a large volume.[141] He says he has never noticed any of them; but it is evident he recurs to them with complacency.

He talked to-day of a very different kind of letter, which appears to have made a profound impression on him; he has promised to show it to me; it is from a Mr. Sheppard, inclosing him a prayer offered up for Byron, by the wife of Mr. Sheppard, and sent since her death. He says he never was more touched than on perusing it, and that it has given him a better opinion of human nature.

The following is the copy of the letter and prayer, which Lord Byron has permitted me to make.[142]

"To Lord Byron.

"Frome, Somerset, Nov. 21, 1821.

"my lord,

"More than two years since, a lovely and beloved wife was taken from me, by lingering disease, after a very short union. She possessed unvarying gentleness and fortitude, and a piety so retiring as rarely to disclose itself in words, but so influential as to produce uniform benevolence of conduct. In the last hour of life, after a fare-

[141] See *To Lord Byron*, ed. George Paston and Peter Quennell (New York, 1939).

[142] Moore, *Life*, pp. 542-43, had published this letter in 1830, with Byron's reply.

well look on a lately-born and only infant, for whom she had evinced inexpressible affection, her last whispers were, 'God's happiness!—God's happiness!'

"Since the second anniversary of her decease, I have read some papers which no one had seen during her life, and which contain her most secret thoughts. I am induced to communicate to your Lordship a passage from these papers, which there is no doubt refers to yourself, as I have more than once heard the writer mention your agility on the rocks at Hastings.

" 'Oh, my God, I take encouragement from the assurance of thy word, to pray to Thee in behalf of one for whom I have lately been much interested. May the person to whom I allude (and who is now, we fear, as much distinguished for his neglect of Thee as for the transcendant talents thou hast bestowed on him), be awakened to a sense of his own danger, and led to seek that peace of mind in a proper sense of religion, which he has found this world's enjoyment unable to procure! Do Thou grant that his future example may be productive of far more extensive benefit than his past conduct and writings have been of evil; and may the Sun of Righteousness, which we trust will, at some future period, arise on him, be bright in proportion to the darkness of those clouds which guilt has raised around him, and the balm which it bestows, healing and soothing in proportion to the keenness of that agony which the punishment of his vices has inflicted on him! May the hope that the sincerity of my own efforts for the attainment of holiness, and the approval of my own love to the Great Author of religion, will render this prayer, and every other for the welfare of mankind, more efficacious,—cheer me in the path of duty; but, let me not forget, that while we are permitted to animate ourselves to exertion by every innocent motive, these are but the lesser streams which may serve to increase the current, but which, deprived of the grand fountain of good, (a deep conviction of inborn sin, and firm belief in the efficacy of Christ's death for the salvation of those who trust in him, and really wish to serve him,) would soon dry up, and leave us barren of every virtue as before.—*Hastings, July* 31, 1814.'

"There is nothing, my Lord, in this extract which, in a literary sense, can at all interest you; but it may, perhaps, appear to you

66

worthy of reflection how deep and expansive a concern for the happiness of others the Christian faith can awaken in the midst of youth and prosperity. Here is nothing poetical and splendid, as in the expostulatory homage of M. Delamartine; but here is the *sublime*, my Lord; for this intercession was offered, on your account, to the supreme *Source* of happiness. It sprang from a faith more confirmed than that of the French poet, and from a charity which, in combination with faith, showed its power unimpaired amidst the languors and pains of approaching dissolution. I will hope that a prayer, which, I am sure, was deeply sincere, may not always be unavailing.

"It would add *nothing*, my Lord, to the fame with which your genius has surrounded you, for an unknown and obscure individual to express his admiration of it. I had rather be numbered with those who wish and pray, that 'wisdom from above,' and 'peace,' and 'joy,' may enter such a mind.

"JOHN SHEPPARD."

On reading this letter and prayer, which Byron did aloud, before he consigned it to me to copy, and with a voice tremulous from emotion, and a seriousness of aspect that showed how deeply it affected him, he observed, "Before I had read this prayer, I never rightly understood the expression, so often used, 'The beauty of holiness.' This prayer and letter has done more to give me a good opinion of religion, and its professors, than all the religious books I ever read in my life.

"Here were two most amiable and exalted minds offering prayers and wishes for the salvation of one considered by three parts of his countrymen to be beyond the pale of hope, and charitably doomed to everlasting torments. The religion that prays and hopes for the *erring* is the true religion, and the only one that could make a convert of me; and I date (continued Byron) my first impressions against religion to having witnessed how little its votaries were actuated by any true feeling of Christian charity. Instead of lamenting the disbelief, or pitying the transgressions (or at least their consequences) of the sinner, they at once cast him off, dwell with acrimony on his errors, and, not content with foredooming him to eternal punishment hereafter, endeavour, as much as they can, to

67

render his earthly existence as painful as possible, until they have hardened him in his errors, and added hatred of his species to their number. Were all religious people like Mr. Sheppard and the amiable wife he has lost, we should have fewer sceptics: such examples would do more towards the work of conversion than all that ever was written on the subject.

"When Religion supports the sufferer in affliction and sickness, even unto death, its advantages are so visible, that all must wish to seek such a consolation; and when it speaks peace and hope to those who have strayed from its path, it softens feelings that severity must have hardened, and leads back the wanderer to the fold; but when it clothes itself in anger, denouncing vengeance, or shows itself in the pride of superior righteousness, condemning, rather than pitying, all erring brothers, it repels the wavering, and fixes the unrepentant in their sins. Such a religion can make few converts, but may make many dissenters, to its tenets; for in religion, as in everything else, its utility must be apparent, to encourage people to adopt its precepts; and the utility is never so evident as when we see professors of religion supported by its consolations, and willing to extend these consolations to those who have still more need of them —the misguided and the erring."

They who accuse Byron of being an unbeliever are wrong: he is *sceptical*, but not unbelieving; and it appears not unlikely to me that a time may come when his wavering faith in many of the tenets of religion may be as firmly fixed as is now his conviction of the immortality of the soul,—a conviction that he declares every fine and noble impulse of his nature renders more decided. He is a sworn foe to Materialism,[143] tracing every defect to which we are subject, to the infirmities entailed on us by the prison of clay in which the heavenly spark is confined. *Conscience*, he says, is to him another proof of the Divine Origin of Man, as is also his natural tendency to the love of good.[144] A fine day, a moonlight night, or any other fine object in the phenomena of nature, excites (said Byron) strong feelings of religion in all elevated minds, and an out-

[143] See Moore, *Life*, p. 653, on materialism.
[144] Byron was not always convinced of man's "natural tendency to the love of good," nor was Lady Blessington. On her religion, see the introduction to this volume.

68

pouring of the spirit to the Creator, that, call it what we may, is the essence of innate love and gratitude to the Divinity.[145]

There is a seriousness in Byron's manner, when he gets warmed by his subject, that impresses one with the truth of his statements. He observed to me, "I seldom *talk* of religion, but I *feel* it, perhaps, more than those who do. I speak to you on this topic freely, because I know you will neither laugh at, nor enter into a controversy with me. It is strange, but true, that Mrs. Sheppard is mixed up with all my religious aspirations: nothing ever so excited my imagination, and touched my heart, as her prayer. I have pictured her to myself a thousand times in the solitude of her chamber, struck by a malady that generally engrosses all feelings for self, and those near and dear to one, thinking *of*, and praying for *me*, who was deemed by all an outcast. Her purity—her blameless life—and the deep humility expressed in her prayer—render her, in my mind, the most interesting and angelic creature that ever existed, and she mingles in all my thoughts of a future state. I would give anything to have her portrait, though perhaps it would destroy the *beau idéal* I have formed of her. What strange thoughts pass through the mind, and how much are we influenced by adventitious circumstances! The phrase *lovely*, in the letter of Mr. Sheppard, has invested the memory of his wife with a double interest; but beauty and goodness have always been associated in my mind, because, through life, I have found them generally go together. I do not talk of mere beauty (continued Byron) of feature or complexion, but of expression, that looking out of the soul through the eyes, which, in my opinion, constitutes true beauty. Women have been pointed out to me as beautiful who never could have interested my feelings, from their want of countenance, or expression, which means countenance; and others, who were little remarked, have struck me as being captivating, from the force of countenance. A woman's face ought to be like an April day—susceptible of change and variety; but sunshine should often gleam over it, to replace the clouds and showers that may obscure its lustre,—which, poetical description apart (said Byron), in sober prose means, that good-humoured smiles ought to be ready to chase away the expression of pensive-

[145] See my *Byron: The Record of a Quest*, Chapter VI, especially, "The Character of Byron's Deism," pp. 185-98.

69

ness or care that sentiment or earthly ills call forth. Women were meant to be the exciters of all that is finest in our natures, and the soothers of all that is turbulent and harsh. Of what use, then, can a handsome automaton be, after one has got acquainted with a face that knows no change, though it causes many? This is a style of looks I could not bear the sight of for a week; and yet such are the looks that pass in society for pretty, handsome, and beautiful. How beautiful Lady C—— was! She had no great variety of expression, but the predominant ones were purity, calmness, and abstraction. She looked as if she had never *caused* an unhallowed sentiment, or felt one,—a sort of 'moonbeam on the snow,' as our friend Moore would describe her, that was lovely to look on.—[146] Lady A. F[orbes][147] *was* also very handsome. It is melancholy to talk of women in the past tense. What a pity, that of all flowers, none fade so soon as beauty! Poor Lady A. F[orbes] has not got married. Do you know, I once had some thoughts of her as a wife; not that I was in love, as people call it, but I had argued myself into a belief that I ought to marry, and meeting her very often in society, the notion came into my head, not heart, that she would suit me. Moore, too, told me so much of her good qualities, all which was, I believe, quite true, that I felt tempted to propose to her, but did not, whether *tant mieux* or *tant pis*, God knows, supposing my proposal accepted. No marriage could have turned out more unfortunately than the one I made,—that is quite certain; and, to add to my agreeable reflections on this subject, I have the consciousness that had I possessed sufficient command over my own wayward humour, I might have rendered myself so dear and necessary to Lady Byron, that she would not, could not, have left me. It is certainly not very gratifying to my vanity to have been *planté* after so short a union, and within a few weeks after being made a father, —a circumstance that one would suppose likely to cement the attachment. I always get out of temper when I recur to this subject; and yet, *malgré moi*, I find myself continually recurring to it."

[146] Perhaps Lady Cowper, daughter of Lady Melbourne, whom Byron described in 1812 as one of the three "pleasantest persons" he knew, possessing his "most respectful admiration" (*Correspondence*, I, 95, 120); perhaps Lady Charlemont, whose head, Byron thought, "seemed to possess all that sculpture could require for its ideal" (Moore, *Life*, p. 694).

[147] See Byron's letters to Moore on Lady Adelaide Forbes, *LJ*, II, 230-321 and n. 3; III, 86-87; IV, 122.

Byron is a perfect chameleon, possessing the fabulous qualities attributed to that animal, of taking the colour of whatever touches him. He is conscious of this, and says it is owing to the extreme *mobilité* of his nature, which yields to present impressions.[148] It appears to me, that the consciousness of his own defects renders him still less tolerant to those of others,—this perhaps is owing to their attempts to conceal them, more than from natural severity, as he condemns hypocrisy more than any other vice—saying it is the origin of all. If vanity, selfishness, or mundane sentiments, are brought in contact with him, every arrow in the armoury of ridicule is let fly, and there is no shield sufficiently powerful to withstand them. If vice approaches, he assails it with the bitterest gall of satire; but when goodness appears, and that he is assured it is sincere, all the dormant affections of his nature are excited, and it is impossible not to observe, how tender and affectionate[149] a heart his must have been, ere circumstances had soured it. This was never more displayed than in the impression made on him by the prayer of Mrs. Sheppard, and the letter of her husband. It is also evident in the generous impulses that he betrays on hearing of distress or misfortune, which he endeavours to alleviate; and, unlike the world in general, Byron never makes light of the griefs of others, but shows commiseration and kindness.[150] There are days when he excites so strong an interest and sympathy, by showing such undoubtable proofs of good feeling, that every previous impression to his disadvantage fades away, and one is vexed with oneself for ever having harboured them. But, alas! "the morrow comes," and he is no longer the same being. Some disagreeable letter, review, or new example of the slanders with which he has been for years assailed, changes the whole current of his feelings—renders him reckless, Sardonic, and as unlike the Byron of the day before, as if they had nothing in common,—nay, he seems determined to efface any good impression he might have made, and appears angry with himself for having yielded to the kindly feelings that gave birth to it. After such exhibitions, one feels perplexed[151] what opinion to form of him; and the individual who has an opportunity of seeing

---

[148] See *Don Juan*, XVI, xcvii, and my introduction.
[149] Teresa Guiccioli: True.   [150] Teresa Guiccioli: True!
[151] Teresa Guiccioli: Why? perplexed?

Byron very often, and for any length of time, if he or she stated the daily impressions candidly, would find, on reviewing them, a mass of heterogeneous evidence, from which it would be most difficult[152] to draw a just conclusion. The affectionate manner in which he speaks of some of his juvenile companions has a delicacy and tenderness resembling the nature of woman more than that of man, and leads me to think that an extreme sensitiveness, checked by coming in contact with persons incapable of appreciating it,[153] and affections chilled by finding a want of sympathy, have repelled, but could not eradicate, the seeds of goodness that now often send forth blossoms, and, with culture, may yet produce precious fruit.

I am sure, that if ten individuals undertook the task of describing Byron, no two, of the ten, would agree in their verdict respecting him, or convey any portrait that resembled the other, and yet the description of each might be correct, according to his or her received opinion; but the truth is, the chameleon-like character or manner of Byron renders it difficult to portray him; and the pleasure he seems to take in misleading his associates in their estimate of him increases the difficulty of the task. This extraordinary fancy of his has so often struck me, that I expect to see all the persons who have lived with him giving portraits, each unlike the other, and yet all bearing a resemblance to the original at some one time.[154] Like the pictures given of some celebrated actor in his different characters, each likeness is affected by the dress and the part he has to fill. The portrait of John Kemble in Cato[155] resembles not Macbeth nor Hamlet, and yet each is an accurate likeness of that admirable actor in those characters; so Byron, changing every day, and fond of misleading those whom he suspects might be inclined to paint him, will always appear different from the hand of each limner.[156]

During our rides in the vicinity of Genoa, we frequently met several persons, almost all of them English, who evidently had taken

---

[152] Teresa Guiccioli: not at *all*.   [153] Teresa Guiccioli: True!

[154] When the first installment of Lady Blessington's *Conversations* appeared in July 1832, book-length reminiscences or biographies of Byron had been published by Dallas, Galt, Gamba, Hunt, James Kennedy, Medwin, Moore, and William Perry.

[155] Sir Thomas Lawrence's large portrait of Kemble as Cato hung in Lady Blessington's house in St. James's Square (Mrs. Mathews, *Memoirs of Charles Mathews, Comedian* [London, 1839], III, 376).

[156] Teresa Guiccioli: True!

72

that route purposely to see Lord Byron. "Which is he?" "That's he," I have frequently heard whispered as the different groups extended their heads to gaze at him, while he has turned to me—his pale face assuming, for the moment, a warmer tint—and said, "How very disagreeable it is to be so stared at! If you knew how I detest it, you would feel how great must be my desire to enjoy the society of my friends at the Hotel de la Ville, when I pay the price of passing through the town, and exposing myself to the gazing multitude on the stairs and in the anti-chambers." Yet there were days when he seemed more pleased than displeased at being followed and stared at.[157] All depended on the humour he was in. When gay, he attributed the attention he excited to the true cause—admiration of his genius; but when in a less good-natured humour, he looked on it as an impertinent curiosity, caused by the scandalous histories circulated against him, and resented it as such.

He was peculiarly fond of flowers,[158] and generally bought a large bouquet every day of a gardener whose grounds we passed. He told me that he liked to have them in his room, though they excited melancholy feelings, by reminding him of the evanescence of all that is beautiful, but that the melancholy was of a softer, milder character, than his general feelings.

Observing Byron one day in more than usually low spirits, I asked him if any thing painful had occurred. He sighed deeply, and said—"No, nothing new; the old wounds are still unhealed, and bleed afresh on the slightest touch, so that God knows there needs nothing new. Can I reflect on my present position without bitter feelings? Exiled from my country by a species of ostracism —the most humiliating to a proud mind, when *daggers* and not shells were used to ballot, inflicting mental wounds more deadly and difficult to be healed than all that the body could suffer. Then the notoriety (as I call what you would kindly name fame) that follows me, precludes the privacy I desire, and renders me an object of curiosity, which is a continual source of irritation to my feelings. I am bound, by the indissoluble ties of marriage, to *one* who will *not* live with me, and live with one to whom I cannot give a

[157] Cf. *The Idler*, April 4, 1823 (*HVSV*, p. 356), where Byron "did not seem annoyed" by being stared at as he entered Lady Blessington's hotel.
[158] Cf. *The Idler* (*HVSV*, p. 357).

legal right to be my companion, and who, wanting that right, is placed in a position humiliating to her and most painful to me. Were the Contessa Guiccioli and I married, we should, I am sure, be cited as an <u>example of conjugal happiness,[159] and the domestic and retired life we lead would entitle us to respect;</u> but our union, wanting the legal and religious part of the ceremony of marriage, draws on us both censure and blame. She is formed to make a good wife to any man to whom she attached herself. She is fond of retirement—is of a most affectionate disposition—and noble-minded and disinterested to the highest degree. Judge then how mortifying it must be to me to be the cause of placing her in a false position. All this is not thought of when people are blinded by passion, but when passion is replaced by better feelings—those of affection, friendship, and confidence—when, in short, the *liaison* has all of marriage but its forms, then it is that we wish to give it the respectability of wedlock. It is painful (said Byron) to find oneself growing old without—

> that which should accompany old age,
> As honour, love, obedience, troops of friends.

I feel this keenly, reckless as I appear, though there are few to whom I would avow it, and certainly not to a man."

"With all my faults," said Byron one day, "and they are, as you will readily believe, innumerable, I have never traduced the only two women with whom I was ever domesticated, Lady Byron and the Contessa Guiccioli. Though I have had, God knows, reason to complain of Lady Byron's leaving me, and all that her desertion entailed, I defy malice itself to prove that I ever spoke against her;[160] on the contrary, I have always given her credit for the many excellent and amiable qualities she possesses, or at least possessed, when I knew her; and I have only to regret that forgiveness, for real, or imagined, wrongs, was not amongst their number. Of the Guiccioli, I could not, if I would, speak ill; her conduct towards me

[159] Teresa Guiccioli: God bless him!
[160] This was settled policy with Byron: at the time of the separation he secured written statements from Lord Holland, Kinnaird, and Samuel Rogers, certifying that he had never spoken ill of Lady Byron. But Lady Blessington told Crabb Robinson, in 1832: "Byron spared no one, mother, wife, or friend" (*HVSV*, p. 372).

74

has been faultless, and there are few examples of such complete and disinterested affection as she has shown towards me all through our attachment."

I observed in Lord Byron a candour in talking of his own defects, nay, a seeming pleasure in dwelling on them, that I never remarked in any other person: I told him this one day, and he answered, "Well, does not that give you hopes of my amendment?" My reply was, "No; I fear, by continually recapitulating them, you will get so accustomed to their existence, as to conquer your disgust of them. You remind me of Belcour, in the 'West Indian,' when he exclaims, 'No one sins with more repentance, or repents with less amendment than I do.'"[161] He laughed, and said, "Well, only wait, and you will see me one day become all that I ought to be; I am determined to *leave* my sins, and not wait until *they* leave me: I have reflected seriously on all my faults, and that is the first step towards amendment. Nay, I have made more progress than people give me credit for; but, the truth is, I have such a detestation of cant, and am so fearful of being suspected of yielding to its outcry, that I make myself appear rather *worse* than better than I am."[162]

"You will believe me, what I sometimes believe myself, mad," said Byron one day, "when I tell you that I seem to have *two* states of existence, *one* purely contemplative, during which the crimes, faults, and follies of mankind are laid open to my view, (my own forming a prominent object in the picture,) and the other *active*, when I play my part in the drama of life, as if impelled by some power over which I have no control, though the consciousness of doing wrong remains. It is as though I had the faculty of discovering error, without the power of avoiding it. How do you account for this?" I answered, "That, like all the phenomena of thought, it

[161] Cf. Lady Blessington in *Sketches and Fragments*, a little essay entitled "Self-correction," p. 131: "Every one who has reflected on his own errors, and the difficulty of correcting them, will be ready to exclaim with Belcour in the *West Indian*: 'No one sins with more repentance, or repents with less amendment.' It has often been urged, that when a person becomes truly sensible of his errors he can correct them, but this is a very doubtful point." Both passages are slightly misquoted from Richard Cumberland's *West Indian*, III, iii.

[162] Lady Blessington's analysis of Byron's personality is generally similar to Moore's; see *HVSV*, pp. 240-43, which discusses the contradictory elements in Byron, the consequent difficulty of defining his nature, his mobility, his self-defamation, his occasional persuasion of a tendency to madness, his mystifications, the abandon with which he conversed, his inability to conceal or retain.

75

was unaccountable; but that contemplation, when too much indulged, often produced the same effect on the mental faculties that the dwelling on bodily ailments effected in the physical powers—we might become so well acquainted with diseases, as to find all their symptoms in ourselves and others, without the power of preventing or curing them; nay, by the force of imagination, might end in the belief that we were afflicted with them to such a degree as to lose all enjoyment of life, which state is termed hypochondria; but the hypochondria which arises from the belief in mental diseases is still more insupportable, and is increased by contemplation of the supposed crimes or faults, so that the mind should be often relaxed from its extreme tension, and other and less exciting subjects of reflection presented to it. Excess in thinking, like all other excesses, produces re-action, and add the two words 'too much' before the word thinking, in the two lines of the admirable parody of the brothers Smith—

Thinking is but an idle waste of thought,
And nought is every thing, and every thing is nought;

and, instead of parody, it becomes true philosophy."

We both laughed at the abstract subject we had fallen upon; and Byron remarked, "How few would guess the general topics that occupy our conversation!" I added, "It may not, perhaps, be very amusing, but at all events it is better than scandal." He shook his head, and said, "All subjects are good in their way, provided they are sufficiently diversified; but scandal has something so piquant,—it is a sort of cayenne to the mind,—that I confess I like it, particularly if the objects are one's particular friends."

"Of course you know Luttrell," said Lord Byron. "He is a most agreeable member of society, the best sayer of good things, and the most epigrammatic conversationist I ever met: there is a terseness, and wit, mingled with fancy, in his observations, that no one else possesses, and no one so peculiarly understands the *apropos*. His 'Advice to Julia' is pointed, witty, and full of observation, showing in every line a knowledge of society, and a tact rarely met with. Then, unlike all, or most other wits, Luttrell is never obtrusive, even the choicest *bons mots* are only brought forth

76

when perfectly applicable, and then are given in a tone of good breeding which enhances their value."[163]

"Moore is very sparkling in a choice or chosen society (said Byron); with lord and lady listeners he shines like a diamond, and thinks that, like that precious stone, his brilliancy should be reserved *pour le beau monde*. Moore has a happy disposition, his temper is good, and he has a sort of fire-fly imagination, always in movement, and in each evolution displaying new brilliancy. He has not done justice to himself in living so much in society; much of his talents are frittered away in display, to support the character of 'a man of wit about town,' and Moore was meant for something better.[164] Society and genius are incompatible, and the latter can rarely, if ever, be in close or frequent contact with the former, without degenerating: it is otherwise with wit and talent, which are excited and brought into play by the friction of society, which polishes and sharpens both. I judge from personal experience; and as some portion of genius has been attributed to me, I suppose I may, without any extraordinary vanity, quote my ideas on this subject. Well, then, (continued Byron,) if I have any genius, (which I grant is problematical,) all I can say is, that I have always found it fade

[163] Henry Luttrell was an old friend of both Byron and Lady Blessington. On his conversational powers, see *LJ*, V, 81, n. 4. D'Orsay sketched him in 1828. Byron found his *Advice to Julia* "very good indeed" (Moore, *Life*, p. 455).

[164] Cf. *The Idler* (*HVSV*, p. 364). The root of the malice directed here against Moore is undoubtedly to be understood chiefly in terms of the revelations recorded by Crabb Robinson in 1832: "Lady Blessington threatens to expose [Moore], which she could do by repeating Lord Byron's contemptuous words and epigrams against him. One she repeated. Lord Byron used to say: "Tommy makes pretty *sweet* verses—sweet indeed, no wonder—he was fed on plums and sugar-candy by his father, the Dublin grocer'" (*HVSV*, p. 371; see the introduction to the present volume). The only other persons who report Byron's conversational attacks on Moore are Leigh Hunt, Medwin, and Hobhouse, who recorded his dislike (and by implication, his jealousy) of Moore as early as 1814 (*HVSV*, pp. 77-78): "I was abusive of Tom Moore, which I always am before Byron and when a little elevated—whence I hardly know. Byron let out to Kinnaird that he was only laughing at Moore in his last dedication to him [that of *The Corsair*]." For other attacks on Moore recorded by Hobhouse, see *HVSV*, pp. 214-15, 314, 548, 619, n. 74. Hobhouse undoubtedly encouraged Byron in this vein. For Medwin's unsatisfactory relations with Moore, see my *Captain Medwin*; and on Byron, Hunt, and Moore, see Marchand, p. 1026, and *Leigh Hunt's Literary Criticism*, ed. Lawrence H. and Carolyn W. Houtchens (New York, 1956), pp. 334-37.

away, like snow before the sun, when I have been living much in the world. My ideas became dispersed and vague, I lost the power of concentrating my thoughts, and became another being: you will perhaps think a better, on the principle that any change in me must be for the better; but no—instead of this, I became worse, for the recollection of former mental power remained, reproaching me with present inability, and increased the natural irritability of my nature. It must be this consciousness of diminished power that renders old people peevish, and, I suspect, the peevishness will be in proportion to former ability. Those who have once accustomed themselves to think and reflect deeply in solitude, will soon begin to find society irksome; the small money of conversation will appear insignificant, after the weighty metal of thought to which they have been used, and like the man who was exposed to the evils of poverty while in possession of one of the largest diamonds in the world, which, from its size, could find no purchaser, such a man will find himself in society unable to change his lofty and profound thoughts into the conventional small-talk of those who surround him. But, bless me, how I have been holding forth! (said Byron.) Madame de Staël herself never declaimed more energetically, or succeeded better, in *ennuyant* her auditors than I have done, as I perceive you look dreadfully bored. I fear I am grown a sad proser, which is a bad thing, more especially after having been, what I swear to you I once heard a lady call me, a sad poet. The whole of my tirade might have been comprised in the simple statement of my belief that genius shuns society, and that, except for the indulgence of vanity, society would be well disposed to return the compliment, as they have little in common between them.

"Who would willingly possess genius? None, I am persuaded, who knew the misery it entails, its temperament producing continual irritation, destructive alike to health and happiness—and what are its advantages?—to be envied, hated, and persecuted in life, and libelled in death. Wealth may be pardoned (continued Byron), if its possessor diffuses it liberally; beauty may be forgiven provided it is accompanied by folly; talent may meet with toleration if it be not of a very superior order,[165] but genius can hope for no mercy. If

[165] Cf. Lady Blessington's "Night Thought Book": "Talent, like beauty, to

78

it be of a stamp that insures its currency, those who are compelled
to receive it will indemnify themselves by finding out a thousand
imperfections in the owner, and as they cannot approach his elevation, will endeavour to reduce him to their level by dwelling on
the errors from which genius is not exempt, and which forms the
only point of resemblance between them. We hear the errors of men
of genius continually brought forward, while those that belong to
mediocrity are unnoticed; hence people conclude that errors peculiarly appertain to genius, and that those who boast it not, are
saved from them. Happy delusion! but not even this belief can
induce them to commiserate the faults they condemn. It is the fate
of genius to be viewed with severity instead of the indulgence
that it ought to meet, from the gratification it dispenses to others;
as if its endowments could preserve the possessor from the alloy
that marks the nature of mankind. Who can walk the earth, with
eyes fixed on the heavens, without often stumbling over the
hinderances that intercept the path? while those who are intent only
on the beaten road escape. Such is the fate of men of genius: elevated over the herd of their fellow-men, with thoughts that soar
above the sphere of their physical existence, no wonder that they
stumble when treading the mazes of ordinary life, with irritated
sensibility, and mistaken views of all the common occurrences
they encounter."

Lord Byron dined with us to-day: we all observed that he was evidently discomposed: the dinner and servants had no sooner disappeared, than he quoted an attack against himself in some newspaper as the cause.[166] He was very much irritated—much more so
than the subject merited,—and showed how keenly alive he is to
censure, though he takes so little pains to avoid exciting it. This is a
strange anomaly that I have observed in Byron,—an extreme susceptibility to censorious observations, and a want of tact in not
knowing how to steer clear of giving cause to them, that is
extraordinary. He winces under castigation, and writhes in agony

be pardoned, must be obscure and unostentatious" (Madden, I, 237). Much
of the paragraph is Blessingtonian.
  [166] *The Idler* refers twice to Byron's sensitivity to newspaper attacks, April
17 and May 4, 1823, both revelations made, supposedly, when Byron and
Lady Blessington were riding together, not dining (*HVSV*, pp. 359, 365).

under the infliction of ridicule, yet gives rise to attack every day. Ridicule is, however, the weapon he most dreads, perhaps because it is the one he wields with most power; and I observe he is sensitively alive to its slightest approach. It is also the weapon with which he assails all; friend and foe alike come under its cutting point; and the laugh, which accompanies each sally, as a deadly incision is made in some vulnerable quarter, so little accords with the wound inflicted, that it is as though one were struck down by summer lightning while admiring its brilliant play.

Byron likes not contradiction: he waxed wroth to-day, because I defended a friend of mine whom he attacked, but ended by taking my hand, and saying he honoured me for the warmth with which I defended an absent friend, adding with irony, "Moreover, when he is not a poet, or even prose writer, by whom you can hope to be repaid by being handed down to posterity as his defender."

"I often think," said Byron, "that I inherit my violence and bad temper from my poor mother—not that my father, from all I could ever learn, had a much better; so that it is no wonder I have such a very bad one. As long as I can remember anything, I recollect being subject to violent paroxysms of rage,[167] so disproportioned to the cause, as to surprise me when they were over, and this still continues. I cannot coolly view anything that excites my feelings; and once the lurking devil in me is roused, I lose all command of myself. I do not recover a good fit of rage for days after: mind, I do not by this mean that the ill-humour continues, as, on the contrary, that quickly subsides, exhausted by its own violence; but it shakes me terribly, and leaves me low and nervous after. Depend on it, people's tempers must be corrected while they are children; for not all the good resolutions in the world can enable a man to conquer habits of ill-humour or rage, however he may regret having given way to them. My poor mother was generally in a rage every day, and used to render me sometimes almost frantic; particularly when, in her passion, she reproached me with my personal deformity, I have left her presence to rush into solitude, where, unseen, I could vent the rage and mortification I endured, and curse the deformity that I now began to consider as a signal mark of the

167 On Byron's childhood fits of rage, see Moore, *Life*, pp. 5, 13; Medwin, *Conversations*, p. 62.

injustice of Providence. Those were bitter moments: even now, the impression of them is vivid in my mind; and they cankered a heart that I believe was naturally affectionate, and destroyed a temper always disposed to be violent. It was my feelings at this period that suggested the idea of 'The Deformed Transformed.'[168] I often look back on the days of my childhood, and am astonished at the recollection of the intensity of my feelings at that period;—first impressions are indelible. My poor mother, and after her my schoolfellows, by their taunts, led me to consider my lameness as the greatest misfortune, and I have never been able to conquer this feeling. It requires great natural goodness of disposition, as well as reflection, to conquer the corroding bitterness that deformity engenders in the mind, and which, while preying on itself, sours one towards all the world. I have read, that where personal deformity exists, it may be always traced in the face, however handsome the face may be. I am sure that what is meant by this is, that the consciousness of it gives to the countenance an habitual expression of discontent, which I believe is the case; yet it is too bad (added Byron with bitterness) that, because one had a defective foot, one cannot have a perfect face."[169]

He indulges a morbid feeling on this subject that is extraordinary, and that leads me to think it has had a powerful effect in forming his character. As Byron had said that his own position had led to his writing "The Deformed Transformed," I ventured to remind him that, in the advertisement to that drama, he had stated it to have been founded on the novel of "The Three Brothers." He said that both statements were correct, and then changed the subject,[170] without giving me an opportunity of questioning him on the unacknowledged, but visible, resemblances between other of his works and that extraordinary production. It is possible that he is unconscious of the plagiary of ideas he has committed; for his reading is so desultory, that he seizes thoughts which, in passing through the glowing alembic of his mind, become so embellished as

[168] Moore also associates Mrs. Byron's taunting references to her son's lameness and the inception of *The Deformed Transformed*, quoting the famous opening lines (*Life*, p. 13).

[169] It seems doubtful that Byron discussed his lameness with Lady Blessington.

[170] The Advertisement accompanying the play states that it was "founded partly" on the novel.

to lose all identity with the original crude embryos he had adopted. This was proved to me in another instance, when a book that he was constantly in the habit of looking over fell into my hands, and I traced various passages marked by his pencil or by his notes, which gave me the idea of having led to certain trains of thought in his works.[171] He told me that he rarely ever read a page that did not give rise to chains of thought, the first idea serving as the original link on which the others were formed,—[172]

> Awake but one, and lo! what myriads rise.

I have observed, that, in conversation, some trifling remark has often led him into long disquisitions, evidently elicited by it; and so prolific is his imagination, that the slightest spark can warm it.

Comte Pietro Gamba lent me the "Age of Bronze," with a request that his having done so should be kept a profound secret, as Lord Byron, he said, would be angry if he knew it. This is another instance of the love of mystification that marks Byron, in trifles as well as in things of more importance. What can be the motive for concealing a *published* book, that is in the hands of all England?[173]

Byron talks often of Napoleon, of whom he is a great admirer,[174] and says that what he most likes in his character was his want of sympathy, which proved his knowledge of human nature, as those only could possess sympathy who were in happy ignorance of it. I told him that this carried its own punishment with it, as Napoleon found the want of sympathy when he most required it, and that some portion of what he affected to despise, namely, enthusiasm and sympathy, would have saved him from the degradations he twice underwent when deserted by those on whom he counted. Not all Byron's expressed contempt for mankind can induce me to believe that he has the feeling; this is one of the many little artifices which he condescends to make use of to excite surprise in his

---

[171] Cf. Moore, *Life*, pp. 420-21, where the phrasing is similar: "train of thoughts."

[172] With this account of Byron's reading, compare the similar account in *The Idler*, May 13, 1823 (*HVSV*, p. 367).

[173] See the account of the same episode in *The Idler*, May 1, 1823 (*HVSV*, pp. 362-63).

[174] Byron's well-known admiration for Napoleon was described by Medwin, among others. See also *HVSV*. Lady Blessington and D'Orsay were strong Bonapartists.

hearers, and can only impose on the credulous. He is vexed when he discovers that any of his little *ruses* have not succeeded, and is like a spoiled child who finds out he cannot have everything his own way. Were he but sensible of his own powers, how infinitely superior would he be, for he would see the uselessness, as well as unworthiness, of being artificial, and of acting to support the character he wishes to play,—a misanthrope, which nature never intended him for, and which he is not and never will be. I see a thousand instances of good feeling in Byron, but rarely a single proof of stability; his abuse of friends, which is continual, has always appeared to me more inconsistent than ill-natured, and as if indulged in more to prove that he was superior to the partiality friendship engenders, than that they were unworthy of exciting the sentiment. He has the rage of displaying his knowledge of human nature, and thinks this knowledge more proved by pointing out the blemishes than the perfections of the subjects he anatomizes. Were he to confide in the effect his own natural character would produce, how much more would he be loved and respected; whereas, at present, those who most admire the genius will be the most disappointed in the man. The love of mystification is so strong in Byron, that he is continually letting drop mysterious hints of events in his past life: as if to excite curiosity, he assumes, on those occasions, a look and air suited to the insinuation conveyed: if it has excited the curiosity of his hearers, he is satisfied, looks still more mysterious, and changes the subject; but if it fails to rouse curiosity, he becomes evidently discomposed and sulky, stealing sly glances at the person he has been endeavouring to mystify, to observe the effect he has produced. On such occasions I have looked at him a little maliciously, and laughed, without asking a single question; and I have often succeeded in making him laugh too at those mystifications, *manquée* as I called them.[175] Byron often talks of the authors of the "Rejected Addresses," and always in terms of unqualified praise. He says that the imitations, unlike all other imitations, are full of genius, and that the "Cui Bono" has some lines that he should wish to have written. "Parodies," he said, "always gave a bad impression of the original, but in the 'Rejected Addresses' the reverse was

[175] These remarks on "mystification" may have been inspired by a paragraph in Moore's *Life*: see *HVSV*, p. 241.

the fact;" and he quoted the second and third stanzas, in imitation of himself, as admirable, and just what he could have wished to write on a similar subject.[176] His memory is extraordinary,[177] for he can repeat lines from every author whose works have pleased him; and in reciting the passages that have called forth his censure or ridicule, it is no less tenacious. He observed on the pleasure he felt at meeting people with whom he could go over old subjects of interest, whether on persons or literature, and said that nothing cemented friendship or companionship so strongly as having read the same books and known the same people.

I observed that when, in our rides, we came to any fine point of view, Byron paused, and looked at it, as if to impress himself with the recollection of it. He rarely praised what so evidently pleased him, and he became silent and abstracted for some time after, as if he was noting the principal features of the scene on the tablet of his memory.[178] He told me that, from his earliest youth, he had a passion for solitude; that the sea, whether in a storm or calm, was a source of deep interest to him, and filled his mind with thoughts. "An acquaintance of mine," said Byron, laughing, "who is a votary of the lake, or simple school, and to whom I once expressed this effect of the sea on me, said that I might in this case say that the ocean served me as a vast inkstand: what do you think of that as a poetical image? It reminds me of a man who, talking of the effect of Mont Blanc from a distant mountain, said that it reminded him of a giant at his toilet, the feet in water, and the face prepared for the operation of shaving.[179] Such observations prove that from the sublime to the ridiculous there is only one step, and really makes one disgusted with the simple school." Recurring to fine scenery, Byron remarked, "That as artists filled their sketch-books with studies from Nature, to be made use of on after-occasions, so he

[176] James Smith, with his brother Horace, author of *Rejected Addresses*, was a friend of both Byron and Lady Blessington. For James Smith on Byron, see *HVSV*, pp. 62, 69, 132-34; for Byron's admiration of *Rejected Addresses*, see *LJ*, II, 177, 187, the earlier letter published by Moore. Lady Blessington knew James Smith at least as early as 1831 (Connely, *Count D'Orsay*, p. 178).

[177] On Byron's memory, see Medwin, *Conversations*, pp. 154, 265.

[178] Contrast Byron's reaction as described in *The Idler*, May 10, 1823 (*HVSV*, pp. 356-57), when he attacked "the cant of the love of nature."

[179] Cf. Byron as reported by John Galt, *Life of Byron*, p. 269: "Hunt . . . has no perception of the sublimity of Alpine scenery; he calls a mountain a great imposter."

laid up a collection of images in his mind, as a store to draw on when he required them, and he found the pictures much more vivid in recollection, when he had not exhausted his admiration in expressions, but concentrated his powers in fixing them in memory. The end and aim of his life is to render himself celebrated: hitherto his pen has been the instrument to cut his road to renown, and it has traced a brilliant path; this, he thinks, has lost some of its point, and he is about to change it for the sword, to carve a new road to fame. Military exploits occupy much of his conversation, and still more of his attention; but even on this subject there is never the slightest *élan*, and it appears extraordinary to see a man about to engage in a chivalrous, and, according to the opinion of many, a Utopian undertaking, for which his habits peculiarly unfit him, without any indication of the enthusiasm that lead men to embark in such careers.[180] Perhaps he thinks with Napoleon, that "Il n'y a rien qui refroidit, comme l'énthousiasme des autres;" but he is wrong—coldness has in general a sympathetic effect, and we are less disposed to share the feelings of others, if we observe that those feelings are not as warm as the occasion seems to require.

There is something so exciting in the idea of the greatest poet of his day sacrificing his fortune, his occupations, his enjoyments,—in short, offering up on the altar of Liberty all the immense advantages which station, fortune, and genius can bestow, that it is impossible to reflect on it without admiration; but when one hears this same person calmly talk of the worthlessness of the people he proposes to make those sacrifices for,[181] the loans he means to advance, the uniforms he intends to wear, entering into petty details, and always with perfect *sang froid*, one's admiration evaporates, and the action loses all its charms, though the real merit of it still remains. Perhaps Byron wishes to show that his going to Greece is more an affair of *principle* than *feeling*, and as such, more entitled to respect, though perhaps less likely to excite warmer feelings. However this may be, his whole manner and conversation on the

[180] George Finlay, Leicester Stanhope, and others observed this trait in Byron (see *HVSV*, p. 457 and n.).

[181] Byron attacked the modern Greek character in conversation with Thomas Medwin, Thomas Smith, James Kennedy, George Finlay, Julius Millingen, William Parry, and James Hamilton Browne (see *HVSV*, pp. 276; 413; 426-27, 453, 471-72; 457, 553, 555-56; 463-65; 517; 598-99).

subject are calculated to chill the admiration such an enterprise ought to create, and to reduce it to a more ordinary standard.

Byron is evidently in delicate health, brought on by starvation, and a mind too powerful for the frame in which it is lodged. He is obstinate in resisting the advice of medical men[182] and his friends, who all have represented to him the dangerous effects likely to ensue from his present system. He declares that he has no choice but that of sacrificing the body to the mind, as that when he eats as others do he gets ill, and loses all power over his intellectual faculties; that animal food engenders the appetite of the animal fed upon, and he instances the manner in which boxers are fed as a proof, while, on the contrary, a regime of fish and vegetables served to support existence without pampering it. I affected to think that his excellence in, and fondness of, swimming, arose from his continually living on fish, and he appeared disposed to admit the possibility, until, being no longer able to support my gravity, I laughed aloud, which for the first minute discomposed him, though he ended by joining heartily in the laugh, and said,—"Well, Miladi, after this hoax, never accuse me any more of mystifying; you did take me in until you laughed." Nothing gratifies him so much as being told that he grows thin. This fancy of his is pushed to an almost childish extent; and he frequently asks—"Don't you think I get thinner?" or "Did you ever see any person so thin as I am, who was not ill?" He says he is sure no one could recollect him were he to go to England at present, and seems to enjoy this thought very much.

Byron affects a perfect indifference to the opinion of the world, yet is more influenced by it than most people,—not in his conduct, but in his dread of, and wincing under its censures. He was extremely agitated by his name being introduced in the P[ortsmouth] trial, as having assisted in making up the match, and showed a degree of irritation that proves he is as susceptible as ever to newspaper attacks, notwithstanding his boasts of the contrary.[183] This

[182] Lady Blessington had discussed Byron with his physician (see Mrs. Moore, p. 486).
[183] Lady Blessington read Byron's account of the Portsmouth trial in his letter of March 28, 1823, where he denied any liaison with Lord Portsmouth's bride, but he told Hobhouse that at the ceremony he "laughed all the time, and gave her left hand away" and told Lady Byron that when he led the bride

susceptibility will always leave him at the <u>mercy</u> of all who may choose to write against him,[184] however insignificant they may be.

I noticed Byron one day more than usually irritable, though he endeavoured to suppress all symptoms of it. After various sarcasms on the cant and hypocrisy of the times, which was always the signal that he was suffering from some attack made on him, he burst forth in violent invectives against America, and said that she now rivalled her mother country in cant, as he had that morning read an article of abuse, copied from an American newspaper, alluding to a report that he was going to reside there. We had seen the article, and hoped that it might have escaped his notice, but unfortunately he had perused it, and its effects on his temper were visible for several days after. He said that he was never sincere in his praises of the Americans, and that he only extolled their navy to pique Mr. Croker.[185] There was something so childish in this avowal, that there was no keeping a serious face on hearing it; and Byron smiled himself, like a petulant spoiled child, who acknowledges having done something to spite a playfellow.

Byron is a great admirer of the poetry of Barry Cornwall, which, he says, is full of imagination and beauty, possessing a refinement and delicacy, that, whilst they add all the charms of a woman's mind, take off none of the force of a man's. He expressed his hope that he would devote himself to tragedy, saying that he was sure he would become one of the first writers of the day.[186]

---

to the altar he "reminded her of his seduction of her" (*HVSV*, pp. 76-77, 619, n. 74). The bride was the daughter of Hanson, Byron's solicitor. Portsmouth was judged insane.

[184] Teresa Guiccioli: false.

[185] Lady Blessington read Byron's praise of the American Navy, following his visit onboard one of the ships in the Mediterranean fleet, in his letter to Murray, May 26, 1822 (Moore, *Life*, p. 559). John Wilson Croker, Secretary to the Admiralty for many years, was also one of Murray's "Elect," and Byron knew that his letter would be read aloud in Albemarle Street and so come sooner or later to the ears of Croker, who did not like Byron. In early 1816 Byron wrote a satiric poem on Croker, which he destroyed, but the *Morning Chronicle* announced its forthcoming publication, and Croker probably saw the announcement (Moore, *Life*, p. 343). He was an early acquaintance of Lord Blessington, knew Lady Blessington as early as 1820 (Madden, I, 259).

[186] "Barry Cornwall," who wrote the English epitaph on Lady Blessington's tomb, was on intimate terms with her as early as January 1833, and very probably knew her earlier, when she was writing her *Conversations*. Byron was not

Talking of marriage, Byron said that there was no real happiness out of its pale. "If people like each other so well," said he, "as not to be able to live asunder, this is the only tie that can ensure happiness—all others entail misery. I put religion and morals out of the question, though of course the misery will be increased tenfold by the influence of both; but admitting persons to have neither (and many such are, by the good-natured world, supposed to exist), still *liaisons*, that are not cemented by marriage, must produce unhappiness, when there is refinement of mind, and that honourable *fierté* which accompanies it. The humiliations and vexations a woman, under such circumstances, is exposed to, cannot fail to have a certain effect on her temper and spirits, which robs her of the charms that won affection; it renders her susceptible and suspicious; her self-esteem being diminished, she becomes doubly jealous of that of him for whom she lost it, and on whom she depends; and if he has feeling to conciliate her, he must submit to a slavery much more severe than that of marriage, without its respectability.[187] Women become *exigeante* always in proportion to their consciousness of a decrease in the attentions they desire; and this very *exigence* accelerates the flight of the blind god, whose approaches, the Greek proverb says, are always made walking, but whose retreat is flying. I once wrote some lines expressive of my feelings on this subject, and you shall have them." He had no sooner repeated the first line than I recollected having the verses in my possession, having been allowed to copy them by Mr. D. Kinnaird the day he received them from Lord Byron.[188] The following are the verses:—

in the habit of praising Bryan Waller Procter's work as enthusiastically as Lady Blessington reports his doing. See *LJ*, V, 37-38, 117, 362; however, Lady Blessington had also read in Moore's *Life* Byron's quietly complimentary remarks in his letter to Murray, January 4, 1821 (*LJ*, V, 217): "I think him very likely to produce a good tragedy, if he keep to a natural style . . ." Procter contributed to Lady Blessington's *Book of Beauty*.

[187] Lady Blessington could speak with authority on the unhappiness of a woman placed in a false position.

[188] The lines cannot be "identical with the 'mere verses of society,' mentioned in the letter to Murray of May 8, 1820," as E. H. Coleridge states (*Poetry*, IV, 549, n. 1), for Byron clearly identifies these as his "Stanzas to the Po," which he did send to Kinnaird (*LJ*, V, 21). E. H. Coleridge prints variant readings from the "MS. Guiccioli." There are differences between all three versions. Did Charles F. Barry present Lady Blessington with a copy of the

Composed Dec. 1, 1819.

Could Love for ever
Run like a river,
And Time's endeavour
   Be tried in vain;
No other pleasure
With this could measure;
And as a treasure
   We'd hug the chain.
But since our sighing
Ends not in dying,
And, formed for flying,
   Love plumes his wing;
Then, for this reason,
Let's love a season;
But let that season be only Spring.

When lovers parted
Feel broken-hearted,
And, all hopes thwarted,
   Expect to die;
A few years older,
Ah! how much colder
They might behold her
   For whom they sigh.
When link'd together,
Through every weather,
We pluck Love's feather
   From out his wing,
He'll sadly shiver,
And droop for ever,
Without the plumage that sped his spring.
   [*or*
Shorn of the plumage which sped his spring.]

---

verses which she published when she returned to Genoa a few years later? At
that time, according to *The Idler* (*HVSV*, p. 370), he offered to her an unpublished "lampoon on a brother poet" written by Byron, which she says she
declined to accept. Kinnaird, who had died in 1830, was a warm and early
friend of Lady Blessington.

Like Chiefs of Faction
His life is action,—
A formal paction,
   Which curbs his reign,
Obscures his glory,
Despot no more, he
Such territory
   Quits with disdain.
Still, still advancing,
With banners glancing,
His power enhancing,
   He must march on:
Repose but cloys him,
Retreat destroys him;
Love brooks not a degraded throne!

Wait not, fond lover!
Till years are over,
And then recover
   As from a dream;
While each bewailing
The other's failing,
With wrath and railing
   All hideous seem;
While first decreasing,
Yet not quite ceasing,
Pause not till teazing
   All passion blight:
If once diminish'd,
His reign is finish'd,—
One last embrace then, and bid good night!

So shall Affection
To recollection
The dear connexion
   Bring back with joy;
You have not waited
Till, tired and hated,
All passion sated,
   Began to cloy.

Your last embraces
Leave no cold traces,—
The same fond faces
  As through the past;
And eyes, the mirrors
Of your sweet errors,
Reflect but rapture; not least, though last!

True separations
Ask more than patience;
What desperations
  From such have risen!
And yet remaining
What is 't but chaining
Hearts which, once waning,
  Beat 'gainst their prison?
Time can but cloy love,
And use destroy love:
The winged boy, Love,
  Is but for boys;
You'll find it torture,
Though sharper, shorter,
To wean, and not wear out your joys.

They are so unworthy the author, that they are merely given as proof that the greatest genius can sometimes write bad verses; as even Homer nods. I remarked to Byron, that the sentiment of the poem differed with that which he had just given me of marriage: he laughed, and said, "Recollect, the lines were written nearly four years ago; and we grow wiser as we grow older: but mind, I still say, that I only approve marriage when the persons are so much attached as not to be able to live asunder, which ought always to be tried by a year's absence before the irrevocable knot was formed. The truest picture of the misery unhallowed *liaisons* produce," said Byron, "is in the 'Adolphe' of Benjamin Constant. I told Madame de Staël that there was more *morale* in that book than in all she ever wrote; and that it ought always to be given to every young woman who had read 'Corinne,' as an antidote.[189] Poor De Staël!

[189] Byron sent a copy of *Adolphe* to Lady Blessington and wrote her that

she came down upon me like an avalanche, whenever I told her any of my amiable truths, sweeping every thing before her, with that eloquence that always overwhelmed, but never convinced. She however, good soul, believed she had convinced, whenever she silenced an opponent; an effect she generally produced, as she, to use an Irish phrase, succeeded in *bothering*, and producing a confusion of ideas that left one little able or willing to continue an argument with her. I liked her daughter very much,"[190] said Byron: "I wonder will she turn out literary?—at all events, though she may not write, she possesses the power of judging the writings of others; is highly educated and clever; but I thought a little given to systems, which is not in general the fault of young women, and, above all, young French women."

One day that Byron dined with us, his chasseur, while we were at table, demanded to speak with him: he left the room, and returned in a few minutes in a state of violent agitation, pale with anger, and looking as I had never before seen him look, though I had often seen him angry. He told us that his servant had come to tell him that he must pass the gate of Genoa (his house being outside the town) before half-past ten o'clock, as orders were given that no one was to be allowed to pass after. This order, which had no personal reference to him, he conceived to be expressly levelled at him, and it rendered him furious: he seized a pen, and commenced a letter to our minister,—tore two or three letters one after the other, before he had written one to his satisfaction; and, in short, betrayed such ungovernable rage, as to astonish all who were present:[191] he seemed very much disposed to enter into a personal contest with the authorities; and we had some difficulty in persuading him to leave the business wholly in the hands of Mr. Hill, the English Minister, who would arrange it much better.

Byron's appearance and conduct, on this occasion, forcibly reminded me of the description given of Rousseau: he declared himself the victim of persecution wherever he went; said that there

---

it contained "some melancholy truths" and that he had first read it "at the desire of Madame de Staël" (*LJ*, VI, 203-04).

[190] See Moore, *Life*, p. 321, n., which confirms the statement.

[191] Similar conduct on the part of Byron in Pisa was described by Medwin (*Conversations*, p. 150), when Byron saw a reprint of Southey's letter to the editor of the *Courier*.

was a confederacy between all governments to pursue and molest him, and uttered a thousand extravagances, which proved that he was no longer master of himself. I now understood how likely his manner was, under any violent excitement, to give rise to the idea that he was deranged in his intellects, and became convinced of the truth of the sentiment in the lines—

> Great wit to madness sure is near allied,
> And thin partitions do their bounds divide.

The next day, when we met, Byron said that he had received a satisfactory explanation from Mr. Hill, and then asked me if I had not thought him mad the night before:—"I assure you," said he, "I often think myself not in my right senses, and this is perhaps the only opinion I have in common with Lady Byron, who, dear sensible soul, not only thought me mad, but tried to persuade others into the same belief."

Talking one day on the difference between men's actions and thoughts, a subject to which he often referred, he observed, that it frequently happened that a man who was capable of superior powers of reflection and reasoning when alone, was trifling and commonplace in society. "On this point," said he, "I speak feelingly, for I have remarked it of myself, and have often longed to know if other people had the same defect, or the same consciousness of it, which is, that while in solitude my mind was occupied in serious and elevated reflections, in society it sinks into a trifling levity of tone, that in another would have called forth my disapprobation and disgust. Another defect of mine is, that I am so little fastidious in the selection, or rather want of selection, of associates, that the most stupid men satisfy me quite as well, nay, perhaps better than the most brilliant; and yet all the time they are with me I feel, even while descending to their level, that they are unworthy of me, and what is worse, that we seem in point of conversation so nearly on an equality, that the effort of letting myself down to them costs me nothing, though my pride is hurt that they do not seem more sensible of the condescension. When I have sought what is called good society, it was more from a sense of propriety and keeping my station in the world, than from any pleasure it gave me, for I have been always disappointed, even in the most brilliant and clever of my acquaintances, by discovering some trait of egoism, or futility, that I was too egoistical and futile to pardon, as I find that we are least disposed to overlook the defects we are most prone to. Do you think as I do on this point?" said Byron. I answered, "That as a clear and spotless mirror reflects the brightest images, so is goodness ever most prone to see good in others; and as a sullied mirror shows its own defects in all that it reflects, so does an impure mind tinge all that passes through it." Byron laughingly said, "That thought of yours is pretty, and just, which all pretty thoughts are not, and I shall pop it into my next poem. But how do you account for this tendency of mine to trifling and levity in conversations, when in solitude my mind is really occupied in serious reflections?" I answered, "That this was the very cause—the bow cannot remain always bent; the thoughts suggested to him in society were the re-action of a mind strained to its bent, and reposing itself after exertion; as also that feeling the inferiority of the persons he mixed with, the great powers were not excited, but lay dormant and supine, collecting their force for solitude." This opinion pleased him, and when I added that great writers were rarely good talkers, and *vice versâ*, he was still more gratified. He said that he disliked every-day topics of conversation; he thought it a waste of time; but that if he met a person with whom he could, as he said, think aloud, and give utterance to his thoughts on abstract subjects, he was sure it would excite the energies of his mind, and awaken sleeping thoughts that he wanted to be stirred up. "I like to go home with a new idea," said Byron; "it sets my mind to work; I enlarge it, and it often gives birth to many others; this one can only do in a *tête-à-tête*. I felt the advantage of this in my rides with Hoppner at Venice;[192] he was a good listener, and his remarks were acute and original; he is besides a thoroughly good man, and I knew he was in earnest when he gave me his opinions. But conversation, such as one finds in society, and, above all, in English society, is as uninteresting as it is artificial, and few can leave the best with the consolation of carrying away with him a new thought, or of leaving behind him an old friend." Here he laughed at his own antithesis, and added, "By Jove, it is true; you know how people abuse or

[192] Cf. Hoppner's account in Moore, *Life*, p. 373.

quiz each other in England, the moment one is absent: each is afraid
to go away before the other, knowing that, as is said in the 'School
for Scandal,' he leaves his character behind.[193] It is this certainty
that excuses me to myself, for abusing my friends and acquaintances
in their absence. I was once accused of this by an *ami intime*, to
whom some devilish good-natured person had repeated what I
had said of him; I had nothing for it but to plead guilty, adding,
'you know you have done the same by me fifty times, and yet you
see I never was affronted, or liked you less for it;' on which he
laughed, and we were as good friends as ever. Mind you (a favourite phrase of Byron's) I never heard that he had abused me, but
I took it for granted, and was right. So much for friends."

I remarked to Byron that his scepticism as to the sincerity and
durability of friendship argued very much against his capability of
feeling the sentiment, especially as he admitted that he had not
been deceived by the *few* he had confided in, consequently his opinion must be founded on *self*-knowledge. This amused him, and he
said that he verily believed that his knowledge of human nature,
on which he had hitherto prided himself, was the criterion by which
I judged so unfavourably of him, as he was sure I attributed his
bad opinion of mankind to his perfect knowledge of *self*. When in
good spirits, he liked badinage very much, and nothing seemed to
please him more than being considered as a *mauvais sujet*: he disclaimed the being so with an air that showed he was far from being
offended at the suspicion. Of love he had strange notions: he said
that most people had *le besoin d'aimer*, and that with this *besoin*
the first person who fell in one's way contented one. He maintained
that those who possessed the most imagination, poets for example,
were most likely to be constant in their attachments, as with the
beau idéal in their heads, with which they identified the object of
their attachment, they had nothing to desire, and viewed their
mistresses through the brilliant medium of fancy, instead of the
common one of the eyes. "A poet, therefore," said Byron, "endows
the person he loves with all the charms with which his mind is
stored, and has no need of actual beauty to fill up the picture.
Hence he should select a woman who is rather good-looking than
beautiful, leaving the latter for those who, having no imagination,

[193] Sir Peter Teazle, II, ii.

require actual beauty to satisfy their tastes. And after all," said he, "where is the actual beauty that can come up to the bright 'imaginings' of the poet? where can one see women that equal the visions, half-mortal, half-angelic, that people his fancy? Love, who is painted blind (an allegory that proves the uselessness of beauty), can supply all deficiencies with his aid; we can invest her whom we admire with all the attributes of loveliness, and though time may steal the roses from her cheek, and the lustre from her eye, still the original *beau idéal*[194] remains, filling the mind and intoxicating the soul with the overpowering presence of loveliness. I flatter myself that my Leila, Zuleika, Gulnare, Medora, and Haidee will always vouch for my taste in beauty: these are the bright creations of my fancy, with rounded forms, and delicacy of limbs, nearly so incompatible as to be rarely, if ever, united; for where, with some rare exceptions, do we see roundness of *contour* accompanied by lightness, and those fairy hands and feet that are at once the type of beauty and refinement. I like to shut myself up, close my eyes, and fancy one of the creatures of my imagination, with taper and rose-tipped fingers, playing with my hair, touching my cheek, or resting its little snowy-dimpled hand on mine. I like to fancy the fairy foot, round and pulpy,[195] but small to diminutiveness, peeping from beneath the drapery that half conceals it, or moving in the mazes of the dance. I detest thin women;[196] and unfortunately all, or nearly all plump women, have clumsy hands and feet, so that I am obliged to have recourse to imagination for my beauties, and there I always find them. I can so well understand the lover leaving his mistress that he might write to her,—I should leave mine, not to write to, but to think of her, to dress her up in the habiliments of my ideal beauty, investing her with all the charms of the latter, and then adoring the idol I had formed. You must have observed that I give my heroines extreme refinement, joined to great simplicity and want of education. Now, refinement and want of education are incompatible, at least I have ever found them

194 Cf. Medwin, *Conversations*, p. 73, where the French phrase occurs in a similar context.

195 The diction at this point does not seem to be Byron's.

196 Cf. Byron to Medwin (*Conversations*, p. 216), on Lady Caroline Lamb's figure: "too thin to be good, and wanted that roundness which elegance and grace would vainly supply."

so: so here again, you see, I am forced to have recourse to imagination; and certainly it furnishes me with creatures as unlike the sophisticated beings of civilized existence, as they are to the still less tempting, coarse realities of vulgar life. In short, I am of opinion that poets do not require great beauty in the objects of their affection; all that is necessary for them is a strong and devoted attachment from the object, and where this exists, joined to health and good temper, little more is required, at least in early youth, though with advancing years men become more *exigeants*." Talking of the difference between love in early youth and in maturity, Byron said, "that, like the measles, love was most dangerous when it came late in life."

Byron had two points of ambition,—the one to be thought the greatest poet of his day, and the other a nobleman and man of fashion, who could have arrived at distinction without the aid of his poetical genius. This often produced curious anomalies in his conduct and sentiments, and a sort of jealousy of himself in each separate character, that was highly amusing to an observant spectator. If poets were talked of or eulogized, he referred to the advantages of rank and station as commanding that place in society by right, which was only accorded to genius by sufferance; for, said Byron, "Let authors do, say, or think what they please, they are never considered as men of fashion in the circles of *haut ton*, to which their literary reputations have given them an *entrée*, unless they happen to be of high birth. How many times have I observed this in London; as also the awkward efforts made by authors to trifle and act the fine gentleman like the rest of the herd in society. Then look at the *faiblesse* they betray in running after great people. Lords and ladies seem to possess, in their eyes, some power of attraction that I never could discover; and the eagerness with which they crowd to balls and assemblies, where they are as *déplacés* as *ennuyés*, all conversation at such places being out of the question, might lead one to think that they sought the heated atmospheres of such scenes as hot-beds to nurse their genius." If men of fashion were praised, Byron dwelt on the futility of their pursuits, their ignorance *en masse*, and the necessity of talents to give lustre to rank and station. In short, he seemed to think that the bays of the author ought to be entwined with a coronet to render either valuable, as,

97

singly, they were not sufficiently attractive; and this evidently arose from *his* uniting, in his own person, rank and genius. I recollect once laughingly telling him that he was fortunate in being able to consider himself a poet amongst lords, and a lord amongst poets. He seemed doubtful as to how he should take the parody, but ended by laughing also.

Byron has often laughed at some *repartie* or joke against himself, and, after a few minutes' reflection, got angry at it; but was always soon appeased by a civil apology, though it was clear that he disliked anything like ridicule, as do most people who are addicted to play it off on others; and he certainly delighted in quizzing and ridiculing his associates. The translation of his works into different languages, however it might have flattered his *amour propre* as an author, never failed to enrage him, from the injustice he considered all translations rendered to his works. I have seen him furious at some passages in the French translation, which he pointed out as proof of the impossibility of the translators understanding the original, and he exclaimed, "*Il traditore! Il traditore!*" (instead of *Il traduttore!*) vowing vengeance against the unhappy traducers as he called them.[197] He declared that every translation he had seen of his poems had so destroyed the sense, that he could not understand how the French and Italians could admire his works, as they professed to do. It proved, he said, at how low an ebb modern poetry must be in both countries. French poetry he detested, and continually ridiculed: he said it was discordant to his ears.

Of his own works, with some exceptions, he always spoke in derision, saying he could write much better, but that he wrote to suit the false taste of the day;[198] and that if now and then a gleam of true feeling or poetry was visible in his productions, it was sure to be followed by the ridicule he could not suppress. Byron was not sincere in this, and it was only said to excite surprise, and show his superiority over the rest of the world. It was this same desire

197 Cf. Byron to Medwin (*Conversations*, p. 161), on Taaffe's translation of Dante: "There's Taaffe is not satisfied with what Cary has done, but he must be *traducing* him too. . . . I have advised him to frontispiece his book with his own head, *Capo di Traditore*. . . ."

198 Cf. E. E. Williams reporting Byron, when Shelley had recited a stanza from *Childe Harold*: "Heavens! Shelley, what infinite nonsense are you quoting?" (*HVSV*, p. 283.) Byron's remarks in his letters on "the false taste of the day" are well known.

of astonishing people that led him to depreciate Shakspeare, which I have frequently heard him do, though from various reflections of his in conversation, and the general turn of his mind, I am convinced that he had not only deeply read, but deeply felt the beauties of our immortal poet.[199]

I do not recollect ever having met Byron that he did not, in some way or other, introduce the subject of Lady Byron. The impression left on my mind was, that she continually occupied his thoughts, and that he most anxiously desired a reconciliation with her. He declared that his marriage was free from every interested motive; and if not founded on love, as love is generally viewed, a wild, engrossing and ungovernable passion, there was quite sufficient liking in it to have insured happiness had his temper been better. He said that Lady Byron's appearance had pleased him from the first moment, and had always continued to please him; and that, had his pecuniary affairs been in a less ruinous state, his temper would not have been excited, as it daily, hourly was, during the brief period of their union, by the demands of insolent creditors whom he was unable to satisfy, and who drove him nearly out of his senses, until he lost all command of himself, and so forfeited Lady Byron's affection. "I must admit," said he, "that I could not have left a very agreeable impression on her mind. With my irascible temper, worked upon by the constant attacks of duns, no wonder that I became gloomy, violent, and, I fear, often personally uncivil, if no worse, and so disgusted her;[200] though, had she really loved me, she would have borne with my infirmities, and made allowance for my provocations. I have written to her repeatedly, and am still in the habit of writing long letters to her, many of which I have sent, but without ever receiving an answer, and others that I did not send, because I despaired of their doing any good. I will show you some of them, as they may serve to throw a light on my feelings." The next day Byron sent me the letter addressed to Lady

[199] Numerous others had heard Byron depreciate Shakespeare (see *HVSV*). Prothero identifies over 150 quotations from Shakespeare in Byron's *LJ*, from 22 plays.

[200] See Lady Byron, writing to Augusta Leigh in October 1815, concerning Byron's "excessive horrors on this subject [a bailiff had slept in the house], which he seems to regard as if no mortal had ever experienced anything so shocking . . ." (*HVSV*, p. 137).

Byron, which has already appeared in "Moore's Life."[201] He never could divest himself of the idea that she took a deep interest in him; he said that their child must always be a bond of union between them, whatever lapse of years or distance might separate them;[202] and this idea seemed to comfort him. And yet, notwithstanding the bond of union a child was supposed to form between the parents, he did not hesitate to state, to the gentlemen of our party, his more than indifference towards the mother of his illegitimate daughter.[203] Byron's mental courage was much stronger in his study than in society. In moments of inspiration, with his pen in his hand, he would have dared public opinion, and laughed to scorn the criticisms of all the *litterati*, but with reflection came doubts and misgivings; and though in general he was tenacious in not changing what he had once written, this tenacity proceeded more from the fear of being thought to *want* mental courage, than from the existence of the quality itself. This operated also on his actions as well as his writings; he was the creature of impulse; never reflected on the possible or probable results of his conduct, until that conduct had drawn down censure and calumny on him, when he shrunk with dismay, "frightened at the sounds himself had made."

This sensitiveness was visible on all occasions, and extended to all his relations with others: did his friends or associates become the objects of public attack, he shrunk from the association, or at least from any public display of it, disclaimed the existence of any particular intimacy, though in secret he felt good-will to the persons. I have witnessed many examples of this, and became convinced that his friendship was much more likely to be retained by those who stood well in the world's opinion, than by those who had even undeservedly forfeited it.[204] I once made an observation to him on

[201] Moore, *Life*, p. 581, letter of November 17, 1821.

[202] Byron made this point in the letter to Lady Byron which he showed to Lady Blessington.

[203] Lady Blessington told Crabb Robinson (*HVSV*, p. 371) that Claire Clairmont "was hated intensely by Lord Byron; indeed, he also could not endure Miss Clairmont though she had a child by him—she forced herself on him, and declared she would have a child by the greatest poet of the age!"

[204] This would seem to be a malicious invention of Lady Blessington, who of course did not stand "well in the world's opinion." See my introduction on Byron's supposed tendency to disclaim friendships. It is also true that in Europe there was little that Byron could do directly to influence events in

this point, which was elicited by something he had said of persons with whom I knew he had once been on terms of intimacy, and which he wished to disclaim: his reply was, "What the deuce good can I do them against public opinion? I shall only injure myself, and do them no service." I ventured to tell him, that this was precisely the system of the English whom he decried; and that self-respect, if no better feeling operated, ought to make us support in adversity those whom we had led to believe we felt interested in. He blushed, and allowed I was right; "though," added he, "you are *singular* in both senses of the word, in your opinion, as I have had proofs; for at the moment when I was assailed *by all* the vituperation of the press in England at the separation, a friend of mine, who had written a complimentary passage to me, either by way of dedication or episode (I forget which he said), sup-pressed it on finding public opinion running hard against me: he will probably produce it if he finds the quicksilver of the barometer of my reputation mounts to *beau fixe*; while it remains, as at present, at variable, it will never see the light, save and except I die in Greece, with a sort of demi-poetic and demi-heroic *renommée* attached to my memory."

Whenever Byron found himself in a difficulty,—and the occasions were frequent,—he had recourse to the example of others, which induced me to tell him that few people had so much profited by friends as he had; they always served "to point a moral and adorn a tale," being his illustrations for all the errors to which human nature is heir, and his apologetic examples whenever he wished to find an excuse for unpoetical acts of worldly wisdom. Byron rather encouraged than discouraged such observations; he said they had novelty to recommend them, and has even wilfully provoked their recurrence. Whenever I gave him my opinions, and still oftener when one of the party, whose sentiments partook of all

England, other than by his writing. He did not of course shrink from association with Hobhouse, when he was in Newgate, although he had no sympathy with the "pack of blackguards," as he called them (*LJ*, IV, 410), for whom Hobhouse had sacrificed himself; he did not shrink from Moore or Scrope Davies, when they had been forced to flee England because of their debts; he stood up for Shelley; he chose the radical John Hunt for his publisher. Similar examples are too numerous to mention.

the chivalric honor, delicacy, and generosity of the *beau idéal* of the poetic character, expressed his, Byron used to say, "Now for a Utopian system of the good and beautiful united; Lord B. ought to have lived in the heroic ages, and if all mankind would agree to act as *he* feels and acts, I agree with you we should all be certainly better, and, I do believe, happier than at present;[205] but it would surely be absurd for a few—and to how few would it be limited—to set themselves up 'doing as they would be done by,' against a million who invariably act *vice versâ*. No; if goodness is to become *à-la-mode*,—and I sincerely wish it were possible,—we must have a fair start, and all begin at the same time, otherwise it will be like exposing a few naked and unarmed men against a multitude in armour." Byron was never *de bonne foi* in giving such opinions; indeed the whole of his manner betrayed this, as it was playful and full of *plaisanterie*, but still he wanted the accompaniment of habitual acts of disinterested generosity to convince one that his practice was better than his theory. He was one of the many whose lives prove how much more effect *example* has than precept. All the elements of good were combined in his nature, but they lay dormant for want of emulation to excite their activity. He was the slave of his passions, and he submitted not without violent, though, alas! unsuccessful, struggles to the chains they imposed; but each day brought him nearer to that age when reason triumphs over passion —when, had life been spared him, he would have subjugated those unworthy tyrants, and asserted his empire over that most rebellious of all dominions—self.

Byron never wished to live to be old; on the contrary, I have frequently heard him express the hope of dying young; and I remember his quoting Sir William Temple's opinion,—that life is like wine; who would drink it pure must not draw it to the dregs,—as

[205] Contrast the tone of Byron's letter to Moore, April 2, 1823 (*LJ*, VI, 181), on Lord Blessington, who had paid Captain Jenkins £10,000 for the right to install in a London house the woman who was to become the Countess of Blessington: "Mountjoy seems very good-natured, but is much tamed, since I recollect him in all the glory of gems and snuff-boxes, and uniforms, and theatricals, and speeches in our house . . . and sitting to Stroelling, the painter . . . to be depicted as one of the heroes of Agincourt, 'with his long sword, saddle, bridle, Whack fal de,' etc., etc." On the relation between virtue and happiness in the mind of Lady Blessington, see my introduction.

being his way of thinking also.[206] He said, it was a mistaken idea
that passions subsided with age, as they only changed, and not for
the better, Avarice usurping the place vacated by Love, and Suspicion filling up that of Confidence. "And this," continued Byron,
"is what age and experience brings us. No; let me not live to be
old: give me youth, which is the fever of reason, and not age, which
is the palsy. I remember my youth, when my heart overflowed
with affection towards all who showed any symptom of liking towards me; and now, at thirty-six, no very advanced period of life, I
can scarcely, by raking up the dying embers of affection in that
same heart, excite even a temporary flame to warm my chilled feelings."[207] Byron mourned over the lost feelings of his youth, as we
regret the lost friends of the same happy period; there was something melancholy in the sentiment, and the more so, as one saw that
it was sincere. He often talked of death, and never with dread. He
said that its certainty furnished a better lesson than all the philosophy of the schools, as it enabled us to bear the ills of life, which
would be unbearable were life of unlimited duration. He quoted
Cowley's lines—

O Life! thou weak-built isthmus, which doth proudly rise
Up betwixt two eternities![208]

as an admirable description, and said they often recurred to his
memory. He never mentioned the friends of whom Death had deprived him without visible emotion: he loved to dwell on their merits, and talked of them with a tenderness as if their deaths had been
recent, instead of years ago. Talking of some of them, and deplor-
ing their loss, he observed, with a bitter smile, "But perhaps it is as
well that they are gone: it is less bitter to mourn their deaths than
to have to regret their alienation; and who knows but that, had they
lived, they might have become as faithless as some others that I

[206] In Byron's "Second Letter . . . on . . . Bowles's Strictures," not pub-
lished until 1835, Byron had quoted from Sir William Temple's *Of Poetry*
(*LJ*, V, 590), the only reference to Temple in *LJ*, *Correspondence*, *Poetry*, or
HVSV. Childe Harold and other Byronic heroes had drunk life to its lees.

[207] Byron expressed similar sentiments in his "Lines to the Countess of
Blessington."

[208] Misquoted from Cowley's "Life and Fame." Byron's notes to "Hints from
Horace" express a very low opinion of Cowley, referred to only once in *LJ*
and not at all in *Correspondence* or *HVSV*.

have known. Experience has taught me that the only friends that we can call our own—that can know no change—are those over whom the grave has closed: the seal of death is the only seal of friendship. No wonder, then, that we cherish the memory of those who loved us, and comfort ourselves with the thought that they were unchanged to the last. The regret we feel at such afflictions has something in it that softens our hearts, and renders us better. We feel more kindly disposed to our fellow-creatures, because we are satisfied with ourselves—first, for being able to excite affection, and, secondly, for the gratitude with which we repay it,—to the memory of those we have lost; but the regret we prove at the alienation or unkindness of those we trusted and loved, is so mingled with bitter feelings, that they sear the heart, dry up the fountain of kindness in our breasts, and disgust us with human nature, by wounding our self-love in its most vulnerable part—the showing that we have failed to excite affection where we had lavished ours. One may learn to bear this uncomplainingly, and with outward calm; but the impression is indelible, and he must be made of different materials to the generality of men, who does not become a cynic, if he become nothing worse, after once suffering such a disappointment."[209]

I remarked that his early friends had not given him cause to speak feelingly on this subject, and named Mr. Hobhouse as a proof: he answered. "Yes, certainly, he has remained unchanged, and I believe is unchangeable; and, if friendship, as most people imagine, consists in telling one truth—unvarnished, unadorned truth—he is indeed a friend; yet, hang it, I must be candid, and say I have had many other, and more agreeable, proofs of Hobhouse's friendship than the truths he always told me; but the fact is, I wanted him to sugar them over a little with flattery, as nurses do the physic given to children; and he never would, and therefore I have never felt quite content with him, though, *au fond*, I respect him the more for his candour, while I respect myself very much less for my weakness in disliking it.

"William Bankes is another of my early friends. He is very clever, very original, and has a fund of information: he is also very good-

[209] On Lady Blessington's disappointments and cynicism, see my introduction.

natured; but he is not much of a flatterer.[210] How unjust it is to accuse you ladies of loving flattery so much; I am quite sure that we men are quite as much addicted to it, but have not the amiable candour, to show it, as you all do. Adulation is never disagreeable when addressed to ourselves, though let us hear only half the same degree of it addressed to another, and we vote the addresser a parasite, and the addressed a fool for swallowing it. But even though we may doubt the sincerity or the judgment of the adulator, the incense is nevertheless acceptable, as it proves we must be of some importance to induce him to take the trouble of flattering us. There are two things that we are all willing to take, and never think we can have too much of (continued Byron)—money and flattery; and the more we have of the *first* the more we are likely to get of the second, as far as I have observed, at all events in England, where I have seen wealth excite an attention and respect that virtue, genius, or valour would fail to meet with.[211]

"I have frequently remarked (said Byron), that in no country have I seen *pre-eminence* so universally followed by envy, jealousy, and all uncharitableness, as in England; those who are deterred by shame from openly attacking, endeavour to depreciate it, by holding up mediocrity to admiration, on the same principle that women, when they hear the beauty of another justly extolled, either deny, or assent with faint praise, to her claims, and lavish on some merely passable woman the highest encomiums, to prove they are not envious. The English treat their celebrated men as they do their climate, abuse them amongst themselves, and defend them out of *amour propre*, if attacked by strangers. Did you ever know a person of powerful abilities really liked in England? Are not the persons most popular in society precisely those who have no qualities to excite envy? Amiable, good-natured people, but negative characters; their very goodness (if mere good-nature can be called goodness) being caused by the want of any positive excellence, as

[210] Cf. Byron to William Bankes, March 6, 1807, which Lady Blessington had read in Moore's *Life,* p. 41: "Your critique is valuable for many reasons: in the first place, it is the only one in which flattery has borne so slight a part; in the *next*, I am *cloyed* with insipid compliments."

[211] Teresa Guiccioli approved in the margin: "True." Lady Blessington had written in *Sketches and Fragments,* p. 126: "In London . . . money is the *primum mobile. . . .*"

white is produced by the absence of colour. People feel themselves equal, and generally think themselves superior to such persons; hence, as they cannot wound vanity, they become popular; all agree to praise them, because *each* individual, while praising, administers to his own self-complacency, from his belief of superiority to him whom he praises. Notwithstanding their faults, the English, (said Byron,) that is to say, the well bred and well educated among them, are better calculated for the commerce of society than the individuals of other countries, from the simple circumstance that they *listen*. This makes one cautious of *what* one says, and prevents the hazarding the *mille petits riens* that escape when one takes courage from the noise of all talking together, as in other places; and this is a great point gained. In what country but England could the epigrammatic repartées and spiritual anecdotes of a Jekyll have flourished?[212] Place him at a French or Italian table, supposing him *au fait* of the languages, and this, our English Attic bee, could neither display his honey nor his sting; both would be useless in the hive of drones around him. St. Evremond,[213] I think it is, who says that there is no better company than an Englishman who talks, and a Frenchman who thinks; but give me the man who *listens*, unless he can talk like a Jekyll, from the overflowing of a full mind, and not, as most of one's acquaintances do, make a noise like drums, from their emptiness. An animated conversation has much the same effect on me as champaigne —it elevates and makes me giddy, and I say a thousand foolish things while under its intoxicating influence: it takes a long time to sober me after; and I sink, under re-action, into a state of depression—half cross, half hippish, and out of humour with myself and the world. I find an interesting book the only sedative to restore me to my wonted calm; for, left alone to my own reflections, I feel so ashamed of myself—*vis-à-vis* to myself—for my levity and overexcitement, that all the follies I have uttered rise up in judgment against me, and I am as sheepish as a schoolboy, after his first degrading abandonment to intemperance."

[212] Joseph Jekyll (1753-1837) was an old friend of Lady Blessington (see my introduction).
[213] Not mentioned elsewhere by Byron.

"Did you know Curran? (asked Byron)—he was the most wonderful person I ever saw. In him was combined an imagination the most brilliant and profound, with a flexibility and wit that would have justified the observation applied to [Ward], that his heart was in his head.[214] I remember his once repeating some stanzas to me, four lines of which struck me so much, that I made him repeat them twice, and I wrote them down before I went to bed:

> While Memory, with more than Egypt's art
> Embalming all the sorrows of the heart,
> Sits at the altar which she raised to woe,
> And feeds the source whence tears eternal flow![215]

I have caught myself repeating these lines fifty times; and, strange to say, they suggested an image on memory to me, with which they have no sort of resemblance in any way, and yet the idea came while repeating them; so unaccountable and incomprehensible is the power of association. My thought was—Memory, the mirror which affliction dashes to the earth, and, looking down upon the fragments, only beholds the reflection multiplied." He seemed pleased at my admiring his idea.* I told him that his thoughts, in comparison with those of others, were eagles brought into competition with sparrows. As an example, I gave him my definition of Memory, which I said resembled a telescope bringing distant objects near to us. He said the simile was good; but I added it was mechanical, instead of poetical, which constituted the difference be-

---

* E'en as a broken mirror which the glass
In every fragment multiplies, and makes
A thousand images of one that was, &c.
    Childe Harold, Canto iii. St. 33.

[214] See Byron's letter to Moore, October 2, 1813, read by Lady Blessington in Moore's *Life*, p. 196, where Byron praised Curran's imagination and humor, although declining to define it. The man whose heart was said to be in his head is probably John William Ward (later Lord Dudley), of whom Rogers wrote: "Ward has no heart, they say; but I deny it;/ He has a heart, and gets his speeches by it." The couplets below, supposedly quoted by Curran to Byron, seem much too sentimental for the taste of Curran, who said to Moore upon the latter's marriage (*LJ*, IV, 371-372): "'so—I hear—you have married a pretty woman—and a very good creature too—an excellent creature—pray—um—*how do you pass your evenings?*'" Curran, who died in 1817, had visited in the house of Lady Blessington's father, when she was still a child (Madden, I, 25).

[215] From Burton's *Anatomy of Melancholy*. See *Poetry*, II, 236, n. 2.

tween excellence and mediocrity, as between the eagle and sparrow. This amused him, though his politeness refused to admit the verity of the comparison.

Talking of tact, Byron observed that it ought to be added to the catalogue of the cardinal virtues, and that our happiness frequently depended more on it than all the accredited ones. "A man (said he) may have prudence, temperance, justice, and fortitude: yet wanting tact may, and must, render those around him *uncomfortable* (the English synonyme for unhappy); and, by the never-failing retributive justice of Nemesis, be unhappy himself, as all are who make others so. I consider tact the real *panacea* of life, and have observed that those who most eminently possessed it were remarkable for feeling and sentiment; while, on the contrary, the persons most deficient in it were obtuse, frivolous, or insensible. To possess tact it is necessary to have a fine perception, and to be sensitive; for how can we know what will pain another without having some criterion in our own feelings, by which we can judge of his? Hence, I maintain that our tact is always in proportion to our sensibility."

Talking of love and friendship, Byron said, that "friendship may, and often does, grow into love, but love never subsides into friendship."[216] I maintained the contrary, and instanced the affectionate friendship which replaces the love of married people; a sentiment as tender, though less passionate, and more durable than the first. He said, "You should say more *enduring*; for, depend on it, that the good-natured passiveness, with which people submit to the conjugal yoke, is much more founded on the philosophical principle of what can't be cured must be endured, than the tender friendship you give them credit for. Who that has felt the all-engrossing passion of love (continued he) could support the stagnant calm you refer to for the same object? No, the humiliation of discovering the frailty of our own nature, which is in no instance more proved than by the short duration of violent love, has something so painful in it, that, with our usual selfishness, we feel, if not a repugnance, at least an indifference to the object that once charmed, but can no longer charm us, and whose presence brings mortifying recollections; nay, such is our injustice, that we transfer the blame

[216] Byron expressed this idea twice in reference to Lady Melbourne; see Moore, *Life*, pp. 206, 377.

108

of the weakness of our own natures to the person who had not power to retain our love, and discover blemishes in her to excuse our inconstancy. As indifference begets indifference, vanity is wounded at both sides; and though good sense may induce people to support and conceal their feelings, how can an affectionate friendship spring up like a phœnix, from the ashes of extinguished passion? I am afraid that the friendship, in such a case, would be as fabulous as the phœnix,[217] for the recollection of burnt-out love would remain too mortifying a memento to admit the successor, friendship." I told Byron that this was mere sophistry, and could not be his real sentiments; as also that, a few days before, he admitted that passion subsides into a better, or at least a more durable feeling. I added, that persons who had felt the engrossing love he described, which was a tempestuous and selfish passion, were glad to sink into the refreshing calm of milder feelings, and looked back with complacency on the storms they had been exposed to, and with increased sympathy to the person who had shared them. The community of interest, of sorrows, and of joys added new links to the chain of affection, and habit, which might wear away the gloss of the selfish passion he alluded to, gave force to friendship, by rendering the persons every day more necessary to each other. I added, that dreadful would be the fate of persons, if, after a few months of violent passion, they were to pass their lives in indifference, merely because their new feelings were less engrossing and exciting than the old.[218] "Then (said Byron), if you admit that the violent love does, or must, subside in a few months, and, as in coursing, that we are mad for a minute to be melancholy for an hour, would it not be wiser to choose the friend, I mean the person most calculated for friendship, with whom the long years are to be spent, than the idol who is to be worshipped for some months, and then hurled from the altar we had raised to her, and left defaced and disfigured by the smoke of the incense she had received? I maintained that as the idols are chosen nearly always for their per-

[217] It is difficult to imagine Byron seriously using the cliché of the phoenix, which he ridiculed elsewhere at least three times: *LJ*, II, 147; V, 557, n.; *HVSV*, p. 60.

[218] Contrast Lady Blessington in her "Night Thought Book" (Madden, I, 211): "Love-matches are made by people who are content, for a month of honey, to condemn themselves to a life of vinegar."

109

sonal charms, they are seldom calculated for friendship; hence the disappointment that ensues, when the violence of passion has abated, and the discovery is made that there are no solid qualities to replace the passion that has passed away with the novelty that excited it. When a man chooses a friend in a woman, he looks to her powers of conversation, her mental qualities, and agreeability; and as these win his regard the more they are known, love often takes the place of friendship, and certainly the foundation on which he builds is more likely to be lasting; and, in this case, I admit that affection, or, as you more prettily call it, tender friendship, may last for ever." I replied that I believe the only difference in our opinions is, that I denied that friendship could not succeed love, and that nothing could change my opinion. "I suppose (said Byron) that a woman, like

> A man, convinced against his will
> Is of the same opinion still—

so that all my fine commentaries on my text have been useless; at all events I hope you give me credit for being *ingenious,* as well as *ingenuous* in my defence. Clever men (said Byron) commit a great mistake in selecting wives who are destitute of abilities; I allow that *une femme savante* is apt to be a bore, and it is to avoid this that people run into the opposite extreme, and condemn themselves to pass their lives with women who are incapable of understanding or appreciating them. Men have an idea that a clever woman must be disputative and dictatorial, not considering that it is only pretenders who are either, and that this applies as much to one sex as the other. Now, my *beau idéal* would be a woman with talent enough to be able to understand and value mine, but not sufficient to be able to shine herself. All men with pretensions desire this, though few, if any, have courage to avow it: I believe the truth is, that a man must be very conscious of superior abilities to endure the thought of having a rival near the throne, though that rival was his wife; and as it is said that no man is a hero to his valet-de-chambre, it may be concluded that few men can retain their position on the pedestal of genius *vis-à-vis* to one who has been behind the curtain, unless that one is unskilled in the art of judging, and consequently admires the more because she does not understand.

110

Genius, like greatness, should be seen at a distance, for neither will bear a too close inspection. Imagine the hero of a hundred fights in his cotton night-cap, subject to all the infirmities of human nature, and there is an end of his sublimity,[219]—and see a poet whose works have raised our thoughts above this sphere of common everyday existence, and who, Prometheus-like, has stolen fire from heaven to animate the children of clay,—see him in the throes of poetic labour, blotting, tearing, re-writing the lines that we suppose him to have poured forth with Homeric inspiration, and, in the intervals, eating, drinking and sleeping, like the most ordinary mortal, and he soon sinks to a level with them in our estimation. I am sure (said Byron) we can never justly appreciate the works of those with whom we have lived on familiar terms. I have felt this myself, and it applies to poets more than all other writers. They should live in solitude, rendering their presence more desired by its rarity; never submit to the gratification of the animal appetite of eating in company, and be as distinct in their general habits, as in their genius, from the common herd of mankind."[220] He laughed heartily when he had finished this speech, and added, "I have had serious thoughts of drawing up a little code of instructions for my brethren of the craft. I don't think my friend Moore would adopt it, and he, perhaps, is the only exception who would be privileged to adhere to his present regime, as he can certainly pass the ordeal of dinners without losing any of his poetical reputation, since the brilliant things that come from his lips reconcile one to the solid things that go into them."

"We have had 'Pleasures of Hope,' 'Pleasures of Memory,' 'Pleasures of Imagination,' and 'Pleasures of Love.'[221] I wonder that no one has thought of writing Pleasures of Fear (said Byron). It surely is a poetical subject, and much might be made of it in good hands." I answered, "Why do you not undertake it?" He replied, "Why, I have endeavoured through life to make believe that I am unac-

---

[219] Teresa Guiccioli: *Mystification si Elles sont vrai.*

[220] This and the two sentences preceding may have been suggested by Moore, *Life*, p. 180.

[221] The first three are by Campbell, Rogers, and Akenside, in that order. A poetic miscellany was published by Dobell in 1721 entitled *The Pleasures of Coition . . . With some other Love-Pieces.* For Byron on the "pleasurable sensation" of fear (and of hope), see Moore, *Life*, p. 483.

quainted with the passion, so I must not now show an intimacy with it, lest I be accused of <u>cowardice, which is, I believe, the only charge that has not yet been brought against me. But, joking apart,</u>[222] it would be a fine subject, and has more of the true sublime than any of the other passions. I have always found more difficulty in hitting on a subject than in filling it up, and so I dare say do most people; and I have remarked that I never could make much of a subject suggested to me by another. I have sometimes dreamt of subjects and incidents (continued he), nay nearly filled up an outline of a tale while under the influence of sleep, but have found it too wild to work up into anything. Dreams are strange things; and here, again, is one of the incomprehensibilities of nature. I could tell you extraordinary things of dreams, and as true as extraordinary, but you would laugh at my superstition. Mine are always troubled and disagreeable; and one of the most fearful thoughts that ever crossed my mind during moments of gloomy scepticism, has been the possibility that the *last* sleep may not be dreamless.[223] Fancy an endless dream of horror—it is too dreadful to think of—this thought alone would lead the veriest clod of animated clay that ever existed to aspirations after immortality. The difference between a religious and irreligious man (said Byron) is, that the one sacrifices the present to the future; and the other, the future to the present." I observed, that grovelling must be the mind that can content itself with the *present*; even those who are occupied only with their pleasures find the insufficiency of it, and must have something to look forward to in the morrow of the future, so unsatisfying is the to-day of the present! Byron said that he agreed with me, and added, "The belief in the immortality of the soul is the only true panacea for the ills of life."

"You will like the Italian women (said Byron), and I advise you to cultivate their acquaintance. They are natural, frank, and good-natured, and have none of the affectation, petitesse, jealousy and malice, that characterize our more polished countrywomen. This gives a raciness to their ideas as well as manners, that to me is peculiarly pleasing; and I feel with an Italian woman as if she was a

[222] Teresa Guiccioli: Oh! Joking apart here is the truth.
[223] Cf. Hamlet's soliloquy, III, i, 64-68. For one of Byron's bad dreams, see Moore, *Life*, p. 204.

full-grown child, possessing the buoyancy and playfulness of infancy with the deep feeling of womanhood; none of that conventional *maniérisme* that one meets with from the first patrician circles in England, justly styled the marble age, so cold and polished,
to the second and third coteries, where a course caricature is given
of the unpenetrated and *impenetrable* mysteries of the *first*. Where
dulness, supported by the *many*, silences talent and originality, up-
held by the few, Madame de Staël used to say, that our great balls
and assemblies of hundreds in London, to which all flocked, were
admirably calculated to reduce all to the same level, and were got
up with this intention. In the torrid zone of suffocating hundreds,
mediocrity and excellence had equal chances, for neither could be
remarked or distinguished; conversation was impracticable, reflection put *hors de combat*, and common sense, by universal accord,
sent to Coventry;[224] so that after a season in London one doubted
one's own identity, and was tempted to repeat the lines in the child's
book, 'If I be not I, who can I be?' So completely was one's faculties
reduced to the conventional standard. The Italians know not this
artificial state of society; their circles are limited and social; they
love or hate; but then they 'do their hating gently;' the clever
among them are allowed a distinguished place; the less endowed
admires, instead of depreciating, what he cannot attain; and all
and each contribute to the general stock of happiness. Misanthropy is unknown in Italy, as are many of the other exotic passions,
forced into flower by the hot-beds of civilization; and yet in *moral*
England you will hear people express their horror of the freedom
and immorality of the Italians, whose errors are but as the weeds
that a too warm sun brings forth, while ours are the stinging-nettles
of a soil rendered rank by its too great richness. Nature is all-
powerful in Italy, and who is it that would not prefer the sins of
her exuberance to the crimes of art? Lay aside ceremony, and meet
them with their own warmth and frankness, and I answer for it you
will leave those whom you sought as acquaintances, friends, instead
of, as in England, scarcely retaining as acquaintances those with
whom you had started in life as friends. Who ever saw in Italy the
nearest and dearest relations bursting asunder all the ties of con-

[224] That is, excluded from society (see *The Oxford Companion to English
Literature*).

113

sanguinity, from some worldly and interested motive? And yet this so frequently takes place in England, that, after an absence of a year of two, one dare hardly enquire of a sister after a sister, or a brother after a brother, as one is afraid to be told—not that they are dead—but that they have cut each other."[225]

"I ought to be an excellent comic writer (said Byron), if it be true, as some assert, that melancholy people succeed best in comedy, and gay people in tragedy; and Moore would make, by that rule, a first-rate tragic writer. I have known, among amateur authors, some of the gayest persons, whose compositions were all of a melancholy turn; and for myself, some of my nearest approaches to comic have been written under a deep depression of spirits.[226] This is strange, but so is all that appertains to our strange natures; and the more we analyze the anomalies in ourselves or others, the more incomprehensible they appear. I believe (continued Byron) the less we reflect on them the better, at least I am sure those that reflect the least are the happiest. I once heard a clever medical man say, that if a person were to occupy himself a certain time in counting the pulsations of his heart, it would have the effect of accelerating its movements, and, if continued, would produce disease. So it is with the mind and nature of man; our examinations and reflections lead to no definitive conclusions, and often engender a morbid state of feeling, that increases the anomalies for which we sought to account. We know that we live (continued Byron), and to live and to suffer are, in my opinion, synonymous. We know also that we shall die, though the how, the when, and the where, we are ignorant of; the whole knowledge of man can pierce no farther, and centuries revolving on centuries have made us no wiser. I think it was Luther who said that the human mind was like a drunken man on horseback—prop it on one side, and it falls on the other: who that has entered into the recesses of his own mind, or examined all that is exposed in the minds of others, but must have discovered this tendency to weakness, which is generally in proportion to the strength in some other faculty. Great imagination is seldom accom-

225 In July 1831, Lady Blessington's sister, Ellen, who had recently ceased to be the mistress of Manners Sutton, Speaker of the House, in order to become his wife, had "thrown [her] overboard." Lady Blessington's preference for Italy over England is witnessed by the number of years she chose to live there.
226 Cf. Byron to Moore, November 16, 1821, Moore, *Life*, p. 542 and n. 3.

panied by equal powers of reason, and *vice versâ*, so that we rarely possess superiority in any one point, except at the expense of another. It is surely then unjust (continued Byron, laughing,) to render poets responsible for their want of common sense, since it is only by the excess of imagination they can arrive at being poets, and this excess debars reason; indeed the very circumstance of a man's yielding to the vocation of a poet ought to serve as a voucher that he is no longer of sound mind."

Byron always became gay when any subject afforded him an opportunity of ridiculing poets; he entered into it *con amore*, and generally ended by some sarcasm on the profession, or on himself. He has often said, "We of the craft are all crazy, but *I* more than the rest; some are affected by gaiety, others by melancholy, but all are more or less touched, though few except myself have the candour to avow it, which I do to spare my friends the pain of sending it forth to the world. This very candour is another proof that I am not of sound mind (continued he), for people will be sure to say how far gone he must be, when he admits it;[227] on the principle that when a belle or beau owns to thirty-five, the world gives them credit for at least seven years more, from the belief that if we seldom speak the truth of others, we never do of ourselves, at least on subjects of personal interest or vanity."

Talking of an acquaintance, Byron said,—"Look at ——, and see how he gets on in the world—he is as unwilling to do a bad action as he is incapable of doing a good: fear prevents the first, and *méchanceté* the second.[228] The difference between —— and me is, that I abuse many, and really, with one or two exceptions, (and, mind you, *they are males,*) hate none; and he abuses none and hates many, if not all. Fancy—in the Palace of Truth, what good fun it would be, to hear him, while he believed himself uttering the most honied compliments, giving vent to all the spite and rancour that has been pent up in his mind for years, and then to see the person he has been so long flattering hearing his real sentiments for the first time: this would be rare fun! Now, I would appear to

[227] Teresa Guiccioli: True!

[228] This may be Southey; see p. 156, where the word *méchanceté* appears in a discussion involving him, and *LJ*, VI, 389, where Byron attacks Southey on the basis of good and bad actions done in their respective lifetimes.

great advantage in the Palace of Truth," continued Byron, "though you look ill-naturedly incredulous; for while I thought I was vexing friends and foes with spiteful speeches, I should be saying good-natured things, for, *au fond*, I have no malice, at least none that lasts beyond the moment." Never was there a more true observation: Byron's is a fine nature,[229] spite of all the weeds that may have sprung up in it; and I am convinced that it is the excellence of the poet, or rather let me say, the effect of that excellence, that has produced the defects of the man. In proportion to the admiration *one* has excited, has been the severity of the censure bestowed on the other, and often most unjustly. The world has burnt incense before the poet, and heaped ashes on the head of the man. This has revolted and driven him out of the pale of social life: his wounded pride has avenged itself, by painting his own portrait in the most sombre colours, as if to give a still darker picture than has yet been drawn by his foes, while glorying in forcing even from his foes an admiration as unbounded for his genius as has been their disapprobation for his character. Had his errors met with more mercy, he might have been a less grand poet, but he would have been a more estimable man; the good that is now dormant in his nature would have been called forth, and the evil would not have been excited. The blast that withers the rose destroys not its thorns, which often remain, the sole remembrancer of the flower they grow near; and so it is with some of our finest qualities,—blighted by unkindness, we can only trace them by the faults their destruction has made visible.

Lord Byron, in talking of his friend, Le Comte Pietro Gamba, (the brother of La Contessa Guiccioli,) whom he had presented to us soon after our arrival at Genoa, remarked, that he was one of the most amiable, brave, and excellent young men, he had ever encountered, with a thirst for knowledge, and a distinterestedness rarely to be met with. "He is my grand *point d'appui* for Greece," said he, "as I know he will neither deceive nor flatter me." We have found Le Comte Pietro Gamba exactly what Lord Byron had described him; sensible, mild, and amiable, devotedly attached to Lord B., and dreaming of glory and Greece.[230] He is extremely good-look-

---

[229] Teresa Guiccioli: Oh! True!

[230] The portrait of Pietro Gamba agrees with Byron's judgment of him as expressed elsewhere.

ing, and Lord Byron told us he resembled his sister very much, which I dare say increased his partiality for him not a little.

Habit has a strong influence over Byron: he likes routine, and detests what he calls being put out of his way. He told me that any infringement on his habitual way of living, or passing his time, annoyed him.[231] Talking of thin women, he said, that if they were young and pretty, they reminded him of dried butterflies; but if neither, of spiders, whose nets would never catch him were he a fly, as they had nothing tempting. A new book is a treasure to him, provided it is really new; for having read more than perhaps any man of his age, he can immediately discover a want of originality, and throws by the book in disgust at the first wilful plagiary he detects.

Talking of Mr. Ward,* Lord Byron said—"Ward is one of the best-informed men I know, and, in a *tête-à-tête*, is one of the most agreeable companions. He has great originality, and, being *tres distrait*, it adds to the piquancy[232] of his observations, which are sometimes somewhat *trop naïve*, though always amusing. This *naïveté* of his is the more piquant from his being really a good-natured man, who unconsciously thinks aloud. Interest Ward on a subject, and I know no one who can talk better. His expressions are concise without being poor, and terse and epigrammatic without being affected. He can compress (continued Byron) as much into a few words as any one I know; and if he gave *more* of his attention to his associates, and *less* to himself, he would be one of the few whom one could praise, without being compelled to use the conjunction *but*. Ward has bad health, and unfortunately, like all valetudinarians, it occupies his attention too much, which will probably bring on a worse state," continued Byron, "that of confirmed egoism,—a malady, that, though not to be found in the catalogue of ailments to which man is subject, yet perhaps is more to be dreaded than all that are."

* Now Lord Dudley.
[231] Cf. Moore, *Life*, p. 44, on Byron's "decided taste for that sort of regular routine of life—bringing round the same occupation at the stated periods,—which formed so much the system of his existence during the greater part of his residence abroad."
[232] Cf. Byron in his journal of November 23, 1813, which Lady Blessington had read in Moore's *Life*, p. 204: "But I like Ward. He is *piquant* . . ." Lady Blessington had known Ward, who succeeded to the title on April 5, 1823, in Naples, where she rented the Villa Gallo from him. He died on March 6, 1833.

I observed that egoism is in general the malady of the aged; and that, it appears, we become occupied with our own existence in proportion as it ceases to be interesting to others. "Yes," said Byron, "on the same principle as we see the <u>plainest people the vainest</u>,—nature giving them vanity and self-love to supply the want of that admiration they never can find in others. I can therefore pity and forgive the vanity of the ugly and deformed, whose sole consolation it is; but the handsome, whose good looks are mirrored in the eyes of all around them, should be content with that, and not indulge in such egregious vanity as they give way to in general. But to return to Ward," said Byron, "and this is not *apropos* to vanity, for I never saw any one who has less. He is not properly appreciated in England. The English can better understand and enjoy the *bons mots* of a *bon vivant*, who can at all times set the table in a roar,[233] than the neat *répliques* of Ward, which, exciting reflection, are more likely to silence the rabble-riot of intemperance. They like better the person who makes them laugh, though often at their own expense, than he who forces them to think,—an operation which the mental faculties of few of them are calculated to perform: so that poor Ward, finding himself undervalued, sinks into self, and this, at the long run, is dangerous:—

> For well we know, the mind, too finely wrought,
> Preys on itself, and is o'erpower'd by thought.

"There are many men in England of superior abilities, (continued Byron,) who are lost from the habits and inferiority of their associates. Such men, finding that they cannot raise their companions to their level, are but too apt to let themselves down to that of the persons they live with; and hence many a man condescends to be merely a wit, and man of pleasure, who was born for better things. Poor Sheridan[234] often played this character in society; but he maintained his superiority over the herd, by having established a literary and political reputation; and as I have heard him more than once say, when his jokes have drawn down plaudits from compan-

[233] Cf. Hamlet on Yorick, V, i, 210: "wont to set the table on a roar." The index to *LJ* lists nineteen quotations from *Hamlet*. In *The Repealers* Lord Albany [Alvanley] is able "to set the table in a roar" (*Works*, I, 257).

[234] Sheridan, whose conversational powers figure large in *LJ*, was repeatedly termed "poor" Sheridan by Byron: see *LJ*, II, 320, 397; IV, 80.

ions, to whom, of an evening at least, sobriety and sadness were alike unknown,—'It is some consolation, that if I set the table in a roar, I can at pleasure set the senate in a roar;'[235] and this was muttered while under the influence of wine, and as if apologizing to his own mind for the profanation it was evident he felt he had offered to it at the moment. Lord A[lvan]ley[236] is a delightful companion, (said Byron,) brilliant, witty, and playful; he can be irresistibly comic when he pleases, but what could he not be if he pleased? for he has talents to be anything. I lose patience when I see such a man throw himself away; for there are plenty of men, who could be witty, brilliant, and comic, but who could be nothing else, while he is all these, but could be much more. How many men have made a figure in public life, without half his abilities! But indolence and the love of pleasure will be the bane of A[lvanle]y, as it has been of many a man of talent before."

The more I see of Byron, the more am I convinced that all he says and does should be judged more leniently than the sayings and doings of others—as his proceed from the impulse of the moment, and never from premeditated malice. He cannot resist expressing whatever comes into his mind; and the least shade of the ridiculous is seized by him at a glance, and portrayed with a facility and felicity that must encourage the propensity to ridicule, which is inherent in him. All the malice of his nature has lodged itself on his lips and the fingers of his right hand[237]—for there is none I am persuaded to be found in his heart, which has more of good than most people give him credit for, except those who have lived with him on habits of intimacy. He enters into society as children do their play-ground, for relaxation and amusement, after his mind has been strained to

---

[235] See above, p. 118, n. 233.
[236] Alvanley, the friend of D'Orsay's who figured in Lady Blessington's novel *The Repealers* as Lord Albany, succeeded Brummell as the reigning dandy. In his letter of April 5, 1823 (*LJ*, VI, 189), Byron informed Lord Blessington that he and Alvanley had belonged to Watier's Club "at the time . . . of its greatest glory." In *The Repealers* (*Works*, I, 257), he has apparently declined into a mere gourmet: "To hear him descant on the mysteries of the *cuisine*, one would suppose that he thought of nothing else, and yet he is, perhaps, one of the best informed men in England, full of talent, and with powers of being satirical, from the lightness and *plaisanterie* of his *coup de pattes*, that few ever possessed without abusing; but he is so thoroughly good-natured, that, unlike the generality of wits, he prefers his friends to his jokes, and suppresses many a one calculated to set the table in a roar."
[237] Teresa Guiccioli: True.

its utmost stretch, and that he feels the necessity of unbending it. Ridicule is his play; it amuses him perhaps the more that he sees it amuses others, and much of its severity is mitigated by the boyish glee, and laughing sportiveness, with which his sallies are uttered. All this is felt when he is conversing, but unfortunately it cannot be conveyed to the reader: the narrator would therefore deprecate the censure his sarcasms may excite, in memory of the smiles and gaiety that palliated them when spoken.

Byron is fond of talking of Napoleon; and told me that his admiration of him had much increased since he had been in Italy, and witnessed the stupendous works he had planned and executed. "To pass through Italy without thinking of Napoleon, (said he,) is like visiting Naples without looking at Vesuvius." Seeing me smile at the comparison, he added—"Though the works of one are indestructible, and the other destructive, still one is continually reminded of the power of both." "And yet (said I) there are days, that, like all your other favourites, Napoleon does not escape censure." "That may be, (said Byron,) but I find fault, and quarrel with Napoleon, as a lover does with the trifling faults of his mistress, from excessive liking, which tempts me to desire that he had been all faultless; and, like the lover, I return with renewed fondness after each quarrel. Napoleon (continued Byron) was a grand creature, and though he was hurled from his pedestal, after having made thrones his footstool, his memory still remains, like the colossal statue of the Memnon, though cast down from its seat of honour, still bearing the ineffaceable traces of grandeur and sublimity to astonish future ages.[238] When Metternich (continued Byron) was depreciating the genius of Napoleon, in a circle at Vienna where his word was a law and his nod a decree, he appealed to John William Ward,[239] if Bonaparte had not been greatly overrated.—Ward's answer was as courageous as admirable. He replied, that 'Napoleon had rendered past glory doubtful, and future fame impossible.' This was expressed in French, and such pure French, that all present were struck with admiration, no less with the thought than with the

[238] Lord Blessington suggested to Byron that he write an epic on Napoleon (see my introduction). D'Orsay and Lady Blessington were devoted Bonapartists.
[239] Ward was in Vienna for three months in 1817 (*DNB*).

120

mode of expressing it." I told Byron that this reminded me of a reply made by Mr. Ward to a lady at Vienna, who somewhat rudely remarked to him, that it was strange that all the best society at Vienna spoke French as well as German, while the English scarcely spoke French at all, or spoke it ill. Ward answered, that the English must be excused for their want of practice, as the French army had not been twice to London to teach them, as they had been at Vienna. "The coolness of Ward's manner (said Byron) must have lent force to such a reply: I have heard him say many things worth remembering, and the neatness of their expression was as remarkable as the justness of the thought. It is a pity (continued Byron) that Ward has not written anything: his style, judging by letters of his that I have seen, is admirable, and reminded me of Sallust."[240]

Having, one day, taken the liberty of (what he termed) scolding Lord Byron, and finding him take it with his usual good-nature, I observed that I was agreeably surprised by the patience with which he listened to my lectures; he smiled, and replied, "No man dislikes being lectured by a woman, provided she be not his mother, sister, wife, or mistress: first, it implies that she takes an interest in him, and, secondly, that she does not think him irreclaimable: then, there is not that air of superiority in women when they give advice, that men, particularly one's contemporaries, affect; and even if there was, men think their own superiority so acknowledged, that they listen without humiliation to the *gentler*, I don't say weaker, sex. There is one exception, however, for I confess I could not stand being lectured by Lady ——; but then she is neither of the weak nor gentle sex—she is a nondescript,—having all the faults of both sexes, without the virtues of either. Two lines in the 'Henriade,'[241] de-

[240] Byron was familiar with the *Conspiracy of Cataline* and the *War of Jugurtha*: see *LJ*, V, 153; *Poetry*, VI, 299 and n. The style of Ward's letters in no way resembles that of Sallust, who, according to the *Encyclopædia Britannica* (11th ed.), took Thucydides for his model "in the introduction of philosophizing reflections and speeches, and in the brevity of his style, sometimes bordering upon obscurity. His fondness for old words and phrases, in which he imitated his contemporary Cato, was ridiculed as an affectation. . . ." Perhaps it might be said, although not very convincingly, that Ward the epigrammatist (but not Ward the letter writer) shared with Sallust the quality of "rhetorical exaggeration," attributed to him by the *Britannica*. See *Letters to 'Ivy' from the First Earl of Dudley*, ed. S. H. Romilly (London, 1905).

[241] Voltaire's early epic, *La Henriade*, II, 63-64. The anonymous lady may be Lady Holland.

scribing Catherine de Medicis, seem made for Lady —— (continued Byron)—

> Possédant en un mot, pour n'en pas dire plus,
> Les défauts de son sexe et peu de ses vertus."

I remember only one instance of Byron's being displeased with my frankness. We were returning on horseback from Nervi, and in defending a friend of mine, whom he assailed with all the slings and arrows of ridicule and sarcasm, I was obliged to be more severe than usual; and having at that moment arrived at the turn of the road that led to Albaro, he politely, but coldly, wished me good bye, and galloped off. We had scarcely advanced a hundred yards, when he came galloping after us, and reaching out his hand, said to me, "Come, come, give me your hand, I cannot bear that we should part so formally: I am sure what you have said was right, and meant for my good; so God bless you, and to-morrow we shall ride again, and I promise to say nothing that can produce a lesson." We all agreed that we had never seen Byron appear to so much advantage. He gives me the idea of being the man the most easily to be managed I ever saw: I wish Lady Byron had discovered the means, and both might now be happier.

Lord Byron told me that La Contessa Guiccioli had repeatedly asked him to discontinue Don Juan, as its immorality shocked her, and that she could not bear that anything of the kind should be written under the same roof with her. "To please her (said Byron) I gave it up for some time, and have only got permission to continue it on condition of making my hero a more moral person.[242] I shall end by making him turn Methodist;[243] this will please the English, and be an *amende honorable* for his sins and mine. I once got an anonymous letter, written in a very beautiful female hand (said Byron), on the subject of Don Juan, with a beautiful illustrative drawing, beneath which was written—'When Byron wrote the first Canto of Don Juan, Love, that had often guided his pen, resigned it to Sensuality—and Modesty, covering her face with her

[242] Cf. Byron to Murray, July 8, 1822, and to Moore, August 27, 1822 (*LJ*, VI, 95, 109), where the phrasing is slightly similar.
[243] Cf. *The Idler* (*HVSV*, p. 363); Hunt, John Hamilton Browne, and James Kennedy made this point (*HVSV*, pp. 332, 400, xxxiv).

veil, to hide her blushes and dry her tears, fled from him for ever.' The drawing (continued Byron) represented Love and Modesty turning their backs on wicked Me,—and Sensuality, a fat, flushed, wingless Cupid, presenting me with a pen. Was not this a pretty conceit? at all events, it is some consolation to occupy the attention of women so much, though it is but by my faults; and I confess it gratifies me. Apropos to Cupid—it is strange (said Byron) that the ancients, in their mythology, should represent Wisdom by a woman, and Love by a boy! how do you account for this? I confess I have little faith in Minerva, and think that Wisdom is, perhaps, the last attribute I should be inclined to give woman; but then I do allow, that Love would be more suitably represented by a female than a male; for men or boys feel not the passion with the delicacy and purity that women do; and this is my real opinion, which must be my peace-offering for doubting the wisdom of your sex."

Byron is infirm of purpose—decides without reflection—and gives up his plans if they are opposed for any length of time; but, as far as I can judge of him, though he yields, he does it not with a good grace: he is a man likely to show that such a sacrifice of self-will was offered up more through indolence than affection, so that his yielding can seldom be quite satisfactory, at least to a delicate mind. He says that all women are *exigéante*, and apt to be dissatisfied: he is, as I have told him, too selfish and indolent not to have given those who had more than a common interest in him cause to be so. It is such men as Byron who complain of women; they touch not the chords that give sweet music in woman's breast, but strike—with a bold and careless hand—those that jar and send forth discord. Byron has a false notion on the subject of women; he fancies that they are all disposed to be tyrants, and that the moment they know their power they abuse it. We have had many arguments on this point—I maintaining that the more disposed men were to yield to the empire of woman, the less were they inclined to exact, as submission disarmed, and attention and affection enslaved them.

Men are capable of making great sacrifices, who are not willing to make the lesser ones, on which so much of the happiness of life depends. The great sacrifices are seldom called for, but the minor ones are in daily requisition; and the making them with cheerfulness and grace enhances their value, and banishes from the domestic circle the various misunderstandings, discussions, and coldnesses, that arise to embitter existence, where a little self-denial might have kept them off. Woman is a creature of feeling,—easily wounded, but susceptible of all the soft and kind emotions: destroy this sensitiveness, and you rob her of her greatest attraction; study her happiness, and you insure your own.

"One of the things that most pleases me in the Italian character (said Byron) is the total absence of that belief which exists so generally in England in the mind of each individual, that the circle in which he lives, and which he dignifies by calling *The World*, is occupied with him and his actions—an idea founded on the extreme vanity that characterizes the English, and that precludes the possibility of living for oneself or those immediately around one. How many of my *soi-disant* friends in England are dupes to this vanity (continued Byron)—keeping up expensive establishments which they can ill afford—living in crowds, and with people who do not suit them—feeling *ennuyés* day after day, and yet submitting to all this tiresome routine of vapid reunions,—living, during the fashionable season, if living it can be called, in a state of intermitting fever, for the sake of being considered to belong to a certain set.[244] During the time I passed in London, I always remarked that I never met a person who did not tell me how bored he or she had been the day or night before at Lady This or Lady That's; and when I've asked, 'Why do you go if it bores you?' the invariable answer has been—'One can't help going; it would be so odd not to go.' Old and young, ugly and handsome, all have the rage in England of losing their identity in crowds; and prefer conjugating the verb *ennuyer*,[245] *en masse*, in heated rooms, to conning it over in privacy in a purer atmosphere. The constancy and perseverance with which our compatriots support fashionable life have always been to me a subject of wonder, if not of admiration, and proves what they might be capable of in a good cause. I am curious to know (continued Byron) if the rising generation will fall into the

[244] The sentence describes rather precisely Lady Blessington's situation in 1832.
[245] Cf. Byron to Hodgson, October 13, 1811 (*LJ*, II, 55; Moore, *Life*, p. 141): ". . . any thing to cure me of conjugating the accursed verb '*ennuyer*.'"

124

same inane routine; though it is to be hoped the march of intellect will have some influence in establishing something like society, which has hitherto been only to be found in country-houses. I spent a week at Lady J[erse]y's once,[246] and very agreeably it passed; the guests were well chosen—the host and hostess on 'hospitable thoughts intent'—the establishment combining all the luxury of a *maison montée en prince* with the ease and comfort of a well-ordered home. How different do the same people appear in London and in the country!—they are hardly to be recognised. In the latter they are as natural and unaffected[247] as they are insipid or over-excited in the former. A certain place (continued Byron) not to be named to 'ears polite,'[248] is said to be paved with good intentions, and London (viewing the effect it produces on its fashionable inhabitants) may really be supposed to be paved by evil passions, as few can touch its *pavé* without contamination. I have been reading Lord John Russell's Essays on London Society,[249] and find them clever and amusing (said Byron), but too microscopic for my taste: he has, however, treated the subject with a lightness and playfulness best suited to it, and his reflections show an accuracy of observation that proves he is capable of better things. He who would take a just view of the world must neither examine it through a microscope nor a magnifying-glass. Lord John is a sensible and amiable man, and bids fair to distinguish himself.

"Do you know Hallam? (said Byron.) Of course I need not ask you if you have read his 'Middle Ages:' it is an admirable work, full of research, and does Hallam honour.[250] I know no one capable

[246] Byron visited the Jerseys at Middleton in the summer of 1812 (Moore, *Life*, pp. 165-66).

[247] This is contrary to the picture of country life painted in *Don Juan*, at Norman Abbey.

[248] Cf. the same phrase above, p. 46.

[249] Thomas Moore had informed Byron of the authorship of Lord John Russell's book, published anonymously, *Essays and Sketches of Life and Character by a Gentleman who has left his Lodgings* (1820). Moore wrote: "Lord [John] Russell, as you will see by his volume of Essays, if it reaches you, has a very sly, dry, and pithy way of putting sound truths upon politics and manners. . . ." He was an early and warmly admired friend of Lady Blessington. See her tribute to him, Madden, I, 100.

[250] Henry Hallam's name does not appear in *LJ*, *Correspondence*, or *HVSV*. Byron ironically praised him in *English Bards*, ll. 513, 548, "classic HALLAM, much renowned for Greek," "honest HALLAM," and referred noncommittally to

of having written it except him; for, admitting that a writer could be found who could bring to the task his knowledge and talents, it would be difficult to find one who united to these his research, patience, and perspicuity of style. The reflections of Hallam are at once just and profound—his language well chosen and impressive. I remember (continued Byron) being struck by a passage, where, touching on the Venetians, he writes—"Too blind to avert danger, too cowardly to withstand it, the most ancient government of Europe made not an instant's resistance: the peasants of Underwald died upon their mountains—the nobles of Venice clung only to their lives.' This is the style in which history ought to be written, if it is wished to impress it on the memory; and I found myself, on my first perusal of the 'Middle Ages,' repeating aloud many such passages as the one I have cited, they struck my fancy so much. Robertson's State of Europe, in his 'Charles the Fifth,' is another of my great favourites (continued Byron);[251] it contains an epitome of information. Such works do more towards the extension of knowledge than half the ponderous tomes that lumber up our libraries: they are the rail-roads to learning; while the others are the neglected old roads that deter us from attempting the journey.

"It is strange (said Byron) that we are in general much more influenced by the opinions of those whose sentiments ought to be a matter of indifference to us, than by that of near or dear friends; nay, we often do things totally opposed to the opinions of the latter (on whom much, if not all, our comfort depends), to cultivate that of the former, who are or can be nothing in the scale of our happiness. It is in this opposition between our conduct and our affections that much of our troubles originates; it loosens the bonds of affection between us and those we ought to please, and fails to excite any good-will in those whom our vanity leads us to wish to propitiate, because they are regardless of us and of our actions. With all our selfishness, this is a great mistake (continued Byron); for, as

---

his *Europe in the Middle Ages* in *Don Juan*, XII, xxx. Lady Blessington had met Hallam in 1827 in Florence. D'Orsay sketched him on March 5, 1828.

[251] In the list of his early reading (Moore, *Life*, p. 47), which Lady Blessington had seen, Byron listed first under the heading of Biography Dr. William Robertson's *Charles the Fifth*, which may have provided him details for his account of the sack of Rome, 1527, in *The Deformed Transformed*. Byron described Charles V in his "Ode to Napoleon Buonaparte," viii.

I take it for granted, we have all some feelings of natural affection for our kindred or friends, and consequently wish to retain theirs; we never wound or offend them without its re-acting on ourselves, by alienating them from us: hence *selfishness* ought to make us study the wishes of those to whom we look for happiness; and the principle of doing as you would be done by, a principle which, if acted upon, could not fail to add to the stock of general good, was founded in wisdom and knowledge of the selfishness of human nature."

Talking of Mr. D. K[innaird], Byron said, "My friend Dug is a proof that a good heart cannot compensate for an irritable temper: whenever he is named, people dwell on the last and pass over the first; and yet he really has an excellent heart, and a sound head, of which I, in common with many others of his friends, have had various proofs. He is clever too, and well informed, and I do think would have made a figure in the world, were it not for his temper, which gives a dictatorial tone to his manner, that is offensive to the *amour propre* of those with whom he mixes; and when you alarm that (said Byron), there is an end of your influence.[252] By tacitly admitting the claims of vanity of others, you make at least acquiescent beholders of your own, and this is something gained; for, depend on it, disguise it how we will, vanity is the prime mover in most, if not all, of us, and some of the actions and works that have the most excited our admiration have been inspired by this passion, that *none* will own to, yet that influences *all*.

"The great difference between the happy and unhappy (said Byron) is, that the former are afraid to contemplate death, and the latter look forward to it as a release from suffering. Now as death is inevitable, and life brief and uncertain, unhappiness, viewed in this point, is rather desirable than otherwise; but few, I fear, derive consolation from the reflection. I think of death often (continued Byron), as I believe do most people who are not happy, and view it as a refuge 'where the wicked cease from troubling, and the weary

[252] The critical and condescending tone of this account of Kinnaird is not typical of Byron's other references to him, although Henry Fox reported, March 31, 1823, that Byron "thinks of going to England, and his desire to do so is rather roused by perceiving Douglas Kinnaird does not wish it." Lady Blessington wrote unsympathetically of Kinnaird in her *Idler in France* (see my introduction).

are at rest.' There is something calm and soothing to me in the thought of death; and the only time that I feel repugnance to it is on a fine day, in solitude, in a beautiful country, when all nature seems rejoicing in light and life. The contrast then between the beautiful and animated world around me, and the dark narrow grave, gives a chill to the feelings; for, with all the boasted philosophy of man, his physical *being* influences his notions of that state where they can be felt no more. The nailed down coffin, and the dark gloomy vault, or grave, always mingle with our thoughts of death; then the decomposition of our mortal frames, the being preyed on by reptiles, add to the disgusting horror of the picture, and one has need of all the hopes of immortality to enable one to pass over this bridge between the life we know and the life we hope to find.

"Do you know (said Byron) that when I have looked on some face that I love, imagination has often figured the changes that death must one day produce on it—the worm rioting on lips now smiling, the features and hues of health changed to the livid and ghastly tints of putrefaction; and the image conjured up by my fancy, but which is as true as it is a fearful anticipation of what *must* arrive, has left an impression for hours that the actual presence of the object, in all the bloom of health, has not been able to banish: this is one of *my* pleasures of imagination."

Talking of hypochondriasm, Byron said, that the world had little compassion for two of the most serious ills that human nature is subject to,—mental or bodily hypochondriasm: "Real ailments may be cured, (said he,) but imaginary ones, either moral or physical, admit of no remedy. People analyze the supposed causes of maladies of the mind; and if the sufferer be rich, well born, well looking, and clever in any way, they conclude he, or she, can have no cause for unhappiness; nay, assign the cleverness, which is often the source of unhappiness, as among the adventitious gifts that increase, or ought to increase, felicity, and pity not the unhappiness they cannot understand. They take the same view of imaginary physical ailments, never reflecting that 'happiness (or health) is often but in opinion;' and that he who believes himself wretched or ill suffers perhaps more than he who has real cause for wretchedness, or who is labouring under disease with less acute sensibility to feel his trou-

128

bles, and nerves subdued by ill health, which prevents his suffering from bodily ills as severely as does the hypochondriac from imaginary ones. The irritability of genius (continued Byron) is nothing more or less than a delicacy of organization, which gives a susceptibility to impressions to which coarser minds are never subject, and cultivation and refinement but increase it, until the unhappy victim becomes a prey to mental hypochondriasm."

Byron furnished a melancholy illustration of the fate of genius; and while he dwelt on the diseases to which it is subject, I looked at his fine features, already marked by premature age, and his face "sicklied o'er with the pale cast of thought," and stamped with decay, until I felt that *his* was no hypothetical statement. Alas!—

> Noblest minds
> Sink soonest into ruin, like a tree
> That, with the weight of its own golden fruitage,
> Is bent down to the dust.

"Do you know Mackintosh? (asked Lord Byron)—his is a mind of powerful calibre. Madame de Staël used to extol him to the skies, and was perfectly sincere in her admiration of him, which was not the case with all whom she praised. Mackintosh also praised her: but his is a mind that, as Moore writes, 'rather loves to praise than blame,' for with a judgment so comprehensive, a knowledge so general, and a critical acumen rarely to be met with, his sentences are never severe. He is a powerful writer and speaker; there is an earnestness and vigour in his style, and a force and purity in his language, equally free from inflation and loquacity.[253] Lord Erskine is, I know, a friend of yours (continued Byron), and a most gifted person he is. The Scotch are certainly very superior people; with intellects naturally more acute than the English, they are better edu-

[253] Sir James Mackintosh wrote: "Madame de Staël treats me as the person she most delights to honour; I am generally ordered with her to dinner, as one orders beans and bacon: she is one of the few persons who surpass expectation; she has every sort of talent . . ." (quoted in *LJ*, II, 229, n.). Although Sydney Smith agreed that "his chief foible was indiscriminate praise," he also paid tribute to his great powers of mind, chiefly evident in his conversation, as did Samuel Rogers (see *LJ*, II, 236, n. 1). Byron dined with de Staël and Mackintosh on October 3, 1813, and on March 1, 1814, when Erskine was also present (*LJ*, II, 273, 390). It does not appear that Lady Blessington knew Mackintosh.

129

cated and make better men of business. Erskine is full of imagination, and in this he resembles your countrymen, the Irish, more than the Scotch. The Irish would make better poets, and the Scotch philosophers; but this excess of imagination gives a redundancy to the writings and speeches of the Irish that I object to: they come down on one with similes, tropes, and metaphors, a superabundance of riches that makes one long for a little plain matter of fact. An Irishman, of course I mean a clever one, (continued Byron,) educated in Scotland, would be perfection, for the Scots professors would prune down the over-luxuriant shoots of his imagination, and strengthen his reasoning powers. I hope you are not very much offended with me for this critique on your countrymen (continued Byron); but, *en revanche*, I give you *carte blanche* to attack mine, as much as you please, and will join in your strictures to the utmost extent to which you wish to go. Lord Erskine is, or was, (said Byron,)—for I suppose age has not improved him more than it generally does people,—the most brilliant person imaginable;— quick, vivacious, and sparkling, he spoke so well that I never felt tired of listening to him, even when he abandoned himself to that subject of which all his other friends and acquaintances expressed themselves so fatigued—*self.* His egoism was remarkable,[254] but there was a *bonhommie* in it that showed he had a better opinion of mankind than they deserved; for it implied a belief that his listeners could be interested in what concerned him, whom they professed to like. He was deceived in this (continued Byron), as are all who have a favourable opinion of their fellow-men: in society all and each are occupied with self, and can rarely pardon any one who presumes to draw their attention to other subjects for any length of time. Erskine had been a great man, and he knew it; and in talking so continually of self, imagined that he was but the echo of fame. All his talents, wit, and brilliancy were insufficient to excuse this weakness in the opinion of his friends; and I have seen bores, acknowledged bores, turn from this clever man, with every

[254] "In society Erskine was widely known for his brilliancy, his puns, and his extraordinary vanity. His egotism gained him such titles as Counsellor Ego, Baron Ego of Eye . . ." (*LJ*, II, 391, n. 5). On Lord Erskine's early intimacy with Lady Blessington, see Madden, II, 512-14, who prints some short and amusing poems given by Erskine to Lady Blessington (II, 392-94). On Erskine and Byron, see Moore, *Life*, p. 166.

symptom of *ennui*, when he has been reciting an interesting anecdote, merely because he was the principal actor in it.

"This fastidiousness of the English," continued Byron, "and habit of pronouncing people bores, often impose on strangers and stupid people, who conceive that it arises from delicacy of taste and superior abilities. I never was taken in by it, for I have generally found that those who were the most ready to pronounce others bores, had the most indisputable claims to that title in their own persons. The truth is," continued Byron, "the English are very envious, they are *au fond*, conscious that they are dreadfully dull—being loquacious without liveliness, proud without dignity, and *brusque* without sincerity; they never forgive those who show that they have made the same discovery,[255] or who occupy public attention, of which they are jealous. An Englishman rarely condescends to take the trouble of conciliating admiration (though he is jealous of esteem), and he as rarely pardons those who have succeeded in attaining it. They are jealous," continued Byron, "of popularity of every sort, and not only depreciate the talents that obtain it, whatever they may be, but the person who possesses them. I have seen in London, in one of the circles the most *récherche*, a literary man *à la mode* universally attacked by the *élite* of the party, who were damning his merits with faint praise, and drawing his defects into notice, until some other candidate for approbation as a conversationist, a singer, or even a dancer, was named, when all fell upon him—proving that a superiority of tongue, voice, or heel was as little to be pardoned as genius or talent. I have known people," continued Byron, "talk of the highest efforts of genius as if they had been within the reach of each of the common-place individuals of the circle; and comment on the acute reasonings of some logician as if they could have made the same deductions from the same premises, though ignorant of the most simple syllogism. Their very ignorance of the subjects on which they pronounce is perhaps the cause of the fearless decisions they give, for, knowing nought, they think everything easy: but this impertinence," continued Byron, "is difficult to be borne by those who know 'how painful 'tis to climb,'

[255] Cf. Lady Blessington's "Night Thought Book": "Society seldom forgives those who have discovered the emptiness of its pleasures . . ." (Madden, I, 241).

131

and who having, by labour, gained some one of the eminences in literature—which, alas! as we all know, are but as mole-hills compared to the acclivity they aim at ascending—are the more deeply impressed with the difficulties that they have yet to surmount. I have never yet been satisfied with any one of my own productions; I cannot read them over without detecting a thousand faults; but when I read critiques upon them by those who could *not* have written them, I lose my patience.

"There is an old and stupid song," said Byron, "that says—'Friendship with woman is sister to love.' There is some truth in this; for let a man form a friendship with a woman, even though she be no longer young or handsome, there is a softness and tenderness attached to it that no male friendship can know. A proof of this is, that Lady M[elbourne], who might have been my mother, excited an interest in my feelings that few young women have been able to awaken. She was a charming person—a sort of modern Aspasia,²⁵⁶ uniting the energy of a man's mind with the delicacy and tenderness of a woman's. She wrote and spoke admirably, because she felt admirably. Envy, malice, hatred, or uncharitableness, found no place in her feelings. She had all of philosophy, save its moroseness, and all of nature, save its defects and general *faiblesse;* or if some portion of *faiblesse* attached to her, it only served to render her more forbearing to the errors of others. I have often thought, that, with a little more youth, Lady M[elbourne] might have turned my head, at all events she often turned my heart, by bringing me back to mild feelings, when the demon passion was strong within me. Her mind and heart were as fresh as if only sixteen summers had flown over her, instead of four times that number: and the mind and heart always leave external marks of their state of health. Goodness is the best cosmetic that has yet been discovered,²⁵⁷ for I am of opinion that, not according to our friend Moore—

²⁵⁶ The biographies of Lady Blessington and of D'Orsay do not mention Lady Melbourne, who was sixty-two when Byron met her in 1812. She died six years later, in 1818. It was supposed that the father of Lady Melbourne's son William Lamb was the third Earl of Egremont. Lady Blessington, Byron's "Irish Aspasia," would naturally take a sympathetic view of this "modern Aspasia."

²⁵⁷ Lady Blessington used no cosmetics of any kind.

As the shining casket's worn,
The gem within will tarnish too,—

but, *au contraire*, the decay of the gem will tarnish the casket—the sword will wear away the scabbard.[258] Then how rare is it to see age give its experience without its hardness of heart! and this was Lady M[elbourne]'s case. She was a captivating creature, *malgré* her eleven or twelve lustres, and I shall always love her.

"Did you know William Spencer, the Poet of Society, as they used to call him?" said Byron. "His was really what your countrymen call an elegant mind, polished, graceful, and sentimental, with just enough gaiety to prevent his being lachrymose, and enough sentiment to prevent his being too anacreontic. There was a great deal of genuine fun in Spencer's conversation, as well as a great deal of refined sentiment in his verses. I liked both, for both were perfectly aristocratic in their way; neither one nor the other was calculated to please the *canaille*, which made me like them all the better.[259] England was, after all I may say against it, very delightful in my day; that is to say, there were some six or seven very delightful people among the hundred commonplace that one saw every day,—seven stars, the pleiades, visible when all others had hid their diminished heads; and look where we may, where can we find so many stars united elsewhere? Moore, Campbell, Rogers, Spencer, as poets; and how many conversationists to be added to the galaxy of stars,—one set irradiating our libraries of a morning, and the other illuminating our dining-rooms of an evening! All this was, and would be, very delightful, could you have confined the stars within their own planets; but alas! they were given to wander into other spheres, and often set

[258] Cf. Byron's "So, We'll Go No More A-Roving," l. 5: "For the sword outwears its sheath."
[259] William Robert Spencer lent Moore the pistols used in his famous duel with Jeffrey and belonged to Watier's Club with Byron and Brummell (its perpetual president). Of him Byron wrote (*LJ*, V, 433): "Sotheby I say had seized upon me by the button and the heart-strings, and spared neither. W. Spencer, who likes fun, and don't dislike mischief, saw my case, and coming up to us both, took me by the hand, and pathetically bade me farewell: 'for,' said he, 'I see it is all over with you.' Sotheby then went away. 'Sic me servavit Apollo.'" A review of Spencer's *Poems* (1811) is reprinted in *LJ*, II, 413-20. There we read of the volume: "It consists chiefly of 'Vers de Société,' calculated to prove very delightful to a large circle of fashionable acquaintance, and pleasing to a limited number of vulgar purchasers." On Spencer's relations with Lady Blessington, see Madden, II, 288-89, and my introduction.

in the arctic circles, the frozen zones of nobility. I often thought at that time," continued Byron, "that England had reached the pinnacle,—that point where, as no advance can be made, a nation must retrograde,—and I don't think I was wrong. Our army had arrived at a state of perfection before unknown; Wellington's star was in the ascendant, and all others paled before its influence. We had Grey, Grenville, Wellesley, and Holland in the House of Peers, and Sheridan, Canning, Burdett, and Tierney[260] in the Commons. In society we were rich in poets, then in their zenith, now alas! fallen into the sear and yellow leaf; and in wits of whom one did not speak in the past tense. Of these, those whom the destroyer Time has not cut off he has mutilated; the wine of their lives has turned sour,—and lost its body, and who is there to supply their places? The march of intellect has been preceded by pioneers, who have levelled all the eminences of distinction, and reduced all to the level of decent mediocrity.

"It is said that as people grow old they magnify the superiority of past times, and detract from the advantages of the present: this is natural enough; for admitting that the advantages were equal, we view them through a different medium,—the sight, like all the other senses, loses its fine perceptions, and nought looks as bright through the dim optics of age as through the bright ones of youth; but as I have only reached the respectable point of middle age," continued Byron, "I cannot attribute my opinion of the falling off of the present men to my senility; and I really see or hear of no young men, either in the literary or political fields of London, who promise to supply the places of the men of my time—no successional crop to replace the passing or the past." I told Byron that the march of intellect had rendered the spread of knowledge so general, that young men abstained from writing, or at least from publishing, until they thought they had produced something likely to obtain attention, which was now much more difficult to be obtained than formerly, as people grew more fastidious every day. He would not agree to this, but maintained that mediocrity was the distinguishing feature of the present times, and that we should see no more

260 Byron refers twice in *LJ* to George Tierney (II, 372; VI, 187), the second time in a letter to Lord Blessington. Tierney is not mentioned in the biographies of Lady Blessington and D'Orsay.

134

men like those of his day. To hear Byron talk of himself, one would suppose that instead of thirty-six he was sixty years old: there is no affectation in this, as he says he feels all the languor and exhaustion of age.[261]

Byron always talks in terms of high admiration of Mr. Canning; says he is a man of superior abilities, brilliant fancy, cultivated mind, and most effective eloquence; and adds, that Canning only wanted to be born to a good estate to have made a great statesman. "Fortune," continued Byron, "would have saved him from tergiversation, the bare suspicion of which is destructive to the confidence a statesman ought to inspire. As it is," said he, "Canning is brilliant but not great, with all the elements in him that constitute greatness."[262]

Talking of Lord ———,[263] Byron observed, that his success in life was a proof of the weight that fortune gave a man, and his popularity a certain sign of his mediocrity: "the first," said Byron, "puts him out of the possibility of being suspected of mercenary motives; and the second precludes envy; yet you hear him praised at every side for his independence!—and a great merit it is truly," said he, "in a man who has high rank and large fortune,—what can he want, and where could be the temptation to barter his principles, since he already has all that people seek in such a traffic? No, I see no merit in Lord ———'s independence; give me the man who is poor and untitled, with talents to excite temptation, and honesty to resist it, and I will give him credit for independence of principle, because he deserves it.[264] People," continued Byron, "talk to you of Lord ———'s high character,—in what does it consist? Why, in being, as I before said, put by fortune and rank beyond the power of temptation,—having an even temper, thanks to a cool

[261] Cf. *The Idler* (*HVSV*, p. 357).

[262] Although George Canning had no large inherited fortune, his wife brought with her in 1800 £100,000, the bulk of which, however, was spent over the years. Canning returned to high office following the suicide of Castlereagh in 1822. Shortly afterwards Byron wrote of Canning: "I am not at all sorry that *he* is in power, for he is worth all the rest in point of talent, and, of course, will hardly be fool enough to go very far wrong" (*LJ*, VI, 162). He was a frequent guest at Lady Blessington's house in St. James's Square.

[263] Probably the 3rd Lord Landsdowne (1780-1863) (see Madden, II, 246, 503, and my introduction, p. 78.

[264] Byron reports a similar distinction made by Sheridan, talking of himself (*LJ*, V, 437).

head and a colder heart!—and a mediocrity of talents that insures his being 'content to live in decencies for ever,' while it exempts him from exciting envy or jealousy, the followers of excellence."

Byron continually reverts to Sir Walter Scott, and always in terms of admiration for his genius, and affection for his good qualities; he says that he never gets up from the perusal of one of his works, without finding himself in a better disposition; and that he generally reads his novels three times. "I find such a just mode of thinking," said Byron, "that I could fill volumes with detached thoughts from Scott, all, and each, full of truth and beauty. Then how good are his definitions! Do you remember, in 'Peveril of the Peak,' where he says, 'Presence of mind is courage. Real valour consists, not in being insensible to danger, but in being prompt to confront and disarm it.'[265] How true is this, and what an admirable distinction between moral and physical courage!"

I complimented him on his memory, and he added:—"My memory is very retentive, but the passage I repeated I read this morning for the third time. How applicable to Scott's works is the observation made by Madame du Deffand on Richardson's Novels, in one of her letters to Voltaire: 'La morale y est en action, et n'a jamais été traitée d'une manière plus intéressante. On meurt d'envie d'être parfait après cette lecture, et l'on croit que rien n'est si aisé.'[266] I think," continued Byron, after a pause, "that Scott is the only very successful genius that could be cited as being as generally beloved as a man, as he is admired as an author; and, I must add, he deserves it, for he is so thoroughly good-natured, sincere, and honest, that he disarms the envy and jealousy his extraordinary genius must excite. I hope to meet Scott once more before I die; for,

[265] The index to *LJ* indicates that Byron quoted from fifteen of Scott's works and referred to numerous others, but *Peveril of the Peak* (1822) is not among them, nor do I find that Byron made any reference elsewhere to this novel.

[266] I do not find that Byron referred elsewhere to the Marquise du Deffand. It may be significant that Byron refused to speak or to write in French to D'Orsay (*HVSV*, p. 352; *LJ*, VI, 190). It is clearly significant, however, that the scissors of Mme. du Deffand were displayed in the library at Seamore Place (Connely, p. 159), where the *Conversations* was written, and that Lady Blessington quoted her in *The Repealers* (*Works*, I, 282). For the French quotation, see *Correspondence Complète de la Marquise du Deffand*, ed. M. de Lescure (Paris, 1865), I, 243, a letter to Voltaire. There are important parallels, of course, between the lives and interests of Lady Blessington and those of the Marquise du Deffand.

worn out as are my affections, he still retains a strong hold for them."

There was something highly gratifying to the feelings in witnessing the warmth and cordiality that Byron's countenance and manner displayed when talking of Sir W. Scott; it proved how capable he was of entertaining friendship,—a sentiment of which he so frequently professed to doubt the existence:[267] but in this, as on many other points, he never did himself justice; and the turn for ridicule and satire implanted in his nature led him to indulge in observations in which his real feelings had no share. Circumstances had rendered Byron suspicious; he was apt to attribute every mark of interest or good-will shown to him as emanating from vanity, that sought gratification by a contact with his poetical celebrity;[268] this encouraged his predilection for hoaxing, ridiculing, and doubting friends and friendship. But as Sir W. Scott's own well-earned celebrity put the possibility of such a motive out of the question, Byron yielded to the sentiment of friendship in all its force for him, and never named him but with praise and affection. Byron's was a proud mind, that resisted correction, but that might easily be led by kindness; his errors had been so severely punished, that he became reckless and misanthropic, to avenge the injustice he had experienced; and, as misanthropy was foreign to his nature, its partial indulgence produced the painful state of being continually at war with his better feelings, and of rendering him dissatisfied with himself and others.

Talking of the effects that ingratitude and disappointments produced on the character of the individual who experienced them, Byron said, "that they invariably soured the nature of the person, who, when reduced to this state of acidity, was decried as a cynical, ill-natured brute. People wonder," continued he, "that a man is sour who has been feeding on acids all his life. The extremes of adversity and prosperity produce the same effects; they harden the heart, and enervate the mind; they render a person so selfish, that, occupied solely with his own pains or pleasures, he ceases to feel for others;

[267] For Lady Blessington on "a world where friendship is little known," see my introduction.
[268] Byron at times may well have suspected Lady Blessington's motives in this very fashion.

137

hence, as sweets turn to acids as well as sours, excessive prosperity may produce the same consequences as adversity."

His was a nature to be bettered by prosperity, and to be rendered obstinate by adversity. He invoked Stoicism to resist injustice, but its shield repelled not a single blow aimed at his peace, while its appearance deprived him of the sympathy for which his heart yearned. Let those, who would judge with severity the errors of this wayward child of genius, look back at his days of infancy and youth, and ask themselves whether, under such unfavourable auspices, they could have escaped the defects that tarnish the lustre of his fame,—defects rendered more obvious by the brightness they partially obscured, and which, without that brightness, had perhaps never been observed.

An eagle confined in a cage could not have been more displaced than was Byron in the artificial and conventional society that disgusted him with the world; like that daring bird, he could fearlessly soar high, and contemplate the sun, but he was unfit for the busy haunts of men; and he, whose genius could people a desert, pined in the solitude of crowds.[269] The people he saw resembled not the creatures his fancy had formed, and, with a heart yearning towards his fellow-men, pride and a false estimate of mankind repelled him from seeking their sympathy, though it deprived them not of his, as not all his assumed Stoicism could subdue the kind feelings that spontaneously showed themselves when the misfortunes of others were named. Byron warred only with the vices and follies of his species; and if he had a bitter jest and biting sarcasm for these, he had pity and forbearance for affliction, even though deserved, and forgot the cause in the effect. Misfortune was sacred in his eyes, and seemed to be the last link of the chain that connected him with his fellow-men. I remember hearing a person in his presence revert to the unhappiness of an individual known to all the party present, and, having instanced some proofs of the unhappiness, observe, that the person was not to be pitied, for he had brought it on himself by misconduct. I shall never forget the expression of Byron's face; it glowed with indignation, and, turning to the person who had excited it, he said, "If, as you say, this heavy

269 Cf. *Childe Harold*, III; especially stanzas lxix and lxxiii.

138

misfortune has been caused by ——'s misconduct, then is he doubly to be pitied, for he has the reproaches of conscience to embitter his draught. Those who have lost what is considered the right to pity in losing reputation and self-respect, are the persons who stand most in need of commiseration; and yet the charitable feelings of the over-moral would deny them this boon; reserving it for those on whom undeserved misfortunes fall, and who have that *within* which renders pity superfluous, have also respect to supply its place. Nothing so completely serves to demoralise a man as the certainty that he has lost the sympathy of his fellow-creatures; it breaks the last tie that binds him to humanity, and renders him reckless and irreclaimable.[270] This," continued Byron, "is my moral; and this it is that makes me pity the guilty and respect the unfortunate."

While he spoke, the earnestness of his manner, and the increased colour and animation of his countenance, bore evident marks of the sincerity of the sentiments he uttered: it was at such moments that his native goodness burst forth, and pages of misanthropic sarcasms could not efface the impression they left behind, though he often endeavoured to destroy such impressions by pleasantries against himself.

"When you go to Naples you must make acquaintance with Sir William Drummond," said Byron, "for he is certainly one of the most erudite men, and admirable philosophers now living. He has all the wit of Voltaire, with a profundity that seldom appertains to wit, and writes so forcibly, and with such elegance and purity of style, that his works possess a peculiar charm. Have you read his 'Academical Questions?' if not, get them directly, and I think you will agree with me, that the preface to that work alone would prove Sir William Drummond an admirable writer. He concludes it by the following sentence, which I think one of the best in our language:—'Prejudice may be trusted to guard the outworks for a short space of time, while Reason slumbers in the citadel; but if the latter sink into a lethargy, the former will quickly erect a standard for herself. Philosophy, wisdom, and liberty, support each other: he who will not reason is a bigot; he who cannot is a fool; and he who dares not is a slave.'[271] Is not the passage admirable?"

[270] This is quite Blessingtonian.
[271] Byron had known Drummond in the Alfred Club and had read his *Oedipus*

continued Byron; "how few could have written it, and yet how few read Drummond's works! they are too good to be popular. His 'Odin' is really a fine poem, and has some passages that are beautiful, but it is so little read that it may be said to have dropped stillborn from the press, a mortifying proof of the bad taste of the age. His translation of Persius is not only very literal, but preserves much of the spirit of the original; a merit that, let me tell you, is very rare at present, when translations have about as much of the spirit of the original as champaigne diluted with three parts of water may be supposed to retain of the pure and sparkling wine. Translations, for the most part, resemble imitations, where the marked defects are exaggerated, and the beauties passed over, always excepting the imitations of Mathews," continued Byron, "who seems to have continuous chords in his mind, that vibrate to those in the minds of others, as he gives not only the look, tones, and manners of the persons he personifies, but the very train of thinking, and the expressions they indulge in; and, strange to say, this modern Proteus succeeds best when the imitated is a person of genius, or great talent, as he seems to identify himself with him. His imitation of Curran, can hardly be so called—it is a *continuation*, and is inimitable. I remember Sir Walter Scott's observing, that Mathews' imitations were of the *mind*, to those who had the key;[272] but as the majority had it not, they were contented with admiring those of the person,

---

Judaicus (1811). His *Satires of Persius* had appeared in 1798, his *Academical Questions* in 1805, his *Odin* in 1817. For his admiration of Byron's "extraordinary talents and genius," see Madden, II, 491. Lady Blessington, who met him in Naples, thought him to be "one of the most intellectual men of his day" and associated him with Voltaire (Madden, I, 386, 387). Medwin had heard Byron "speak more than once of his Academical Questions" (*Captain Medwin*, p. 223). After reading *Odin*, Lady Blessington, in a letter to the author, April 24, 1825, compared it to the work of Michelangelo, Shakespeare, and Milton, and informed Drummond that he was "the first poet" of the age (Madden, I, 473). The quoted sentences appear in Byron's note to *Childe Harold*, IV, cxxvii.

272 For Sir Walter Scott on Charles Mathews's remarkable imitation of Curran, see *LJ*, II, 272, n. Byron lunched with Mathews and Scott on September 14, 1815, the last day that Scott ever saw Byron (*HVSV*, p. 131). Mathews was an early friend of Lord and Lady Blessington; Charles James Mathews, son of the comedian, joined the Blessingtons in Naples, in November 1823. Coleridge is reported to have said of the elder Mathews, " 'You call him a mimic: I define him as a comic poet acting his own poems' " (Julian Charles Young, *Personal Reminiscences by Chorley, Planché, and Young*, ed. Richard H. Stoddard [New York, 1874], p. 252).

140

and pronounced him a mimic who ought to be considered an accurate and philosophic observer of human nature, blessed with the rare talent of intuitively identifying himself with the mind of others. But, to return to Sir William Drummond," continued Byron, "he has escaped all the defects of translators, and his Persius resembles the original as nearly in feeling and sentiment as two languages so dissimilar in idiom will admit. Translations almost always disappoint me; I must, however, except Pope's 'Homer,' which has more of the spirit of Homer than all the other translations put together, and the Teian bard himself might have been proud of the beautiful odes which the Irish Anacreon has given us.

"Of the wits about town, I think," said Byron, "that George Colman was one of the most agreeable; he was *toujours prêt*, and after two or three glasses of champaigne, the quicksilver of his wit mounted to *beau fixe*. Colman has a good deal of tact; he feels that convivial hours were meant for enjoyment, and understands society so well, that he never obtrudes any private feeling, except hilarity, into it. His jokes are all good, and *readable*, and flow without effort, like the champaigne that often gives birth to them, sparkle after sparkle, and brilliant to the last. Then one is sure of Colman," continued Byron, "which is a great comfort; for to be made to cry when one had made up one's mind to laugh, is a *triste* affair. I remember that this was the great drawback with Sheridan; a little wine made him melancholy, and his melancholy was contagious; for who could bear to see the wizard, who could at will command smiles or tears, yield to the latter without sharing them, though one wished that the exhibition had been less public?[273] My feelings were never more excited than while writing the Monody on Sheridan, —every word that I wrote came direct from the heart.[274] Poor Sherry! what a noble mind was in him overthrown by poverty! and to see the men with whom he had passed his life, the dark souls whom his genius illumined, rolling in wealth, the Sybarites whose

[273] Byron comments on Sheridan's weeping, distinguishes between his and George Colman's company in his "Detached Thoughts" (*LJ*, II, 240-41, n.). Lady Blessington knew Colman as early as 1819 (Madden, I, 255-56).
[274] For an analysis of Byron's relations with Sheridan, see *Poetry*, IV, 69-70. Byron wrote to Murray, September 29, 1816: "The Monody was written by request of Mr. K[innaird] for the theatre. I did as well as I could; but where I have not my choice I pretend to answer for nothing" (*LJ*, III, 365-66).

slumbers a crushed rose-leaf would have disturbed, leaving him to die on the pallet of poverty, his last moments disturbed by the myrmidons of the law.[275] Oh! it was enough to disgust one with human nature, but above all with the nature of those who, professing liberality, were so little acquainted with its twin-sister generosity.

"I have seen poor Sheridan weep, and good cause had he," continued Byron. "Placed by his transcendent talents in an elevated sphere, without the means of supporting the necessary appearance, to how many humiliations must his fine mind have submitted, ere he had arrived at the state in which I knew him, of reckless jokes to pacify creditors of a morning, and alternate smiles and tears of an evening, round the boards where ostentatious dulness called in his aid to give a zest to the wine that often maddened him, but could not thaw the frozen current of their blood. Moore's Monody on Sheridan," continued Byron, "was a fine burst of generous indignation, and is one of the most powerful of his compositions. It was as daring as my 'Avatar,' which was bold enough, and, God knows, true enough, but I have never repented it. Your countrymen behaved dreadfully on that occasion; despair may support the chains of tyranny, but it is only baseness that can sing and dance in them,[277] as did the Irish on the [King]'s visit. But I see you would prefer another subject,[278] so let us talk of something else, though this cannot be a humiliating one to you personally, as I know your husband did not make one among the rabble at that Saturnalia.

"The Irish are strange people," continued Byron, "at one moment overpowered by sadness, and the next elevated to joy; impressionable as heated wax, and like it changing each time that it is

[275] Shortly before his death, Sheridan wrote to Rogers to inform him that bailiffs were prepared to take the rugs off his floors and arrest him (*Poetry*, IV, 73, n. 1, quoted from Moore's *Life of Sheridan*, 1825).

[276] Moore's "Lines on the Death of SH-R-D-N" clearly implied that the Prince Regent should have provided financial aid to "that high-gifted man, / The pride of the palace, the bower, and the hall." Although Byron's attack on George IV, occasioned by his visit to Ireland, is indeed "bold," Byron did not publish it: he directed Moore to have twenty copies privately and anonymously printed in Paris. It was first published in Medwin's *Conversations*.

[277] Cf. "The Irish Avatar," stanza 7: "this dance in thy chain" (*Poetry*, IV, 555).

[278] Lady Blessington's sympathies were chiefly with the English, as *The Repealers* makes very clear.

142

warmed. The dolphin, when shone upon by the sun, changes not its hues more frequently than do your mobile countrymen, and this want of stability will leave them long what centuries have found them—slaves. I liked them before the degradation of 1822,[279] but the dance in chains disgusted me. What would Grattan and Curran have thought of it?[280] and Moore, why struck he not the harp of Erin to awaken the slumbering souls of his supine countrymen?[281]

[279] George IV visited Dublin in 1821 (August), not 1822.

[280] The names of Grattan and Curran appear indignantly together in the same line in stanza 29 of "The Irish Avatar" and are also associated in one of Byron's "Detached Thoughts" (*LJ*, II, 271, n.).

[281] At this time, as Moore explained later, he did not write against the Irish when they welcomed the King; he "discharged" his "Irish rage on the Neapolitans . . . 'Aye, down to the dust with them, slaves as they are.'" The poem is entitled "Lines on the Entry of the Austrians into Naples, 1821" (see *The Letters of Thomas Moore*, II, 786 and nn.).

LORD BYRON.

To those who only know Byron as an author, it would be difficult, if not impossible, to convey a just impression of him as a man. In him the elements of good and evil were so strongly mixed,[1] that an error could not be detected that was not allied to some good quality; and his fine qualities, and they were many, could hardly be separated from the faults that sullied them. In bestowing on Byron a genius as versatile as it was brilliant and powerful, Nature had not denied him warmth of heart, and the kind affections that beget, while they are formed to repay friendship; but a false *beau idéal* that he had created for himself, and a wish of exciting wonder, led him into a line of conduct calculated to lower him in the estimation of superficial observers, who judge from appearances, while those who had opportunities of observing him more nearly, and who made allowance for his besetting sin, (the assumption of vices and errors, that he either had not, or exaggerated the appearance of,)[2] found in him more to admire than censure, and to pity than condemn. In his severest satires, however much of malice there might be in the expression, there was little in the feeling that dictated them; they came from the imagination and not from the heart, for in a few minutes after he had unveiled the errors of some friend or acquaintance, he would call attention to some of their good quali-

---

[1] Cf. *Lara*, ll. 289-90: "In him inexplicably mixed appeared / Much to be loved and hated, sought and feared."

[2] Many who knew Byron best agreed. Cf. Moore's *Life* (*HVSV*, p. 241): "this fancy for self-defamation," carried to "perverse length."

Lady Blessington wrote in her "Night Thought Book," kept in 1834 and 1835: "The great majority of men are actors, who prefer an assumed part to that which Nature had assigned them. They seek to be something, or to appear something which they are not, and even stoop to the affectation of defects rather than display real estimable qualities which belong to them" (Madden, I, 242).

ties with as much apparent pleasure as he had dwelt on their defects. A nearly daily intercourse of ten weeks[3] with Byron left the impression on my mind, that if an extraordinary quickness of perception prevented his passing over the errors of those with whom he came in contact, and a natural incontinence of speech[4] betrayed him into an exposure of them, a candour and good-nature, quite as remarkable, often led him to enumerate their virtues, and to draw attention to them. It may be supposed, that with such powerful talents, there was less excuse for the attacks he was in the habit of making on his friends and acquaintances;[5] but those very talents were the cause; they suggested a thousand lively and piquant images to his fancy, relative to the defects of those with whom he associated; and he had not self-command sufficient to repress the sallies that he knew must show at once his discrimination and talents for ridicule, and amuse his hearers, however they might betray a want of good-nature and sincerity.

There was no premeditated malignity in Byron's nature; though constantly in the habit of exposing the follies and vanity of his friends, I never heard him blacken their reputations, and I never felt an unfavourable impression from any of the censures he bestowed, because I saw they were aimed at follies, and not character. He used frequently to say that people hated him more for exposing their follies than if he had attacked their moral characters, adding, "Such is the vanity of human nature, that men would prefer being defamed to being ridiculed, and would much sooner pardon the first than the second. There is much more folly than vice in the world," said Byron. "The appearance of the latter is often assumed by the dictates of the former, and people pass for being vicious who are only foolish. I have seen such examples," continued he, "of this in the world, that it makes one rather incredulous as to the extent of actual vice; but I can believe any thing of the capabilities of vanity and folly, having witnessed to what length they can go. I have seen women compromise their honour (in appearance only)

[3] Teresa Guiccioli: No!
[4] Cf. Moore's *Life* (*HVSV*, p. 242): "the utter powerlessness of retention with which he promulgated his every thought and feeling,—more especially if at all connected with the subject of self. . . ."
[5] This was a facet of Byron not called forth by most of those with whom he talked.

145

for the triumph (and a hopeful one) of rivalling some contemporary belle; and men sacrifice theirs, in reality, by false boastings for the gratification of vanity. All, all is vanity and vexation of spirit,"[6] added he; "the first being the legitimate parent of the second, an offspring that, school it how you will, is sure to turn out a curse to its parent."

"Lord Blessington has been talking to me about Mr. Galt,"[7] said Lord Byron, "and tells me much good of him. I am pleased at finding he is as amiable a man as his recent works prove him to be a clever and intelligent author. When I knew Galt, years ago, I was not in a frame of mind to form an impartial opinion of him; his mildness and equanimity struck me even then; but, to say the truth, his manner had not deference enough[8] for my then aristocratical taste, and finding I could not awe him into a respect sufficiently profound for my sublime self, either as a peer or an author, I felt a little grudge towards him that has now completely worn off. There is a quaint humour and observance of character in his novels that interest me very much, and when he chooses to be pathetic he fools one to his bent, for I assure you the 'Entail' beguiled me of some portion of watery humours, yclept tears, 'albeit unused to the melting mood.' What I admire particularly in Galt's works," continued Byron, "is, that with a perfect knowledge of human nature and its frailties and legerdemain tricks, he shows a tenderness of heart which convinces one that *his* is in the right place, and he has a sly caustic humour that is very amusing. All that Lord Blessington has been telling me of Galt has made me reflect on the striking difference between his (Lord B.'s) nature and my own. I had an excellent opportunity of judging Galt, being shut up on

[6] Byron quoted from Ecclesiastes at least once in his letters (*LJ*, II, 373).

[7] On the relations between Byron and John Galt, with whom the poet quarreled in December 1813, bringing their friendship to its final end, see *HVSV*, pp. xii-iv. Galt had made an insulting remark about Lady Oxford to Byron's face (see Byron's last letter to Galt, December 11, 1813 [*LJ*, II, 304-06]). Byron does not seem to have made written reference to Galt after this year. There are no references by name to any of Galt's novels. The novelist, however, was an early friend of Lady Blessington and dedicated the second edition of *Sir Andrew Wylie* (1822) to Lord Blessington, with his Lordship's portrait added. He had served as the model for the character of Lord Sandiford in the novel. *The Entail*, mentioned below, was published in 1823. See also above, p. 51.

[8] Teresa Guiccioli: *Bah! Il n'a pas dis* [sic] *cela.*

146

board ship with him for some days; and though I saw he was mild, equal, and sensible, I took no pains to cultivate his acquaintance further than I should with any common-place person, which he was not; and Lord Blessington in London, with a numerous acquaintance, and 'all appliances to boot,' for choosing and selecting, has found so much to like in Galt, *malgré* the difference of their politics, that his liking has grown into friendship.

"I must say that I never saw the milk of human kindness overflow in any nature to so great a degree, as in Lord Blessington's," continued Byron. "I used, before I knew him well, to think that Shelley was the most amiable person I ever knew, but I now think that Lord B. bears off the palm,[9] for he has been assailed by all the temptations that so few can resist, those of unvarying prosperity, and has passed the ordeal victoriously,—a triumphant proof of the extraordinary goodness of his nature, while poor Shelley had been tried in the school of adversity only, which is not such a corrupter as is that of prosperity. If Lord B. has not the power, Midas-like, of turning whatever he touches into gold," continued Byron, "he has at least that of turning all into good. I, alas! detect only the evil qualities of those that approach me, while he discovers the amiable. It appears to me, that the extreme excellence of his own disposition prevents his attributing evil to others; I do assure you," continued Byron, "I have thought better of mankind since I have known him intimately." The earnestness of Byron's manner convinced me that he spoke his real sentiments relative to Lord B., and that his commendations were not uttered with a view of gratifying me, but flowed spontaneously in the honest warmth of the moment. A long, daily and hourly knowledge of the person he praised, has enabled me to judge of the justice of the commendation, and Byron never spoke more truly than when he pronounced Lord B.'s a faultless nature. While he was speaking, he continually looked back, for fear that the person of whom he spoke should overhear his remarks, as he was riding behind, at a little distance from us.

"Is Lady —— as restless and indefatigable as ever? (asked Byron.)—She is an extraordinary woman, and the most thorough-

[9] It is not easy to imagine Byron seriously making this comparison. Is the slight echo of Falstaff in any way meaningful below? "I shall think the better of myself, and thee, during my life—I for a valiant lion, and thou for a true prince" (*I Henry Fourth*, II, iv, 302-04).

paced manœuvrer I ever met with; she cannot make or accept an invitation, or perform any of the common courtesies of life, without manœuvring, and has always some plan in agitation, to which all her acquaintance are made subservient. This is so evident, that she never approached me that I did not expect her to levy contributions on my muse, the only disposable property I possessed; and I was as surprised as grateful at finding it was not pressed into the service for compassing some job, or accomplishing some mischief. Then she passes for being clever, when she is only cunning: her life has been passed in giving the best proof of want of cleverness, that of intriguing to carry points not worth intriguing for, and that must have occurred in the natural course of events without any manœuvring on her part. Cleverness and cunning are incompatible— I never saw them united; the latter is the resource of the weak, and is only natural to them: children and fools are always cunning, but clever people never. The world, or rather the persons who compose it, are so indolent, that when they see great personal activity, joined to indefatigable and unshrinking exertion of tongue, they conclude that such effects must proceed from adequate causes, never reflecting that real cleverness requires not such aids; but few people take the trouble of analyzing the actions or motives of others, and least of all when such others have no envy-stirring attractions. On this account Lady ——'s manœuvres are set down to cleverness; but when she was young and pretty they were less favourably judged. Women of a certain age (continued Byron) are for the most part bores or *méchantes*. I have known some delightful exceptions, but on consideration they were past the certain age, and were no longer, like the coffin of Mahomet hovering between heaven and earth, that is to say, floating between maturity and age, but had fixed their persons on the unpretending easy chairs of *vieillesse*, and their thoughts neither on war nor conquest, except the conquest of self. Age is beautiful when no attempt is made to modernize it. Who can look at the interesting remains of loveliness without some of the same tender feelings of melancholy with which we regard a fine ruin? Both mark the triumph of the mighty conqueror Time; and whether we examine the eyes, the windows of the soul, through which love and hope once sparkled, now dim and languid, showing only resignation, or the ruined casements of

148

the abbey or castle through which blazed the light of tapers, and the smoke of incense offered to the Deity, the feelings excited are much the same, and we approach both with reverence,—always (interrupted Byron) provided that the old beauty is not a specimen of the florid Gothic,—by which I mean restored, painted, and varnished,—and that the abbey or castle is not whitewashed; both, under such circumstances, produce the same effect on me, and all reverence is lost; but I do seriously admire age when it is not ashamed to let itself be seen, and look on it as something sanctified and holy, having passed through the fire of its passions, and being on the verge of the grave.

"I once (said Byron) found it necessary to call up all that could be said in favour of matured beauty, when my heart became captive to a *donna* of forty-six, who certainly excited as lively a passion in my breast as ever it has known; and even now the autumnal charms of Lady [Oxford] are remembered by me with more than admiration.[10] She resembled a landscape by Claude Lorraine, with a setting sun, her beauties enhanced by the knowledge that they were shedding their last dying beams, which threw a radiance around. A woman (continued Byron) is only grateful for her *first* and *last* conquest. The first of poor dear Lady [Oxford]'s was achieved before I entered on this world of care, but the *last* I do flatter myself was reserved for me, and a *bonne bouche* it was."

I told Byron that his poetical sentiments of the attractions of matured beauty had, at the moment, suggested four lines to me; which he begged me to repeat, and he laughed not a little when I recited the following lines to him:—

> Oh! talk not to me of the charms of youth's dimples,
> There's surely more sentiment center'd in wrinkles.
> They're the triumphs of time that mark beauty's decay,
> Telling tales of years past, and the few left to stay.

"I never spent an hour with Moore (said Byron) without being ready to apply to him the expression attributed to Aristophanes, 'You have spoken roses;' his thoughts and expressions have all the beauty

---

[10] Lady Oxford was in fact only forty in 1812, when Byron met her. Medwin has Byron refer to the "autumn of [her] beauty." Her first lover, following her marriage in 1794, seems to have been Sir Francis Burdett.

and freshness of those flowers, but the piquancy of his wit, and the readiness of his repartees, prevent one's ear being cloyed by too much sweets,[11] and one cannot 'die of a rose in aromatic pain' with Moore, though he does speak roses, there is such an endless variety in his conversation. Moore is the only poet I know (continued Byron) whose conversation equals his writings; he comes into society with a mind as fresh and buoyant as if he had not expended such a multiplicity of thoughts on paper; and leaves behind him an impression that he possesses an inexhaustible mine equally brilliant as the specimens he has given us. Will you, after this frank confession of my opinion of your countryman, ever accuse me of injustice again? You see I can render justice when I am not forced into its opposite extreme by hearing people overpraised, which always awakes the sleeping Devil in my nature, as witness the desperate attack I gave your friend Lord —— the other day, merely because you all wanted to make me believe he was a model, which he is not; though I admit he is not *all* or *half* that which I accused him of being. Had you dispraised, probably I should have defended him."

"I will give you some stanzas I wrote yesterday (said Byron); they are as simple as even Wordsworth himself could write, and would do for music."

The following are the lines:—

To ——.[12]

But once I dared to lift my eyes—
　To lift my eyes to thee;
And since that day, beneath the skies,
　No other sight they see.

In vain sleep shuts them in the night—
　The night grows day to me;
Presenting idly to my sight
　What still a dream must be.

[11] Contrast Lady Blessington as reported by Crabb Robinson in 1832 (*HVSV*, p. 371): "Lord Byron used to say: 'Tommy makes pretty *sweet* verses—sweet indeed, no wonder—he was fed on plums and sugar-candy by his father, the Dublin grocer.'"

[12] E. H. Coleridge believes that these lines were "probably" addressed to Lady Blessington (*Poetry*, IV, 564, n. 1).

A fatal dream—for many a bar
Divides thy fate from mine;
And still my passions wake and war,
But peace be still with thine.

"No one writes songs like Moore (said Byron). Sentiment and imagination are joined to the most harmonious versification, and I know no greater treat than to hear him sing his own compositions; the powerful expression he gives to them, and the pathos of the tones of his voice, tend to produce an effect on my feelings that no other songs, or singer, ever could. [Caroline Lamb] used to write pretty songs,[13] and certainly has talent, but I maintain there is more poesy in her prose, at least more fiction, than is to be met with in a folio of poetry. You look shocked at what you think my ingratitude towards her, but if you knew half the cause I have to dislike her, you would not condemn me. You shall however know some parts of that serio-comic drama, in which I was forced to play a part; and, if you listen with candour, you must allow I was more sinned against than sinning."

The curious history that followed this preface is not intended for the public eye, as it contains anecdotes and statements that are calculated to give pain to several individuals—the same feeling that dictates the suppression of this most curious episode in Byron's London life, has led to the suppression of many other piquant and amusing disclosures made by him, as well as some of the most severe poetical portraits that ever were drawn of some of his supposed friends,[14] and many of his acquaintances. The vigour with which they are sketched proves that he entered into every fold of the characters of the originals, and that he painted them *con amore*, but he could not be accused of being a flattering portrait painter.

The disclosures made by Byron could never be considered *confidential*, because they were always at the service of the first listener who fell in his way, and who happened to know anything of the parties he talked of. They were not confided with any injunc-

[13] For some of Lady Caroline Lamb's songs, see Isaac Nathan, *Fugitive Pieces and Reminiscences of Lord Byron* (London, 1829). I can find no evidence that Lady Blessington knew her personally.
[14] These probably included the poem on Rogers, "Question and Answer."

151

tion to secrecy,[15] but were indiscriminately made to his chance companions,—nay, he often declared his decided intention of writing copious notes to the Life he had given to his friend Moore, in which *the whole truth* should be declared of, for, and against, himself and others.

Talking of this gift to Mr. Moore, he asked me if it had made a great sensation in London, and whether people were not greatly alarmed at the thoughts of being shown up in it? He seemed much pleased in anticipating the panic it would occasion, naming all the persons who would be most alarmed.

I told him that he had rendered the most essential service to the cause of morality by his confessions, as a dread of similar disclosures would operate [more] in putting people on their guard in reposing dangerous confidence in men, than all the homilies that ever were written; and that people would in future be warned by the phrase of "beware of being *Byroned*," instead of the old cautions used in past times. "This (continued I) is a sad antithesis to your motto of *Crede Byron*." He appeared vexed at my observations, and it struck me that he seemed uneasy and out of humour for the next half-hour of our ride. I told him that his gift to Moore had suggested to me the following lines:—

> The ancients were famed for their friendship we're told,
> Witness Damon and Pythias, and others of old;
> But, Byron, 'twas thine friendship's power to extend,
> Who surrender'd thy Life for the sake of a friend.

He laughed heartily at the lines, and, in laughing at them, recovered his good-humour.

"I have never," said Byron, "succeeded to my satisfaction in an epigram; my attempts have not been happy, and knowing Greek as I do, and admiring the Greek epigrams, which excel all others, it is mortifying that I have not succeeded better: but I begin to think that epigrams demand a peculiar talent, and that talent I decidedly have not. One of the best in the English language is that of Rogers on [Ward]; it has the true Greek talent of expressing by implication what is wished to be conveyed.

[15] Cf. Medwin in the preface to his *Conversations*, p. xvi: "They were communicated . . . without any injunctions to secrecy. . . ."

> [Ward] has no heart they say, but I deny it:
> He has a heart—he gets his speeches by it.[16]

This is the *ne plus ultra* of English epigrams." I told Byron that I had copied Roger's thought, in two lines on an acquaintance of mine, as follows:—

> The charming Mary has no mind they say;
> I prove she has—it changes every day.

This amused him, and he repeated several epigrams, very clever, but which are too severe to be given in these pages. The epigrams of Byron are certainly not equal to his other poetry, they are merely clever, and such as any person of talent might have written, but who except him, in our day, could have written Childe Harold? No one; for admitting that the same talent exists, (which I am by no means prepared to admit) the possessor must have experienced the same destiny, to have brought it to the same perfection. The reverses that nature and circumstances entailed on Byron served but to give a higher polish and a finer temper to his genius. All that marred the perfectibility of the man, had perfected the poet, and this must have been evident to those who approached him, though it had escaped his own observation. Had the choice been left him, I am quite sure he would not have hesitated a moment in choosing between the renown of the poet, even at the price of the happiness of the man, as he lived much more in the future than in the present, as do all persons of genius. As it was, he felt dissatisfied with his position, without feeling that it was the whetstone that sharpened his powers; for with all his affected philosophy, he was a philosopher but in theory, and never reduced it to practice. One of the strangest anomalies in Byron was the exquisite taste displayed in his descriptive poetry, and the total want of it that was so visible in his modes of life. Fine scenery seemed to produce little effect on his feelings,[17] though his descriptions are so glowing, and the elegancies and comforts of refined life he appeared to as little understand as value. This last did not arise from a contempt of them, as might be imagined, but from an ignorance of what constituted

[16] Cf. Medwin, *Conversations*, p. 210. The epigram was well known.
[17] See above, p. 40, and my *Byron: The Record of a Quest*, pp. 32-33, and Chapter II, "Byron's Laughter."

153

them. I have seen him apparently delighted with the luxurious inventions in furniture, equipages, plate, &c. common to all persons of a certain station or fortune, and yet after an inquiry as to their prices—an inquiry so seldom made by persons of his rank, shrink back alarmed at the thought of the expense, though there was nothing alarming in it, and congratulate himself that he had no such luxuries, or did not require them. I should say that a bad and vulgar taste predominated in all Byron's equipments, whether in dress or in furniture. I saw his bed at Genoa, when I passed through in 1826, and it certainly was the most gaudily vulgar thing I ever saw; the curtains in the worst taste, and the cornice having his family motto of "Crede Byron" surmounted by baronial coronets. His carriages and his liveries were in the same bad taste,[18] having an affectation of finery, but *mesquin* in the details, and tawdry in the *ensemble*; and it was evident that he piqued himself on them, by the complacency with which they were referred to.[19] These trifles are touched upon, as being characteristic of the man, and would have been passed by, as unworthy of notice, had he not shown that they occupied a considerable portion of his attention. He has even asked us if they were not rich and handsome, and then remarked that no wonder they were so, as they cost him a great deal of money. At such moments it was difficult to remember that one was speaking to the author of Childe Harold. If the poet was often forgotten in the levities of the man, the next moment some original observation, cutting repartee, or fanciful simile, reminded one that he who could be ordinary in trifles, (the only points of assimilation between him and the common herd of men,)

[18] Barry, who had purchased some of Byron's furniture (Marchand, p. 1090), had also taken Byron's house in Albaro and was living there as late as October 1826 (Marchand, note to p. 1089, l. 37), when he proudly showed Hobhouse the table at which Byron dined. One of Byron's coaches was copied from a coach used by Napoleon, complete with "*lit de repos*, . . . library, a plate-chest, and every apparatus for dining" (quoted by Marchand, p. 603). For a description of Lady Blessington's traveling carriage, see *The Idler in Italy*, I, 41-43, and Connely, p. 56 ("a gypsy's dream"); its equipment was similar to that of Byron's. The Blessingtons normally traveled with so many carriages that the party and their rolling stock were described by an eyewitness as the "Blessington circus" (Michael Sadleir, *The Strange Life of Lady Blessington* [Boston, 1933], p. 54). For a discussion of her own vulgar taste, see the introduction to this volume.

[19] Teresa Guiccioli: Mensonges *mais ce sont des mensonges pour plaire a dorset* [sic; i.e., D'Orsay].

154

was only ordinary when he descended to their level; but when once on subjects worthy his attention, the great poet shone forth, and they who had felt self-complacency at noting the futilities that had lessened the distance between him and them, were forced to see the immeasurable space which separated them, when he allowed his genius to be seen. It is only Byron's pre-eminence as a poet that can give interest to such details as the writer has entered into: if they are written without partiality, they are also given in no unfriendly spirit; but his defects are noted with the same feeling with which an astronomer would remark the specks that are visible even in the brightest stars, and which having examined more minutely than common observers, he wishes to give the advantages of his discoveries, though the specks he describes have not made him overlook the brightness of the luminaries they sullied, but could not obscure.

"You know —— of course, (said Byron,) every one does. I hope you don't like him; water and oil are not more antipathetic than he and I are to each other. I admit that his abilities are great; they are of the very first order; but he has that which almost always accompanies great talents, and generally proves a counterbalance to them—an overweening ambition, which renders him not over nice about the means, as long as he attains the end; and this facility will prevent his ever being a truly great man, though it may abridge his road to what is considered greatness—official dignity. You shall see some verses in which I have not spared him, and yet I have only said what I believe to be strictly correct. Poets are said to succeed best in fiction; but this I deny; at least I always write best when truth inspires me, and my satires, which are founded on truth, have more spirit than all my other productions, for they were written *con amore*. My intimacy with the —— family (continued Byron) let me into many of ——'s secrets, and they did not raise him in my estimation.

"One of the few persons in London, whose society served to correct my predisposition to misanthropy, was Lord Holland.[20] There

[20] The degree of Byron's intimacy with Lord Holland is suggested by the fact that the poet showed to him, and to M. G. Lewis, Moore, Rogers, and Lady Melbourne, the letter which Lord Sligo wrote describing Byron's mysterious adventure with the Turkish girl in Athens, on her way to her death. At the time of the separation proceedings, Byron requested letters from three of his

is more benignity, and a greater share of the milk of human kindness in his nature than in that of any man I know, always excepting Lord B——. Then there is such a charm in his manners, his mind is so highly cultivated, his conversation so agreeable, and his temper so equal and bland, that he never fails to send away his guests content with themselves and delighted with him. I never (continued Byron) heard a difference of opinion about Lord Holland; and I am sure no one could know him without liking him. Lord Erskine,[21] in talking to me of Lord Holland, observed, that it was his extreme good-nature alone that prevented his taking as high a political position as his talents entitled him to fill. This quality (continued Byron) will never prevent ——'s rising in the world; so that his talents will have a fair chance.

"It is difficult (said Byron) when one detests an author not to detest his works. There are some that I dislike so cordially, that I am aware of my incompetency to give an impartial opinion of their writings. Southey, *par exemple*, is one of these. When travelling in Italy, he was reported to me as having circulated some reports much to my disadvantage, and still more to that of two ladies of my acquaintance; all of which, through the kind medium of some good-natured friends, were brought to my ears; and I have vowed eternal vengeance against him,[22] and all who uphold him; which vengeance has been poured forth, in phials of wrath, in the shape of epigrams and lampoons, some of which you shall see. When any one attacks me, on the spur of the moment I sit down and write all the *méchanceté* that comes into my head; and, as some of these sallies have merit, they amuse me, and are too good to be torn or

---

friends, Holland, Rogers, and Kinnaird, to reply to the charge that he had encouraged members of his circle to abuse Lady Byron in public. For D'Orsay's complimentary sketch of Lord Holland, an old friend or acquaintance of Lord Blessington, see Madden, II, 503. Macaulay's magnificent tribute to Lord Holland is in agreement with that of Byron (see *Miscellaneous Works of Lord Macaulay*, ed. Lady Trevelyan [New York, n.d.], "Lord Holland," especially III, 147-51).

[21] Lord Erskine was an early and intimate friend of Lady Blessington (Madden, II, 512).

[22] Henry Crabb Robinson recorded in his diary in 1832 (*HVSV*, p. 371), "Lady Blessington says that Byron's hatred of Southey originated in Southey's saying that Lord Byron was *the lover of two sisters*, Mrs. Shelley and Miss Clairmont—not that he was offended by the immorality imputed to him, but the bad taste of loving so vulgar a woman as Mrs. Shelley."

burned, and so are kept, and see the light long after the feeling that dictated them has subsided. All my malice evaporates in the effusions of my pen: but I dare say those that excite it would prefer any other mode of vengeance. At Pisa, a friend told me that Walter Savage Landor[23] had declared he either would not, or could not, read my works. I asked my officious friend if he was sure which it was that Landor said, as the *would not* was not offensive, and the *could not* was highly so. After some reflection, he, of course *en ami*, chose the most disagreeable signification; and I marked down Landor in the tablet of memory as a person to whom a *coup-de-pat* must be given in my forthcoming work, though he really is a man whose brilliant talents and profound erudition I cannot help admiring as much as I respect his character—various proofs of the generosity, manliness, and independence of which has [*sic*] reached me; so you see I can render justice (*en petite comité*) even to a man who says he could not read my works; this, at least, shows some good feeling, if the *petit* vengeance of attacking him in my work cannot be defended; but my attacking proves the truth of the observation made by a French writer—that we don't like people for the merit we discover in them, but for that which they find in us."

When Byron was one day abusing —— most vehemently, we accused him of undue severity; and he replied, he was only deterred from treating him much more severely by the fear of being indicted under the Act of cruelty to Animals!

"I am quite sure (said Byron) that many of our worst actions and our worst thoughts are caused by friends. An enemy can never do as much injury, or cause as much pain: if he speaks ill of one, it is set down as an exaggeration of malice, and therefore does little harm, and he has no opportunity of telling one any of the disagreeable things that are said in one's absence; but a friend has such an amiable candour in admitting the faults least known, and often unsuspected, and of denying or defending with *acharnement* those that can neither be denied nor defended, that he is sure to do one mischief. Then he thinks himself bound to retail and detail every dis-

---

[23] Byron's chief references to Landor, an old friend of Lady Blessington, were disparaging ones alluding to his friendship with Southey (see *LJ*, VI, 389; *Poetry*, IV, 484-85; VI, 445). Byron and Landor seem never to have met personally. Landor, whom Lady Blessington met after she met Byron, became one of her most devoted friends.

agreeable remark or story he hears, and generally under the injunction of secrecy; so that one is tormented without the power of bringing the slanderer to account, unless by a breach of confidence. I am always tempted to exclaim, with Socrates, 'My friends! there are no friends!' when I hear and see the advantages of friendship.[24] It is odd (continued Byron) that people do not seem aware that the person who repeats to a friend an offensive observation, uttered when he was absent, without any idea that he was likely to hear it, is much more blamable than the person who originally said it; of course I except a friend who hears a charge brought against one's honour, and who comes and openly states what he has heard, that it may be refuted: but this friends seldom do; for, as that Queen of egoists, La Marquise du Deffand, truly observed— 'Ceux qu'on nomme amis sont ceux par qui on n'a pas à craindre d'être assassiné, mais qui laisseroient faire les assassins.'[25] Friends are like diamonds; all wish to possess them: but few can or will pay their price; and there never was more wisdom embodied in a phrase than in that which says—'Defend me from my friends, and I will defend myself from my enemies.'"

Talking of poetry, (Byron said) that "next to the affected simplicity of the Lake School, he disliked prettinesses, or what are called flowers of poetry; they are only admissible in the poetry of ladies, (said he,) which should always have a sprinkling of dew-gemmed leaves and flowers of rainbow hues, with tuneful birds and gorgeous butterflies—" Here he laughed like a child, and added, "I suppose you would never forgive me if I finished the sentence,—sweet emblems of fair woman's looks and mind." Having joined in the laugh, which was irresistible from the mock heroic air he assumed, I asked him how he could prove any resemblance between tuneful birds, gorgeous butterflies, and woman's face or mind. He immediately replied, "Have I not printed a certain line, in which I

24 Cf. Lady Blessington in a letter to Landor in 1832 (J. F. Molloy, *The Most Gorgeous Lady Blessington*, p. 227): ". . . I live in a world where friendship is little known, and were it not for one or two individuals like yourself, I might be tempted to exclaim with Socrates, 'My friends, there are no friends.'"

25 See above, p. 136, n. 266. The similarities between Lady Blessington and the cynical Madame du Deffand are clearly implied in a sketch of the latter in Madden, II, 504-06.

say, 'the music breathing from her face?'[26] and do not all, even philosophers, assert, that there is harmony in beauty, nay, that there is no
beauty without it? Now tuneful birds are musical; *ergo*, that simile
holds good as far as the face, and the butterfly must stand for the
mind, brilliant, light, and wandering. I say nothing of its being the
emblem of the soul, because I have not quite made up my mind that
women have souls; but, in short, flowers and all that is fragile and
beautiful must remind one of women. So do not be offended with
my comparison.

"But to return to the subject, (continued Byron,) you do not, cannot like what are called flowers in poetry. I try to avoid them as
much as possible in mine, and I hope you think that I have succeeded." I answered that he had given oaks to Parnassus instead of
flowers,[27] and while disclaiming the compliment it seemed to gratify him.

"A successful work (said Byron) makes a man a wretch for life:
it engenders in him a thirst for notoriety and praise, that precludes
the possibility of repose; this spurs him on to attempt others, which
are always expected to be superior to the first; hence arise disappointment, as expectation being too much excited is rarely gratified,
and, in the present day, one failure is placed as a counterbalance
to fifty successful efforts. Voltaire was right (continued Byron)
when he said that the fate of a literary man resembled that of the
flying fish; if he dives in the water the fish devour him, and if he
rises in the air he is attacked by the birds. Voltaire (continued
Byron) had personal experience of the persecution a successful author must undergo; but *malgré* all this, he continued to keep alive
the sensation he had excited in the literary world, and, while at Ferney, thought only of astonishing Paris. Montesquieu has said 'that
moins on pense plus on parle.'[28] Voltaire was a proof, indeed I
have known many (said Byron), of the falseness of this observation,
for who ever wrote or talked as much as Voltaire? But Montesquieu, when he wrote his remark, thought not of literary men; he

[26] *The Bride of Abydos*, I, 179. Moore, *Life*, p. 218, discusses the variants
of this line.

[27] Teresa Guiccioli: Pah.

[28] Byron had read Montesquieu's *Esprit des Lois*; see *LJ*, I, 172, and Moore,
Life, p. 47.

was thinking of the *bavards* of society, who certainly think less and talk more than all others. I was once very much amused (said Byron) by overhearing the conversation of two country ladies, in company with a celebrated author, who happened to be that evening very taciturn: one remarked to the other, how strange it was that a person reckoned so clever, should be so silent! and the other answered, Oh! he has nothing left to say, he has sold all his thoughts to his publishers. This you will allow was a philosophical way of explaining the silence of an author.

"One of the things that most annoyed me in London (said Byron) was the being continually asked to give my opinion on the works of contemporaries. I got out of the difficulty as well I could, by some equivocal answer that might be taken in two ways; but even this prudence did not save me, and I have been accused of envy and jealousy of authors, of whose works, God knows, I was far from being envious. I have also been suspected of jealousy towards ancient as well as modern writers; but Pope, whose poems I really envy, and whose works I admire, perhaps more than any living or dead English writer, they have never found out that I was jealous of, nay, probably, as I always praise him, they suppose I do not seriously admire him, as insincerity on all points is universally attributed to me.

"I have often thought of writing a book to be filled with all the charges brought against me in England (said Byron); it would make an interesting folio, with my notes, and might serve posterity as a proof of the charity, good-nature, and candour of Christian England in the nineteenth century. Our laws are bound to think a man innocent until he is proved to be guilty; but our English society condemn him before trial, which is a summary proceeding that saves trouble.[29]

"However, I must say, (continued Byron,) that it is only those to whom any superiority is accorded, that are prejudged or treated with undue severity in London, for mediocrity meets with the utmost indulgence, on the principle of sympathy, 'a fellow-feeling makes them wondrous kind.' The moment my wife left me, I was

[29] This attack on English society is of the kind which appears frequently in the other writings of Lady Blessington.

assailed by all the falsehoods that malice could invent or slander publish; how many wives have since left their husbands, and husbands their wives, without either of the parties being blackened by defamation, the public having the sense to perceive that a husband and wife's living together or separate can only concern the parties, or their immediate families! but in *my case*, no sooner did Lady Byron take herself off than my character went off, or rather was carried off, not by force of arms, but by force of tongues and pens too; and there was no crime too dark to be attributed to me by the moral English, to account for so very common an occurrence as a separation in high life. I was thought a devil, because Lady Byron was allowed to be an angel; and that it formed a pretty antithesis, *mais hélas!* there are neither angels nor devils on earth, though some of one's acquaintance might tempt one into the belief of the existence of the latter. After twenty, it is difficult to believe in that of the former, though the *first* and *last* object of one's affection have some of its attributes. Imagination (said Byron) resembles hope —when unclouded, it gilds all that it touches with its own bright hue: mine makes me see beauty whenever youth and health have impressed their stamp; and after all I am not very far from the goddess, when I am with her handmaids, for such they certainly are. Sentimentalists may despise 'buxom health, with rosy hue,' which has something dairy-maid like, I confess, in the sound, (continued he)—for buxom, however one may like the reality, is not euphonious, but I have the association of plumpness, rosy hue, good spirits, and good humour, all brought before me in the homely phrase; and all these united give me a better idea of beauty than lanky languor, sicklied o'er with the pale cast of thought, and bad health, and bad humour, which are synonymous, making to-morrow cheerless as to-day. Then see some of our fine ladies, whose nerves are more active than their brains, who talk sentiment, and ask you to 'administer to a mind diseased, and pluck from the memory a rooted sorrow,' when it is the body that is diseased, and the rooted sorrow is some chronic malady: these, I own (continued Byron), alarm me, and a delicate woman, however prettily it may sound, harrows up my feelings with a host of shadowy ills to come, of vapours, hysterics, nerves, megrims, intermitting fevers, and all the ills that wait upon

161

poor *weak* women, who, when sickly, are generally weak in more senses than one. The best dower a woman can bring is health and good humour; the latter, whatever we may say of the triumphs of mind, depends on the former, as, according to the old poem—

> Temper ever waits on health,
> As luxury depends on wealth.

But mind (said Byron) when I object to delicate women, that is to say, to women of delicate *health*, alias *sickly*, I don't mean to say that I like coarse, fat ladies, *à la Rubens*,[30] whose minds must be impenetrable, from the mass of matter in which they are incased. No! I like an active and healthy mind, in an active and healthy person, each extending its beneficial influence over the other, and maintaining their equilibrium, the body illumined by the light within, but that light not let out by any 'chinks made by time;' in short, I like, as who does not, (continued Byron,) a handsome healthy woman, with an intelligent and intelligible mind, who can do something more than what is said a French woman can only do, *habille, babille,* and *dishabille,* who is not obliged to have recourse to dress, shopping and visits, to get through a day, and soirées, operas, and flirting to pass an evening. You see, I am moderate in my desires; I only wish for perfection.[31]

"There was a time (said Byron) when fame appeared the most desirable of all acquisitions to me; it was my 'being's end and aim,' but now—how worthless does it appear! Alas! how true are the lines—

> La Nominanza è color d'erba,
> Che viene e va; e quei la discolora
> Per cui vien fuori della terra acerba.[32]

---

[30] For Byron's unfavorable opinion of Rubens' women, see *LJ*, III, 332; IV, 107, the latter letter in Moore's *Life*, p. 352. In the discussion of the relation between a woman's health, beauty, and good humor, the sentiments seem to be those of Byron, although we may suspect some degree of self-portraiture by Lady Blessington, who also disliked Rubens' models.

[31] Teresa Guiccioli: *C'était son cas alors.*

[32] Lady Blessington appears not to have known Italian in 1823; Gell offered to teach her the language the following year (Madden, I, 345); she quotes some Italian in *The Repealers* (*Works*, I, 257, 258).

And dearly is fame bought, as all have found who have acquired even a small portion of it,—

> Che seggendo in piuma
> In Fama non si vien, ne sotto coltre.

No! with sleepless nights, excited nerves, and morbid feelings, is fame purchased, and envy, hatred, and jealousy follow the luckless possessor.

> O ciechi, il tanto affaticar che giova?
> Tutti tornate alla gran madre antica,
> E il vostro nome appena si ritrova.

Nay, how often has a tomb been denied to those whose names have immortalized their country, or else granted when shame compelled the tardy justice! Yet, after all, fame is but like all other pursuits, ending in disappointment—its worthlessness only discovered when attained,[33] and

> Sensa la qual chi sua vita consuma
> Cotal vestigio in terra di se lascia
> Qual fummo in aere, ed in acqua la schiuma.

"People complain of the brevity of life, (said Byron,) should they not rather complain of its length, as its enjoyments cease long before the halfway-house of life is passed, unless one has the luck to die young, ere the illusions that render existence supportable have faded away, and are replaced by experience, that dull monitress, that ever comes too late? While youth steers the bark of life, and passion impels her on, experience keeps aloof; but when youth and passion are fled, and that we no longer require her aid, she comes to reproach us with the past, to disgust us with the present, and to alarm us with the future.

"We buy wisdom with happiness, and who would purchase it at such a price? To be happy, we must forget the past, and think not

---

[33] Teresa Guiccioli: *Le sens de l'auteur est fausse—c'est le contraire.* (This comment appears at the bottom of the page, not clearly attached to any single statement, and may perhaps refer to one or both of the two paragraphs following.)

of the future; and who that has a soul, or mind, can do this?[34] No one (continued Byron); and this proves, that those who have either, know no happiness on this earth. Memory precludes happiness, whatever Rogers may say to the contrary, for it borrows from the past, to imbitter the present,[35] bringing back to us all the grief that has most wounded, or the happiness that has most charmed us; the first leaving its sting, and of the second,—

> Nessun maggior dolore,
> Che ricordarsi del tempo felice,
> Nulla miseria.

Let us look back (continued Byron) to those days of grief, the recollection of which now pains us, and we shall find that time has only cicatrized, but not effaced the scars; and if we reflect on the happiness, that seen through the vista of the past seems now so bright, memory will tell us that, at the actual time referred to, we were far from thinking so highly of it, nay,—that at that very period, we were obliged to draw drafts on the future, to support the then present, though now that epoch, tinged by the rays of memory, seems so brilliant, and renders the present more sombre by contrast. We are so constituted (said Byron) that we know not the value of our possessions until we have lost them.[36] Let us think of the friends that death has snatched from us, whose loss has left aching voids in the heart never again to be filled up; and memory will tell us that we prized not their presence, while we were blessed with it, though, could the grave give them back, now that we had learnt to estimate their value, all else could be borne, and we believe (because it is impossible) that happiness might once more be ours. We should live with our friends, (said Byron,) not as the worldly-

---

[34] Cf. Manfred's opening speech, ll. 9-10: "But Grief should be the Instructor of the wise; / Sorrow is Knowledge . . . ," and his quest for "forgetfulness."

[35] Cf. Lady Blessington's "Night Thought Book": "Memory seldom fails when its office is to show us the tombs of our buried hopes" (Madden, I, 240).

[36] Cf. Lady Byron in a letter to Byron, February 7, 1816 (Elwin, p. 397): "It is unhappily your disposition to consider what you have as worthless—what you have lost as invaluable." Cf. also Lady Blessington in a letter to Mrs. Charles Mathews, following the death of Lord Blessington: ". . . I feel this dreadful blow with even more bitterness, because it appears to me that, while I possessed the inestimable blessing I have lost, I was not to the full sensible of its value. . . . We are, God help us, too apt to underrate the good we have . . . until some cruel blow . . . draws the veil from our eyes . . ." (Molloy, pp. 182-83).

minded philosopher says, as though they may one day become our enemies, but as though we may one day lose them; and this maxim, strictly followed, will not only render our lives happier while together, but will save the survivors from those bitter pangs that memory conjures up, of slights and unkindnesses offered to those we have lost, when too late for atonement, and arms remorse with double force because it is too late." It was in such conversations that Byron was seen in his natural character; the feeling, the tenderness of his nature shone forth at such moments, and his natural character, like the diamond when breathed upon, though dimmed for a time, soon recovered its purity, and showed its original lustre, perhaps the more for having been for a moment obscured.

How much has Byron to unlearn ere he can hope for peace! Then he is proud of his false knowledge. I call it false, because it neither makes him better nor happier, and true knowledge ought to do the former, though I admit it cannot the latter. We are not relieved by the certainty that we have an incurable disease; on the contrary, we cease to apply remedies, and so let the evil increase. So it is with human nature: by believing ourselves devoted to selfishness, we supinely sink into its withering and inglorious thraldom; when, by encouraging kindly affections, without analyzing their source, we strengthen and fix them in the heart, and find their genial influence extending around, contributing to the happiness and well-being of others, and reflecting back some portion to ourselves. Byron's heart is running to waste for want of being allowed to expend itself on his fellow-creatures; it is naturally capacious, and teeming with affection; but the worldly wisdom he has acquired has checked its course, and it preys on his own happiness by reminding him continually of the aching void in his breast. With a contemptible opinion of human nature, he requires a perfectibility in the persons to whom he attaches himself, that those who think most highly of it never expect: he gets easily disgusted, and when once the persons fall short of his expectations, his feelings are thrown back on himself, and, in their re-action, create new bitterness. I have remarked to Byron that it strikes me as a curious anomaly, that he, who thinks ill of mankind, should require more from it than do those who think well of it *en masse;* and that each new disappointment at discovery of baseness sends him back to solitude with some of the feelings with which a savage creature would seek its lair; while those who judge it more favourably, instead of feeling bitterness at the disappointments we must all experience, more or less, when we have the weakness to depend wholly on others for happiness, smile at their own delusion, and blot out, as with a sponge, from memory that such things were, and were most sweet while we believed them, and open a fresh account, a new leaf in the ledger of life, always indulging in the hope that it may not be balanced like the last. We should judge others not by self, for that is deceptive, but by their general conduct and character. We rarely do this, because that with *le besoin d'aimer*, which all ardent minds have, we bestow our affections on the first person that chance throws in our path, and endow them with every good and noble quality, which qualities were unknown to them, and only existed in our own imaginations. We discover, when too late, our own want of discrimination; but, instead of blaming ourselves, we throw the whole censure on those whom we had overrated, and declare war against the whole species because we had chosen ill, and "loved not wisely, but too well." When such disappointments occur,—and, alas! they are so frequent as to inure us to them,—if we were to reflect on all the antecedent conduct and modes of thinking of those in whom we had "garnered up our hearts," we should find that *they* were in general consistent, and that *we* had indulged erroneous expectations, from having formed too high an estimate of them, and consequently were disappointed.

A modern writer has happily observed that "the sourest disappointments are made out of our sweetest hopes, as the most excellent vinegar is made from damaged wine." We have all proved that hope ends but in frustration, but this should only give us a more humble opinion of our own powers of discrimination, instead of making us think ill of human nature: we may believe that goodness, disinterestedness, and affection exist in the world, although we have not had the good fortune to encounter them in the persons on whom we had lavished our regard. This is the best, because it is the safest and most consolatory philosophy; it prevents our thinking ill of our species, and precludes that corroding of our feelings which is the inevitable result; for as we all belong to the family of human nature, we cannot think ill of it without deteriorating our own. If we have had the misfortune to meet with some persons whose ingratitude and baseness might serve to lower our opinion of our fellow-creatures, have we not encountered others whose nobleness, generosity, and truth might redeem them? A few such examples,—nay, one alone,—such as I have had the happiness to know, has taught me to judge favourably of mankind; and Byron, with all his scepticism as to the perfectibility of human nature, allowed that the person to whom I allude was an exception to the rule of the belief he had formed as to the selfishness or worldly-mindedness being the spring of action in man.

The grave has closed over *him* who shook Byron's scepticism in perfect goodness,[37] and established for ever my implicit faith in it; but, in the debts of gratitude engraved in deep characters on memory, the impression his virtues have given me of human nature is indelibly registered,—an impression of which his conduct was the happiest illustration, as the recollection of it must ever be the antidote to misanthropy. We have need of such examples to reconcile us to the heartless ingratitude that all have, in a greater or less degree, been exposed to, and which is so calculated to disgust us with our species. How, then, must the heart reverence the memory of those who, in life, spread the shield of their goodness between us and sorrow and evil, and, even in death, have left us the hallowed recollection of their virtues, to enable us to think well of our fellow-creatures!

> Of the rich legacies the dying leave,
> Remembrance of their virtues is the best.

We are as posterity to those who have gone before us—the *avant-coureurs* on that journey that we must all undertake. It is permitted us to speak of *absent* friends with the honest warmth of commendatory truth; then surely we may claim that privilege for the *dead*, —a privilege which every grateful heart must pant to establish, when the just tribute we pay to departed worth is but as the outpourings of a spirit that is overpowered by its own intensity, and whose praise or blame falls equally unregarded on "the dull cold ear of death." They who are in the grave cannot be flattered; and

[37] Byron may have conceded, in conversation with Lady Blessington, the saintly character of Lord Blessington, but nowhere else do we hear of it.

if their qualities were such as escaped the observance of the public eye, are not those who, in the shade of domestic privacy, had opportunities of appreciating them, entitled to one of the few consolations left to survivors—that of offering the homage of admiration and praise to virtues that were beyond all praise, and goodness that, while in existence, proved a source of happiness, and, in death, a consolation, by the assurance they have given of meeting their reward?

Byron said to-day that he had met, in a French writer, an idea that had amused him very much, and that he thought had as much truth as originality in it: he quoted the passage, "La curiosité est suicide de sa nature, et l'amour n'est que la curiosité." He laughed, and rubbed his hands, and repeated, "Yes, the Frenchman is right. Curiosity kills itself; and love is only curiosity, as is proved by its end."

I told Byron that it was in vain that he affected to believe what he repeated, as I thought too well of him to imagine him to be serious.

"At all events," said Byron, "you must admit that, of all passions, love is the most selfish. It begins, continues, and ends in selfishness.[38] Who ever thinks of the happiness of the object apart from his own, or who attends to it? While the passion continues, the lover wishes the object of his attachment happy, because, were she visibly otherwise, it would detract from his own pleasures. The French writer understood mankind well, who said that they resembled the grand Turk in an opera, who, quitting his sultana for another, replied to her tears, 'Dissimulez votre peine, et respectez mes plaisirs.'[39] This," continued Byron, "is but too true a satire on men; for when love is over,

A few years older,
Ah! how much colder
He could behold her
For whom he sigh'd![40]

[38] Cf. *Don Juan*, IX, lxxiii, referring to the relations between Catherine the Great and Juan: ". . . Love is vanity, / Selfish in its beginning as its end. . . ."
[39] Madame du Deffand, *Correspondence*, II, 135.
[40] From Byron's "Could Love for ever," stanza 2, a poem which expresses sentiments similar to those placed in Byron's mouth here and in the following two paragraphs.

"Depend on it, my doggrel rhymes have more truth than most that I have written. I have been told that love never exists without jealousy;[41] if this be true, it proves that love must be founded on selfishness, for jealousy surely never proceeds from any other feeling than selfishness. We see that the person we like is pleased and happy in the society of some one else, and we prefer to see her unhappy with us, than to allow her to enjoy it: is not this selfish? Why is it," continued Byron, "that lovers are at first only happy in each other's society? It is, that their mutual flattery and egoism gratify their vanity; and not finding this stimulus elsewhere, they become dependent on each other for it. When they get better acquainted, and have exhausted all their compliments, without the power of creating or feeling any new illusions, or even continuing the old, they no longer seek each other's presence from preference; habit alone draws them together, and they drag on a chain that is tiresome to both, but which often neither has the courage to break. We have all a certain portion of love in our natures, which portion wė invariably bestow on the object that most charms us, which, as invariably is, self; and though some degree of love may be extended to another, it is only because that other administers to our vanity; and the sentiment is but a reaction,—a sort of electricity that emits the sparks with which we are charged to another body;—and when the retorts lose their power—which means, in plain sense, when the flattery of the recipient no longer gratifies us—and yawning, that fearful abyss in love, is visible, the passion is over. Depend on it," continued Byron, "the only love that never changes its object is self-love; and the disappointments it meets with make a more lasting impression than all others."

I told Byron that I expected him to-morrow to disprove every word he had uttered to-day. He laughed, and declared that his profession of faith was contained in the verses, "Could love for ever;" that he wished he could think otherwise, but so it was.

Byron affects scepticism in love and friendship, and yet is, I am persuaded, capable of making great sacrifices for both. He has an unaccountable passion for misrepresenting his own feelings and motives, and exaggerates his defects more than any enemy could do:

[41] Cf. Lady Blessington's "Night Thought Book": "Love often reillumines his extinguished flame at the torch of jealousy" (Madden, I, 244).

169

he is often angry because we do not believe all he says against himself, and would be, I am sure, delighted to meet some one credulous enough to give credence to all he asserts or insinuates with regard to his own misdoings.[42]

If Byron were not a great poet, the charlatanism of affecting to be a Satanic character, in this our matter-of-fact nineteenth century, would be very amusing: but when the genius of the man is taken into account, it appears too ridiculous, and one feels mortified at finding that he, who could elevate the thoughts of his readers to the empyrean, should fall below the ordinary standard of everyday life, by a vain and futile attempt to pass for something that all who know him rejoice that he is not; while, by his sublime genius and real goodness of heart, which are made visible every day, he establishes claims on the admiration and sympathy of mankind that few can resist. If he knew his own power, he would disdain such unworthy means of attracting attention, and trust to his merit for commanding it.

"I know not when I have been so much interested and amused," said Byron, "as in the perusal of [D'Orsay's] journal: it is one of the choicest productions I ever read, and is astonishing as being written by a minor, as I find he was under age when he penned it. The most piquant vein of pleasantry runs through it; the ridicules—and they are many—of our dear compatriots are touched with the pencil of a master; but what pleases me most is, that neither the reputation of man nor woman is compromised, nor any disclosures made that could give pain. He has admirably penetrated the secret of English *ennui*," continued Byron, "a secret that is one to the English only, as I defy any foreigner, blessed with a common share of intelligence, to come in contact with them without discovering it. The English know that they are <u>*ennuyés*</u>, but vanity prevents their discovering that they are <u>*ennuyeux*</u>, and they will be little disposed to pardon the person who enlightens them on this point.[43] [Count

[42] Frequently attested Byronic qualities (see above, p. 75, n. 162).
[43] Cf. Byron's letter to Lord Blessington, April 5, 1823 (*LJ*, VI, 187-88): "The most singular thing is, *how* he should have penetrated *not* the *fact*, but the *mystery* of the English *ennui* at two-and-twenty . . . *Il faut être Français*, to effect this . . . . Altogether, your friend's Journal is a very formidable production. Alas! our dearly beloved countrymen have only discovered that they are tired, and not that they are tiresome; and I suspect that the communication of the latter unpleasant verity will not be better received than truths usually are."

170

D'Orsay] ought to publish this work," continued Byron, "for two reasons: the first, that it will be sure to get known that he has written a piquant journal, and people will imagine it to be a malicious libel, instead of being a playful satire, as the English are prone to fancy the worst, from a consciousness of not meriting much forbearance; the second reason is, that the impartial view of their foibles, taken by a stranger who cannot be actuated by any of the little jealousies that influence the members of their own coteries, might serve to correct them, though I fear *réflexion faite*, there is not much hope of this. It is an extraordinary anomaly," said Byron, "that people who are really naturally inclined to good, as I believe the English are, and who have the advantages of a better education than foreigners receive, should practise more ill-nature and display more heartlessness than the inhabitants of any other country. This is all the effect of the artificial state of society in England, and the exclusive system has increased the evils of it tenfold. We accuse the French of frivolity," continued Byron, "because they are governed by *fashion;* but this extends only to their dress, whereas the English allow it to govern their pursuits, habits, and modes of thinking and acting: in short, it is the Alpha and Omega of all they think, do, or will: their society, residences, nay, their very friends, are chosen by this criterion, and old and tried friends, wanting its stamp, are voted *de trop.* Fashion admits women of more than dubious reputations, and well-born men with none, into circles where virtue and honour, not *à la mode*, might find it difficult to get placed; and if (on hearing the reputation of Lady This, or Mrs. That or rather want of reputation, canvassed over by their associates) you ask why they are received, you will be told it is because they are seen every where—they are the fashion.[44]—I have known," continued Byron, "men and women in London received in the first circles, who, by their birth, talents, or manners, had no one claim to such a distinction, merely because they had been seen in one or two houses, to which, by some manœuvring, they got the *entrée;* but I must add, they were not remarkable for good looks, or superiority in any way, for if they had been, it would have elicited attention to their want of other claims, and closed the doors

[44] The discussion of women of dubious reputation who are admitted into fashionable society is very Blessingtonian, although Byron would agree.

171

of fashion against them. I recollect," said Byron, "on my first entering fashionable life, being surprised at the (to me) unaccountable distinctions I saw made between ladies placed in peculiar and precisely similar situations. I have asked some of the fair leaders of fashion, 'Why do you exclude Lady ——, and admit Lady ——, as they are both in the same scrape?' With that amiable indifference to cause and effect that distinguishes the generality of your sex, the answer has invariably been, 'Oh! we admit Lady —— because all our set receive her; and exclude Lady —— because they will not.' I have pertinaciously demanded, 'Well, but you allow their claims are equal?' and the reply has been, 'Certainly; and we believe the excluded lady to be the better of the two.' *Mais que voulez-vous?* she is not received, and the other is; it is all chance or luck: and this," continued Byron, "is the state of society in London, and such the line of demarcation drawn between the pure and the impure, when chance or luck, as Lady —— honestly owned to me, decided whether a woman lost her caste or not. I am not much of a prude," said Byron, "but I declare that, for the general good, I think that all women who had forfeited their reputations ought to lose their places in society; but this rule ought never to admit of an exception: it becomes an injustice and hardship when it does, and loses all effect as a warning or preventive. I have known young married women, when cautioned by friends on the probability of losing caste by such or such a step, quote the examples of Lady This, or Mrs. That, who had been more imprudent, (for imprudence is the new name for guilt in England,) and yet that one saw these ladies received every where, and vain were precepts with such examples. People may suppose," continued Byron, "that I respect not morals, because unfortunately I have sometimes violated them: perhaps from this very circumstance I respect them the more, as we never value riches until our prodigality has made us feel their loss; and a lesson of prudence coming from him who had squandered thousands, would have more weight than whole pages written by one who had not personal experience: so I maintain that persons who have *erred* are most competent to point out errors. It is my respect for morals that makes me so indignant against its vile substitute cant, with which I wage war, and this the good-natured world chooses to consider as a sign of my wickedness. We are all the creatures of cir-

172

cumstance," continued Byron; "the greater part of our errors are caused, if not excused, by events and situations over which we have had little control; the world see the faults, but they see not what led to them: therefore I am always lenient to crimes that have brought their own punishment, while I am a little disposed to pity those who think they atone for their own sins by exposing those of others, and add cant and hypocrisy to the catalogue of their vices. Let not a woman who has gone astray, *without detection,* affect to disdain a less fortunate, though not more culpable, female. She who is unblemished should pity her who has fallen, and she whose conscience tells her she is not spotless should show forbearance; but it enrages me to see women whose conduct is, or has been, infinitely more blamable than that of the persons they denounce, affecting a prudery towards others that they had not in the hour of need for themselves. It was this forbearance towards her own sex that charmed me in Lady Melbourne: she had always some kind interpretation for every action that would admit of one, and pity or silence when aught else was impracticable.

"Lady ——, beautiful and spotless herself, always struck me as wanting that pity she could so well afford. Not that I ever thought her ill-natured or spiteful; but I thought there was a certain severity in her demarcations, which her acknowledged purity rendered less necessary. Do you remember my lines in the Giaour,[45] ending with—

> No: gayer insects fluttering by
> Ne'er droop the wing o'er those that die;
> And lovelier things have mercy shown
> To every failing but their own;
> And every woe a tear can claim
> Except an erring sister's shame.

"These lines were suggested by the conduct I witnessed in London from women to their erring acquaintances—a conduct that led me to draw the conclusion, that their hearts are formed of less penetrable stuff than those of men."[46]

[45] Ll. 416-21.
[46] The preceding sketch of London society, while it does not do violence to Byron's usually expressed opinions, seems colored by Lady Blessington's

Byron has not lived sufficiently long in England, and has left it at too young an age, to be able to form an impartial and just estimate of his compatriots.[47] He was a busy actor, more than a spectator, in the circles which have given him an unfavourable impression; and his own passions were, at that period, too much excited to permit his reason to be unbiassed in the opinions he formed. In his hatred of what he calls cant and hypocrisy he is apt to denounce as such all that has the air of severity; and which, though often painful in individual cases, is, on the whole, salutary for the general good of society. This error of Byron's proceeds from a want of actual personal observation, for which opportunity has not been afforded him, as the brief period of his residence in England, after he had arrived at an age to judge, and the active part he took in the scenes around him, allowed him not to acquire that perfect knowledge of society, manners, and customs, which is necessary to correct the prejudices that a superficial acquaintance with it is so apt to engender, even in the most acute observer, but to which a powerful imagination, prompt to jump at conclusions, without pausing to trace cause and effect, is still more likely to fall into. Byron sees not that much of what he calls the usages of cant and hypocrisy are the fences that protect propriety, and that they cannot be invaded without exposing what it is the interest of all to preserve. Had he been a calm looker on, instead of an impassioned actor in the drama of English fashionable life, he would probably have taken a less harsh view of all that has so much excited his ire, and felt the necessity of many of the restraints which fettered him.

A two years' residence in Greece, with all the freedom and personal independence that a desultory rambling life admits of and gives a taste for,—in a country where civilization has so far retrograded that its wholesome laws, as well as its refinement, have disappeared, leaving license to usurp the place of liberty,—was little calculated to prepare a young man of three-and-twenty for the conventional habits and restraints of that artificial state of society which extreme civilization and refinement beget. No wonder then that

---

bitter social defeats, which effectively denied her entrance into circles that admitted those less talented than she and no more virtuous.

[47] Teresa Guiccioli: not sufficiently!? *all his life* except 2 years when he left England for the last time in 1816 *à l'age de 28 ans.*

174

it soon became irksome to him, and that, like the unbroken courser of Arabia, when taken from the deserts where he had sported in feedom, he spurned the puny meshes which ensnared him, and pined beneath the trammels that intercepted his liberty.

Byron returned to England in his twenty-third year, and left it before he had completed his twenty-eighth, soured by disappointments and rendered reckless by a sense of injuries. "He who fears not is to be feared," says the proverb; and Byron, wincing under all the obloquy which malice and envy could inflict, felt that its utmost malignity could go no farther, and became fixed in a fearless braving of public opinion, which a false spirit of vengeance led him to indulge in, turning the genius, that could have achieved the noblest ends, into the means of accomplishing those which were unworthy of it.[48] His attacks on the world are like the war of the Titans against the gods,—the weapons he aims fall back on himself. He feels that he has allowed sentiments of pique to influence and deteriorate his works; and that the sublime passages in them, which now appear like gleams of sunshine flitting across the clouds that sometimes obscure the bright luminary, might have been one unbroken blaze of light, had not worldly resentment and feelings dimmed their lustre.

This consciousness of misapplied genius has made itself felt in Byron,[49] and will yet lead him to redeem the injustice he has done it; and when he has won the guerdon of the world's applause, and satisfied that craving for celebrity which consumes him, reconciled to that world, and at peace with himself, he may yet win as much esteem for the man as he has hitherto elicited admiration for the poet. To satisfy Byron, the admiration must be unqualified; and, as I have told him, this depends on himself: he has only to choose a subject for his muse, in which not only received opinions are not wounded, but morality is inculcated; and his glowing genius, no longer tarnished by the stains that have previously blemished it, will shine forth with a splendour, and insure that universal applause, which will content even his ambitious and as-

[48] Teresa Guiccioli: Why unworthy?
[49] More than once Byron referred to the false taste of the age, which he felt he had helped to corrupt by the publication of his non-satiric poetry; but there is no recorded evidence that he ever felt he had "misapplied" his genius in writing his mature satires.

175

piring nature. He wants some one to tell him what he *might* do, what he *ought* to do, and what so doing he would become. I have told him: but I have not sufficient weight or influence with him to make my representations effective; and the task would be delicate and difficult for a male friend to undertake, as Byron is pertinacious in refusing to admit that his works have failed in morality,[50] though in his heart I am sure he feels it.

Talking of some one who was said to have fallen in love, "I suspect," said Byron, "that he must be indebted to your country for this phrase, 'falling in love;' it is expressive and droll: they also say falling ill; and, as both are involuntary, and, in general, equally calamitous, the expressions please me. Of the two evils, the falling ill seems to me to be the least; at all events I would prefer it; for as, according to philosophers, pleasure consists in the absence of pain, the sensations of returning health (if one does recover) must be agreeable; but the recovery from love is another affair, and resembles the awaking from an agreeable dream. Hearts are often only lent, when they are supposed to be given away," continued Byron; "and are the loans for which people exact the most usurious interest. When the debt is called in, the borrower, like all other debtors, feels little obligation to the lender, and, having refunded the principal, regrets the interest he has paid.[51] You see," said Byron, "that, *à l'Anglaise*, I have taken a mercantile view of the tender passion; but I must add that, in closing the accounts, they are seldom fairly balanced, 'e ciò sa 'l tuo dottore.'[52] There is this difference between the Italians and others," said Byron, "that the end of love is not with them the beginning of hatred, which certainly is, in general, the case with the English, and, I believe, the French: this may be accounted for from their having less vanity; which is also the rea-

[50] Teresa Guiccioli: And he was in the right and sincere. (Cf. Byron to Murray, December 25, 1822 [*LJ*, VI, 155]: "*Don Juan* will be known by and bye, for what it is intended,—a *Satire* on *abuses* of the present states of Society, and not an eulogy of vice. . . .")

[51] Cf. *Don Juan*, IX, lxii, describing Catherine the Great:

> She could repay each amatory look you lent
>   With interest, and, in turn, was wont with rigour
> To exact of Cupid's bills the full amount
> At sight, nor would permit you to discount.

[52] Teresa Guiccioli: *Conversations imaginaires et rien autre.* (This comment, appearing at the bottom of the page, presumably refers to all the marked lines.)

son why they have less ill-nature in their compositions; for vanity, being always on the *qui vive*, up in arms, ready to resent the least offence offered to it, precludes good temper."

I asked Byron if his partiality for the Italians did not induce him to overlook other and obvious reasons for their not beginning to hate when they ceased to love: first, the attachments were of such long duration that age arrived to quell angry feelings, and the gradations were so slow, from the first sigh of love to the yawn of expiring affection, as to be almost imperceptible to the parties; and the system of domesticating in Italy established a habit that rendered them necessary to each other. Then the slavery of *serventism*, the jealousies, carried to an extent that is unknown in England, and which exists longer than the passion that is supposed to excite, if not excuse, them, may tend to reconcile lovers to the exchange of friendship for love; and, rejoicing in their recovered liberty, they are more disposed to indulge feelings of complacency than hatred.

Byron said, "Whatever may be the cause, they have reason to rejoice in the effect; and one is never afraid in Italy of inviting people together who have been known to have once had warmer feelings than friendship towards each other, as is the case in England, where, if persons under such circumstances were to meet, angry glances and a careful avoidance of civility would mark their kind sentiments towards each other."

I asked Byron if what he attributed to the effects of wounded vanity might not proceed from other and better feelings, at least on the part of women? Might not shame and remorse be the cause? The presence of the man who had caused their dereliction from duty and virtue calling up both, could not be otherwise than painful and humiliating to women who were not totally destitute of delicacy and feeling; and that this most probably was the cause of the coldness he observed between persons of opposite sexes in society.

"You are always thinking of and reasoning on the *English*," answered Byron: "mind, I refer to Italians, and with them there can be neither shame nor remorse, because, in yielding to love, they do not believe they are violating either their duty or religion; consequently a man has none of the reproaches to dread that awaits him in England when a lady's conscience is *awakened*,—which, by the by, I have observed it seldom is until *affection* is laid asleep,

177

which," continued Byron, "is very convenient to herself, but very much the reverse to the unhappy man."

I am sure that much of what Byron said in this conversation was urged to vex me. Knowing my partiality to England and all that is English, he has a childish delight in exciting me into an argument; and as I as yet know nothing of Italy, except through books, he takes advantage of his long residence in, and knowledge of the country, to vaunt the superiority of its customs and usages, which I never can believe he prefers to his own. A wish of vexing or astonishing the English is, I am persuaded, the motive that induces him to attack Shakspeare; and he is highly gratified when he succeeds in doing either, and enjoys it like a child. He says that the reason why he judges the English women so severely is, that, being brought up with certain principles, they are doubly to blame in not making their conduct accord with them; and that, while punishing with severity the transgressions of persons of their own sex in humble positions, they look over the more glaring misconduct and vices of the rich and great—that not the crime, but its detection, is punished in England, and, to avoid this, hypocrisy is added to want of virtue.[53]

"You have heard, of course," said Byron, "that I was considered mad in England; my most intimate friends in general, and Lady Byron in particular, were of this opinion;[54] but it did not operate in my favour in their minds, as they were not, like the natives of eastern nations, disposed to pay honour to my supposed insanity or folly. They considered me a *mejnoun*, but would not treat me as one. And yet, had such been the case, what ought to excite such pity and forbearance as a mortal malady that reduces us to more than childishness—a prostration of intellect that places us in the dependence of even menial hands? Reason," continued Byron, "is so unreasonable, that few can say that they are in possession of it. I have often doubted my own sanity; and, what is more, wished for insanity—[55]anything—to quell memory, the never-dying worm that

---

[53] Cf. the pregnant "country girl in a close cap/ And scarlet cloak" brought in to be judged at Norman Abbey amid all the hypocrisy assembled there (*Don Juan*, XVI, lxi-lxvii).

[54] See *Don Juan*, I, xxvii (*Poetry*, VI, 21 and n. 1): "For Inez called some druggists and physicians,/ And tried to prove her loving lord was *mad*."

[55] Teresa Guiccioli: *Insanity? C'était le malheur qui [il] redoutait au delà de tout. Comment a-t-il pu dire qu'il l'avait désiré?*

178

feeds on the heart, and only calls up the *past* to make the *present* more insupportable. Memory has for me

> The vulture's ravenous tooth,
> The raven's funereal song.

There is one thing," continued Byron, "that increases my discontent, and adds to the rage that I often feel against self. It is the conviction that the events in life that have most pained me—that have turned the milk of my nature into gall—have not depended on the persons who tortured me,—as I admit the causes were inadequate to the effects:—it was my own nature, prompt to receive painful impressions, and to retain them with a painful tenacity, that supplied the arms against my peace. Nay, more, I believe that the wounds inflicted were not, for the most part, premeditated; or, if so, that the extent and profundity of them were not anticipated by the persons who aimed them. There are some natures that have a predisposition to grief, as others have to disease; and such was my case. The causes that have made me wretched would probably not have discomposed, or, at least, more than discomposed, another. We are all differently organized; and that I feel *acutely* is no more my fault (though it is my misfortune) than that another feels not, is his. We did not make ourselves; and if the elements of unhappiness abound more in the nature of one man than another, he is but the more entitled to our pity and forbearance. Mine is a nature," continued Byron, "that might have been softened and ameliorated by prosperity, but that has been hardened and soured by adversity." Prosperity and adversity are the fires by which moral chemists try and judge human nature; and how few can pass the ordeal! Prosperity corrupts, and adversity renders ordinary nature callous; but when any portion of excellence exists, neither can injure. The first will expand the heart, and show forth every virtue, as the genial rays of the sun bring forth the fruit and flowers of the earth; and the second will teach sympathy for others, which is best learned in the school of affliction.

"I am persuaded (said Byron) that education has more effect in quelling the passions than people are aware of. I do not think this is achieved by the powers of reasoning and reflection that education is supposed to bestow; for I know by experience how little either can influence the person who is under the tyrant rule of passion. My opinion is, that education, by expanding the mind, and giving sources of tasteful occupation, so fills up the time, that leisure is not left for the passions to gain that empire that they are sure to acquire over the idle and ignorant. Look at the lower orders, and see what fearful proofs they continually furnish of the unlimited power passion has over them. I have seen instances, and particularly in Italy, among the lower class, and of your sex, where the women seemed for the moment transformed into Medeas;[56] and so ungoverned and ungovernable was their rage, that each appeared grand and tragic for the time, and furnished me, who am rather an amateur in studying nature under all her aspects, with food for reflection. Then the upper classes, too, in Italy, where the march of intellect has not advanced by rail-roads and steam-boats, as in polished, happy England; and where the women remain children in mind long after maturity had stamped their persons!—see one of their stately dames under the influence of the green-eyed monster, and one can believe that the Furies were not fabulous. This is amusing at first, but becomes, like most amusements, rather a bore at the end; and a poor *cavalier servente* must have more courage than falls to the share of most, who would not shut his eyes against the beauty of all *damas* but his own, rather than encounter an explosion of jealousy. But the devil of it is, there is hardly a possibility of avoiding it, as the Italian women are so addicted to jealousy, that the poor *serventi* are often accused of the worst intentions for merely performing the simple courtesies of life;[57] so that the system of *serventism* imposes a thousand times more restraint and slavery than marriage ever imposed, even in the most moral countries:[58] indeed, where the morals are the most respected and cultivated, (continued Byron,) there will be the least jealousy or suspicion, as morals are to the enlightened what religion is to the ignorant—their safeguard from committing wrong, or suspecting it.

[56] See Byron on Margarita Cogni (the Fornarina), who on at least one occasion looked "like Medea alighted from her chariot . . ." (*LJ*, IV, 333).

[57] According to Byron, Teresa Guiccioli, who never consented to be introduced to Lady Blessington during her visit, was "seized with a furious fit of Italian jealousy."

[58] See Byron to Hoppner, January 31, 1820 (Moore, *Life*, p. 434), on the slavery of *serventism* in Ravenna, "a dreadfully moral place."

So you see, bad as I am supposed to be, I have, by this admission, proved the advantages of morals and religion.

"But to return to my opinion of the effect education has in extending the focus of ideas, and, consequently, of curbing the intensity of the passions. I have remarked that well-educated women rarely, if ever, gave way to any ebullitions of them; and this is a grand step gained in conquering their empire, as habit in this, as well as in all else, has great power. I hope my daughter will be well educated; but of this I have little dread, as her mother is highly cultivated, and certainly has a degree of self-control that I never saw equalled. I am certain that Lady Byron's first idea is, what is due to herself; I mean that it is the undeviating rule of her conduct. I wish she had thought a little more of what is due to others. Now my besetting sin is a want of that self-respect,—which she has in *excess;* and that want has produced much unhappiness to us both. But though I accuse Lady Byron of an excess of self-respect, I must in candour admit, that if any person ever had an excuse for an extraordinary portion of it, she has; as in all her thoughts, words, and deeds, she is the most decorous woman that ever existed,[59] and must appear—what few, I fancy, could—a perfect and refined gentlewoman, even to her *femme-de-chambre.* This extraordinary degree of self-command in Lady Byron produced an opposite effect on me. When I have broken out, on slight provocations, into one of my ungovernable fits of rage, her calmness piqued and seemed to reproach me; it gave her an air of superiority that vexed, and increased my *mauvaise humeur.* I am now older and wiser, and should know how to appreciate her conduct as it deserved, as I look on self-command as a positive virtue, though it is one I have not courage to adopt."

Talking of his proposed expedition to Greece, Byron said that, as the moment approached for undertaking it, he almost wished he had never thought of it.[60] "This (said Byron) is one of the

[59] Cf. Samuel Rogers to Byron in March 1816 (*HVSV*, pp. 166-67): "The very first time I saw you after that event, you said . . . 'that wherever the wrong lay, it did not lie with Lady Byron; that Lady B. had been faultless in thought, word, and deed.'" This represents Byron's usual stance in conversation on the subject.

[60] In July 1823, shortly before sailing for Greece, Byron confessed to Barry his banker (*HVSV*, p. 381) that "he would not go on the Greek expedition even then but that 'Hobhouse and the others would laugh at him.'"

many scrapes into which my poetical temperament has drawn me. You smile; but it is nevertheless true. No man, or woman either, with such a temperament, can be quiet. Passion is the element in which we live; and without it we but vegetate. All the passions have governed me in turn, and I have found them the veriest tyrants;—like all slaves, I have reviled my masters, but submitted to the yoke they imposed. I had hoped (continued Byron) that avarice, that old gentlemanly vice,[61] would, like Aaron's serpent, have swallowed up all the rest in me; and that now I am descending into the vale of years, I might have found pleasure in golden realities, as in youth I found it in golden dreams, (and let me tell you, that, of all the passions, this same decried *avarice* is the most consolatory, and, in nine cases out of ten, lasts the longest, and is the latest,) when up springs a new passion,—call it love of liberty, military ardour, or what you will,—to disgust me with my strong box, and the comfortable contemplation of my *moneys*,—nay, to create wings for my golden darlings, that may waft them away from me for ever; and I may awaken to find that this, my present ruling passion, as I have always found my last, was the most worthless of all, with the soothing reflection that it has left me *minus* some thousands. But I am fairly in for it, and it is useless to repine; but, I repeat, this scrape, which may be my last, has been caused by my poetical temperament,—the devil take it, say I."[62]

Byron was irresistibly comic when commenting on his own errors or weaknesses. His face, half laughing and half serious, archness always predominating in its expression, added peculiar force to his words.

"Is it not pleasant (continued Byron) that my eyes should never open to the folly of any of the undertakings passion prompts me to engage in, until I am so far embarked that retreat (at least with honour) is impossible, and my *mal à propos sagesse* arrives, to scare away the enthusiasm that led to the undertaking, and which is so requisite to carry it on? It is all an up-hill affair with me afterwards: I cannot, for my life, *échauffer* my imagination again; and

[61] Cf. *Don Juan*, I, ccxvi: "So for a good old-gentlemanly vice,/ I think I must take up with avarice." See also Pratt, the *Variorum Don Juan*, IV, 51, note to this stanza. When Byron knew Lady Blessington he was gathering money for use in the Greek cause.
[62] Teresa Guiccioli: *Mystifications que tout cela! ou inventions!*

my position excites such ludicrous images and thoughts in my own mind, that the whole subject, which, seen through the veil of passion, looked fit for a sublime epic, and I one of its heroes, examined now through reason's glass, appears fit only for a travestie, and my poor self a Major Sturgeon, marching and countermarching, not from Acton to Ealing, or from Ealing to Acton,[63] but from Corinth to Athens, and from Athens to Corinth. Yet, hang it, (continued he,) these very names ought to chase away every idea of the ludicrous; but the laughing devils will return, and make a mockery of everything, as with me there is, as Napoleon said, but one step between the sublime and the ridiculous. Well, *if I do* (and this *if* is a grand *peut-être* in my future history) outlive the campaign, I shall write two poems on the subject—one an epic, and the other a burlesque,[64] in which none shall be spared, and myself least of all: indeed, you must allow (continued Byron) that if I take liberties with my friends, I take still greater ones with myself; therefore they ought to bear with me, if only out of consideration for my impartiality. I am also determined to write a poem in praise of avarice, (said Byron,) as I think it a most ill-used and unjustly decried passion:—mind, I do not call it a vice,—and I hope to make it clear that a passion which enables us to conquer the appetites, or, at least, the indulgence of them; that triumphs over pride, vanity, and ostentation; that leads us to the practice of daily self-denial, temperance, sobriety, and a thousand other praiseworthy practices, ought not to be censured, more especially as all the sacrifices it commands are endured without any weak feeling of reference to others, though to others all the reward of such sacrifices belongs."[65]

Byron laughed very much at the thought of this poem, and the censures it would excite in England among the matter-of-fact, credulous class of readers and writers. Poor Byron! how much <u>more</u> pains did he bestow to take off the gloss from his own qualities,

---

[63] Lady Blessington may have read Byron's reference in his speech on the Framework Bill (*LJ*, II, 427) to Major Sturgeon's "marchings and countermarchings," in Samuel Foote's play, *The Mayor of Garratt* (1763), alluded to a number of times in Byron's letters.

[64] As Byron parted from Trelawny in Greece on September 6, 1823, he said (*HVSV*, p. 434): "If things are farcical they will do for *Don Juan*; if heroical, you shall have another canto of *Childe Harold*." Lady Blessington may have read a similar remark in Kennedy's *Conversations* (*HVSV*, p. 427).

[65] On avarice, see Pratt, the *Variorum Don Juan*, IV, 51.

183

than others do to give theirs a false lustre! In his hatred and contempt of hypocrisy and cant, he outraged his own nature, and rendered more injustice to himself than even his enemies ever received at his hands. His confessions of errors were to be received with caution; for he exaggerated not only his misdeeds but his opinions; and, fond of tracing springs of thought to their sources, he involved himself in doubts, to escape from which he boldly attributed to himself motives and feelings that had passed, but like shadows, through his mind, and left unrecorded, mementos that might have redeemed even more than the faults of which he accused himself. When the freedom with which Byron remarked on the errors of his friends draws down condemnation from his readers, let them reflect on the still greater severity with which he treated his own, and let this mistaken and exaggerated candour plead his excuse.

"It is odd (said Byron) that I never could get on well in conversation with literary men: they always seemed to think themselves obliged to pay some neat and appropriate compliment to my last work, which I, as in duty bound, was compelled to respond to, and bepraise theirs.[66] They never appeared quite satisfied with my faint praise, and I was far from being satisfied at having been forced to administer it; so mutual constraint ensued, each wondering what was to come next, and wishing each other (at least I can answer for myself) at the devil. Now Scott, though a giant in literature, is unlike literary men; he neither expects compliments nor pays them in conversation. There is a sincerity and simplicity in his character and manner that stamp any commendation of his as truth, and any praise one might offer him must fall short of his deserts; so that there is no *gêne* in his society. There is nothing in him that gives the impression I have so often had of others, who seemed to say, 'I praise you that you may do the same by me.' Moore is a delightful companion, (continued Byron;) gay without being boisterous, witty without effort, comic without coarseness, and sentimental without being lachrymose. He reminds one (continued Byron) of the fairy, who, whenever she spoke, let diamonds fall

[66] This paragraph, with its praise of Scott and Moore, in that order, seems to be founded on Byron's "Detached Thoughts," No. 53 (*LJ*, 435): "In general, I do not draw well with literary men: not that I dislike them, but I never know what to say to them after I have praised their last publication. There are several exceptions, to be sure . . . such as Scott, and Moore. . . ."

from her lips. My *tête-à-tête* suppers with Moore are among the most agreeable impressions I retain of the hours passed in London: they are the redeeming lights in the gloomy picture; but they were,

Like angel visits, few and far between;[67]

for the great defect in my friend Tom is a sort of fidgety unsettledness, that prevents his giving himself up, *con amore*, to any one friend, because he is apt to think he might be more happy with another: he has the organ of locomotiveness largely developed, as a phrenologist would say, and would like to be at three places instead of one. I always felt, with Moore, the desire Johnson expressed, to be shut up in a post-chaise, *tête-à-tête* with a pleasant companion,[68] to be quite sure of him. He must be delightful in a country-house, at a safe distance from any other inviting one, when one could have him really to oneself, and enjoy his conversation and his singing, without the perpetual fear that he is expected at Lady This or Lady That's, or the being reminded that he promised to look in at Lansdowne House or Grosvenor Square. The wonder is, *not* that he is *récherché*, but that he wastes himself on those who can so little appreciate him, though they value the *éclat* his reputation gives to their stupid *soirées*. I have known a dull man live on a *bon mot* of Moore's for a week; and I once offered a wager of a considerable sum that the reciter was *guiltless* of understanding its point, but could get no one to accept my bet.

"Are you acquainted with the family of ——? (asked Byron.) The commendation formerly bestowed on the Sydney family might be reversed for them, as all the sons are virtuous, and all the daughters brave. I once (continued he) said this, with a grave face, to a

[67] Campbell's *Pleasures of Hope*, II, 378. Lady Blessington quoted the line in her *Idler in France*, I, 328; in her *Ella Stratford; or, the Orphan Child* (Philadelphia, n.d.), p. 12, where "the joys were 'like angel visits, few and far between' "; and in a letter of August 15, 1832, to Mrs. Mathews, where her "heart . . . is only preserved from corroding, by knowing that such hearts as yours exist, though like Angel visits they are few and far between—" (from the autograph letter in the Princeton University Library).

[68] A variant of Dr. Johnson's phrase also appears in the Swiss Journal for Augusta (Moore, *Life*, p. 313; *LJ*, III, 356): "a Bull nearly leapt into the Charaban—'agreeable companion in a post-chaise. . . .'" Byron informed Lady Hardy that J. Wedderburn Webster "actually (no jest I assure you) advertised for an 'agreeable companion in a post chaise' in the Genoa Gazette" (*Cornhill Magazine*, LXIV [January 1928], 45).

near relation of theirs, who received it as a compliment, and told me I was very good. I was in old times fond of mystifying, and paying equivocal compliments; but 'was is not is' with me, as God knows, in any sense, for I am now cured of mystifying,[69] as well as of many others of my mischievous pranks: whether I am a *better* man for my self-correction remains to be proved; I am quite sure that I am not a more agreeable one. I have always had a strong love of mischief in my nature, (said Byron,) and this still continues, though I do not very often give way to its dictates. It is this lurking devil that prompts me to abuse people against whom I have not the least malicious feeling, and to praise some whose merits (if they have any) I am little acquainted with; but I do it in the mischievous spirit of the moment to vex the person or persons with whom I am conversing.[70] Is not this very childish? (continued Byron;) and, above all, for a poet, which people tell me I am? All I know is, that, if I am, poets can be greater fools than other people. We of the craft—poets, I mean—resemble paper-kites; we soar high into the air, but are held to earth by a cord, and our flight is restrained by a child—that child is self. We are but grown children, having all their weakness, and only wanting their innocence; our thoughts soar, but the frailty of our natures brings them back to earth. What should we be without thoughts? (continued Byron;) they are the bridges by which we pass over time and space. And yet, perhaps, like troops flying before the enemy, we are often tempted to destroy the bridges we have passed, to save ourselves from pursuit. How often have I tried to shun thought! But come, I must not get gloomy; my thoughts are almost always of the sombre hue, so that I ought not to be blamed (said he, laughing) if I steal those of others, as I am accused of doing; I cannot have any more disagreeable ones than my own, at least as far as they concern myself.

"In all the charges of plagiary brought against me in England, (said Byron,) did you hear me accused of stealing from Madame de Staël the opening lines of my 'Bride of Abydos?' She is supposed to have borrowed her lines from Schlegel, or to have stolen them

[69] This seems doubtful (see my introduction).
[70] See similar comments made about Byron by Hobhouse and Kinnaird, *HVSV*, p. xi.

from Goethe's 'Wilhelm Meister;'[71] so you see I am a third or fourth hand stealer of stolen goods. Do you know de Staël's lines? (continued Byron;) for if I am a thief, she must be the plundered, as I don't read German, and do French; yet I could almost swear that I never saw her verses when I wrote mine, nor do I even now remember them. I think the first began with 'Cette terre,' &c. &c. but the rest I forget; as you have a good memory, perhaps you would repeat them."

I did so, and they are as follows:—

———Cette terre, où les myrtes fleurissent,
Où les rayons des cieux tombent avec amour,
Où des sons enchanteurs dans les airs retentissent,
Où la plus douce nuit succède au plus beau jour.

"Well (said Byron) I do not see any point of resemblance, except in the use of the two unfortunate words land and myrtle, and for using these new and original words I am a plagiarist! To avoid such charges, I must invent a dictionary for myself. Does not this charge prove the liberal spirit of the hypercritics in England? If they knew how little I value their observations, or the opinions of those that they can influence, they would be perhaps more spiteful, and certainly more careful in producing better proofs of their charges; the one of the Staël's I consider a triumphant refutation for me.

"I often think (said Byron) that were I to return to England, I should be considered, in certain circles, as having a *très mauvais ton,* for I have been so long out of it that I have learned to say what I think, instead of saying only what, by the rules of convenience, people are permitted to think. For though England tolerates the liberty of the press, it is far from tolerating liberty of thought or of speech; and since the progress of modern refinement, when delicacy of words is as remarkable as indelicacy of actions, a plain-speaking man is sure to get into a scrape. Nothing amuses me more than to see refinement *versus* morals, and to know that people are shocked *not* at crimes, but their detection. The Spartan boy, who suffered the animal he had secured by theft to prey on his vitals, evinced not more constancy in concealing his sufferings than do the English in suppressing all external symptoms of what they must

[71] See *LJ*, II, 304, n. 2, and 490.

feel, and on many occasions, when Nature makes herself felt through the expression of her feelings, would be considered almost as a crime.[72] But I believe crime is a word banished from the vocabulary of *haut-ton*, as the vices of the rich and great are called errors, and those of the poor and lowly only, crimes.

"Do you know ——? (asked Byron.) He is the king of prosers. I called him 'he of the thousand tales,' in humble imitation of Boccaccio, whom I styled 'he of the hundred tales of love:'—*mais, hélas!* ——'s are not tales of love, or that beget love; they are born of dulness, and inciting sleep, they produce the same effect on the senses that the monotonous sound of a waterfall never fails to have on mine. With —— one is afraid to speak, because whatever is said is sure to bring forth a reminiscence, that as surely leads to interminable recollections,

> Dull as the dreams of him who swills vile beer.

Thus (continued Byron), —— is so honourable and well-intentioned a man that one can find nothing bad to say of him, except that he is a bore; and as there is no law against that class of offenders, one must bear with him. It is to be hoped, that, with all the modern improvements in refinement, a mode will be discovered of getting rid of bores, for it is too bad that a poor wretch can be punished for stealing your pocket-handkerchief or gloves, and that no punishment can be inflicted on those who steal your time, and with it your temper and patience, as well as the bright thoughts that might have entered into the mind, (like the Irishman who lost a fortune before he had got it,) but were frighted away by the bore. Nature certainly (said Byron) has not dealt charitably by ——, for, independent of his being the king of prosers, he is the ugliest person possible, and when he talks, breathes not of Araby the blest: his heart is good, but the stomach is none of the best, judging from its exhalations. His united merits led me to attempt an epigram on them, which, I believe, is as follows:—

> When conversing with ——, who can disclose
> Which suffers the most—eyes, ears, or the nose?

[72] Cf. Lady Blessington's "Night Thought Book": "Society, in its Spartan morality, punishes its members severely for the detection of their vices, but crime itself has nothing but detection to apprehend at its hands" (Madden, I, 246).

"I repeated this epigram (continued Byron) to him as having been made on a mutual friend of ours, and he enjoyed it, as we all do some hit on a friend. I have known people who were incapable of saying the least unkind word against friends, and yet who listened with evident (though attempted to be suppressed) pleasure to the malicious jokes or witty sarcasms of others against them; a proof that, even in the best people, some taints of the original evil of our natures remain. You think I am wrong (continued Byron) in my estimate of human nature; you think I analyze my own evil qualities and those of others too closely, and judge them too severely. I have need of self-examination to reconcile me to all the incongruities I discover, and to make me more lenient to faults that my tongue censures, but that my heart pardons, from the consciousness of its own weakness."

We should all do well to reflect on the frailty of man, if it led us more readily to forgive his faults, and cherish his virtues;—the one, alas! are inextirpable, but the others are the victories gained over that most difficult to be conquered of all assailants—self; to which victory, if we do not decree a triumph, we ought to grant an ovation; but, unhappily, the contemplation of human frailty is too apt to harden the heart, and oftener creates disgust than humility. "When we dwell on vices with mockery and bitterness, instead of pity, we may doubt the efficacy of our contemplation; and this," said I to Byron, "seems to me to be your case; for when I hear your taunting reflections on the discoveries you make in poor, erring human nature; when you have explored and exposed every secret recess of the heart, you appear to me like a fallen angel, sneering at the sins of men, instead of a fellow man pitying them. This it is that makes me think you analyze too deeply; and I would at present lead you to reflect only on the good that still remains in the world, —for be assured there is much good, as an antidote to the evil that you know of."

Byron laughed, and said, "You certainly do not spare me; but you manage to wrap up your censures in an envelope almost complimentary, and that reconciles me to their bitterness, as children are induced to take physic by its being disguised in some sweet substance. The fallen angel is so much more agreeable than demon, as others have called me, that I am rather flattered than affronted;

189

I ought, in return, to say something *très aimable* to you, in which angelic at least might be introduced, but I will not, as I never can compliment those that I esteem.—But to return to self;—you know that I have been called not only a demon, but a French poet has addressed me as *chantre d'enfer,*[73] which, I suppose, he thinks very flattering. I dare say his poem will be done into English by some Attic resident, and, instead of a singer of hell, I shall be styled a hellish singer, and so go down to posterity."

He laughed at his own pun, and said he felt half disposed to write a quizzing answer to the French poet, in which he should mystify him.

"It is no wonder (said Byron) that I am considered a demon, when people have taken it into their heads that I am the hero of all my own tales in verse. They fancy one can only describe what has actually occurred to oneself, and forget the power that persons of any imagination possess of identifying themselves, for the time being, with the creations of their fancy. This is a peculiar distinction conferred on me, for I have heard of no other poet who has been identified with his works. I saw the other day (said Byron) in one of the papers a fanciful simile about Moore's writings and mine. It stated that Moore's poems appeared as if they ought to be written with crow-quills, on rose-coloured paper, stamped with Cupids and flowers; and mine on asbestos, written by quills from the wing of an eagle:—you laugh, but I think this a very sublime comparison,—at least, so far as I am concerned,—it quite consoles me for 'chantre d'enfer.' By the bye, the French poet is neither a philosopher nor a logician: as he dubs me by this title merely because I doubt that there is an *enfer,*—ergo, I cannot be styled the *chantre* of a place of which I doubt the existence.[74] I dislike French verse so much (said Byron) that I have not read more than a few lines of the one in which I am dragged into public view. He calls me,

[73] Byron quoted the phrase from Lamartine's "L'Homme—à Lord Byron," *Premières Méditationes Poétiques,* in his letter to Moore, July 13, 1820; Lady Blessington may have read it in Moore's *Life,* p. 451 (*LJ,* V, 51).

[74] Cf. Byron to Moore, July 13, 1820 (Moore, *Life,* p. 451; *LJ,* V, 51), referring to Lamartine's *chantre d'enfer:* "A pretty title to give a man for doubting if there be any such place." See also Medwin's report of Byron on Lamartine's poem, p. 228, which does not always agree with Lady Blessington, who observed of the French poet in Florence that he "dressed so perfectly like a gentleman that one never would suspect him to be a poet" (*The Idler in Italy,* II, 476).

(said Byron,) 'Esprit mystérieux, mortel, ange ou démon;' which I call very uncivil, for a well-bred Frenchman, and moreover one of the craft: I wish he would let me and my works alone, for I am sure I do not trouble him or his, and should not know that he existed, except from his notice of me, which some good-natured friend has sent me. There are some things in the world, of which, like gnats, we are only reminded of the existence by their stinging us; this was his position with me."

Had Byron read the whole of the poem addressed to him by M. de Lamartine, he would have been more flattered than offended by it, as it is not only full of beauty, but the admiration for the genius of the English poet, which pervades every sentiment of the ode, is so profound, that the epithet which offended the morbid sensitiveness of Byron would have been readily pardoned. M. de Lamartine is perhaps the only French poet who could have so justly appreciated, and gracefully eulogized, our wayward child of genius; and having written so successfully himself, his praise is more valuable. His "Meditations" possess a depth of feeling which, tempered by a strong religious sentiment that makes the Christian rise superior to the philosopher, bears the impress of a true poetical temperament, which could not fail to sympathize with all the *feelings*, however he might differ from the *reasonings* of Byron. Were the works of the French poet better known to the English bard he could not, with even all his dislike to French poetry, have refused his approbation to the writings of M. de Lamartine.

Talking of solitude—"It has but one disadvantage (said Byron), but that is a serious one,—it is apt to give one too high an opinion of oneself. In the world we are sure to be often reminded of every known or supposed defect we may have; hence we can rarely, unless possessed of an inordinate share of vanity, form a very exalted opinion of ourselves, and, in society, woe be to him who lets it be known that he thinks more highly of himself than of his neighbours, as this is a crime that arms every one against him. This was the rock on which Napoleon foundered; he had so often wounded the *amour propre* of others, that they were glad to hurl him from the eminence that made him appear a giant and those around him pigmies. If a man or woman has any striking superiority, some great defect or weakness must be discovered to counterbalance it, that their con-

191

temporaries may console themselves for their envy, by saying, 'Well, if I have not the genius of Mr. This, or the beauty or talents of Mrs. That, I have not the violent temper of the one, or the overweening vanity of the other.' But, to return to solitude, (said Byron,) it is the only fool's paradise on earth: there we have no one to remind us of our faults, or by whom we can be humiliated by comparisons. Our evil passions sleep, because they are not excited; our productions appear sublime, because we have no kind and judicious friend to hint at their defects, and to point out faults of style and imagery where we had thought ourselves most luminous: these are the advantages of solitude, and those who have once tasted them, can never return to the busy world again with any zest for its feverish enjoyments. In the world (said Byron) I am always irritable and violent; the very noise of the streets of a populous city affect my nerves: I seemed in a London house 'cabined, cribbed, confined, and felt like a tiger in too small a cage:'[75] apropos of tigers, did you ever observe that all people in a violent rage, walk up and down the place they are in, as wild beasts do in their dens? I have particularly remarked this, (continued he,) and it proved to me, what I never doubted, that we have much of the animal and the ferocious in our natures, which, I am convinced, is increased by an over-indulgence of our carnivorous propensities. It has been said that, to enjoy solitude, a man must be superlatively good or bad: I deny this, because there are no superlatives in man,—all are comparative or relative; but, had I no other reason to deny it, my own experience would furnish me with one. God knows I never flattered myself with the idea of being superlatively good, as no one better knows his faults than I do mine; but, at the same time, I am as unwilling to believe that I am superlatively bad, yet I enjoy solitude more than I ever enjoyed society, even in my most youthful days."

I told Byron, that I expected he would one day give the world a collection of useful aphorisms, drawn from personal experience. He laughed and said—"Perhaps I may; those are best suited to advise others who have missed the road themselves, and this has been my case. I have found friends false,—acquaintances malicious,—

[75] For numerous statements of the opposite point of view, that a city, specifically London, is the only place to spend one's life, see my *Byron: The Record of a Quest*, Chapter III, "Town Versus Country."

relations indifferent,—and nearer and dearer connexions perfidious. Perhaps much, if not all this, has been caused by my own waywardness; but that has not prevented my feeling it keenly. It has made me look on friends as partakers of prosperity,—censurers in adversity,—and absentees in distress; and has forced me to view acquaintances merely as persons who think themselves justified in courting or cutting one, as best suits them. But relations I regard only as people privileged to tell disagreeable truths, and to accept weighty obligations, as matters of course. You have now (continued Byron) my unsophisticated opinion of friends, acquaintances, and relations; of course there are always exceptions, but they are rare, and exceptions do not make the rule. All that I have said are but reiterated truisms that all admit to be just, but that few, if any, act upon; they are like the death-bell that we hear toll for others, without thinking that it must soon toll for us;[76] we know that others have been deceived, but we believe that we are either too clever, or too *loveable*, to meet the same fate: we see our friends drop daily around us, many of them younger and healthier than ourselves, yet we think that we shall live to be old, as if we possessed some stronger hold on life than those who have gone before us. Alas! life is but a dream from which we are only awakened by death. All else is illusion; changing as we change, and each cheating us in turn, until death withdraws the veil, and shows us the dread reality. It is strange (said Byron) that feeling, as most people do, life a burthen, we should still cling to it with such pertinacity. This is another proof of animal feeling; for if the divine spirit that is supposed to animate us mastered the animal nature, should we not rejoice at laying down the load that has so long oppressed us, and beneath which we have groaned for years, to seek a purer, brighter existence? Who ever reached the age of twenty-five (continued Byron) without feeling the *tædium vitæ* which poisons the little enjoyment that we are allowed to taste? We begin life with the hope of attaining happiness; soon discovering that to be unattainable, we seek pleasure as a poor substitute; but even this eludes our grasp, and we end by desiring respose, which death alone can give."

[76] If this is an echo of the famous sermon by John Donne, it seems to be one of two references that Byron made to Donne: the other is in "To Lord Thurlow" (*Poetry*, VII, 19).

I told Byron that the greater part of our chagrins arose from disappointed hopes; that, in our pride and weakness, we considered happiness as our birthright, and received infliction as an injustice; whereas the latter was the inevitable lot of man, and the other but the *ignis fatuus* that beguiles the dreary path of life, and sparkles but to deceive. I added that while peace of mind was left us, we could not be called miserable. This greatest of all earthly consolations depends on ourselves; whereas for happiness we rely on others: but, as the first is lasting, and the second fleeting, we ought to cultivate that of which nought but our own actions can deprive us, and enjoy the other as we do a fine autumnal day, that we prize the more, because we know it will soon be followed by winter.

"Your philosophy is really admirable (said Byron) if it were possible to follow it; but I suspect that you are among the number of those who preach it the most, and practise it the least, for you have too much feeling to have more than a theoretical knowledge of it. For example, how would you bear the ingratitude and estrangement of friends—of those in whom you had garnered up your heart?[77] I suspect that, in such a case, feeling would beat philosophy out of the field; for I have ever found that philosophy, like experience, never comes until one has ceased to require its services. I have (continued Byron) experienced ingratitude and estrangement from friends; and this, more than all else, has destroyed my confidence in human nature. It is thus from individual cases that we are so apt to generalize. A few persons on whom we have lavished our friendship, without ever examining if they had the qualities requisite to justify such a preference, are found to be ungrateful and unworthy, and instead of blaming our own want of perception in the persons so unwisely chosen, we cry out against poor human nature: one or two examples of ingratitude and selfishness prejudice us against the world; but six times the number of examples of goodness and sincerity fail to reconcile us to it,—so much more susceptible are we of evil impressions than of good. Have you not observed (said Byron) how much more prone people are to remember injuries than benefits? The most essential services are soon forgotten; but some trifling and often unintentional offence is rarely

[77] Lady Blessington knew very well "the ingratitude and estrangement of friends" (see Madden, II, 422, 429, and my introduction).

194

pardoned, and never effaced from the memory. All this proves that we have a strong and decided predisposition to evil; the tendencies and consequences of which we may conceal, but cannot eradicate. I think ill of the world, (continued Byron,) but I do not, as some cynics assert, believe it to be composed of knaves and fools. No, I consider that it is, for the most part, peopled by those who have not talents sufficient to be the first, and yet have one degree too much to be the second."

Byron's bad opinion of mankind is not, I am convinced, genuine; and it certainly does not operate on his actions, as his first impulses are always good, and his heart is kind and charitable. His good deeds are never the result of reflection, as the heart acts before the head has had time to reason. This cynical habit of decrying human nature is one of the many little affectations to which he often descends; and this impression has become so fixed in my mind, that I have been vexed with myself for attempting to refute opinions of his which, on reflection, I was convinced were not his real sentiments, but uttered either from a foolish wish of display, or from a spirit of contradiction, which much influences his conversation. I have heard him assert opinions one day, and maintain the most opposite, with equal warmth, the day after: this arises not so much from insincerity, as from being wholly governed by the feeling of the moment: he has no fixed principle of conduct or of thought,[78] and the want of it leads him into errors and inconsistencies, from which he is only rescued by a natural goodness of heart, that redeems, in some degree, what it cannot prevent. Violence of temper tempts him into expressions that might induce people to believe him vindictive and rancorous; he exaggerates all his feelings when he gives utterance to them; and here the imagination, that has led to his triumph in poetry, operates less happily, by giving a stronger shade to his sentiments and expressions. When he writes or speaks at such moments, the force of his language imposes a belief that the feeling which gives birth to it must be fixed in his mind; but see him in a few hours after, and not only no trace of this angry excite-

[78] For numerous other comments on Byron's temperamental *mobilité* and lack of "fixed" principles, see the statements by Mary Shelley, Madame Albrizzi, Stanhope, Moore, Scott, Kennedy, Leigh Hunt, and Trelawny in my *Byron: The Record of a Quest,* pp. 25-29.

195

ment remains, but, if recurred to by another, he smiles at his own exaggerated warmth of expression, and proves, in a thousand ways, that the temper only is responsible for his defects, and not the heart.

"I think it is Diderot (said Byron) who says that, to describe woman, one ought to dip one's pen in the rainbow; and, instead of sand, use the dust from the wings of butterflies to dry the paper. This is a *concetto* worthy of a Frenchman; and, though meant as complimentary, is really by no means so to your sex. To describe woman, the pen should be dipped, not in the rainbow, but in the heart of man, ere more than eighteen summers have passed over his head; and, to dry the paper, I would allow only the sighs of adolescence. Women are best understood by men whose feelings have not been hardened by a contact with the world, and who believe in virtue because they are unacquainted with vice. A knowledge of vice will, as far as I can judge by experience, invariably produce disgust, as I believe, with my favourite poet, that—

> Vice is a monster of such hideous mien,
> That, to be hated, needs but to be seen.

But he who has known it can never truly describe woman as she ought to be described; and, therefore, a perfect knowledge of the world unfits a man for the task. When I attempted to describe Haidee and Zuleika, I endeavoured to forget all that friction with the world had taught me; and if I at all succeeded, it was because I was, and am, penetrated with the conviction that women only know evil from having experienced it through men; whereas men have no criterion to judge of purity or goodness but woman. Some portion of this purity and goodness always adheres to woman, (continued Byron,) even though she may lapse from virtue; she makes a willing sacrifice of herself on the altar of affection, and thinks only of him for whom it is made: while men think of themselves alone, and regard the woman but as an object that administers to their selfish gratification, and who, when she ceases to have this power, is thought of no more, save as an obstruction in their path. You look incredulous, (said Byron;) but I have said what I think, though not all that I think, as I have a much higher opinion of your sex than I have even now expressed."

196

This would be most gratifying could I be sure that, to-morrow or next day, some sweeping sarcasm against my sex may not escape from the lips that have now praised them, and that my credulity, in believing the praise, may not be quoted as an additional proof of their weakness. This instability of opinion, or expression of opinion, of Byron, destroys all confidence in him, and precludes the possibility of those, who live much in his society, feeling that sentiment of confiding security in him, without which a real regard cannot subsist. It has always appeared a strange anomaly to me, that Byron, who possesses such acuteness in discerning the foibles and defects of others, should have so little power either in conquering or concealing his own, that they are evident even to a superficial observer; it is also extraordinary that the knowledge of human nature, which enables him to discover at a glance such defects, should not dictate the wisdom of concealing his discoveries, at least from those in whom he has made them; but in this he betrays a total want of tact, and must often send away his associates dissatisfied with themselves, and still more so with him, if they happen to possess discrimination or susceptibility.

"To let a person see that you have discovered his faults, is to make him an enemy for life," (says Byron); and yet this he does continually: he says, "that the only truths a friend will tell you, are your faults; and the only thing he will give you, is advice." Byron's affected display of knowledge of the world deprives him of commiseration for being its dupe, while his practical inexperience renders him so perpetually. He is at war with the actual state of things, yet admits that all that he now complains of has existed for centuries; and that those who have taken up arms against the world have found few applauders, and still fewer followers. His philosophy is more theoretical than practical, and must so continue, as long as passion and feeling have more influence over him than reflection and reason. Byron affects to be unfeeling, while he is a victim to sensibility; and to be reasonable, while he is governed by imagination only; and so meets with no sympathy from either the advocates of sensibility or reason, and consequently condemns both. "It is fortunate for those (said Byron) whose near connexions are good and estimable; independently of various other advantages

197

that are derived from it, perhaps the greatest of all are the impressions made on our minds in early youth by witnessing goodness, impressions which have such weight in deciding our future opinions. If we witness evil qualities in common acquaintances, the effect is slight, in comparison with that made by discovering them in those united to us by the ties of consanguinity; this last disgusts us with human nature, and renders us doubtful of goodness, a progressive step made in misanthropy, the most fearful disease that can attack the mind.[79] My first and earliest impressions were melancholy,—my poor mother gave them; but to my sister, who, incapable of wrong herself, suspected no wrong in others, I owe the little good of which I can boast; and had I earlier known her, it might have influenced my destiny. Augusta has great strength of mind, which is displayed not only in her own conduct, but to support the weak and infirm of purpose. To me she was, in the hour of need, as a tower of strength. Her affection was my last rallying point, and is now the only bright spot that the horizon of England offers to my view. Augusta knew all my weaknesses, but she had love enough to bear with them. I value not the false sentiment of affection that adheres to one while we believe him faultless; not to love him would then be difficult: but give me the love that, with perception to view the errors, has sufficient force to pardon them,—who can 'love the offender, yet detest the offence;' and this my sister had. She has given me such good advice, and yet, finding me incapable of following it, loved and pitied me but the more, because I was erring.[80] This is true affection, and, above all, true Christian feeling; but how rarely is it to be met with in England! where *amour propre* prompts people to show their superiority by giving advice; and a *mélange* of selfishness and wounded vanity engages them to resent its not being followed; which they do by not only leaving off the *advised*, but by injuring him by every means in their power. Depend on it (continued Byron), the English are the most perfidious friends and unkind relations that the civilized world can produce; and if you have had the misfortune to lay them under weighty obli-

[79] Lady Blessington had greater reason to understand this than Byron had (see my introduction).

[80] Byron was not ordinarily grateful to Augusta for "good" advice, suspecting that she had fallen under the influence of Lady Byron.

gations, you may look for all the injuries that they can inflict, as they are anxious to avenge themselves for the humiliations they suffer when they accept favours. They are proud, but have not sufficient pride to refuse services that are necessary to their comfort, and have too much false pride to be grateful. They may pardon a refusal to assist them, but they never can forgive a generosity which, as they are seldom capable of practising or appreciating, overpowers and humiliates them. With this opinion of the English (continued Byron), which has not been lightly formed, you may imagine how truly I must value my sister, who is so totally opposed to them. She is tenacious of accepting obligations, even from the nearest relations; but, having accepted, is incapable of aught approaching to ingratitude.[81] Poor Lady —— had just such a sister as mine, who, faultless herself, could pardon and weep over the errors of one less pure, and almost redeem them by her own excellence. Had Lady ——'s sister or mine (continued Byron) been less good and irreproachable, they could not have afforded to be so forbearing; but, being unsullied, they could show mercy without fear of drawing attention to their own misdemeanours."

Byron talked to-day of Campbell the poet; said that he was a warm-hearted and honest man; praised his works, and quoted some passages from the "Pleasures of Hope," which he said was a poem full of beauties. "I differ, however, (said Byron,) with my friend Campbell on some points. Do you remember the passage—

> But mark the wretch whose wanderings never knew
> The world's regard, that soothes though half untrue!
> His erring heart the lash of sorrow bore,
> But found not pity when it erred no more."[82]

This, he said, was so far a true picture, those who once erred being supposed to err always,—a charitable, but false, supposition, that the English are prone to act upon.[83] "But (added Byron) I am not prepared to admit, that a man, under such circumstances as

[81] Cf. Lady Blessington's "Night Thought Book": "Most people escape the weight of obligations by Ingratitude." Lady Blessington's sister Ellen, when respectably married, had expressed such ingratitude.
[82] *Pleasures of Hope*, I, 295-98. Lady Blessington first met Campbell in the spring of 1832 (Madden, II, 274, 357).
[83] Lady Blessington also suffered from this supposition.

199

those so poetically described by Campbell, could feel hope; and, judging by my own feelings, I should think that there would be more of envy than of hope in the poor man's mind, when he leaned on the gate, and looked at 'the blossom'd bean-field and the sloping green.' Campbell was, however, right in representing it otherwise (continued Byron). We have all, God knows, occasion for hope to enable us to support the thousand vexations of this dreary existence; and he who leads us to believe in this universal panacea, in which, *par parenthese*, I have little faith, renders a service to humanity. Campbell's 'Lochiel' and 'Mariners' are admirable spirit-stirring productions (said Byron); his 'Gertrude of Wyoming' is beautiful; and some of the episodes in his 'Pleasures of Hope' pleased me so much, that I know them by heart.[84] By the bye (continued he) we must be indebted to Ireland for this mode of expressing the knowing anything by rote, and it is at once so true and poetical, that I always use it. We certainly remember best those passages, as well as events, that interest us most, or touch the heart, which must have given birth to the phrase—'know by heart.' The 'Pleasures of Memory' is a very beautiful poem (said Byron), harmonious, finished, and chaste; it contains not a single meretricious ornament. If Rogers has not fixed himself in the higher fields of Parnassus, he has, at least, cultivated a very pretty flower-garden at its base. Is not this (continued Byron) a poetical image worthy of a *conversazione* at Lydia White's?[85] But, jesting apart, for one ought to be serious in talking of so serious a subject as the pleasures of

[84] Early and late—with lapses, however, or with qualifications—Byron revealed his sympathy with the poetry of Campbell. In 1813 in his *"Gradus ad Parnassum"* he placed him just below Scott and Rogers and on the same level with Moore (*LJ*, II, 344); in 1820 in his "Reply to Blackwood's *Edinburgh Magazine*" he named Campbell as one of the four living poets who could write an heroic couplet (*LJ*, IV, 489); and in 1821 he defended him against Bowles in the Pope-Bowles controversy (*LJ*, V, 543-44) and quoted from *The Pleasures of Hope* (*LJ*, V, 552). "Ye Mariners of England" and "Lochiel's Warning" are among Campbell's better or better-known short poems; Byron referred to Lochiel in *Childe Harold*, III, xxvi. But *Gertrude of Wyoming*, Byron thought, had "no more locality in common with Pennsylvania than with Penmanmaur. It is notoriously full of grossly false scenery, as all Americans declare . . ." (*LJ*, V, 166). From 1820 to 1830 Campbell was editor of *The New Monthly*, in which Lady Blessington's *Conversations* appeared 1832-1833.

[85] Byron satirized Lydia White, the famous bluestocking, in *The Blues*. She died in 1827. Lady Blessington apparently did not know her personally.

memory, which, God knows, never offered any pleasures to me, (mind, I mean memory, and not the poem,) it really always did remind me of a flower-garden, so filled with sweets, so trim, so orderly. You, I am sure, know the powerful poem written in a blank leaf of the 'Pleasures of Memory,' by an unknown author? He has taken my view of the subject, and I envy him for expressing all that I felt; but did not, could not, express as he has done. This wilderness of triste thoughts offered a curious contrast to the *hortus siccus* of pretty flowers that followed it (said Byron), and marks the difference between inspiration and versification.[86]

"Having compared Rogers's poem to a flower-garden," continued Byron, "to what shall I compare Moore's?—to the Valley of Diamonds, where all is brilliant and attractive, but where one is so dazzled by the sparkling on every side that one knows not where to fix, each gem beautiful in itself, but overpowering to the eye from their quantity. Or, to descend to a more homely comparison, though really," continued Byron, "so brilliant a subject hardly admits of any thing homely, Moore's poems (with the exception of the Melodies) resemble the fields in Italy, covered by such myriads of fire-flies shining and glittering around, that if one attempts to seize one, another still more brilliant attracts, and one is bewildered from too much brightness. I remember reading somewhere," said Byron, "a *concetto* of designating different living poets, by the cups Apollo gives them to drink out of. Wordsworth is made to drink from a wooden bowl, and my melancholy self from a skull, chased with gold. Now, I would add the following cups:—To Moore, I would give a cup formed like the lotus flower, and set in brilliants; to Crabbe, a scooped pumpkin;[87] to Rogers, an antique vasé, formed of agate; and to Colman, a champagne glass, as descriptive of

[86] By 1823 Byron, to be sure, had become very bitter toward Rogers, a long-time friend or dinner guest of Lady Blessington; however, Rogers had drifted away from the Blessington circle, back to Holland House and other haunts, and she could speak very bitterly of him to Crabb Robinson (see my introduction).

[87] Byron seems never to have seriously or radically revised the judgment of Crabbe expressed in *English Bards* (1. 858: "Though Nature's sternest Painter, yet the best") and confirmed in his marginalia of 1816: "I consider Crabbe and Coleridge as the first of these times, in point of power and genius" (*Poetry*, I, 365, n. 1). In 1821 Crabbe was still among "the Elect" (*LJ*, V, 373, 392). In view of these comments, Lady Blessington's "scooped pumpkin" seems somewhat rural, even for Crabbe.

201

their different styles.[88] I dare say none of them would be satisfied with the appropriation; but who ever is satisfied with any thing in the shape of criticism? and least of all, poets."

Talking of Shakspeare, Byron said, that he owed one half of his popularity to his low origin, which, like charity, covereth a multitude of sins with the multitude, and the other half, to the remoteness of the time at which he wrote from our own days. All his vulgarisms," continued Byron, "are attributed to the circumstances of his birth and breeding depriving him of a good education; hence they are to be excused, and the obscurities with which his works abound are all easily explained away by the simple statement, that he wrote about 200 years ago, and that the terms then in familiar use are now become obsolete. With two such good excuses, as want of education, and having written above 200 years before our time, any writer may pass muster; and when to these is added the being a sturdy hind of low degree, which to three parts of the community in England has a peculiar attraction, one ceases to wonder at his supposed popularity; I say supposed, for who goes to see his plays, and who, except country parsons, or mouthing, stage-struck, theatrical amateurs, read them?"[89] I told Byron what really was, and is, my impression, that he was not sincere in his depreciation of our immortal bard; and I added, that I preferred believing him insincere, than incapable of judging works, which his own writings proved he must, more than most other men, feel the beauties of. He laughed, and replied, "That the compliment I paid to his writ-

[88] Byron, who referred repeatedly to the theatrical productions of George Colman the Younger and often quoted from them in his letters, paid his tribute to the wit and charm of the man in his "Detached Thoughts," No. 107 (*LJ*, V, 461; Moore's *Life*, p. 183): "I have got very drunk with them both [Colman and Sheridan]; but, if I had to *choose*, and could not have both at a time, I should say, 'let me begin the evening with Sheridan, and finish it with Colman.' Sheridan for dinner—Colman for Supper. Sheridan for Claret or port; but Colman for every thing, from the Madeira and Champaigne at dinner—the Claret with a *layer* of *port* between the Glasses—up to the Punch of the Night, and down to the Grog or Gin and water of day-break." Although this colorful passage may be the source of Lady Blessington's "champagne glass," which does very well for Colman's conversational style, it does not seem particularly appropriate for the style of his poetry, often humorous and coarse. Lady Blessington knew him as early as 1819 (Madden, I, 292).

[89] Byron attacked Shakespeare in conversation with Medwin, Rogers, Moore, George Bancroft, Hobhouse, George Finlay, Hunt, Kennedy, and Stanhope, but never with these persons on the grounds reported by Lady Blessington.

ings was so entirely at the expense of his sincerity, that he had no cause to be flattered; but that, knowing I was one of those who worshipped Shakspeare, he forgave me, and would only bargain that I made equal allowance for his worship of Pope." I observed, "That any comparison between the two was as absurd as comparing some magnificent feudal castle, surrounded by mountains and forests, with foaming cataracts, and boundless lakes, to the pretty villa of Pope, with its sheen lawn, artificial grotto, stunted trees, and trim exotics." He said that my simile[90] was more ingenious than just, and hoped that I was prepared to admit that Pope was the greatest of all modern poets, and a philosopher as well as a poet. I made my peace by expressing my sincere admiration of Pope, but begged to be understood as refusing to admit any comparison between him and Shakspeare; and so the subject ended. Byron is so prone to talk for effect, and to assert what he does not believe, that one must be cautious in giving implicit credence to his opinions. My conviction is, that, in spite of his declarations to the contrary, he admires Shakspeare as much as most of his countrymen do; but that, unlike the generality of them, he sees the blemishes that the freedom of the times in which the great poet lived led him to indulge in in his writings, in a stronger point of view, and takes pleasure in commenting on them with severity, as a means of wounding the vanity of the English. I have rarely met with a person more conversant with the works of Shakspeare than was Byron. I have heard him quote passages from them repeatedly; and in a tone that marked how well he appreciated their beauty, which certainly lost nothing in his delivery of them, as few possessed a more harmonious voice or a more elegant pronunciation than did Byron.[91] Could there be a less equivocal proof of his admiration of our im-

[90] It will be noted that Lady Blessington's "simile" referring to the poetry of Pope, implying artificiality, smallness, and the absence of the sublime, is similar to the contemptuous similes or metaphors placed in the mouth of Byron when describing Moore or his poetry: when Moore speaks, he is like a fairy who lets diamonds fall from her lips (p. 184); his poetry should be written on rose-coloured paper decorated with Cupids and flowers (p. 190); the cup given to him by Apollo is shaped like the lotus flower (p. 201); or, as she told Crabb Robinson, Moore's father the Dublin grocer fed him on plums and sugar candy (*HVSV*, p. 371).

[91] Cf. *The Idler* (*HVSV*, p. 350): "His voice and accent are particularly clear and harmonious, but somewhat effeminate; and his enunciation is so distinct that, though his general tone in speaking is low, not a word is lost."

mortal bard than the tenacity with which his memory retained the finest passages of all his works? When I made this observation to him he smiled, and affected to boast that his memory was so retentive that it equally retained all that he read; but as I had seen many proofs of the contrary, I persevered in affirming what I have never ceased to believe, that, in despite of his professions to the reverse, Byron was in his heart a warm admirer of Shakspeare.

Byron takes a peculiar pleasure in opposing himself to popular opinion on all points; he wishes to be thought as dissenting from the multitude, and this affectation is the secret source of many of the incongruities he expresses. One cannot help lamenting that so great a genius should be sullied by this weakness; but he has so many redeeming points that we must pardon what we cannot overlook, and attribute this error to the imperfectibility of human nature. Once thoroughly acquainted with his peculiarities, much that appeared incomprehensible is explained, and one knows when to limit belief to assertions that are not always worthy of commanding it, because uttered from the caprice of the moment. He declares that such is his bad opinion of the taste and feelings of the English, that he should form a bad opinion of any work that they admired, or any person that they praised; and that their admiration of his own works has rather confirmed than softened his bad opinion of them. "It was the exaggerated praises of the people in England," said he, "that indisposed me to the Duke of Wellington. I know that the same herd, who were trying to make an idol of him, would, on any reverse, or change of opinions, hurl him from the pedestal to which they had raised him, and lay their idol in the dust. I remember," continued Byron, "enraging some of his Grace's worshippers, after the battle of Waterloo, by quoting the lines from Ariosto:—

> Fù il vincer sempre mai laudabil cosa,
> Vincasi ò per fortuna ò per ingregno,[92]

in answer to their appeal to me, if he was not the greatest general that ever existed."

I told Byron that his quotation was insidious, but that the Duke had gained too many victories to admit the possibility of any of

[92] *Orlando Furioso*, XV, 1. It appears that Lady Blessington did not know Italian in 1823.

204

them being achieved more by chance than ability; and that, like his attacks on Shakspeare, he was not sincere in disparaging Wellington, as I was sure he must *au fond* be as proud of him as all other Englishmen are. "What!" said Byron, "could a Whig be proud of Wellington! would this be consistent?"[93]

The whole of Byron's manner, and his countenance on this and other occasions, when the name of the Duke of Wellington has been mentioned, conveyed the impression, that he had not been *de bonne foi* in his censures on him. Byron's words and feelings are so often opposed, and both so completely depend on the humour of the moment, that those who know him well could never attach much confidence to the stability of his sentiments, or the force of his expressions; nor could they feel surprised, or angry, at hearing that he had spoken unkindly of some for whom he really felt friendship. This habit of censuring is his ruling passion, and he is now too old to correct it.

"I have been amused," said Byron, "in reading 'Les Essais de Montaigne,'[94] to find how severe he is on the sentiment of tristesse: we are always severe on that particular passion to which we are not addicted, and the French are exempt from this. Montaigne says that the Italians were right in translating their word tristezza, which means tristesse, into malignité; and this," continued Byron, "explains my méchanceté, for that I am subject to tristesse cannot be doubted; and if that means, as Le Sieur de Montaigne states, *la malignité*, this is the secret of all my evil doings, or evil imaginings, and prob-

[93] For a summary of Byron's expressions on Wellington, see Pratt, the variorum edition of *Don Juan*, IV, 189-93, which quote from Byron's "Detached Thoughts," *LJ*, V, 462: "*Nelson was* a hero: the other [Wellington] is a mere Corporal, dividing with Prussians and Spaniards the luck, which he never deserved. . . ." Wellington was a friend of Lady Blessington, and she asked many favors of him over the years (Madden, II, 162-67). His eldest son, born in 1807, "was one of [her] most intimate friends" (Madden, II, 167). Count D'Orsay made a portrait, a statuette, and a bust of the Duke, who had befriended him in his boyhood.

[94] Outside of *Don Juan*, Byron's references to Montaigne are few, but Leigh Hunt has recorded: "The only great writer of past times, whom he read with avowed satisfaction, was Montaigne"; and James Hamilton Browne stated, of Byron's last voyage to Greece: "He also made it a constant rule to peruse every day one or more of the Essays of Montaigne. This practice, he said, he had pursued for a long time; adding his decided conviction, that more useful general knowledge and varied information were to be derived by an intimate acquaintance with the writings of that diverting author, than by a long and continuous course of study" (*HVSV*, pp. 320, 387).

ably is also the source of my inspiration." This idea appeared to amuse him very much, and he dwelt on it with apparent satisfaction, saying that it absolved him from a load of responsibility, as he considered himself, according to this, as no more accountable for the satires he might write or speak, than for his personal deformity. Nature, he said, had to answer for malignité as well as for deformity; she gave both, and the unfortunate persons on whom she bestowed them were not to be blamed for their effects. Byron said, that Montaigne was one of the French writers that amused him the most, as, independently of the quaintness with which he made his observations, a perusal of his works was like a repetition at school, they rubbed up the reader's classical knowledge. He added, that "Burton's Anatomy of Melancholy" was also excellent, from the quantity of desultory information it contained, and was a mine of knowledge that, though much worked, was inexhaustible.[95] I told him that he seemed to think more highly of Montaigne than did some of his own countrymen; for that when Le Cardinal du Perron "appelloit les Essais de Montaigne le bréviaire des honnêtes gens; le célèbre Huet, évêque d'Avranche, les disoit celui des honnêtes paresseux et des ignorans, qui veulent s'enfariner de quelque teinture des lettres"— Byron said that the critique was severe, but just; for that Montaigne was the greatest plagiarist that ever existed, and certainly had turned his reading to the most account. "But," said Byron, "who is the author that is not, intentionally or unintentionally, a plagiarist? Many more, I am persuaded, are the latter than the former; for if one has read much, it is difficult, if not impossible, to avoid adopting, not only the thoughts, but the expressions of others, which, after they have been some time stored in our minds, appear to us to come forth ready formed, like Minerva from the brain of Jupiter, and we fancy them our own progeny, instead of being those of adoption. I met lately a passage in a French book," continued Byron, "that states, *à propos* of plagiaries, that it was from the preface to the works of Montaigne, by

[95] Byron's copy of Burton's *Anatomy* was purchased by Murray at the sale of the poet's library in 1816, returned to him in 1821 when he requested Murray to send him a copy (*LJ*, V, 392, n. 1). Prothero states (*LJ*, V, 184, n. 1) that Byron was a "devoted admirer" of the book (see Moore, *Life*, p. 48).

Mademoiselle de Gournay, his adopted daughter, that Pascal[96] stole his image of the Divinity:—'C'est un cercle, dont la circonférence est par-tout, et le centre nulle part.' So you see that even the saintly Pascal could steal as well as another, and was probably unconscious of the theft.

"To be perfectly original," continued Byron, "one should think much and read little; and this is impossible, as one must have read much before one learns to think; for I have no faith in innate ideas, whatever I may have of innate predispositions. But after one has laid in a tolerable stock of materials for thinking, I should think the best plan would be to give the mind time to digest it, and then turn it all well over by thought and reflection, by which we make the knowledge acquired our own; and on this foundation we may let our originality (if we have any) build a superstructure, and if not, it supplies our want of it, to a certain degree. I am accused of plagiarism," continued Byron, "as I see by the newspapers. If I am guilty, I have many partners in the crime; for I assure you I scarcely know a living author who might not have a similar charge brought against him, and whose thoughts I have not occasionally found in the works of others; so that this consoles me.

"The book you lent me, Dr. Richardson's 'Travels along the Mediterranean,' "[97] said Byron, "is an excellent work. It abounds in information, sensibly and unaffectedly conveyed, and even without Lord B.'s praises of the author, would have led me to conclude that he was an enlightened, sensible, and thoroughly good man. He is always in earnest," continued Byron, "and never writes for ef-

[96] The indexes to *LJ, Poetry, Correspondence*, and *HVSV* do not reveal any reference made by Byron to Pascal.

[97] Not mentioned in the indexes to *LJ, Poetry, Correspondence*, or *HVSV*. Byron wrote to Murray, September 24, 1821, asking that he send him books of "*Voyages* and *travels*, provided that they are *neither in Greece, Spain, Asia Minor, Albania, nor Italy* . . . : having travelled the countries mentioned, I know that what is said of them can convey nothing further which I desire to know about them." Dr. Robert Richardson's *Travels*, however, also describes places Byron had never seen, Jerusalem, Damascus, and others, along with those with which he was familiar. Richardson was personal physician to the Earl of Belmore and an old friend and former traveling physician of Lord Blessington; he wrote a letter of condolence to Lady. Blessington following the death of her husband (Madden, I, 123); see also Madden, II, 90, and Moore, *Memoirs*, II, 357, which describes a dinner at Lady Blessington's on August 27, 1819, attended by Dr. Richardson.

fect: his language is well chosen and correct; and his religious views unaffected and sincere without bigotry. He is just the sort of man I should like to have with me for Greece—clever, both as a man and a physician; for I require both—one for my mind, and the other for my body, which is a little the worse for wear, from the bad usage of the troublesome tenant that has inhabited it, God help me!

"It is strange," said Byron, "how seldom one meets with clever, sensible men in the professions of divinity or physic! and yet they are precisely the professions that most peculiarly demand intelligence and ability,—as to keep the soul and body in good health requires no ordinary talents. I have, I confess, as little faith in medicine as Napoleon had. I think it has many remedies, but few specifics. I do not know if we arrived at the same conclusion by the same road. Mine has been drawn from observing that the medical men who fell in my way were, in general, so deficient in ability, that even had the science of medicine been fifty times more simplified than it ever will be in our time, they had not intelligence enough to comprehend or reduce it to practice, which has given me a much greater dread of remedies than diseases.[98] Medical men do not sufficiently attend to idiosyncrasy," continued Byron, "on which so much depends, and often hurry to the grave one patient by a treatment that has succeeded with another. The moment they ascertain a disease to be the same as one they have known, they conclude the same remedies that cured the first must remove the second, not making allowance for the peculiarities of temperament, habits, and disposition; which last has a great influence in maladies. All that I have seen of physicians has given me a dread of them, which dread will continue until I have met a doctor like your friend Richardson, who proves himself to be a sensible and intelligent man. I maintain," continued Byron, "that more than half our maladies are produced by accustoming ourselves to more sustenance than is required for the support of nature. We put too much oil into the lamp, and it blazes and burns out; but if we only put enough to feed

[98] After parting from Polidori, Byron never again had his own personal physician until he hired the inexperienced Dr. Bruno, when he was about to sail for Greece in 1823. Of him Byron said to Trelawny: "If he knows little, I pay little . . ." (*HVSV*, p. 380). It was he who bled Byron to death.

the flame, it burns brightly and steadily. We have, God knows, sufficient alloy in our compositions, without reducing them still nearer to the brute by overfeeding. I think that one of the reasons why women are in general so much better than men,—for I do think they are, whatever I may say to the contrary," continued Byron, "is, that they do not indulge in *gourmandise* as men do; and, consequently, do not labour under the complicated horrors that indigestion produces, which has such a dreadful effect on the tempers, as I have both witnessed and felt.

"There is nothing I so much dread as flattery," said Byron; "not that I mean to say I dislike it,—for, on the contrary, if well administered, it is very agreeable,—but I dread it because I know, from experience, we end by disliking those we flatter:[99] it is the mode we take to avenge ourselves for stooping to the humiliation of flattering them. On this account, I never flatter those I really like; and, also, I should be fearful and jealous of owing their regard for me to the pleasure my flattery gave them. I am not so forbearing with those I am indifferent about; for seeing how much people like flattery, I cannot resist giving them some, and it amuses me to see how they swallow even the largest doses. Now, there is ———— and ————; who could live on passable terms with them, that did not administer to their vanity? One tells you all his *bonnes fortunes*, and would never forgive you if you appeared to be surprised at their extent; and the other talks to you of prime ministers and dukes by their surnames, and cannot state the most simple fact or occurrence without telling you that Wellington or Devonshire told him so. One does not," continued Byron, "meet this last *faiblesse* out of England, and not then, I must admit, except among *parvenus*.

"It is doubtful which, vanity or conceit, is the most offensive," said Byron; "but I think conceit is, because the gratification of vanity depends on the suffrages of others, to gain which vain people must endeavour to please; but as conceit is content with its own approbation, it makes no sacrifice, and is not susceptible of humiliation. I confess that I have a spiteful pleasure," continued Byron, "in mortifying conceited people; and the gratification is enhanced

[99] Cf. Lady Blessington's "Night Thought Book": "Flattery is always acceptable, however we may despise the flatterer, because it implies an acknowledgment of our superiority."

209

by the difficulty of the task. One of the reasons why I dislike society is, that its contact excites all the evil qualities of my nature, which, like the fire in the flint, can only be elicited by friction. My philosophy is more theoretical then practical:[100] it is never at hand when I want it; and the puerile passions that I witness in those whom I encounter excite disgust when examined near, though, viewed at a distance, they only create pity:—that is to say, in simple homely truth," continued Byron, "the follies of mankind, when they touch *me* not, I can be lenient to, and moralize on; but if they rub against my own, there is an end to the philosopher. We are all better in solitude, and more especially if we are tainted with evil passions, which, God help us! we all are, more or less," said Byron. "They are not then brought into action: reason and reflection have time and opportunity to resume that influence over us which they rarely can do if we are actors in the busy scene of life; and we grow better, because we believe ourselves better. Our passions often only sleep when we suppose them dead; and we are not convinced of our mistake till they awake with renewed strength, gained by repose. We are, therefore, wise when we choose solitude, where 'passions sleep and reason wakes;' for if we cannot conquer the evil qualities that adhere to our nature, we do well to encourage their slumber. Like cases of acute pain, when the physician cannot remove the malady he administers soporifics.

"When I recommend solitude," said Byron, "I do not mean the solitude of country neighbourhood, where people pass their time *à dire, redire, et médire.* No! I mean a regular retirement, with a woman that one loves, and interrupted only by a correspondence with a man that one esteems, though if we put plural of man, it would be more agreeable for the correspondence. By this means, friendships would not be subject to the variations and estrangements that are so often caused by a frequent personal intercourse;[101] and we might delude ourselves into a belief that they were sincere, and might be lasting—two difficult articles of faith

[100] Cf. p. 197: "His philosophy is more theoretical than practical. . . ."
[101] The life described by Byron here is essentially that which he had established for himself in Genoa and elsewhere in Europe, usually moving in a very small circle of friends or acquaintants. Moore comments on the difficulty which Byron's sensitive nature had in maintaining day-to-day associations with people over an extended period of time (see *HVSV*, p. 237).

in my creed of friendship. Socrates and Plato," continued Byron, "ridiculed Laches,[102] who defined fortitude to consist in remaining firm in the ranks opposed to the enemy; and I agree with those philosophers in thinking that a retreat is not inglorious, whether from the enemy in the field or in the town, if one feels one's own weakness, and anticipates a defeat. I feel that society is my enemy, in even more than a figurative sense: I have not fled, but retreated from it; and if solitude has not made me better, I am sure it has prevented my becoming worse, which is a point gained.

"Have you ever observed," said Byron, "the extreme dread that *parvenus* have of aught that approaches to vulgarity?[103] In manners, letters, conversation, nay, even in literature, they are always superfine; and a man of birth would unconsciously hazard a thousand dubious phrases sooner than a *parvenu* would risk the possibility of being suspected of one. One of the many advantages of birth is, that it saves one from this hypercritical gentility, and he of noble blood may be natural without the fear of being accused of vulgarity. I have left an assembly filled with all the names of *haut ton* in London, and where little but names were to be found, to seek relief from the ennui that overpowered me, in a—cyder cellar: —are you not shocked?—and have found there more food for speculation than in the vapid circles of glittering dulness I had left.[104]

—— or —— dared not have done this; but I had the patent of nobility to carry me through it, and what would have been deemed originality and spirit in me, would have been considered a natural bias to vulgar habits in them. In my works, too, I have dared to pass the frozen molehills—I cannot call them Alps, though they are frozen eminences—of high life, and have used common thoughts and common words to express my impressions; where poor —— would have clarified each thought, and double-refined each sentence, until he had reduced them to the polished and cold temperature of the illuminated houses of ice that he loves to frequent; which

[102] In the dialogue of that name; not mentioned in the indexes to *LJ*, *Poetry, Correspondence*, or *HVSV*.

[103] Lady Blessington had this same dread (see my introduction). For Byron on vulgarity ("worse than downright *blackguardism*") and the "shabby-genteel," see his "Second Letter . . . on . . . Bowles's Strictures . . . ," *LJ*, V, 591-92, not published until 1835.

[104] Cf. Byron to Moore, September 5, 1813: "I am so sick of the other ["high life"], that I quite sigh for a cider-cellar . . ." (*LJ*, II, 261).

have always reminded me of the palace of ice built to please an empress, cold, glittering, and costly. But I suppose that —— and —— like them, from the same cause that I like high life below stairs, not being born to it:—there is a good deal in this. I have been abused for dining at Tom Cribb's,[105] where I certainly was amused, and have returned from a dinner where the guests were composed of the magnates of the land, where I had nigh gone to sleep—at least my intellect slumbered—so dullified was I and those around me, by the soporific quality of the conversation, if conversation it might be called. For a long time I thought it was my constitutional melancholy[106] that made me think London society so insufferably tiresome; but I discovered that those who had no such malady found it equally so; the only difference was that they yawned under the nightly inflictions, yet still continued to bear them, while I writhed, and 'muttered curses not loud but deep' against the well-dressed automatons, that threw a spell over my faculties, making me doubt if I could any longer feel or think; and I have sought the solitude of my chamber, almost doubting my own identity, or, at least, my sanity; such was the overpowering effect produced on me by exclusive society in London. Madame de Staël was the only person of talent I ever knew who was not overcome by it; but this was owing to the constant state of excitement she was kept in by her extraordinary self-complacency, and the mystifications of the dandies, who made her believe all sorts of things. I have seen her entranced by them, listening with undisguised delight to exaggerated compliments, uttered only to hoax her, by persons incapable of appreciating her genius, and who doubted its existence from the facility with which she received mystifications which would have been detected in a moment by the most common-place woman in the room.[107] It is thus genius and talent are judged of," continued Byron, "by those who, having neither, are incapable of understanding

[105] Byron dined with his old friend Thomas Cribb the pugilist, champion of all England, on November 24, 1813 (*LJ*, II, 345-46; Moore, *Life*, pp. 206-07).

[106] For Byron on his "constitutional depression of Spirits," the "depression of Spirits . . . which I have some reason to believe constitutional," see *LJ*, V, 370, 459-60; the first phrase in Moore, *Life*, p. 531.

[107] See Byron's "Detached Thoughts," No. 29 (*LJ*, V, 423): "I liked the Dandies; they were always very civil to *me*, though in general they disliked literary people, and persecuted and mystified Mᵉ. de Staël . . . damnably" (in Moore, *Life*, p. 303). The two literary ladies never met. See also p. 27, above.

them; and a punster may glory in puzzling a genius of the first order, by a play on words that was below his comprehension, though
suited to that of the most ordinary understandings. Madame de
Staël had no tact; she would believe anything, merely because she
did not take the trouble to examine, being too much occupied
with self, and often said the most *mal à propos* things, because she
was thinking not of the person she addressed, but of herself.[108] She
had a party to dine with her one day in London, when Sir James
and Lady —— entered the drawing-room, the lady dressed in a
green gown, with a shawl of the same verdant hue, and a bright red
turban. Madame de Staël marched up to her in her eager manner,
and exclaimed, 'Ah, mon Dieu, miladi! comme vous ressemblez à
un perroquet!' The poor lady looked confounded: the company
tried, but in vain, to suppress the smiles the observation excited;
but all felt that the making it betrayed a total want of tact in
the 'Corinne.'

"Does the cant of sentiment still continue in England?" asked
Byron. "'Childe Harold' called it forth; but my 'Juan' was well calculated to cast it into shade, and had that merit, if it had no other;
but I must not refer to the Don, as that, I remember, is a prohibited
subject between us. Nothing sickens me so completely," said Byron,
"as women who affect sentiment in conversation.[109] A woman
without sentiment is not a woman; but I have observed, that those
who most display it in words have least of the reality. Sentiment,
like love and grief, should be reserved for privacy; and when I hear
women *affichant* their sentimentality, I look upon it as an allegori-

108 However, Madame de Staël understood the theory of conversation very
well, as she revealed in her *L'Allemagne*: "To succeed in conversation, we
must possess the tact of perceiving clearly, and at every instant, the impression
made on those with whom we converse. . . . We must be able to note and
arrest half-formed censures as they pass over the countenance of the listeners,
by hastening to dissipate them before self-love be engaged against us. There
is no area in which vanity displays itself under such a variety of forms as in
conversation" (quoted by Madden, I, 134).

109 Cf. Byron on the reason why Teresa Guiccioli persuaded him to discontinue *Don Juan* (*LJ*, V, 321; Moore, *Life*, p. 516): "it arises from the wish
of all women to exalt the *sentiment* of the passions, and to keep up the illusion
which is their empire. Now *Don Juan* strips off this illusion, and laughs at that
and most other things. I never knew a woman who did *not* protect *Rousseau*,
nor one who did not dislike de Grammont, Gil Blas, and all the *comedy* of the
passions, when brought out naturally." Lady Blessington's style never permitted her to "affect sentiment in conversation."

cal mode of declaring their wish of finding an object on whom they could bestow its superfluity. I am of a jealous nature," said Byron, "and should wish to call slumbering sentiment into life in the woman I love, instead of finding that I was chosen, from its excess and activity rendering a partner ·in the firm indispensable. I should hate a woman," continued Byron, "who could laugh at or ridicule sentiment, as I should, and do, women who have not religious feelings: and, much as I dislike bigotry, I think it a thousand times more pardonable in a woman than irreligion. There is something unfeminine in the want of religion, that takes off the peculiar charm of woman. It inculcates mildness, forbearance, and charity,—those graces that adorn them more than all others," continued Byron, "and whose beneficent effects are felt, not only on their minds and manners, but are visible in their countenances, to which they give their own sweet character. But when I say that I admire religion in women," said Byron, "don't fancy that I like sectarian ladies, distributors of tracts, armed and ready for controversies, many of whom only preach religion, but do not practise it. No; I like to know that it is the guide of woman's actions, the softener of her words, the soother of her cares, and those of all dear to her, who are comforted by her, —that it is, in short, the animating principle to which all else is referred. When I see women professing religion and violating its duties—mothers turning from erring daughters, instead of staying to reclaim,—sisters deserting sisters,[110] whom, in their hearts, they know to be more pure than themselves,—and wives abandoning husbands on the ground of faults that they should have wept over, and redeemed by the force of love,—then it is," continued Byron, "that I exclaim against the cant of false religion, and laugh at the credulity of those who can reconcile such conduct with the dictates of a creed that ordains forgiveness, and commands that 'if a man be overtaken in a fault, ye which are spiritual restore such a one in the spirit of meekness; considering thyself, lest thou also be tempted;' and that tells a wife, that 'if she hath an husband that believeth not, and if he be pleased to dwell with her, let her not leave him. For the unbelieving husband is sanctified by the wife,' &c.[111] Now,

[110] On Lady Blessington's relations with her sister, see my introduction.
[111] Teresa Guiccioli: how true how good. (This marginal comment presumably refers to all of Byron's remarks on good women. The quotations are

214

people professing religion either believe, or do not believe, such creeds," continued Byron. "If they believe, and act contrary to their belief, what avails their religion, except to throw discredit on its followers, by showing that they practice not its tenets? and if they inwardly disbelieve, as their conduct would lead one to think, are they not guilty of hypocrisy? It is such incongruities between the professions and conduct of those who affect to be religious that puts me out of patience," continued Byron, "and makes me wage war with cant,[112] and not, as many suppose, a disbelief or want of faith in religion. I want to see it *practised*, and to know, which is soon made known by the conduct, that it dwells in the heart, instead of being on the lips only of its votaries. Let me not be told that the mothers, sisters, and wives, who violate the duties such relationships impose, are good and religious people: let it be admitted that a mother, sister, or wife, who deserts instead of trying to lead back the stray sheep to the flock, cannot be truly religious, and I shall exclaim no more against hypocrisy and cant, because they will no longer be dangerous. Poor Mrs. Sheppard tried more, and did more, to reclaim me," continued Byron, "than ——:[113] but no; as I have been preaching religion, I shall practice one of its tenets, and be charitable; so I shall not finish the sentence."

It appears to me that Byron has reflected much on religion and that many, if not all, the doubts and sarcasms he has expressed on it are to be attributed only to his enmity against its false worshippers. He is indignant at seeing people professing it governed wholly by worldly principles in their conduct; and fancies that he is serving the true cause by exposing the votaries that he thinks dishonour it. He forgets that in so exposing and decrying them, he is breaking through the commandments of charity he admires, and says ought to govern our actions towards our erring brethren; but that he reflects deeply on the subject of religion and its duties, is, I hope, a

from Galatians, 6:1, and I Corinthians, 7:13, the latter slightly misquoted, but both from the King James version.)

[112] Cf. Byron in his *Letter . . . on the Rev. W. L. Bowles's Strictures* (*LJ*, V, 542; Moore, *Life*, p. 690): "The truth is, that in these days the grand 'primum mobile' of England is *cant*; cant political, cant poetical, cant religious, cant moral; but always *cant*, multiplied through all the varieties of life. It is the fashion. . . ."

[113] Perhaps Lady Byron.

step gained in the right path, in which I trust he will continue to advance: and which step I attribute, as does he, to the effect the prayer of Mrs. Sheppard had on his mind, and which, it is evident, has made a lasting impression, by the frequency and seriousness with which he refers to it.

"There are two blessings of which people never know the value until they have lost them," said Byron, "health and reputation. And not only is their loss destructive to our own happiness, but injurious to the peace and comfort of our friends. Health seldom goes without temper accompanying it; and, that fled, we become a burden on the patience of those around us, until dislike replaces pity and forbearance. Loss of reputation entails still greater evils. In losing caste, deservedly or otherwise," continued Byron, "we become reckless and misanthropic: we cannot sympathize with those, from whom we are separated by the barrier of public opinion, and pride becomes 'the scorpion, girt by fire,' that turns on our own breasts the sting prepared for our enemies.[114] Shakspeare says, that 'it is a bitter thing to look into happiness through another man's eyes;'[115] and this must he do," said Byron, "who has lost his reputation. Nay, rendered nervously sensitive by the falseness of his position,[116] he sees, or fancies he sees, scorn or avoidance in the eyes of all he encounters; and, as it is well known that we are never so jealous of the respect of others as when we have forfeited our own, every mark of coldness or disrespect he meets with, arouse a host of angry feelings, that prey upon his peace. Such a man is to be feared," continued Byron; "and yet how many such have the world made! how many errors have not slander and calumny magnified into crimes of the darkest dye! and, malevolence and injustice having set the condemned seal on the reputation of him who has been judged without a trial, he is driven without the pale of society, a sense of injustice rankling in his heart; and if his hand be not against each man, the hand, or at least the tongue, of each man is against him. The genius and powers of such a man," continued Byron, "act but as fresh incitements to the unsated malice of his calumniators;

[114] *The Giaour*, ll. 422-32, paraphrased.
[115] Slightly misquoted from *As You Like It*, V, ii, 47-49.
[116] Cf. Lady Blessington on "A False Position," "Spartan Moralists," and "The Victims of Society" (Madden, I, 244, 246). See also my introduction on this entire subject.

and the fame they win is but as the flame that consumes the funeral pile, whose blaze attracts attention to the substance that feeds it. Mediocrity is to be desired for those who lose caste, because, if it gains not pardon for errors, it sinks them into oblivion. But genius," continued Byron, "reminds the enemies of its possessor, of his existence, and of their injustice. They are enraged that he on whom they heaped obloquy can surmount it, and elevate himself on new ground, where their malice cannot obstruct his path."

It was impossible not to see that his own position had led Byron to these reflections; and on observing the changes in his expressive countenance while uttering them, who could resist pitying the morbid feelings which had given them birth? The milk and honey that flowed in his breast has been turned to gall by the bitterness with which his errors have been assailed; but even now, so much of human kindness remains in his nature, that I am persuaded the effusions of wounded pride which embody themselves in the biting satires that escape from him, are more productive of pain to him who writes, than to those on whom they are written. Knowing Byron as I do, I could forgive the most cutting satire his pen ever traced, because I know the bitter feelings and violent reaction which led to it; and that, in thus avenging some real or imagined injury on individuals, he looks on them as a part of that great whole, of which that world which he has waged war with, and that he fancies has waged war with him, is composed. He looks on himself like a soldier in action, who, without any individual resentment, strikes at all within his reach, as component parts of the force to which he is opposed. If this be indefensible, and all must admit that it is so, let us be merciful even while we are condemning; and let us remember what must have been the heart-aches and corroding thoughts of a mind so sensitive as Byron's, ere the last weapons of despair were resorted to, and the fearful sally, the forlorn hope attack, on the world's opinions, made while many of those opinions had partisans within his own breast, even while he stood in the last breach of defeated hope, to oppose them. The poison in which he has dipped the arrows aimed at the world has long been preying on his own life, and has been produced by the deleterious draughts administered by that world, and which he has quaffed to the dregs, until it has turned the once healthful current of his existence into deadly venom, poison-

217

ing all the fine and generous qualities that adorned his nature.[117] He feels what he might have been, and what he is, and detests the world that has marred his destiny. But, as the passions lose their empire, he will think differently: the veil which now obscures his reason will pass away, like clouds dispelled by the sun; he will learn to distinguish much of good, where he has hitherto seen only evil; and no longer braving the world, and, to enrage it, assuming faults he has not, he will let the good qualities he has make themselves known, and gain that good-will and regard they were formed to conciliate.

"I often, in imagination, pass over a long lapse of years," said Byron, "and console myself for present privations, in anticipating the time when my daughter will know me by reading my works; for, though the hand of prejudice may conceal my portrait from her eyes,[118] it cannot hereafter conceal my thoughts and feelings, which will talk to her when *he* to whom they belonged has ceased to exist. The triumph will then be mine; and the tears that my child will drop over expressions wrung from me by mental agony,— the certainty that she will enter into the sentiments which dictated the various allusions to her and myself in my works,—consoles me in many a gloomy hour. Ada's mother has feasted on the smiles of her infancy and growth, but the tears of her maturity shall be mine."

I thought it a good opportunity to represent to Byron, that this thought alone should operate to prevent his ever writing a page which could bring the blush of offended modesty to the cheek of his daughter; and that, if he hoped to live in her heart, unsullied by aught that could abate her admiration, he ought never more to write a line of "Don Juan." He remained silent for some minutes, and then said, "You are right; I never recollected this. I am jealously tenacious of the undivided sympathy of my daughter; and that work, ('Don Juan,') written to beguile hours of *tristesse* and wretch-

[117] Cf. *Childe Harold*, III, vii and ix: "My springs of life were poisoned. . . . His [cup of life] had been quaffed too quickly, and he found/ The dregs were wormwood. . . ."

[118] Byron said to Medwin (*Conversations*, p. 101): "I hear that my name is not mentioned in her [Ada's] presence; that a green curtain is always kept over my portrait, as over something forbidden. . . ." Lady Noel's will specified that Ada was not to be shown Byron's portrait until she reached the age of twenty-one.

edness, is well calculated to loosen my hold on her affection. I will write no more of it;[119]—would that I had never written a line!"

There is something tender and beautiful in the deep love with which poor Byron turns to his daughter. This is his last resting-place, and on her heart has he cast his last anchor of hope. When one reflects that he looks not to consolation from her during his life, as he believes her mother implacable, and only hopes that, when the grave has closed over him, his child will cherish his memory, and weep over his misfortunes, it is impossible not to sympathize with his feelings. Poor Byron! why is he not always true to himself? Who can, like him, excite sympathy, even when one knows him to be erring? But he shames one out of one's natural and better feelings by his mockery of self. Alas!—

> His is a lofty spirit, turn'd aside
> From its bright path by woes, and wrongs, and pride;
> And onward in its new, tumultuous course,
> Borne with too rapid and intense a force
> To pause one moment in the dread career,
> And ask—if such could be its native sphere?

How unsatisfactory is it to find one's feelings with regard to Byron varying every day! This is because he is never two days the same. The day after he has awakened the deepest interest, his manner of scoffing at himself and others destroys it, and one feels as if one had been duped into a sympathy, only to be laughed at.

"I have been accused (said Byron) of thinking ill of women. This has proceeded from my sarcastic observations on them in conversation, much more than from what I have written. The fact is, I always say whatever comes into my head, and very often say things to provoke people to whom I am talking. If I meet a romantic person, with what I call a too exalted opinion of women, I have a peculiar satisfaction in speaking lightly of them; not out of pique to

---

[119] If Byron said anything like this to Lady Blessington, there were surely other reasons in addition to those stated. On May 8, 1823, two days after finishing the first draft of Canto XVI, he started Canto XVII, writing only 14 stanzas, but taking them to Greece with him, where on March 4, 1824, he reported that the press of business in Greece had kept him from continuing *Don Juan*; a similar explanation, lack of time, had been made on July 14, 1823, the day after he embarked on the *Hercules*.

your sex, but to mortify their champion; as I always conclude, that when a man over-praises women, he does it to convey the impression of how much they must have favoured him, to have won such gratitude towards them;[120] whereas there is such an abnegation of vanity in a poor devil's decrying women,—it is such a proof positive that they never distinguished him, that I can overlook it. People take for gospel all I say, and go away continually with false impressions. *Mais n'importe!* it will render the statements of my future biographers more amusing; as I flatter myself I shall have more than one. Indeed, the more the merrier, say I. One will represent me as a sort of sublime misanthrope, with moments of kind feeling. This, *par exemple*, is my favourite *rôle*. Another will portray me as a modern Don Juan; and a third (as it would be hard if a votary of the Muses had less than the number of the Graces for his biographers) will, it is to be hoped, if only for opposition sake, represent me as an *amiable*, ill-used gentleman,[121] 'more sinned against than sinning.' Now, if I know myself, I should say, that I have no character at all. By the bye, this is what has long been said, as I lost mine, as an Irishman would say, before I had it; that is to say, my reputation was gone, according to the good-natured English, before I had arrived at years of discretion, which is the period one is supposed to have found one. But, joking apart, what I think of myself is, that I am so changeable, being every thing by turns and nothing long,—I am such a strange *mélange* of good and evil, that it would be difficult to describe me. There are but two sentiments to which I am constant,—a strong love of liberty, and a detestation of cant, and neither is calculated to gain me friends. I am of a wayward, uncertain disposition, more disposed to display the

120 Essentially these same sentiments were reported by Teresa Guiccioli, describing an occasion when Medwin engaged in a sentimental "tirade" exalting the female sex, whereupon Byron attacked in the manner described by Lady Blessington (*HVSV*, p. 278).

121 Cf. Byron to Moore, March 10, 1817 (*LJ*, IV, 72-74; Moore, *Life*, pp. 343-44): "I wish you would also add, what you know, that I was not, and, indeed, am not even *now*, the misanthropical and gloomy gentleman he [Jeffrey] takes me for, but a facetious companion, well to do with those with whom I am intimate, and as loquacious and laughing as if I were a much cleverer fellow.

"I suppose now I shall never be able to shake off my sables in public imagination, more particularly since my moral ° ° [Clytemnestra?] clove down my fame." For other views of Byron's character, see *LJ*, IV, 73, n. 1.

defects than the redeeming points in my nature; this, at least, proves that I understand mankind, for they are always ready to believe the evil, but not the good; and there is no crime of which I could accuse myself, for which they would not give me implicit credit. What do you think of me?" (asked he, looking seriously in my face.)

I replied, "I look on you as a spoilt child of genius, an epicycle in your own circle." At which he laughed, though half disposed to be angry.

"I have made as many sacrifices to liberty (continued Byron) as most people of my age; and the one I am about to undertake is not the least, though, probably, it will be the last; for, with my broken health, and the chances of war, Greece will most likely terminate my mor[t]al career. I like Italy, its climate, its customs, and, above all, its freedom from cant of every kind, which is the *primum mobile* of England:[122] therefore it is no slight sacrifice of comfort to give up the tranquil life I lead here, and break through the ties I have formed, to engage in a cause, for the successful result of which I have no very sanguine hopes. You will think me more superstitious than ever (said Byron) when I tell you, that I have a presentiment that I shall die in Greece.[123] I hope it may be in action, for that would be a good finish to a very *triste* existence, and I have a horror to death-bed scenes; but as I have not been famous for my luck in life, most probably I shall not have more in the manner of my death, and that I may draw my last sigh, not on the field of glory, but on the bed of disease. I very nearly died when I was in Greece in my youth;[124] perhaps as things have turned out, it would have been well if I had; I should have lost nothing, and the world very little, and I would have escaped many cares, for God knows I have had

[122] See above, p. 215, n. 112.

[123] It seems rather certain that Byron had premonitions that he might die in Greece: just before sailing he instructed Teresa to write his life in Italy (*HVSV*, p. 379); on July 16, 1823, he talked with Pietro Gamba about the uncertainty of the future, asking him, "Where shall we be in a year?" (*HVSV*, p. 381); about three months before his death he discussed with Stanhope the question of his biography, suggesting Hobhouse and Gamba as possible biographers; and he discussed with Fletcher the problem of his burial should he die in Greece (*HVSV*, p. 495). According to Medwin (p. 91), he said: "I mean to return to Greece, and shall in all probability die there."

[124] Byron was very ill of a fever in Patras in 1810, being saved only by Nature, Jove, and Nicolo his faithful dragoman, as Byron explained (see Marchand, I, 260; Medwin, p. 91; and Byron's n. 11 to *Childe Harold*, II [*Poetry*, II, 175]).

enough of one kind or another: but I am getting gloomy, and looking either back or forward is not calculated to enliven me. One of the reasons why I quiz my friends in conversation is, that it keeps me from thinking of myself: you laugh, but it is true."

Byron had so unquenchable a thirst for celebrity, that no means were left untried that might attain it: this frequently led to his expressing opinions totally at variance with his actions and real sentiments, and *vice versâ*, and made him appear quite inconsistent and puerile. There was no sort of celebrity that he did not, at some period or other, condescend to seek, and he was not over nice in the means, provided he obtained the end. This weakness it was that led him to accord his society to many persons whom he thought unworthy the distinction, fancying that he might find a greater facility in astonishing them, which he had a childish propensity to do, than with those who were more on an equality with him.[125] When I say persons that he thought unworthy of his society, I refer only to their stations in life, and not to their merits, as the first was the criterion by which Byron was most prone to judge them, never being able to conquer the overweening prejudices in favour of aristocracy that subjugated him.[126] He expected a deferential submission to his opinions from those whom he thought he honoured by admitting to his society; and if they did not seem duly impressed with a sense of his condescension, as well as astonished at the versatility of his powers and accomplishments, he showed his dissatisfaction by assuming an air of superiority, and by opposing their opinions in a dictatorial tone, as if from his fiat there was no appeal. If, on the contrary, they appeared willing to admit his superiority in all respects, he was kind, playful, and good-humoured, and only showed his own sense of it by familiar jokes, and attempts at hoaxing, to which he was greatly addicted.

An extraordinary peculiarity in Byron was his constant habit of disclaiming friendships, a habit that must have been rather humili-

[125] It is indeed true that Byron enjoyed the more colorful forms of human life, often choosing the company of boxers, actors, and adventurers, but not for the reason stated by Lady Blessington.

[126] Byron had only two close friends who were members of the aristocracy or hereditary nobility: Lord Clare and Lord Holland, if either of these may be counted as close friendships. Lady Blessington, of course, cultivated the aristocracy at every opportunity.

ating to those who prided themselves on being considered his friends.[127] He invariably, in conversing about the persons supposed to stand in that relation to him, drew a line of demarcation; and Lord Clare, with Mr. Hobhouse and Moore, were the only persons he allowed to be within its pale. Long acquaintance, habitual correspondence, and reciprocity of kind actions, which are the general bonds of friendship, were not admitted by Byron to be sufficient claims to the title of friend;[128] and he seized with avidity every opportunity of denying this relation with persons for whom, I am persuaded, he felt the sentiment, and to whom he would not have hesitated to have given all proof but the *name*, yet who, wanting this, could not consistently with delicacy receive aught else.

This habit of disclaiming friendships was very injudicious in Byron, as it must have wounded the *amour propre* of those who liked him, and humiliated the pride and delicacy of all whom he had ever laid under obligations, as well as freed from a sense of what was due to friendship, those who, restrained by the acknowledgement of that tie, might have proved themselves his zealous defenders and advocates. It was his aristocratic pride that prompted this ungracious conduct, and I remember telling him, *apropos* to his denying friendships, that all the persons with whom he disclaimed them, must have less vanity, and more kindness of nature, than fall to the lot of most people, if they did not renounce the sentiment, which he disdained to acknowledge, and give him proofs that it no longer operated on them. His own morbid sensitiveness did not incline him to be more merciful to that of others; it seemed, on the contrary, to render him less so, as if every feeling was concentrated in self alone, and yet this egoist was capable of acts of generosity, kindness, and pity for the unfortunate: but he appeared to think, that the physical ills of others were those alone which he was called on to sympathize with; their moral ailments he entered not into, as he considered his own to be too ele-

[127] See my introduction.
[128] Upon occasion Byron was capable of taking the position described. See his letter of 1823 to an anonymous correspondent, probably Mary Shelley, where he distinguishes between true friendships, limited to Lord Clare and Moore and unaccountably omitting Hobhouse, and "men-of-the-world friendships," of which he says he has had many (*LJ*, VI, 175; Moore, *Life*, pp. 574-75). This is to be understood, probably, as an expression of high idealism in friendship.

223

vated to admit of any reciprocity with those of others.[129] The immeasurable difference between his genius and that of all others he encountered had given him a false estimate of their feelings and characters; they could not, like him, embody their feelings in language that found an echo in every breast, and hence he concluded they have neither the depth nor refinement of his. He forgot that this very power of sending forth his thoughts disburthened him of much of their bitterness, while others, wanting it, felt but the more poignantly what is unshared and unexpressed. I have told Byron that he added ingratitude to his other faults, by scoffing at, and despising his countrymen, who have shared all his griefs, and enjoyed all his biting pleasantries; he has sounded the diapason of his own feelings, and found the concord in theirs, which proves a sympathy he cannot deny, and ought not to mock: he says, that he values not their applauses or sympathy; that he who describes passions and crimes, touches chords, which vibrate in every breast, not that either pity or interest is felt for him who submits to this moral anatomy; but that each discovers the symptoms of his own malady and feels and thinks only of self, while analyzing the griefs or pleasures of an other.

When Byron had been one day repeating to me some epigrams and lampoons, in which many of his friends were treated with great severity, I observed that, in case he died, and that these *proofs of friendship* came before the public, what would be the feelings of those so severely dealt by, and who previously had indulged the agreeable illusion of being high in his good graces!

"That (said Byron) is precisely one of the ideas which most amuses me. I often fancy the rage and humiliation of my quondam friends at hearing the truth (at least from me) for the first time, and when I am beyond the reach of their malice. Each individual will enjoy the sarcasms against his friends, but that will not console him for those against himself. Knowing the affectionate dispositions of my *soi-disant* friends, and the mortal chagrin my death would occasion them, I have written my thoughts of each, purely as a consolation for them in case they survive me. Surely this is philanthropic, for a more effectual means of destroying all regret for the dead could

[129] Cf. Lara, Manfred, and other Byronic heroes who sternly and proudly decline the aid or sympathy of others.

224

hardly be found than discovering, after their decease, memorials in which the surviving friends were treated with more sincerity than flattery. What grief (continued Byron, laughing while he spoke) could resist the charges of ugliness, dulness, or any of the thousand nameless defects, personal or mental, to which flesh is heir, coming from one *ostentatiously loved, lamented, and departed,* and when reprisals or recantations are impossible! Tears would soon be dried, lamentations and eulogiums changed to reproaches, and many faults would be discovered in the dear departed that had previously escaped detection. If half the observations (said Byron) which friends make on each other were *written* down instead of being said, how few would remain on terms of friendship! People are in such daily habits of commenting on the defects of friends, that they are unconscious of the unkindness of it; which only comes home to their business and bosoms when they discover that *they* have been so treated, which proves that *self* is the only medium for feeling or judging of, or for, others. Now I *write down,* as well as speak, my sentiments of those who believe that they have gulled me; and I only wish (in case I die before them) that I could return to witness the effect my posthumous opinions of them are likely to produce on their minds. What good fun this would be! Is it not disinterested in me to lay up this source of consolation for my friends, whose grief for my loss might otherwise be too acute? You don't seem to value it as you ought (continued Byron, with one of his sardonic smiles, seeing that I looked, as I really felt, surprised at his avowed insincerity).[130] I feel the same pleasure in anticipating the rage and mortification of my *soi-disant* friends, at the discovery of my real sentiments of them, that a miser may be supposed to feel while making a will that is to disappoint all the expectants who have been toadying him for years. Then only think how amusing it will be, to compare my posthumous with my previously given opinions, one throwing ridicule on the other. This will be delicious, (said he, rubbing his hands,) and the very anticipation of it charms me. Now this, by your grave face, you are disposed to call very wicked,

[130] Teresa Guiccioli: *tout cela mystification!* (This comment, written at the bottom of the page, presumably refers to the entire account of posthumous publication and Byron's ghostly glee. Byron also "suspected her sincerity," as Teresa explained [*HVSV,* p. 354].)

nay, more, very mean; but wicked or mean, or both united, it is human nature, or at least my nature."

Should various poems of Byron that I have seen ever meet the public eye, and this is by no means unlikely, they will furnish a better criterion for judging his real sentiments than all the notices of him that have yet appeared.

Each day that brought Byron nearer to the period fixed on for his departure for Greece seemed to render him still more reluctant to undertake it. He frequently expressed a wish to return to England, if only for a few weeks, before he embarked, and yet had not firmness of purpose sufficient to carry his wishes into effect. There was a helplessness about Byron, a sort of abandonment of himself to his destiny,[131] as he called it, that common-place people can as little pity as understand. His purposes in visiting England, previous to Greece, were vague and undefined, even to himself; but from various observations that he let fall, I imagined that he hoped to establish something like an amicable understanding, or correspondence, with Lady Byron, and to see his child, which last desire had become a fixed one in his mind. He so often turned with a yearning heart to his wish of going to England before Greece, that we asked him why, being a free agent, he did not go. The question seemed to embarrass him. He stammered, blushed, and said,—

"Why, true, there is no reason why I should not go; but yet I want resolution to encounter all the disagreeable circumstances which might, and most probably would, greet my arrival in England. The host of foes that now slumber, because they believe me out of their reach, and that their stings cannot touch me, would soon awake with renewed energies to assail and blacken me. The press, that powerful engine of a licentious age, (an engine known only in civilized England as an invader of the privacy of domestic life,) would pour forth all its venom against me, ridiculing my person, misinterpreting my motives, and misrepresenting my actions. I can mock at all these attacks when the sea divides me from them, but on the spot, and reading the effect of each libel in the alarmed

---

[131] See Moore, *Life*, p. 592, where he discusses Byron's superstitious sense of "approaching doom" at the time of his sailing and summarizes his last conversation with Barry: "That he had not fixed to go to England, in preference [to going at once to Greece], seemed one of his deep regrets. . . ."

faces of my selfishly-sensitive friends, whose common attentions, under such circumstances, seem to demand gratitude for the personal risk of abuse incurred by a contact with the attacked delinquent,— No, this I could not stand, because I once endured it, and never have forgotten what I felt under the infliction. I wish to see Lady Byron and my child, because I firmly believe I shall never return from Greece, and that I anxiously desire to forgive, and be forgiven, by the former, and to embrace Ada. It is more than probable (continued Byron) that the same amiable consistency,—to call it by no harsher name,—which has hitherto influenced Lady B.'s adherence to the line she had adopted, of refusing all explanation, or attempt at reconciliation, would still operate on her conduct. My letters would be returned unopened, my daughter would be prevented from seeing me, and any step, I might, from affection, be forced to take to assert my right of seeing her once more before I left England, would be misrepresented as an act of the most barbarous tyranny and persecution towards the mother and the child; and I should be driven again from the British shore, more vilified, and with even greater ignominy, than on the separation. Such is my idea of the justice of public opinion in England, (continued Byron,) and, with such woeful experience as I have had, can you wonder that I dare not encounter the annoyances I have detailed? But if I live, and return from Greece with something better and higher than the reputation or glory of a poet, opinions may change, as the successful are always judged favourably of in our country; my laurels may cover my faults better than the bays have done, and give a totally different reading to my thoughts, words, and deeds."

With such various forms of pleasing as rarely fall to the lot of man, Byron possessed the counterbalance to an extraordinary degree, as he could disenchant his admirers almost as quickly as he had won their admiration. He was too observant not to discover, at a glance, the falling off in the admiration of those around him, and resented as an injury the decrease in their esteem, which a little consideration for their feelings, and some restraint in the expression of his own, would have prevented. Sensitive, jealous, and exigent himself, he had no sympathy or forbearance for those weaknesses in others. He claimed admiration not only for his genius, but for his defects, as a sort of right that appertained solely to him. He was conscious of this *faiblesse*, but wanted either power or inclination to correct it, and was deeply offended if others appeared to have made the discovery.

There was a sort of mental reservation in Byron's intercourse with those with whom he was on habits of intimacy that he had not tact enough to conceal, and which was more offensive when the natural flippancy of his manner was taken into consideration. His incontinence of speech on subjects of a personal nature, and with regard to the defects of friends, rendered this display of reserve on other points still more offensive;[132] as, after having disclosed secrets which left him, and some of those whom he professed to like, at the mercy of the discretion of the person confided in, he would absolve him from the best motive for secrecy—that of implied confidence—by disclaiming any sentiment of friendship for those so trusted. It was as though he said, I think aloud, and you hear my thoughts; but I have no feeling of friendship towards you, though you might imagine I have from the confidence I repose. Do not deceive yourself; few, if any, are worthy of my friendship: and only one or two possess even a portion of it. I think not of you but as the first recipient for the disclosures that I have *le besoin* to make, and as an admirer whom I can make administer to my vanity, by exciting in turn surprise, wonder, and admiration; but I can have no sympathy with you.

Byron, in all his intercourse with acquaintances, proved that he wanted the simplicity and good faith of uncivilized life, without having acquired the tact and fine perception that throws a veil over the artificial coldness and selfishness of refined civilization, which must be concealed to be rendered endurable. To keep alive sympathy, there must be a reciprocity of feelings; and this Byron did not, or would not, understand. It was the want of this, or rather the studied display of the want, that deprived him of the affection that would otherwise have been unreservedly accorded to him, and which he had so many qualities calculated to call forth. Those who have known Byron only in the turmoil and feverish excitation of a London life, may not have had time or opportunity to be

---

[132] Teresa Guiccioli: *C'était precisement son idée en parlant a Lady Blessington? Il ne voulait pas qu'elle se fît allusions sur ses sentiments.* (This comment may refer to the entire paragraph.)

struck with this defalcation in his nature; or, if they observed it, might naturally attribute it to the artificial state of society in London, which more or less affects all its members; but when he was seen in the isolation of a foreign land, with few acquaintances, and fewer friends, to make demands either on his time or sympathy, this extreme egoism[133] became strikingly visible, and repelled the affection that must otherwise have replaced the admiration to which he never failed to give birth.

Byron had thought long and profoundly on man and his vices,—natural and acquired;—he generalized and condemned *en masse*, in theory; while, in practice, he was ready to allow the exceptions to his general rule. He had commenced his travels ere yet age or experience had rendered him capable of forming a just estimate of the civilized world he had left, or the uncivilized one he was exploring: hence he saw both through a false medium, and observed not that their advantages and disadvantages were counterbalanced. Byron wished for that Utopian state of perfection which experience teaches us it is impossible to attain,—the simplicity and good faith of savage life, with the refinement and intelligence of civilization. Naturally of a melancholy temperament, his travels in Greece were eminently calculated to give a still more sombre tint to his mind, and tracing at each step the marks of degradation which had followed a state of civilization still more luxurious than that he had left; and surrounded with the fragments of arts that we can but imperfectly copy, and ruins whose original beauty we can never hope to emulate, he grew into a contempt of the actual state of things, and lived but in dreams of the past, or aspirations of the future. This state of mind, as unnatural as it is uncommon in a young man, destroyed the bonds of sympathy between him and those of his own age, without creating any with those of a more advanced. With the young he could not sympathize, because they felt not like him; and with the old, because that, though their reasonings and reflections arrived at the same conclusions, they had not journeyed by the same road. They had travelled by the beaten one of experience, but he had abridged the road, having been hurried over it by the passions which were still unexhausted, and ready to go in search

[133] Teresa Guiccioli: *Egoisme pour Elle.*

229

of new discoveries. The wisdom thus prematurely acquired by Byron being the forced fruit of circumstances and travail acting on an excitable mind, instead of being the natural production ripened by time, was, like all precocious advantages, of comparatively little utility; it influenced his words more than his deeds, and wanted that patience and forbearance towards the trangressions of others that is best acquired by having suffered from and repented our own.

It would be a curious speculation to reflect how far the mind of Byron might have been differently operated on, had he, instead of going to Greece in his early youth, spent the same period beneath the genial climate, and surrounded by the luxuries of Italy. We should then, most probably, have had a "Don Juan" of a less reprehensible character, and more excusable from the youth of its author, followed, in natural succession, by atoning works produced by the autumnal sun of maturity, and the mellowing touches of experience, instead of his turning from the more elevated tone of "Childe Harold" to "Don Juan." Each year, had life been spared him, would have corrected the false wisdom that had been the bane of Byron, and which, like the fruit so eloquently described by himself as growing on the banks of the Dead Sea, that was lovely to the eye, but turned to ashes when tasted, was productive only of disappointment to him, because he mistook it for the real fruit its appearance resembled, and found only bitterness in its taste.

There was that in Byron which would have yet nobly redeemed the errors of his youth, and the misuse of his genius, had length of years been granted him; and, while lamenting his premature death, our regret is rendered the more poignant by the reflection, that we are deprived of works which, tempered by an understanding arrived at its meridian, would have had all the genius, without the immorality[134] of his more youthful productions, which, notwithstanding their defects, have formed an epoch in the literature of his country.

[134] Teresa Guiccioli: *Immorality!! Heureusement ses flatteries à l'hypocrisie et au cant n'ont pas profité à l'auteur; n'ont pas produit les consequences qu'elle esperer [sic] de ces insinuations et exaggerations.*

TEXTUAL NOTES

The list following provides a collation of the present text, based on Henry Colburn's London edition of 1834, and the text of *The New Monthly Magazine and Literary Journal*, July 1832-December 1833. In the variant readings listed below, the revised version regularly appears first, preceded by page and paragraph numbers of the present edition, separated by a period. *The New Monthly* version is followed by volume, page, and paragraph number, the first two of these separated by a comma, the last separated by a period. A paragraph is numbered zero when it is the first paragraph that ends on a page but begins on the page before.

3   *added.*
7. 1, palazzo *for* chateau, 35, 6. 1.
11. 0, said Byron *added.*
12. 0, resemblance *for* semblance, 35, 9. 0.
13. 1, selfishness *for* egotism, 35, 9. 1.
14. 2, a few *for* three, 35, 10. 1.
17. 3, Lady Blessington, Miss Power, and Comte D'Orsay *for* Lady B----, Miss P----, and C---- D----, 35, 12. 4.
18. 0, two *for* ten, 35, 13. 0.
28. 1, the dislike *for* it, 35, 19. 1.
35. 0, displaying his wit and astonishing his hearers *for* display and astonishing, 35, 23. 2.
42. 0, and as I do not wish my poor fame to be either *preserved* or *pickled*, I have lived on and written my Memoirs *for* and as I lived on, and do not wish my poor fame to be either *preserved* or *pickled*, I have written my Memoirs, 35, 133. 0.
44. 2, selfishness *for* egotism, 35, 134. 1.
52. 2, with Byron *added.*
52. 2, his *for* Byron's, 35, 140. 1.
59. 0, thus while we nurse *for* and while we nurse, 35, 145. 0.
59. 2, which ought only *for* that ought only, 35, 145. 2.
62. 0, selfishness *for* egoism, 35, 228. 2.
63. 0, and his *for* and that his, 35, 229. 1.
71. 1, fabulous qualities attributed to that animal *for* qualities attributed to that fabulous animal, 35, 235. 1.
73. 2, new. Can *for* new, and yet can, 35, 236. 4.
81. 0, be always traced *for* always be traced, 35, 305. 1.
81. 0, yet it *for* for it, 35, 305. 1.
81. 0, is too bad *for* would be too bad, 35, 305. 1.
81. 0, one cannot *for* one could not, 35, 305. 1.
82. 0, passages marked by his pencil or by his notes, which *for* passages that, 35, 306. 1.
88. 1, which accompanies *for* that accompanies, 35, 310. 2.
92. 2, the description given of *added.*
94. 0, egoism *for* egotism, 35, 314. 1.
94. 0, egoistical *for* egotistical, 35, 314. 1.
99. 0, astonishing people *for* astonishing, 35, 318. 1.
99. 0, reflections of his *for* of his reflections, 35, 318. 1.
99. 1, said he *added.*

102. 0, a million *for* the million, 35, 521. 1.
104. 1, for his candour *added*.
104. 1, for my weakness in disliking it *for* for this weakness of mine, 35, 523. 1.
107. 1, wit *for* tenderness, 35, 524. 1.
109. 0, for the recollection *for* as the recollection, 35, 526. 0.
113. 0, course caricature *for* coarse caricature, 35, 529. 0.
113. 0, Where dulness *for* When dullness, 35, 529. 0.
113. 0, place *for* place, and, 35, 529. 0.
115. 2, person he *for* persons he, 35, 531. 0.
119. 1, after his mind *for* when his mind, 35, 533. 2.
122. 1, more severe *for* more frank, 35, 535. 1.
122. 2, beautiful illustrative drawing *for* beautiful drawing, 35, 535. 2.
124. 1, establishments which they *for* establishments they, 35, 536. 3.
130. 0, will join in *for* will join you in, 35, 540. 2.
130. 0, egoism *for* egotism, 35, 541. 0.
131. 1, envious, they are *for* envious, being, 35, 541. 1.
133. 1, where can we find *for* where is the place that we can find, 35, 543. 0.
138. 2, Stoicism could subdue *for* Stoicism could conceal, 37, 215. 3.
144. 1, observing him *for* judging him, 37, 219. 0.
147. 1, discovers the amiable *for* discovers the good, 37, 221. 0.
148. 0, are made subservient *for* are subservient, 37, 221. 1.
148. 0, her life *for* though her life, 37, 221. 1.
148. 0, fine ruin *for* fine view, 37, 222. 0.
149. 2, recited *for* repeated, 37, 222. 2.
152. 2, operate *for* operate more, 37, 309. 4.
152. 2, for the sake of a friend *for* for the sake of thy friend, 37, 310. 0.
153. 0, All that marred the perfectibility *for* Circumstances, in marring the perfectibility, 37, 310. 2.
153. 0, those who approached him *for* all who approached him, 37, 310. 2.
153. 0, even at the price of the happiness of the man *for* and the happiness of the man, even at the price of happiness, 37, 310. 2.
164. 0, may say *for* may say or write, 37, 317. 2.
166. 1, goodness, disinterestedness, and affection exist in the world *for* there exist goodness, disinterestedness, and affection in the world, 38, 144. 0.
167. 0, the selfishness *for* selfishness, 38, 144. 0.
169. 1, egoism *for* egotism, 38, 146. 0.
173. 0, I am a little disposed *for* I am little disposed, 38, 148. 0.
173. 0, more culpable *for* less culpable, 38, 149. 0.
175. 1, which now appear *for* that now appear, 38, 150. 2.
177. 4, reproaches *for* reproach, 38, 152. 3.
180. 0, ignorant *for* the ignorant, 38, 305. 1.
186. 0, steal those *for* steal them, 38, 309. 1.
189. 2, explored and exposed *for* explored, 38, 311. 2.
190. 0, *chantre d'enfer* for *chantre d'enfers*, 38, 312. 1.
191. 1, tempered by *for* though tempered by, 38, 313. 0.
193. 0, view acquaintances *for* view my acquaintances, 38, 314. 1.
195. 1, stronger shade *for* darker shade, 39, 33. 1.
195. 1, a belief that *for* a belief which, 39, 33. 1.
197. 1, human nature, which *for* human nature that, 39, 34. 1.
205. 1, humour of the moment *for* humours of the moment, 39, 39. 3.
206. 0, for if one *for* and if one, 39, 40. 1.
207. 1, accused of plagiarism *for* accused of plagiary, 39, 41. 0.
216. 1, every mark . . . arouse *for* every mark . . . arouses, 39, 414. 1.
218. 2, that this thought *for* which this thought, 39, 415. 2.

221. 2, moral career *for* mortal career, 39, 417. 2.
221. 2, a horror to death-bed scenes *for* a horror of death-bed scenes, 39, 417. 2.
221. 2, I would have escaped *for* I should have escaped, 39, 417. 2.
223. 1, egoist *for* egotist, 39, 418. 2.
224. 0, they have *for* they had, 39, 418. 2.
224. 1, died, and that *for* died, and, 39, 418. 3.
225. 0, a will that is *for* a will which is, 39, 419. 1.
228. 1, surprise *for* your surprise, 39, 421. 1.
229. 0, egoism *for* egotism, 39, 421. 2.
229. 1, ere yet age *for* ere age, 39, 421. 3.

"Part the Second," p. 144 of the book, does not appear in the journal and does not coincide with the beginning of any installment. The point of division occurs twelve paragraphs into the sixth installment, February 1833 (XXXVII, 218). Editor's notes have been deleted at head of first installment, XXXV, 5, and at XXXV, 134, 144; XXXVII, 217. The motto at the head of the first two installments, "Nothing extenuate,/ Nor set down aught in malice," has been replaced in the book by Goethe's German.

The Conversations originally appeared in eleven installments: July, August, September, October, December, 1832; February, March, June, July, September, and December, 1833.

INDEX

Nota bene: page references in italics refer to the editor's introduction only. Pagination begins anew with Lady Blessington's text.

literary works: "And canst thou bare thy breast," 34; *Book of Beauty* (ed.), 97, *100-101*; *Conversations of Byron*, modern critics on, *3-6*, *112*, *113*; nineteenth century reviews of, *6*, *112*; Leigh Hunt on, 6; Hobhouse on, *6-7*; Teresa Guiccioli on, 7, *109-11*; Henry Crabb Robinson on, 7; Fulke Greville on, 7; Byron's friends in, *23-24*; origins of, *90-91*; Gell on, *111*; Madden on, *111*; uniqueness of, *113*; *Desultory Thoughts and Reflections*, 31; *Ella Stratford*, 82; *Idler in France*, 77ff; *Idler in Italy*, 26ff, *40-41*, *52-54*, *64*ff; *Journal of a Tour through the Netherlands to Paris*, *18-19*; "Lines on the Death of Byron," 65; *Magic Lantern*, *12-16*, *17*, *43*; "MS. book" lent to Thomas Moore, *39-40*, *52*, *97*; "Night Thought Book," *84-90*; *Repealers*, 9, *31-32*, *92*, *101*, *104-105*; *Sketches and Fragments*, *16-18*; "Soliloquy of Tasso," *74*; *The Two Friends*, *92*; "When I ask'd for a verse," *46-47*

Blessington, Earl of, 7, *11-12*, 23, *28-38*, *52*, *62*, *63*, *66*, *70*, *72*, *79*, *94*, *97*, *106*, *112*; 14, 15-18, 101-102, 146-47, 156

Boccaccio, 188

Bolivar, *37*, *61*, *63*, *66*, *93*

Bonaparte, Jerome, 72

Bonaparte, Napoleon, *see* Napoleon

Borgia, Lucretia, *75-76*

Boswell, James, 3

Brougham, Henry, *24*

Bulwer, Edward, *91*, *113-14*

Burdett, Sir Frances, *23*, *33*, *78*; *61-62*, 134

Burghersh, Lord, *71*, *77*

Burton, Robert, 206

Byron, Allegra, 50

Byron, Augusta Ada, *45*, *48*, *77*; 7, 7n, 60, 61, 218, 226

Byron, Mrs. Catherine Gordon (the poet's mother), 80-81, 198

Byron, George Gordon, 6th Lord:
personal traits, habits, posses-
sions, opinions, etc., of: age, old, 102-103, 134, 148-49; Americans, 87; anger or rage, 80, 92, 98, 181, 195; antiquities, 32; appearance, 5-6, 6n; aristocracy, 54, 62-64, 97, 211; Aspasia, 132; authors, the craft of, 24, 38, 111, 115, 186, 191; avarice, 27-28, 32-33, 103, 183; biography, 42, 72, 220; bitterness, 46; cant, 12, 13, 15, 29, 87, 172-73, 174 187-88, 213, 215, 220, 221; chameleon character, 71-72, 220; charities, 32; childhood, 81; Christians, 67-69; comedy, 114, 183; conceit, 209-210; Cupid, 123; death, 101, 102, 103, 104, 112, 127-28, 193, 221; defamation of self, 183-84, 195; diet, 14, 18, 35-36, 86; dilettantes, 31-32; dreams, 112; dress, 6, 40-41; education, 179-80, 181; English character, 38-39, 62, 124, 129, 131, 170-73, 204; English country life, 38, 125; English society, 79, *84*, *107*, *111*; 38-39, 94-95, 105-106, 113-14, 118, 124, 131, 133-34, 160-61, 198-99, 212; enthusiasm, lack of, 85-86; epigrams, 152, 224; fame, 85, 162-63, 222; fear, pleasures of, 111-12; flattery, 209; flippancy, 7, 10, 19, 43, 228; flowers, 73; folly, 145; frankness, 13; friends, desertion of, 62, 103-104, 192-93, 194; friendship, 24, 43, 72, 93-94, 108-110, 132, 157-58, 169, 210-11, 224-25; friendship, denial of, 93; 53-54, 100-101, 222-23; genius, 77-79, 129, 144; "God save the King," 46; goodness, natural, 68, 139, 144, 195; gossip, 13, 28, 76; Greek character, 85; Greek War of Independence, 85-86, 181-83, 221, 226; health, 86, 216, 221; horsemanship, 28, 40-41, 64; hypochondria, 128-29; imagination, 49, 114-15; incontinence of speech, 145, 151-52, 228; indiscreetness, 51; infirmity of purpose, 123; ingratitude, 137, 194; insanity, 75, 178; intellect, march of, 38, 134; intol-

erance, 71; Irish character, 130, 142-43; Italian character, 29; Italian society, 112-13, 124, 177, 180; kindness, 71; Lake school of poets, 52, 53, 84, 158; literary men, 184; literature, 43; love, 95-96, 97, 108-110, 132, 168-69, 176; malice, lack of, 119, 144; manner, 7; man of fashion, 20, 45, 97; marksmanship, 28; marriage, 74, 88, 91; materialism, 68; memory, 84, 107, 164, 178-79, 200-201; Minerva, 123; misanthropy, 82-83, 95, 192-95, 229; misfortune, 138-39; misrepresentation of self, 169-70; mobility, 47, 71; money, 105; morality of his works, 26; moral severity of English, 29; music, 32; mystification, 47, 83, 86, 212; newspaper attacks, 79, 86-87, 101, 226-27; parvenus, 211; persiflage, 20; physicians, 208; plagiarism, 81, 117, 186-87, 206-207; poetical temperament, 49; poets, 115; praise, love of, 28, 54, 105; raconteur, 36; religion, 112, 214-15; repentance, 75; reputation, 216-17; ridicule, 13, 33, 34, 43, 71, 80, 98, 115, 119, 120, 145; romance, 35; routine habitual, 117; sarcasm, 33; scandal, 95; scenery, 40, 45-46, 68-69, 84-85, 153; Scotch character, 129-30; selfishness, 15, 44, 71, 127, 168, 198; self-portraiture, 190; sentiment, 33, 34, 35, 45-47; serventism, 180; skepticism, 68; society, 77-78, 93-94, 192, 210; solitude, 49, 78, 84, 93-94, 191-92, 210-11; stoicism, 46, 138; suicide, 42; superstition, 30-31; suspiciousness, 32; swimming, 28, 45; tact, 108; taste, false or vulgar, 98, 153-54; temper, 27; tourists, English, 8, 10, 72-73; translation of poetry, 98; understanding of character of others, 27, 44; unhappiness, 49, 64, 73, 127, 138, 164; vanity, 45, 71, 209; vice, 145; voice, 6-7, 7n; will, 61; women, 69-70, 88, 95-97, 110, 117, 121, 123-24, 148-49, 161-62, 172-73,

180, 196, 213-14, 219-26; women, English, 39, 65, 113; women, Italian, 112-13, 180; women, literary, 22; youth, 103, 134

works: Age of Bronze, 82; "Beneath Blessington's eyes," *44, 46, 97; Beppo, 75; Bride of Abydos, 96,* 159n, 186-87, 196; "But once I dared to lift my eyes," *44,* 150; *Childe Harold, 36, 53, 64, 67, 73, 74;* 153, 154, 213, 230; *Corsair, 96;* "Could Love for ever," 89-91; *Deformed Transformed,* 81; "Detached Thoughts," 76; *Don Juan, 36, 58-59, 59n, 60, 66, 74, 110, 111;* 48, 96, 122-23, 196, 213, 218-19, 230; "Dream" *90; English Bards,* 12; "Farewell," 51; *Giaour, 96,* 173; "Irish Avatar," 142; "Lines on Hearing that Lady Byron was Ill," *45, 96;* 55; *Manfred, 53; Marino Faliero, 74;* "Memoirs," said to have been copied, 7, 8; 42, 152; "Monody on . . . Sheridan," 141; *Parisina, 74;* "Question and Answer," *68, 79, 98 and n; Sardanapalus, 77;* "To the Countess of Blessington," *44, 46, 97; Two Foscari, 75;* "When we two parted," *51*

Byron, Lady (the poet's wife), *34, 35, 45, 46, 47, 48,* 76-77; 12, 18-19, 20-22, 33, 51, 55-60, 61, 70, 73-74, 99-100, 160-61, 178, 181, 218, 226

Cain, *62*

Campbell, Thomas, *91, 96;* 111, 133, 199-200

Canning, George, *23, 33;* 134, 135

Carbonari movement, *74*

Carlisle, Lord, *66*

Castlereagh, Lord, *24*

Charlemont, Lord, *78*

Chorley, Henry, *69*

Clairmont, Claire, *95, 99;* 100, 156

Clare, Lord, *223*

Claude, Lorraine, *26;* 149

Clermont, Mrs., *12n,* 18-19

Coleridge, S. T., *95*

Colman, George, *23;* 141, 201

Johnson, Dr. Samuel, *35, 51*; 3, 20, 31, 36, 185

Keats, John, 52
Kemble, John Philip, *24*; 72
Kinnaird, Douglas, *7, 24, 35, 51, 62, 77-78*; 7, 7n, 16, 88, 127
Kinnaird, Lord, 7

Lamartine, *67-68, 69, 70; 67,* 190-91
Lamb, Lady Caroline, *52, 94*; 151
Landor, Walter Savage, *69-70, 91, 95, 96*; 157
Lanfranchi, Palazzo, *69*
Lansdowne, Lord, *24, 78*; 135n, 185
Lawrence, Sir Thomas, 8, *25, 103, 104*
Leeds, Duke of, 30
Leigh, Augusta, *48*; 19, 30, 198, 199
Liberal, The, 27; 53
Literary Gazette, 12, 17, 18
Lockhart, John Gibson, *68*
Lushington, Dr. and Mrs. Stephen, *19*
Luther, Martin, 114
Luttréll, Henry, *7, 24, 72, 79, 80*; 76-77

Mackintosh, Sir James, 129
Madden, R. R., *20*
Mameluke, *36*; 41
Manfrini Palace, 75
Mathews, Charles, *24, 29, 100-101*; 140-41
Mathews, Mrs. Charles, *20, 21, 25-26*
Mathews, Charles James, *20, 21-22, 29-31*
Maurice (Byron's boatman in Geneva), 27
Medwin, Thomas, *64, 91, 95, 98, 99-100*; 3n
Melbourne, Lady Elizabeth, 132-33, 173
Melbourne, second Viscount, *94, 100, 105*
Metternich, Prince, 120
Mezzophanti, *76*
Michelangelo, *67*
Milton, John, *67, 107*
Mocenigo, Palazzo, *74*
Montaigne, 205-206

Montesquieu, 159-60
Montgomery, Colonel Hugh, *24, 41, 45, 47-48*; 20-22
Moore, Thomas, *7, 24, 25, 26, 51, 61, 75, 95, 96-97, 97n, 98*; 7, 7n, 9-10, 38, 42n, 46, 77, 111, 114, 129, 132-33, 141, 142, 143, 149-52, 184-85, 190, 201, 223

Napoleon, *19, 37, 49, 57, 61*; 25, 36, 82, 120, 191, 208
New Monthly, The, 84, 91
Noel-Hill, William, *41, 71*; 14, 14n, 15, 92, 93
Norton, Mrs. Caroline, *94, 100, 104, 105-106*

Osborne, Lord Sidney Godolphin, 30, 30n
Oxford, Lady, *52*; 149

Palmerston, Lord, *25*
Paradiso, Il, *43*
Parr, Dr. Samuel, 8, *25, 34*
Pascal, 207
Patmore, P. G., *94, 95*
Perry, James, *25*
Petrarch, 75
Plato, 211
Polidori, Dr. William, *25*
Pope, Alexander, 141, 160, 203
Portsmouth, Lord, 86
Power, Edmund (father of Lady Blessington), *9-10*
Power, Ellen, *see* Sutton, Mrs. Manners
Power, Mary Ann, *27-28, 92, 96*; 16
Power, Robert (brother), 92
Purves, Mrs. Home (Ellen Power), *see* Sutton, Mrs. Manners

Redding, Cyrus, *55n*
Richardson, Dr. Robert, 207-208
Richardson, Samuel, 136
Robinson, Henry Crabb, 7, 95ff
Rochefoucault, *84*
Rogers, Samuel, *7, 24, 68, 79, 80, 95, 98 and n*; 12, 111, 133, 152, 164, 200-201

239

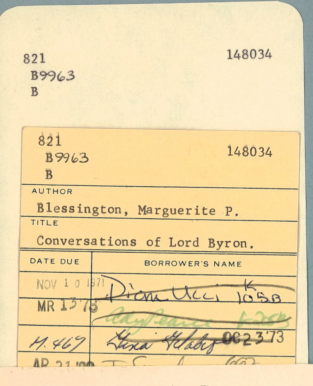